HOW SOVEREIGN IS GOD?

HOW SOVEREIGN IS GOD?

A Non-Partisan Exploration

JON K. NEWTON

Foreword by Barry Chant

RESOURCE *Publications* · Eugene, Oregon

HOW SOVEREIGN IS GOD?
A Non-Partisan Exploration

Copyright © 2025 Jon K. Newton. All rights reserved. Except for brief quotations in critical publications or reviews, no part of this book may be reproduced in any manner without prior written permission from the publisher. Write: Permissions, Wipf and Stock Publishers, 199 W. 8th Ave., Suite 3, Eugene, OR 97401.

Resource Publications
An Imprint of Wipf and Stock Publishers
199 W. 8th Ave., Suite 3
Eugene, OR 97401

www.wipfandstock.com

PAPERBACK ISBN: 979-8-3852-4587-1
HARDCOVER ISBN: 979-8-3852-4588-8
EBOOK ISBN: 979-8-3852-4589-5

12/08/25

To all the speakers and authors who have provoked me
to think more deeply about divine sovereignty since
my Christian conversion in 1966

CONTENTS

Foreword by Barry Chant | ix
Preface | xiii
Introduction | xv

PART 1   **BIBLICAL SURVEY | 1**

CHAPTER 1   GOD'S SOVEREIGNTY IN CREATION AND PROVIDENCE | 3

CHAPTER 2   DELEGATION AND PROBATION | 15

CHAPTER 3   REBELLION AND JUDGMENT | 37

CHAPTER 4   GUIDANCE AND MANAGEMENT | 65

CHAPTER 5   ELECTION | 88

CHAPTER 6   VICTORY | 126

CHAPTER 7   THE FINAL GOAL | 157

PART TWO   **THEOLOGICAL AND PRACTICAL DISCUSSION | 185**

CHAPTER 8   GOD AND OTHER ACTORS | 187

CHAPTER 9   DIVINE SOVEREIGNTY IN HUMAN LIVING | 243

CHAPTER 10	PRAYER AND THE SOVEREIGNTY OF GOD	271
CHAPTER 11	OUR PART IN GOD'S PLAN	299
	CONCLUSIONS	312

Bibliography | 323

Subject Index | 329

Scripture Index | 343

FOREWORD

Dr Jon Newton's *How Sovereign is God?* offers an expansive and comprehensive discussion on the question of the sovereignty of God. The author demonstrates a wide-ranging knowledge of the Scriptures—the Old Testament narrative in particular—and offers perceptive insights on his topic. He analyses what the phrase 'sovereignty of God' means and what the implications are for everyone, believer and unbeliever alike. He necessarily addresses such perennial questions as freedom of the will, the problem of suffering, the character of God, the place of divine judgement, the nature of love and many others. He shows a broad awareness of both evangelical and liberal writings on the subject.

Even readers of a non-theological bent will find much to think about as they peruse these pages. Common questions such as, 'Why does God allow suffering?' and, 'If God is sovereign, what is the point of praying?' and, 'If God is sovereign, why doesn't he just step in and fix things?' are addressed both directly and indirectly. The author's biblical exegesis is clearly undergirded by pastoral concerns. This is not theology in a vacuum.

So what is original about the book? Why yet another treatise on this vital topic? Well, no two publications are the same, and Newton adds refreshing insights and observations on many of the excellent works that have gone before. More significantly, as a Pentecostal author he is not afraid to tackle questions like that of divine healing (which he addresses in a practical manner), the place of supernal acts in the purpose of God, the work of the Holy Spirit and both strengths and weaknesses in some areas of contemporary Pentecostalism. I would like to read more of his perspective on the gifts and power of the Holy Spirit in the light of God's sovereign purpose and perhaps also on the prominence in the teaching of Jesus on the power of faith. Are there grounds here for another volume?

The author does not hold back from affirming God's sovereign role as Judge of all the earth. He simply and plainly asserts that evil must be addressed and cannot be glossed over. His identification of some contemporary practices as deserving the justice of God may seem offensive, but this is consistent with his overall argument; being offended is insufficient reason for rejecting his thesis.

Naturally, the apparent dichotomy between God's sovereignty and humanity's autonomy permeates the book. In a nutshell, Newton shows how it is possible to reconcile both realities, even if our personal sensibilities may sometimes be disturbed.

I'm impressed with the astounding amount of time and energy Newton must have put in to prepare this work. Yet there is nothing arrogant about his approach. This absence of dogmatism is refreshing and commendable, although he is not averse to making bold affirmations here and there.

As a teaching manual about the nature and relevance of God's sovereignty, this volume has much to offer and is well worth investment of both time and money by readers, particularly those involved in the ministry of the Word.

In conclusion, I want to make three observations. First, when all is said and done, intellectually satisfying answers to questions about such matters as God's sovereignty ultimately lie outside human reach. Moses put it well when he said, 'The secret things belong to the LORD our God, but the things that are revealed belong to us' (Deuteronomy 29:29); as did Paul, 'Oh, the depth of the riches and wisdom and knowledge of God! How unsearchable are his judgments and how inscrutable his ways!' (Romans 11:33).

Second, in spite of this, the Scriptures encourage us to think through such issues as deeply as we can. We are to love God not only with all our hearts but also with all our minds (Mark 12:30). Newton has done well to follow this injunction in relation to the sovereignty of God.

Interestingly, the apparent inconsistency of these two propositions is actually consistent with the whole revelation of God. Examples are obvious. The Bible is written by humans yet its content is deistic. Jesus is both perfectly human and yet perfectly divine. Tragedy is usually the result of human failing yet 'the Lord has done it' (Amos 3:6).

So there is a third option. The Holy Spirit brings to us godly insight and understanding. If we are to grasp the wonders of the inextricable fusion between humanity, destiny, eternity and sovereignty, our constant prayer must also be for God to enlighten us with the spirit of wisdom and revelation in the knowledge of Christ (Ephesians 1:15-23). Such knowledge is spiritually discerned.

This is not just a lazy option. It requires serious prayer and serious thought. It is a willingness to explore the essence of a God who not only shows love but who by nature essentially, profoundly and inextricably is love. This perfect love is a profound mystery, displayed through the cross. And as with every other expression of true love—a man's love for his wife, a mother's love for her child—we may receive it, relish it, marvel at it and know it beyond question, yet not begin to understand it.

So, regarding God's sovereign purpose through the cross, we heed the call of God to reason together (Isaiah 1:18) but we are not so foolish as to believe we comprehend it all.

As Charles Wesley put it so well:

> 'Tis mystery all: the Immortal dies:
> Who can explore His strange design?
> In vain the firstborn seraph tries
> To sound the depths of love divine.
> 'Tis mercy all! Let earth adore,
> Let angel minds inquire no more.
> Amazing love, how can it be
> That thou, my God, shouldst die for me?

Jon Newton's book is infused with this conviction and I am honoured to commend it.

Dr Barry Chant, author and teacher
Founding President of Tabor College, Australia.

PREFACE

THIS BOOK REFLECTS A lifetime of reflection, study and experience. As a young Christian in Sydney, Australia, in the late 1960s, I was exposed to strong expressions of Calvinist theology espoused by other young people and leading theologians, especially from Moore College, the Anglican theological school for the Diocese of Sydney. At the same time, I was also attracted to a Pentecostal form of Christianity. These two streams seemed incompatible, but both had important insights into the Bible and the ways of God. Later I had a strong 'flirtation' with Calvinist theology in my thirties, but when I sat down and studied the Scriptures as part of a theology degree, I became convinced that classical Calvinism had an inadequate explanation of Scripture in relation to God and humanity. I have, however, gained much value from Calvinist authors and indeed from Calvin himself. I have also learned much from Arminian, and even Open Theist, authors. In this book I hope to draw on all such insights but also to learn directly from the Bible itself in a non-partisan way, though aware of the challenges involved and not wishing to be hopelessly naïve. As a Pentecostal scholar, I am obviously influenced by Pentecostal perspectives as well.

All Scripture quotations, unless otherwise indicated, are taken from the Holy Bible, New International Version®, NIV®. Copyright ©1973, 1978, 1984, 2011 by Biblica, Inc.™ Used by permission of Zondervan. All rights reserved worldwide. www.zondervan.com The "NIV" and "New International Version" are trademarks registered in the United States Patent and Trademark Office by Biblica, Inc.™

While no English translation captures everything in the original text perfectly, I believe that doctrinal claims must survive examination from any credible translation of Scripture.

I want to thank several great scholars who commented on the first draft of the book, namely Dr Barry Chant (Founder and former Principal of Tabor College) and Associate Professor Jeff Aernie, Director of the School of Ministry and Theology at Alphacrucis University College. I also thank Kerrie Stevens, the Librarian of Alphacrucis University College, for proofreading this manuscript. I have made several changes to this book as a result of their helpful suggestions. But I bear the full responsibility for everything written here, including changes I failed to make in response to their advice.

INTRODUCTION

WE LIVE IN A CONFUSING and confused age. Things are changing rapidly and unpredictably, and no one really knows where it is all heading. The world often seems meaningless, threatening, insecure, and chaotic. Technological changes have opened up all kinds of new possibilities; who would have thought, even at the dawn of the 21st century, that someone could hold in their hand a small device that plays movies and music, keeps you up-to-date with the latest news, allows you to communicate instantly with people all over the globe, lets you manage your bank accounts, takes better photos than many cameras, does incredible calculations, tells you the time in every large city of the world, gives you answers to almost any factual question, and incidentally . . . acts as a phone? On the other hand, we are threatened with new pandemics, changing political boundaries, an unpredictable new balance of power, terrorism, wars, polarizing opinions, and unpredictable climate change. Is there any sense in all this?

Many commentators simply conclude that there is no meaning or control; the universe is, and always has been, random, even absurd. Get used to it! Others call for governments to somehow *take control* and sort out the mess. Recently citizens of democratic countries were willingly giving up many freedoms for a season to get some kind of protection from the COVID-19 virus. Authoritarian countries gave their citizens no choice. But governments floundered in their use of this newfound power and there was increasing resistance to mandatory vaccination, for example.

It's certainly hard for the ordinary person to see God's hand in it all. Is the world even out of God's control? Is it madness to believe in the sovereignty of God when evil and turmoil seem to be affecting people all over the world?

This question is more pressing for Christians than perhaps any other kind of religious believer. Muslims have a more fatalistic way of referring everything back to a distant and controlling deity, though that doesn't stop some of them launching violent jihad in the name of Allah, taking advantage of the current confusion and turmoil. Hindus and Buddhists often tend to turn inward, looking for personal tranquility in defiance of the world. But Christians believe in a God who is all-loving, all-powerful and all-wise, which seems ridiculously naïve, if not illogical, to many.

The other factor here is the increasingly common "watered-down" idea of God in our western Christian world. The idea of God as Judge is largely incomprehensible to many people. One researcher has described common thinking as envisaging "God as Heavenly Butler," that is, a Grand Old Man in the sky who doesn't interfere with your life but is on hand when you need help.[1] This concept reminds me of Feuerbach's idea of God as a projection of humans driven by the desire to have a father-figure "up there" looking after them.[2]

This is why I think we need to consider again what the Bible teaches about God, and particularly about God's sovereignty. Does God know and care about the confusion we are experiencing? Can God help us find answers and meaning in the midst of it all as we seek to live our own lives and participate productively in society? What kind of God do we worship, or question, anyway? Does God just exist to meet our needs? Where is God taking us, if anywhere? Are we accountable to God, and if so, how? I think this is a good time in history to ask these sorts of questions and see what answers we can find in Scripture, and judging by some recent publications, others are also on a similar journey.

The late D. Martyn Lloyd-Jones, the long-serving pastor of Westminster Chapel in London, a man soaked in Puritan theology, wrote,

> There is no greater ground of security in this world of time than to feel that you are a part of the grand plan and purpose of God. None of these things are accidental, none of them are fortuitous. It does not matter what may happen in the future, nothing can disturb this plan.[3]

And coming from an opposing theological camp, Robert Shank writes,

---

1. Philip Hughes, *Putting Life Together*, 142.
2. Cf. Kendall, *Out of the Comfort Zone*, 7.
3. Lloyd-Jones, *The Assurance of Our Salvation*, 18.

> The sovereignty of God is an unfailing encouragement that lights the path of the just and affords assurance to all the faithful. . . . He who "works all things after the counsel of his own will" is at work in the world in these momentous times, moving inexorably toward fulfillment of an eternal purpose that antedates creation and gives meaning to human history.[4]

So, the question I'm asking is,

HOW SOVEREIGN IS GOD?

On the face of it, this is a ludicrous question. How can God, at least the God of the Bible, be any less than sovereign? As A.W. Pink put it, "To say that God is sovereign is to declare that God *is* God."[5] Stanley Grenz contends, "unless God exercises sovereignty, history will have proven that God is in fact not God at all."[6] And even physicist Isaac Newton declared, "The supreme God is an eternal, infinite, and absolute perfect being; but a being, however perfect, without dominion is not the Lord God."[7] The God described in Scripture, is almighty, enthroned, all knowing and totally free to do whatever He[8] decides. God is not responsible or accountable to anyone outside Himself whereas all creation is responsible and accountable to God.

Popular devotion often says, 'God is in control,' especially in situations where things seem very much 'out of control.' That is supposed to bring comfort and hope; too often (in my experience) it only raises more questions. After all, if God is in control, why are these bad things happening? But what else can we say?

Apart from Calvinists, whose theology is largely built on the idea of God as sovereign in all areas, including salvation, most Christians do not think systematically about the sovereignty of God. Pentecostals (my tribe) rarely even use such language. But divine sovereignty seems to be affirmed and displayed throughout the Bible so we cannot avoid the issue.

---

4. Shank, *Elect in the Son*, 21.
5. Pink, *The Sovereignty of God*, 19; emphasis in the original text.
6. Grenz, *Theology for the Community of God*, 107.
7. Newton, *Principia*, 940–941 as quoted in Vondey, "The Holy Spirit and the Physical Universe", 15.
8. Not all readers will be comfortable with me calling God 'He.' God has no gender but I think the traditional masculine pronoun raises fewer problems than the alternatives. I'm also sticking with the traditional capitalization of pronouns referring to God.

INTRODUCTION

However, the reason I put this title as a question is to raise four key issues. First, what are we really saying when we affirm that God is sovereign? Second, how does God's sovereignty relate to the activity and decisions of other intelligent beings in God's universe: angels, the devil and humans? Third, how credible is it to affirm a robust view of God's sovereignty in such a tumultuous world as this one? And fourth, how does God's sovereignty operate? Or to put it another way, what *kind* of sovereign is God?

The sovereignty of God does not operate in some kind of a vacuum. The relationship between divine sovereignty and human freedom is an ancient problem that is still engaging, and perplexing, good minds. Is God's sovereignty and freedom limited in any way by the free will of angels or humans? Is their freedom limited by His sovereignty? And can God truly foreknow the decisions of free creatures without threatening their freedom? What is free will anyway, and is it a coherent notion?

Such questions will keep raising their heads throughout this book, but will not be addressed exhaustively. Aware of the danger raised by D.A. Carson for systematic theology of "constructing the 'system' too early" or "of overlooking genuine variations of approach and emphasis within the biblical literature,"[9] I intend rather to approach this topic from a perspective of biblical theology, unpacking how specific passages in Scripture shed light on this vast and important topic.

But first, let me explain what I think we are saying when we affirm that God is sovereign. Here are a few definitions offered by other authors.

R.C. Sproul writes,

> As sovereign, God is the supreme authority of heaven and earth . . . Any other authority that exists in the universe is derived from and dependent upon God's authority. . . . He owns the universe. His ownership gives him certain rights. He may do with the universe what is pleasing to his holy will. Likewise, all power in the universe flows from the power of God.[10]

Stanley Grenz puts it somewhat differently:

---

9. Carson, *Divine Sovereignty and Human Responsibility*, 3. Thomas Weinandy offers another caution: treating this as a problem to be solved rather than a mystery to be clarified (Weinandy, *Does God Suffer?*, 32–36). In other words, we can never hope to fully understand God; all we can try to do is understand the issues more clearly.

10. Sproul, *Chosen by God*, 24.

> Strictly speaking God's sovereignty is an eschatological concept. It refers to the bringing to pass of the final goal God has for the world.[11]

Then, in his autobiographical *Surprised by Joy*, the late C.S. Lewis suggested that God is sovereign both *de facto* (by the power of His acts) and *de jure* (by His rights as God) and even if God had no power over us, "we should still owe Him precisely the same kind and degree of allegiance as we do now."[12]

I think that there are three elements to the idea of divine sovereignty:

1. *God's freedom.* Psalm 115:3 contends, "Our God is in heaven; he does whatever pleases him."[13] Karl Barth claimed, "freedom is the prerogative of divine sovereignty."[14] God is not obligated to, or dependent on, any other person or force. His will is only subject to His own character as God. Calvin put it this way: "in his mere generosity he has not been bound by any laws but is free."[15] Or in Pink's words, "He is under no rule or law outside of His own will and nature."[16] This is in contrast to us humans, whose freedom is limited *both* by external forces and circumstances outside our control *and* by our internal drives, habits and motivations.

2. *God's ownership rights.* In some contexts, sovereignty refers to the legal right or claim of a person or group over some territory or sphere. God has absolute rights over His creation. He has the moral and legal right to interact with His creation and dispose of it as He sees fit. As Grenz puts it, "Ultimately God alone has the prerogative to declare what his creation should be."[17] In the case of humanity, God is the absolute Judge; He has the right to judge us and we are totally accountable to Him (not the other way around). As Campbell puts it, "*As a principle*, we have duties to him; he has no duties toward us" [18]

---

11. Grenz, *Theology for the Community of God*, 106.
12. Lewis, *Surprised by Joy*, 185.
13. See also Ps 135:6.
14. *Church Dogmatics* II/1.4 (Johnson, *The Essential Karl Barth*, 172)
15. John Calvin, *Institutes of the Christian Religion*, 929.
16. Pink, *Sovereignty of God*, 21.
17. Grenz, *Theology for the Community of God*, 106.
18. *The Wonderful Decree*, 259; emphasis in the original.

3. *God's rule.* God rules over the universe He has created. All created things depend on Him. Nothing happens without His permission. His purposes prevail and are fulfilled. A strong expression of this can be seen in Calvin, who contends, "there is no erratic power, or action, or motion in creatures, but that they are governed by God's secret plan in such a way that nothing happens except what is knowingly and willingly decreed by him."[19] And Paul Helm argues that God causing all things to work together for the good of His elect (Rom 8:28) "implies control over all contingencies that do or could affect the divine purpose, including the plans and actions of people hostile to or indifferent to it."[20] To put it another way, God is never frustrated.[21]

So the purpose of this book is to establish how much these three points are taught (or implied) in the Christian Bible and how such divine sovereignty operates. For example, as we saw, Stanley Grenz distinguishes between God's sovereignty as a future triumph toward which history is travelling and as a legal claim that God has over all creation even when it is not recognized by humanity. In other words, he suggests that God is not fully *in control* at this stage of history.[22] He affirms the first two elements I have identified but not so much the third. And Roger Olson argues that sovereignty does not equal control. Rather,

> God is in charge of the world including free creatures who sometimes thwart his perfect will. God allows that to happen by an act of self-restriction; he could control creatures meticulously, but he chooses not to for the sake of genuinely loving, reciprocal relationships.[23]

As we will see, a key word here is 'meticulously.'

---

19. Calvin, *Institutes*, 201.

20. Paul Helm, "Classical Calvinist Doctrine of God"; in Bruce A. Ware, *Perspectives on the Doctrine of God*, 25. The Westminster Shorter Catechism states that "God's works of providence are, his most holy, wise, and powerful preserving and governing all his creatures, and all their actions" (as quoted in Helm, *Providence of God*, 31). "Governing" is perhaps better than "control" with its less fortunate connotations.

21. Hence John Piper concludes that God is "the happiest of all beings" (*Desiring God*, 24). But this is not always how the Bible portrays God, as we will see.

22. Grenz, *Theology for the Community of God*, 108–109.

23. Olson, "The Classical Free Will Theist Model of God;" in Ware, *Perspectives on the Doctrine of God*, 155. See also Fretheim, *Suffering of God*, 37.

INTRODUCTION

But a question that may arise in your mind is, why does this matter? God is sovereign whether or not we know, understand or believe it. What practical value does such teaching have for our lives today? The short answer is that the Bible portrays God as sovereign (whatever we conclude that means) so it must be true and relevant. But I want to suggest that our ideas about 'How sovereign is God?' influence our thinking and acting in more ways than you might think, and I will explore some of these in the second part of this book.

Think of the weather, to start with a relatively trivial topic. I plan a boat trip for the weekend and ask God for pleasant weather so that my companions and I can enjoy the experience in safety. What assumptions am I making in praying this way? I seem to be assuming that God actually controls the weather, or at least can do so if He so chooses. I also seem to be assuming that God not only hears my prayer but responds to it; so, for example, God may intervene to avert a storm that would otherwise happen in my area next weekend. Does this mean that God changes His plans because of my prayer? If not, what does it mean to say that God answered my prayer? Did He, for example, influence my thinking so that I prayed what He had already decided would happen? Or is the whole idea that God answers prayer flawed?

Now what if the weather is actually bad and my boat sinks and several people drown, together with others in the region? Do we call that an 'act of God' (to borrow an insurance idiom)? Or do we blame the people concerned for poor decisions, failing to respond to weather forecasts perhaps? Or do we attribute this to the devil? Or global warming? The more you think of these hypotheticals, the more complex it all is.

Or think instead of someone you want to win for Christ. You care about that person and you don't want them to go to hell or miss God's plan for their lives. But does God care? Or is that person not one of God's chosen ones, so that God is willing for them to be lost? Whose responsibility is it whether the person receives Christ, or not? Is it my fault if I don't witness to them faithfully and effectively? Is it their own fault if they choose not to respond to the gospel? Is it the devil who deceives and seduces them? Or could God overrule all this and effectively draw them to Christ if He so chose? Or am I fretting too much because somehow God will save everyone anyway? Every answer to such questions says something about the sovereignty of God as I defined it above. It also has implications for the fourth question I raised, what kind of sovereign is God?

Our thinking about God's sovereignty affects more areas of life than you might think.

THE PLAN OF THIS BOOK

This book approaches this topic in a way different from many other authors. I am not trying to argue for a specific picture or partisan view of God's sovereignty. As you will see, I have read books from various contradictory and competing views about God's sovereignty, and especially the difficult areas of election and salvation. I have tried to think my way into the positions of Calvinists, Arminians and Open Theists especially. I am trying to learn from all and submit to none absolutely. Whether or not I have succeeded, you must judge.

The first part of this book is a biblical theological survey. Using some important relevant themes (creation, providence, probation, judgement, management, election and victory), I try to unpack as accurately as possible what the Old and New Testaments have to say about each, without 'cherry picking' verses out of context.

In the second part of the book, I discuss the implications and issues that arise from the biblical study. What does the sovereignty of God, as described in Scripture, mean for evangelism, prayer, and decision-making, among other things? How does God's sovereignty relate to other actors in the universe or the forces of nature? What does all this tell us about God's nature?

The end result of that discussion should be that our view of God's sovereignty affects what we think about a whole lot of questions. So welcome to the journey!

PART 1

BIBLICAL SURVEY

CHAPTER 1

GOD'S SOVEREIGNTY IN CREATION AND PROVIDENCE

We now know from physics that the universe had a beginning, what scientists call 'the big bang,' a micro-moment when the universe went from nothing to something and began its long journey to the world we know today. Before that there was nothing, or to believers, nothing but God. How long was there nothing but God? Perhaps that's another absurd question because time likely began with the 'big bang.'[1] What Genesis implies, however, is that God had a plan in His mind when He began to create.

GENESIS 1 AND CREATION

The Bible begins with this statement: "In the beginning God created the heavens and the earth" (Gen 1:1). It thus announces that God's position as sovereign Creator is the fundamental reality it will assume throughout, not just in Genesis, but at least the whole Torah (or the Pentateuch). This has usually been understood by the phrase 'creation *ex nihilo*;' that is, God created the world out of nothing.[2] God was not obliged or influenced by any force or person outside Himself when He decided to create

---

1. We'll touch on that later. Helm contends that 'before' in relation to creation is a matter of hierarchy not time (*Providence of God*, 70–71).
2. As Millard Erickson shows, this is clearly implied by the Hebrew and Greek language used of God's creating (Erickson, *Christian Theology*, 394–396). Cf. Wenham, *Genesis 1–15*, 14.

(in contrast to creation narratives of other ancient cultures).[3] As Stanley Grenz puts it, "God is not driven to create, not forced by some sense of compulsion to bring the universe into existence." Not only was God not compelled by anything outside Himself, but "creation is not the product of an *internal* necessity within God."[4] As Daniel Castelo puts it, "The cosmos only exists because God calls it into being and allows it to be."[5] There was literally nothing else in existence until God created.[6]

Genesis 1 unpacks this in a series of 'days' during which God developed the original earth into the form He desired. On each day, we read that "God said," resulting in a new stage in the plan (vv.3,6,9,11,14,20,24,26,29). This implies that the whole creation owed its existence totally to the word of the Creator, expressing His sovereign will.

Other language in Genesis 1 also points to God's sovereignty. God evaluates His own work: "God saw that the light was good" (v.4), and He makes similar comments after creating dry land (v.10), vegetation (v.12), heavenly bodies (v.18), sea creatures and birds (v.21), and land animals (v.25). As Wenham comments, "God the great artist is pictured admiring his handiwork."[7] Finally, contemplating the 'finished' work, "God saw all that he had made, and it was very good" (v.31). God has the last word about the value of His creation.

God separates light from darkness (v.4), waters above and below the vault of sky (v.7), and day from night (vv.14,18). God gives his different creatures names: day and night (v.5), sky (v.8), and land and seas (v.10). He also makes different creatures:[8] the vault (v.7), the sun, moon and stars (v.16), which are seen as "creatures, not gods,"[9] the sea creatures[10]

---

3. Recent scholars have suggested that Genesis 1 was likely written to contradict other creation myths of the ancient world. Cf. Houston, *I Believe in the Creator*, 65; Howard-Brook, *"Come Out, My People!"*, 17–20; Wenham, *Genesis 1–15*, 9.

4. Grenz, *Theology for the Community of God*, 99; emphasis in the original.

5. *Theological Theodicy*, 40.

6. Greg Boyd argues for the 'gap' theory that suggests there was a fall of angelic beings before Genesis 1:2, leading to a conflict comparable to the alternative stories of other ancient Near East cultures (Boyd, *God At War*, 97–113, especially 104). His argument has merit, but it has to be read *into* Genesis 1 rather than being found there, and it still assumes that God created the original universe.

7. Wenham, *Genesis 1–15*, 18.

8. The Hebrew here is *asah*, a different word to *bara*, "create," which is only ever used of God (Wenham, . *Genesis 1–15*, 14).

9. Wenham, *Genesis 1–15*, 21.

10. This includes "the great creatures of the sea" (Gen 1:21), sometimes seen as enemies to be defeated (e.g. Ps 74:13–14), but here just creatures (Wenham, *Genesis*

and birds (v.21),[11] land animals (v.25), and human beings (vv.26,27).[12] He makes the boundaries in which His creatures are to operate: He limits the sea by creating dry land (v.9). He creates living beings to multiply "according to their various kinds" (vv.11,12,21,24,25).

All this language makes it clear that God is not only 'calling the shots' but 'setting the rules' for the whole universe. It implies that behind the natural forces of gravity, life, evolution and others that we see in the natural world lies the creative will of Another.[13]

God is also sovereign in creating humanity, as Gen 1:26–30 makes clear. This is seen not only in the fact of creating humanity but in the details. God determined to create humans "in our image" (vv.26,27), a bold, unprecedented act. God appointed humanity over the rest of creation, or at least over the animate beings specifically (vv.26,28). God created humans as sexual beings, with just two genders – "male and female" (v.27). God blessed them (v.28), indicating His favor and approval. He commissioned them to "be fruitful and increase in number" and "fill the earth" (v.28); unlike some other living beings, humans are specifically permitted (even commanded) to live everywhere in the earth and become a large population. Finally, He determined the diet of human beings (vv.29–30). Clearly God is making the key decisions and setting the rules for this final part of His creation.

Let's recap here in terms of the three elements of divine sovereignty identified in the Introduction. First, God is clearly completely free in all this narrative of creation. God, and God alone, makes the decisions and no reason is given for any of these steps other than the word and action of God Himself.

Second, God affirms His rights over His creation by such actions as naming,[14] separating, approving (evaluating) and appointing boundaries for each of His creatures. In the case of human beings, this takes the form of specific rules for their lives, even down to the food they eat.

And third, God rules. He is the only one making decisions. And all creation is portrayed as obeying His edicts; whatever He commanded

---

1–15, 24).

11. In this case the verse uses *bara*.

12. Both Hebrew terms are used here.

13. Cf Wenham, *Genesis 1–15*, 37–38. This would be true no matter what idea of the processes of creation we hold to.

14. Wenham asserts, "In the OT, to name something is to assert sovereignty over it" (Wenham, *Genesis 1–15*, 19).

was done; "it was so" as verses 11,15 and 24 say. There is no hint of resistance to the will of God.[15] And Wenham suggests there is a 'moral' principle here: "Things are the way they are because God made it so, and men and women should accept his decree."[16]

But fourth, God rules benevolently. Not only is His creation good, but He blesses it (vv.22,28). God creates His world to thrive and grow. And as Wenham points out, in Genesis, God's blessing has power: it "guarantees and effects the hoped-for success."[17]

God as Creator is clearly distinct from the universe He is creating. He is not part of creation, but is "Wholly Other," as Thomas Weinandy puts it.[18] But God is not acting just as a singular Ruler, a kind of lonely individual. In verse 2, the Scripture states, "the Spirit of God was hovering over the waters." We have to be careful not to read back New Testament teaching on the Holy Spirit into this statement.[19] But at least this statement throws a different note into the scene, suggesting at the very least that God does not just dictate events, but gets involved; it's a note of *immanence* balancing the *transcendence* implied in the rest of the narrative.[20] It opens the possibility that God works from *within*, not just from *above*, in relationship to His creation.

Then a note of plurality is introduced in verse 26: "let us make mankind in our image, in our likeness." This suggests some kind of consultation within God; not with angels because "image" and "likeness" are singular here and in verse 27.[21]

More importantly perhaps, God creates living creatures with the power to sustain and multiply themselves. This is seen with the plant world (vv.11–12), sea and sky creatures (vv.20–22) and land animals (vv.24–25) as well as humans (v.28). God releases living creatures to a degree of autonomy by setting up systems of nourishment (vv.29–30) and reproduction by which these creatures can sustain their existence. In

---

15. Contra Boyd, *God At War*, 108.
16. Wenham, *Genesis 1–15*, 21.
17. Wenham, *Genesis 1–15*, 24.
18. *Does God Suffer?*, 46–47.

19. The Hebrew word *ruah* can be translated 'wind' or 'breath.' Hence the NRSV translates "a wind from God swept over the face of the waters" (Gen 1:2b).

20. Theologians try to balance two aspects of God's relationship with creation: God is *transcendent*, that is, different and unique and separate from His creation, 'above' it all; but He is also *immanent* in creation, that is 'inside' it and involved at every level. It's important to affirm both of these truths and not collapse either into the other.

21. Cf. Wenham, *Genesis 1–15*, 27–28.

the case of sky and sea creatures, as well as humans, God even commissions them to multiply and fill the earth by their own God-given power (vv.22,28). And even the earth has such divinely ordained power to produce both vegetation and animals (vv.11,24). All this suggests that God does not constantly dictate to creation but releases it to operate according to the power He has placed within it.[22] This is why we can validly speak of 'laws' of nature. God's sovereignty includes such delegation.[23]

Natural, predictable, law-like forces, created by God, regulate the normal operations of nature. These forces and laws, and the potential built into the natural world, can be researched, understood and (to some degree) controlled and exploited by human investigators, because God appoints His final creation, the human race, to rule over the creation (vv.26,28,29; compare Ps 8:6–8). This enormous move by God has incredible implications which we will discuss in the next chapter.

Meanwhile let's explore other biblical material related to creation and providence.

CREATION AND PROVIDENCE

Many Old Testament passages simply affirm that God created the universe, which implies that He is sovereign in that role. However, Exod 20:11 draws an interesting conclusion from this, relating to God's lordship over time, based on His creation (as in Gen 1:14), which is the basis for the Sabbath law (see Gen 2:2–3). Sabbath observance is thus a recognition of God's sovereignty as Creator.

Psalm 33:6 sums up Genesis 1 when it affirms that the heavens were made by God's word and breath (Heb. *ruah*); the following verse suggests God's control of the seas. Psalm 33:8–9 grounds the call to all people to fear God in His spoken word, affirming God's rights as Creator and Judge. Psalm 19 sees the whole heavens as declaring God's glory and "the work of his hands" (v.1), and the rhythm of the sun is poetically attributed to God (vv.4–6). Psalm 24:1–2 affirms that the earth and all it contains, including "all who live in it," belongs to God by right because He created it.

In the New Testament, there is the same emphasis on God as Creator of all things. Paul, in preaching to the Gentiles, affirms that "the

---

22. Oord pushes this idea strongly, perhaps too strongly, when he attributes agency to the non-human world (Oord, *Uncontrolling Love*, 52–56).

23. This principle is also seen when the heavenly bodies are appointed to "govern the day and the night" (Gen 1:18).

living God... made the heavens and the earth and the sea and everything in them" (Acts 14:15) and "made the world and everything in it" (Acts 17:24). In Revelation also, the heavenly beings worship God because He is the Creator (Rev 4:11).

Three other emphases are seen in Colossians 1. First, creation includes not just the natural visible world but also the invisible, spiritual world (v.16). Second, Jesus Christ is Creator and also heir of all creation (v.16; compare John 1:2–3; 1 Cor 8:6).[24] And third, God in Christ not only created everything but also sustains the creation- "in him all things hold together" (v.17; see also Heb 1:3). And also God will through Christ "reconcile to himself all things, whether things on earth or things in heaven" (v.20). Whatever that means exactly,[25] it shows that God has not abandoned His creation, including the invisible, spiritual creation, but has good plans for its future.

The Bible also says that God is intimately involved with all creation. Unlike Deism, which affirms a God who created the world and then left it to run according to natural laws without any divine interference, Christian theology affirms what is usually called providence. This is the idea that God actively cares for His creation. As John Webster defines it, "Providence is that work of divine love for temporal creatures whereby God ordains and executes their fulfilment in fellowship with himself."[26] Or, as Thomas Jay Oord puts it, providence refers to, "the ways God acts to promote our well-being and the well-being of the whole."[27] And John Piper speaks of "the act of purposefully providing for, or sustaining and governing, the world."[28] Finally, Calvin writes,

> He is also everlasting Governor and Preserver- not only in that he drives the celestial fame as well as its several parts by a universal motion, but also in that he sustains, nourishes, and cares for everything he has made, even to the least sparrow [cf. Matt.10:29].[29]

---

24. Cf. N.T. Wright, *Colossians and Philemon*, 71–73.

25. See the discussion in Wright, *Colossians and Philemon*, 75–78.

26. "On the Theology of Providence" (in Murphy and Ziegler, eds, *The Providence of God*), 158.

27. Oord, *Uncontrolling Love*, 16.

28. Piper, *Providence*, 30.

29. Calvin, *Institutes of the Christian Religion*, 197–198.

A key passage that speaks of creation and providence is Psalm 104.[30] While part of this psalm describes the original creation (vv.5–9,24), it is mainly about God's ongoing providential care of the earth. God controls the weather (vv.3–4). God provides rain and water sources for living creatures (vv.10–13,16). God sustains vegetation for the nourishment of animals and birds (vv.14–18). God maintains the regularity of the heavenly bodies (vv.19–23). Even lions are said to "seek their food from God" (v.21); indeed "all creatures look to you to give them their food at the proper time" (v.27) and depend on God for life (vv.28–30). Indeed, when God hides His face, takes away their breath, or shakes the earth, it is disastrous (vv.29,32). However, He always recreates and renews by His Spirit (v.30). The whole psalm therefore creates a picture of an earth dependent on, and rejoicing in, God's providential care, expressed in His management of all factors that impinge on the lives of His creatures. As Duffield and Van Cleave comment, "even an earth under the curse displays God's design and care to those who are not blinded by unbelief."[31]

However, this psalm also indicates that those creatures are not passive recipients of such care: people cultivate plants (v.14), make bread and wine (v.15), and work during daylight hours (v.23); birds build nests (vv.12,17), lions seek prey (v.21), creatures generally gather what God has provided (v.28).

Such a big view of God's providence is picked up by Jesus in the Sermon on the Mount. He insists that God "causes his sun to rise on the evil and the good, and sends rain on the righteous and the unrighteous" (Matt 5:45). Alluding to God's care of birds and wildflowers, Jesus then exhorts his followers to have a similar trust in God:

> Look at the birds of the air; they do not sow or reap or store away in barns, and yet *your heavenly Father* feeds them. Are you not much more valuable than they? .... And why do you worry about clothes? See how the flowers of the field grow. They do not labor or spin. Yet I tell you that not even Solomon in all his splendor was dressed like one of these. If that is how *God* clothes the grass of the field, which is here today and tomorrow is thrown into the fire, will he not much more clothe you- you of little faith?
>
> (Matt 6:26,28–30; emphasis added)

---

30. Cf. Piper, *Providence*, 221–235.
31. Duffield and Van Cleave, *Foundations of Pentecostal Theology*, 84.

Jesus is not calling believers to an irresponsible passivity, as if they should not work or plan. As Psalm 104 says, people are meant to work with what God provides. But Jesus *is* teaching us to look to God as our Provider. As Piper comments, "the argument is valid only if God really is the one who sees to it that the birds find their worms and the lilies wear their flowers."[32]

This will normally happen through the regular processes God has ordained (Gen 8:22). But, if necessary, God will direct or overrule natural processes to provide for His servants, as when He directed the ravens to supply food for Elijah while he was hiding (1 Kings 17:4–6) or when He moved the Egyptians to give donations of silver and gold and clothing on request to the departing Israelites (Exod 12:35–36).

Paul, in an urgent call to the people of Lystra who had been trying to offer sacrifice to him and Barnabas, points them instead to the one true God as creator and provider:

> "the living God, who made the heavens and the earth and the sea and everything in them. . . . has not left himself without testimony. He has shown kindness by giving you rain from heaven and crops in their seasons; he provides you with plenty of food and fills your hearts with joy.
>
> (Acts 14:15–17).

Later, speaking to the intellectual Athenians, Paul affirms that God "gives everyone life and breath and everything else" (Acts 17:25). God does not depend on our prayers, sacrifices, gifts, or rituals. Rather we depend on Him for everything.

IMPLICATIONS

This all implies that God is infinite in capacity and knowledge. He is the Creator and Lord of creation. He provides for His creation but is not the servant of His creatures. And the way He has set up the operations of the world do not create a picture of an indulgent or soft Deity. If "the lions roar for their prey and seek their food *from God*" (Ps 104:21; emphasis

---

32. Piper, *Providence*, 18.

added), it appears that predation is part of the divine setup.[33] Violence is not alien to God.[34]

Also this revelation shows God as interested in diversity. James Houston comments,

> The energy of God's will, not just the energy of the sun, sustains the biosphere where grass grows and animals feed, and man depends on them for his own food. God's creative power also produces diversity . . . creation is rich in variations.[35]

God has a role for each of His creatures, a fact more evident today with our greater appreciation of the eco-sphere and the interrelationship of all creation. God also displays creativity and variety in what He has made. His mind is fertile, even apparently weird at times when we look at some of His creatures: what kind of Mind thought of cockroaches, elephants, germs, plankton and many others? In Job 38–41, God boasts of His creation, its climate systems and its animals, such as wild donkeys, ostriches and the famous Leviathan. Human beings may not understand all these things, let alone control them, but God does.

The power of the wind, earthquakes, floods, volcanoes and other mighty natural forces shows how powerful God is and how vulnerable we are to divine interventions.[36] The tiny details that control life, down to the subatomic level, often somewhat 'random' and unpredictable, reveal how detailed God's operations can be.[37] As I originally wrote these words (in 2022), a microscopically small virus was wreaking havoc worldwide with astonishing impacts, not just on people's physical and mental health, but on politics and economies.

Jesus promises the twelve, "Are not two sparrows sold for a penny? Yet not one of them will fall to the ground outside your Father's care. And

---

33. Of course, this may be the setup in a *fallen* world which will be restored to a more peaceable state (Isa 11:6). But Psalm 104 itself doesn't say this.

34. Too many nineteenth century Christians left their faith behind when the idea of an original peaceful universe without any form of death or violence was exploded by Darwin's theory. Whatever the truth or otherwise of evolution, it is consistent with Psalm 104.

35. Houston, *I Believe in the Creator*, 15.

36. Cf. Piper, *Providence*, 236, referring especially to Amos 3:6.

37. These affirmations of God's providential control are challenged strongly in Oord, *Uncontrolling Love*. Oord's model of providence is much more open to chance and randomness.

even the very hairs of your head are all numbered" (Matt 10:29–30). This shows how specific and detailed God's providence can be.

Millard Erickson offers another good example from the book of Jonah:

> Everyone and everything (except Jonah) obeyed God's will and plan: the storm, the dice, the sailors, the great fish, the Ninevites, the east wind, the gourd, and the worm. Each part of creation is capable of fulfilling God's purposes for it, but each obeys in a different way.[38]

And a Trinitarian perspective implies that God's providential rule of creation, especially in relation to humanity, affects how we relate to one another. This is where the immanent working of the Spirit of God is so central. The universe is seen as fundamentally personal and relational; and human beings are not *just* organisms, machines, animals, workers, producers, or consumers. Our relationship with God gives a greater depth.[39]

The revelation of God as sovereign Creator should affect the way we talk about the natural world. We talk commonly of 'Mother Nature,' especially in relation to powerful disasters. And a whole ideology has grown up that makes Nature sovereign and rules out any force or agency that is not contained within Nature. But as Piper suggests, the Bible speaks of "a God-entranced world."[40] Millard Erickson points out that the Old Testament never says, "It rained," since "For the Hebrews, rain did not simply happen; God sent the rain."[41] This revelation is central to a biblical Christian worldview focused on God as sovereign. As Houston suggests, "We should see the world as the effects of the Word of God, the expression of His will and purpose."[42]

The biblical revelation of God as Creator and Provider also emphasizes another fact modern people intensely dislike. As Houston puts it, "Man's natural existence is wholly dependent upon the Word of God."[43] If there's one thing we can learn from epidemics, wars, accidents and the

---

38. Erickson, *Christian Theology*, 399.
39. I explore these points more fully in *The Revelation Worldview*, Chapter 5.
40. Piper, *Providence*, 18.
41. Erickson, *Christian Theology*, 374.
42. Houston, *I Believe in the Creator*, 51.
43. Houston, *I Believe in the Creator*, 51.

like, it is that we cannot be sure of tomorrow and our plans are always contingent on forces we cannot control.

The regularity we experience in creation is not always guaranteed. There are times of famine and drought (Acts 11:28; Gen 41:30-31,53-56). Some of these periods are attributed to God: "the matter has been firmly decided by God, and God will do it soon" (Gen 41:32; compare Ps 107:33-35).[44] Sometimes they are also summoned by God's representatives: "there will be neither dew nor rain in the next few years except at my word" (1 Kings 17:1). The breaking of this drought also comes as an answer to Elijah's prayers in 1 Kings 18:41-45 (see also James 5:17-18; Rev 11:6).

A major locust plague (Joel 1-2) is caused by "the army of the Lord" (Joel 2:11) and the people of Israel are exhorted to turn to God and seek Him "with all your heart, with fasting and weeping and mourning" (Joel 2:12) in the hope that "he may turn and relent and leave behind a blessing" (Joel 2:14a), which God promises to do (Joel 2:18-27). The covenant blessings and curses in Leviticus and Deuteronomy likewise give God the credit, or blame, for such weather regularities or their interruption (Lev 26:4,19-20; Deut 28:12,22-24,38-40).

This does not mean that those who suffer from natural disasters are especially targets of God's wrath. As Jesus explained in relation to two disasters of his day, one humanly inflicted and one the result of an accident, those who suffered were not worse sinners than others, but they do function as a warning that "unless you repent, you too will all perish" (Luke 13:3,5). In contrast to the expectation of repentance in response to disasters, Jesus criticizes his generation for not repenting in response to the display of God's power in healing miracles (Matt 11:20-24).

But on the other hand, "Creation . . . is an open system, open ultimately to the goodness and sovereignty of God . . . a view incompatible either with Fate . . . or with chance,"[45] but not with prayer. Since God is the sovereign Provider and Governor of creation, we can appeal to Him in our distresses. Major natural events such as earthquakes, volcanic eruptions, rough seas and storms may sometimes be attributed to God and alleviated in response to prayer (Gen 6:13; 7:11-12; 8:1; 19:24-25; Ps 107:24-30; Rev 8:7-12; 11:13). The disasters that came on Egypt in Exodus 6-12 are a major case in point (see also Ps 105:27-35). It was a

---

44. Calvin even speaks of harmful events in nature as "a sign of his certain and special vengeance" (Calvin, *Institutes of the Christian Religion*, 204).

45. Houston, *I Believe in the Creator*, 107.

windstorm that made a way for the Israelites to cross the Red Sea (Exod 14:21) and the return of the sea to its normal function drowned the Egyptian army (Exod 14:26–28; 15:1,4–10). On the other hand, natural forces may also be harnessed by evil powers. Jesus rebuked the storm that threatened the lives of him and his disciples using language similar to that of casting out demons (Mark 4:37–39; compare 1:25).[46]

Finally, the sovereignty of God in creation and providence, and indeed in history and salvation, tends to, and is meant to, bring God glory.[47] He should, and will, be the One who is viewed as central to everything in His creation. Referring to the future of Israel, Isaiah states,

> For my own sake, for my own sake, I do this.
> How can I let myself be defamed.
> I will not yield my glory to another.

(Isa 48:11).

Some of these points will become more important as this discussion proceeds. But first we need to explore the role of humanity in God's rule of His creation.

---

46. Cf. Boyd, *God At War*, 206.

47. This is the major thrust of John Piper's argument in *Providence*, especially 1–201.

CHAPTER 2

DELEGATION AND PROBATION

SHAKESPEARE EXPRESSES THE WONDER and mystery of human beings in his famous play, *Hamlet*:

> What a piece of work is man! How noble in reason! How infinite in faculties! in form and moving, how express and admirable! in action how like an angel! In apprehension, how like a god! The beauty of the world! the paragon of animals![1]

Human beings are amazing in so many ways, unique among all creatures, capable of astonishing feats, bringing so much of the world under their control. And yet so small compared to the size of the earth, which itself is a relatively tiny part of a vast universe. On what basis, then, do we justify our preeminent agency across the planet and even beyond? An ancient Hebrew poet meditated on this:

> When I consider your heavens,
> the work of your fingers,
> the moon and stars which you have set in place,
> what is mankind that you are mindful of them,
> human beings that you care for them?
> You have made them a little lower than the angels
> and crowned them with glory and honor.
> You have made them rulers over the works of your hands;
> you put everything under their feet
>
> (Ps 8:3–6)

---

1. Shakespeare, *Hamlet*, Act 2, Scene 2.

Only the biblical worldview accounts for the importance of human beings in the scheme of things.

THE HUMAN COMMISSION

Day 6 of the narrative in Genesis 1 concludes with God freely deciding to create a new and unique kind of creature: human beings. They are going to be different to all His other creatures in being created in God's own "image" and "likeness" (Gen 1:26–27). While the meaning of "image" and "likeness" has been debated, it may imply that, "The image makes man God's representative on earth,"[2] in a way analogous to the place of the king in the worldview of many ancient cultures.[3] Moreover, to them God assigned the responsibility to "rule over the fish in the sea and the birds in the sky, over the livestock and all the wild animals, and over all the creatures that move along the ground" (v.26). He then blessed these new creatures (male and female) and commissioned them to multiply, to "fill the earth and subdue it" and rule over all those living creatures (v.28).

This commission is not only unique, in that no other creature has such responsibilities, but it also involves God delegating His authority and power to these created beings. Humankind became a kind of 'vice-regent' over the earth.[4] This is a very serious and consequential step. God was not so directly in control of this planet after this. He had delegated the management of the earth to humanity, at least to some extent. This decision by God makes the question we are dealing with here very important: how much, or in what ways, is God sovereign *now*?

The Hebrew word translated "rule" in verses 26 and 28 (NIV) is *radah*, which means "tread down, subjugate, rule or have dominion." It suggests perhaps that this rule must be somehow imposed, even perhaps against some resistance. It has therefore some similarity with "subdue" in v.28, which translates the Hebrew *kabash*, which means "tread down, conquer, subdue, keep under."[5] However, this does not mean a license to

---

2. Wenham, *Genesis 1–15*, 30–31.

3. And in contrast to them, since in Genesis all humans have this dignity, not just kings.

4. Cf. Wenham, *Genesis 1–15*, 32.

5. In contrast, the word "govern" used in verse 16 of the role of the sun and moon is *mashal* or *memshalah*, which do not seem to have this connotation. These Hebrew definitions and other following are derived from Young's *Analytical Concordance* and Strong's *Exhaustive Concordance* and supported by Holladay (ed.), *Concise Hebrew and*

unlimited domination or exploitation of the non-human world. Rather, as Frédéric Baudin comments,

> In the context of Genesis... these two Hebrew verbs *mashal* and *kābaš* signify that man and woman are called to superintend creation, to manage it properly, with the knowledge and the skill that God granted them in the exercise of their mandate.[6]

We will explore how this delegation and its results affects God's sovereignty in the rest of this book. But let's note some of the implications. First, compared to polytheistic cultures, humans are not created just to serve God, or the gods, and provide for his (or their) needs.[7] Rather, "God is here portrayed as a benevolent creator concerned for man's welfare."[8]

Second, for theodicy: many critics ask how we can believe in a good God in a context of human evil and natural disasters? Part of the answer to that, in a biblical worldview, is to place the responsibility for these evils at the feet of the human race: God put *us* in charge of the earth and we have 'stuffed up.' The current problem of 'anthropogenic' global warming is a good example of this.[9]

Third, there are implications for ethics and human accountability to God. Human beings innately know that they are responsible for the earth, especially now with our debates on the environment and climate change. No one holds pigs responsible for global warming (except to the degree that they emit lots of carbon dioxide). No one expects pigs to come up with a plan to limit emissions. We all know that the responsibility is ours. This implies that we are accountable *to* Someone else, and not just to future generations.

Hence, God gives Israel responsibility to care for the land; for example, by letting it rest every seven years and in the Year of Jubilee (Lev 25:1–7,11), by not eating the fruit of a tree for four years (Lev 19:23–25) and by not harvesting crops to the extreme boundaries so as to leave some for the needy (Lev 19:9–10). Leviticus 25:19 says that as a result,

---

Aramaic Lexicon of the Old Testament. See also Boyd, *God At War*, 106.

6. Frédéric Baudin, *Ecology and the Bible* (translated by Damon Dimauro; Peabody: Hendrickson, 2020), 17. See also Wenham, *Genesis 1–15*, 33.

7. Cf. Wenham, *Genesis 1–15*, 37.

8. Wenham, *Genesis 1–15*, 39.

9. Cf. Baudin, *Ecology and the Bible*, 21–33 for a biblical analysis of the roots of this.

"Then the land will yield its fruit, and you will eat your fill and live there in safety." And part of the reason for the Israelites being exiled was to allow the land to recover and "enjoy its sabbaths" (Lev 26:43).[10] This is applied as a general principle in *Revelation* when the judgment of God comes, "destroying those who destroy the earth" (Rev 11:18). God holds humanity accountable for the care of the earth and we are not licensed to exploit it relentlessly.

But fourth, this momentous decision of God to delegate rule over the earth to humanity potentially limits, or at least modifies, the sovereign activity of God. As John Lennox puts it, God's sovereignty

> is clearly to be understood not in terms of absolute control over human behavior but as a more glorious thing: the devolving of real power to creatures made in God's image, so that they are not mere programmed automata but moral beings with genuine freedom.[11]

There is no evidence in Scripture that God has rescinded this delegation or indeed that He ever will; this becomes a factor in the incarnation later. God made a free choice to submit His world to human government and care. We will see later that this does not *annul* God's sovereignty, but it clearly affects how God's sovereign rule operates. As we saw in Psalm 104, God's providential care of creation continues. To put it another way, God has *delegated* but not *abdicated*. Human beings are accountable to the Creator for their rule of the earth, and part of God's ongoing sovereign rule is to hold us to account, that is judge us, for our actions.

All this is on view in Genesis 2, the story of Adam and Eve.[12] This narrative begins by reaffirming God's creation of "the heavens and the earth" (v.4).[13] It then focuses on an early stage in creation: "now no shrub had yet appeared on the earth and no plant had yet sprung up, for the Lord God had not sent rain on the earth and there was no one to work the ground" (v.5). Perhaps some aspects of creation were 'on hold' until the creation of human beings who would "work the ground." So in verse 7, "the Lord God formed a man from the dust of the ground." The Hebrew for "formed" is *yatsar*, meaning "mould, fashion, make, frame" as

---

10. Cf. Baudin, *Ecology and the Bible*, 47–49.
11. Lennox, *Determined to Believe?*, 45.
12. Of course, many scholars question or reject the historical validity of this story, but the principles are valid even if the story is read as a kind of parable.
13. Using both the Hebrew words found in Genesis 1: *bara* and *asah*

a potter. Then God "breathed into his nostrils the breath of life, and the man became a living being."

This passage affirms God's sovereignty since God did not *have to* make this man and the man will not be made, and not live, except by God's decision. Paul asserts that God personally designed the human body as He planned (1 Cor 12:18; 15:38; compare Ps 139:13–15). And what a design it is! But the language does not convey the idea of a remote dictator just speaking things into existence as Genesis 1 might suggest. Rather God is seen to get 'down and dirty,' shaping this creature as a potter shapes a pot and then breathing into it. This is another way of looking at humanity as made in the image of God, though animals are also said to have the breath of life (Gen 7:22).

The man is placed into a pristine environment, a garden cultivated *by God* with all sorts of possibilities (vv.8–14). God then speaks a further word of delegation: He puts the man "in the Garden of Eden to work it and take care of[14] it" (v.15). This localizes the rule spoken of in Gen 1:26–28 in that the man is in control of the Garden and responsible to God for its upkeep.

The man also has freedom with respect to the trees with one limitation only (v.17). God is being incredibly generous here, granting the early humans huge territory in which to freely operate. They could make their own decisions about all the trees in the garden (Gen 2:16). Within the limitations of their natural capacity (they couldn't fly, for example), Adam and Eve could do whatever they wanted with only one exception.[15] God never intended to micro-manage humanity.

And the man also gets to name "all the livestock, the birds in the sky and all the wild animals" (v.20). This is deliberate: God "brought them to the man to see what he would name them; and whatever *the man* called each living creature, that was its name" (v.19, emphasis added). God's naming showed His sovereignty in Chapter 1 (Gen 1:5,8.10). So man's naming indicates *his* sovereignty (a delegated sovereignty), though of course, when he names the woman (Gen 2:23), that throws a different light on the situation, a point made by the language of "suitable helper" (v.20), "bone of my bones, and flesh of my flesh" (v.23) and "one flesh" (v.24). Clearly the man's relationship with his wife is very different to his relationship with animals.

14. Or "guard it" (Heb *shomrah*). Cf Wenham, *Genesis 1–15*, 67.
15. As Sproul helpfully puts it, humans are free but not autonomous; their freedom is limited by God's sovereignty (Sproul, *Chosen by God*, 42).

Later we see that Jesus shows a new level of dominance over natural events which not only reveals him to be divine but potentially shows what true humanity might look like. He displays both God's sovereignty and the potential of humanity as earth's governor. He resists the temptation to interfere in nature for selfish ends (Matt 4:3-7; Luke 4:3-4,9-12). But he heals the sick and demonized (Matt 4:23-24; 8:16; 11:4; 14:35-36), calms storms (Matt 8:24-27), walks across a lake (Matt 14:25-27), provides food for two large crowds (Matt 14:15-21; 15:32-38; compare 2 Kings 4:42-44) and encourages his followers to reach by faith for a greater level of authority over natural forces (Matt 8:26; 21:18-22). His forgiving and healing of a crippled man is seen by the crowd as due to the fact that God "had given such authority to man" (Matt 9:8), an authority he then delegated to his twelve disciples (Matt 10:1,8). Jesus attributed such authority to the power of the Spirit and the arrival of God's kingdom or rule (Matt 12:28). God's plans for human beings are much bigger than many Christians imagine.

HUMAN PROBATION

Meanwhile the other aspect of this original situation is probation: the man, and by implication, the woman, are faced with a test. They are free "to eat from any tree in the garden" (Gen 2:16), but "not from the tree of the knowledge of good and evil" (v.17). This is not mere advice: "when you eat from it you will certainly die" (v.17). God is actively asserting His sovereign right over His creation, giving and withholding access as He sees fit, testing His newmade man, commanding him with authority, and warning of consequences for disobedience.

But notice three aspects of this situation. First, the man has some kind of free will, to obey or disobey this command. This is clearly implied by God's commanding language. Lennox comments, "Far from diminishing the status of humanity, that prohibition was essential to establish the unique dignity of humans as moral beings."[16] Second, God sets up the test by placing the forbidden tree within reach, so disobedience is a real possibility.

And third, the test and command are not arbitrary: there is a real reason why God places the man under this rule. The reasons are not

---

16. Lennox, *Determined to Believe?*, 45.

spelled out, but I think we can speculate with some confidence.[17] God cannot act contrary to His own nature. This is only implied, at best, in this passage, but is clearly stated elsewhere in the Bible (e.g. James 1:13; Tit 1:2; Heb 6:18; 1 John 1:5). As Geisler puts it, *"Something is not right just because God wills it; He wills it because it is right in accordance with His unchangeable nature."*[18]

To begin with, the name of the forbidden tree, "the tree of the knowledge of good and evil," implies some kind of moral knowledge or awareness. Eating it would imply a desire for such knowledge independent of God, a kind of moral autonomy that would damage their relationship with God as God.[19] Based on what happens in Genesis 2 and 3, we can also suggest, therefore, that God was protecting the innocence and happiness of Adam and Eve. Gen 2:25 expresses their original state well: like little children, they "were both naked, and they felt no shame."[20] But the first result of them eating from the forbidden tree was that, "the eyes of both of them were opened, and they realized that they were naked" (Gen 3:7), with disastrous consequences for their relationship with God and their happiness in general. Shame and guilt have been universal features of the human experience ever since.

Perhaps another reason for the prohibition was as a test of obedience and faith. Would they respect God's right to set the rules? Would they trust God's decision as in their best interests? Clearly God set this test up by creating the forbidden tree, by drawing their attention to it, by putting it within reach, by giving them free will so that they had the possibility of disobedience, *and* by putting the serpent in the garden to tempt them. Why did God do that? Genesis does not state whether or not God knew what the outcome would be, but at least God is seen as taking one awful risk here.

However, the test in itself was not hard. Adam and Eve had no reason to doubt or push back at God. Their needs were met abundantly: they had maximum freedom to eat from the trees in the garden, and indeed to do anything they liked, except eat from the one forbidden tree, and should easily have remained grateful and trusting. It implies that ingratitude is

---

17. According to Wenham, it was not that the fruit was poisonous (Wenham, *Genesis 1–15*, 67).

18. Geisler, *Chosen But Free*, 150 (emphasis in the original).

19. Cf. Wenham, *Genesis 1–15*, 87.

20. Cf. Wenham, *Genesis 1–15*, 88.

the root of sin because that was what the serpent sowed into their minds (compare 2 Sam 12:7–9 and Rom 1:21).

My suggestion is that there was something in God's constitution, perhaps something in God Himself, that necessitated this test. There seems to be an unspoken rule in the moral universe, part of what Sanders calls "the rules of the game,"[21] that everything must be tested. We see that implied in many places in the Bible: it seems that almost every time God did something fresh, there was a test or temptation that the people involved either resisted or succumbed to. There are many examples, as this table illustrates.

Location	God's New Event	Testing or Temptation	Result
Genesis 15–16	Covenant made with Abram including promise of a son	Age and infertility; Sarai's suggestion of a child by Hagar	Birth of Ishmael and consequent conflict
Exodus 14–16	The Exodus event and crossing the Red Sea	Shortages of water and food in the desert	People grumble; God provides
Exodus 25–40	Construction of the Tabernacle	Moses' prolonged absence; people approach Aaron (Exod 32:1)	Golden Calf rebellion and death of 3,000 people
Lev 8–10	Institution of the Aaronic Priesthood	Aaron's two older sons offer "unauthorized fire" (Lev 10:1)	Fire from God consumes them
1 Sam 8–15	Institution of the monarchy with Saul	Saul fails two tests of obedience (1 Sam 13, 15)	Saul's rule is limited and another will become king
2 Sam 6	The ark brought to Jerusalem	The oxen carrying the ark stumble and Uzzah tries to steady it	Uzzah killed by God and the venture is delayed for 3 months
2 Sam 7–12	David's victories and exaltation in Jerusalem	David is tempted and takes Bathsheba and has Uriah killed in battle	Nathan pronounces judgment; David's kingdom will be shaky
1 Kings 5–11	Building of Solomon's temple	Solomon led astray by foreign wives	Prophetic judgment pronounced
Daniel 1–3	Promotion of the four Hebrew young men	Golden statue test	Three youths are loyal to God and vindicated

21. Cf. Sanders, *God Who Risks*, 184, 241. This idea was not derived from Sanders, however.

Location	God's New Event	Testing or Temptation	Result
Job 1–2	Satan gains permission to try Job's faith	Job loses everything but his life	Job remains loyal to God even though he questions God's dealings
Matt 3–4	Jesus baptized and publicly recognized by God	The Spirit leads Jesus "into the wilderness to be tempted by the devil" (Matt 4:1)	Jesus successfully resists the devil's three temptations
Luke 22–23	Satan asks permission to sift the disciples, especially Peter (23:31–32)	Peter promises never to betray Jesus (23:33)	Peter denies Jesus three times
Acts 2–5	Pentecost births a new move and the church with an attitude of generosity	Ananias and Sapphira tempted by Satan to tell lies and withhold offering (5:3,9)	Ananias and Sapphira killed instantly

At the very least, God could only know (or perhaps better, *they* could only know) whether or not Adam and Eve loved and trusted Him by exposing them to such a test.

I suggest that, if they had passed the test, Adam and Eve would have grown in stature and maturity and in their relationship with God. The test was a kind of growing up experience. They were created as physical adults, it seems, but morally they were still children, naked, innocent and immature as opposed to righteous. The passage in Genesis does not spell out this idea of growing to maturity, but it seems implicit in the narrative in which God seems to be teaching Adam (Gen 2:19–20) and in which the potential for development is also implied by the resources described in the region of Eden (Gen 2:10–14).

So what does this all imply about God's sovereignty? God had the freedom to set up the situation as He decided. God had the right to command the human beings and restrict their access to any item He chose. And God himself was controlling or managing the situation by setting up all its ingredients; not only was nothing happening without God's permission, but God seemed to be actively setting up the test, almost willfully creating the possibility of failure for the humans.[22] Perhaps, as

---

22. I'm not saying that God 'decreed' the Fall as such, but He set up the possibility. Debates about this continue, especially among Calvinists who debate whether or not God decreed the reprobation of the 'non-elect' before He created them (cf. Custance, *Sovereignty of Grace*, 74).

Sproul contends, "God must have foreordained the entrance of sin into the world," meaning that "God must have decided to allow it to happen."[23]

TESTING THE ISRAELITES

Similar features can be found in the dealings of God with Israel as they moved through the desert towards their promised land. Psalm 95 talks of the people testing God (Ps 95:9; compare Exod 17:2,7), but Deuteronomy suggests that God was testing *them* and teaching them:

> Remember how the Lord your God led you all the way in the wilderness these forty years, to humble and *test* you *in order to know what was in your heart*, whether or not you would keep his commands. He humbled you, causing you to hunger and then feeding you with manna, which neither you nor your ancestors had known, *to teach you* that man does not live on bread alone but on every word that comes from the mouth of the Lord

(Deut 8:2–3; emphasis added).

Election and testing go hand in hand. It's God's people who are tested by God Himself as He seeks to teach them and bring them to mature faith, obedience and ability to be entrusted with God's authority like the original humans. And these tests usually involve shortages of some kind.

This note is sounded in the very first issue the Israelites face after the Red Sea, a serious water shortage, when "the people grumbled against Moses" (Exod 15:24) and, after solving the problems, "the Lord issued a ruling and instruction for them and put them to the test" (Exod 15:25) involving a challenge and a promise.

The second test of the Israelites involves food. Again the people grumble (Exod 16:2–3). Again God promises to provide sovereignly – "I will rain down bread from heaven" (Exod 16:4). But God tests them with the instructions He gave for collecting the manna in relation to the Sabbath (Exod 16:4–5), a test that some failed by storing up the daily manna or looking for some on the Sabbath day (Exod 16:20,27–28).

The Sinai covenant presents in detail God's rule over His people, His delegation of authority to them and the note of probation. God's initial

---

23. Sproul, *Chosen by God*, 31. Comp Piper, *Providence*, 171–177. This seems to follow from the premise that God knew what would happen and went ahead anyway. It's also implied by the foreordination of Christ's cross (Rev 13:8; 1 Pet 1:11,20). Comp. Helm, *Providence of God*, 101.

speech to them through Moses reminds them of His work in saving them from Egyptian oppression and then appoints them conditionally to a special role:

> Now *if* you obey me fully and keep my covenant, then out of all nations you will be my treasured possession. Although the whole earth is mine, you will be for me a kingdom of priests and a holy nation

(Exod 19:5–6 emphasis added).

Here God asserts His ownership of the whole world but explains His decision to delegate aspects of His rule to the Israelites by appointing them as a divine "kingdom of priests" mediating God's will and blessing to the rest of the world.[24] However, this is conditional on their loyalty to His covenant,[25] so we see both delegation and probation as well as election (God chooses Israel out of all nations for this privilege).

God then dictates the terms of the covenant based on His role as Israel's Savior (Exod 20:2) and the earth's Creator (Exod 20:11). Central to these demands is respect for God as unique, holy and "jealous" (Exod 20:2–7), that is, sovereign. God makes the rules; humans are expected to obey them. And the note of probation is sounded again here when Moses tells the people, "God has come to test you" (Exod 20:20). The theme of what follows is one of delegation: Israel itself is to administer and enforce God's revealed laws.

There is a positive side to this probation. If they attend to the words of the angel sent by God, they will enjoy victory, health, fruitfulness, and secure possession of the promised land (Exod 23:20–31). On the other side, compromise with the Canaanites will bring a snare (Exod 23:32–33). The Israelites formally promise to keep the covenant (Exod 19:8; 24:3,7) as part of a somber ratification ceremony sealed with sacrificial blood (Exod 24: 3–8). But shortly afterwards, they fall into rebellion at the golden calf incident (Exodus 32).

Testing is therefore a major theme of the Pentateuch.

---

24. As Helm comments, "Israel has a mission to the nations" (*Providence of God*, 105).

25. Cf. Calvin, *Institutes*, 929.

TESTING SAUL

The theme of testing extends into the historical books of the Old Testament. One of the clearest examples of delegation and probation is found in the life of Israel's first king, Saul. Saul is clearly and prophetically earmarked as king through the ministry of the final judge, Samuel. The popular demand for a king is itself flawed and rooted in poor motives that amounted to a rejection of God (1 Sam 8:4–20), although anticipated and provided for by Moses in Deuteronomy (17:14–20); both passages seem to anticipate the later centralization and authoritarianism of Solomon. God, however, accedes to this demand and instructs Samuel, "Listen to them and give them a king" (1 Sam 8:22).

The choice of Saul from the unlikely tribe of Benjamin, which had been nearly wiped out in a civil war (1 Sam 9:21; Judg 20–21), is perhaps a good illustration of election. But the choice is vindicated by a story of providential guidance set off by lost donkeys (1 Sam 9:1–20; 10:2,14–16), leading to a prophetic action by Samuel to the astonished Saul (1 Sam 9:15–10:1), and confirmed by several events, including a prophetic encounter during which Saul himself "prophesies" by the Spirit (1 Sam 10:5–6,9–12). Saul is then publicly confirmed as king by a system of lots (1 Sam 10:19–24; compare Prov 16:33; Acts 1:26). Each of these incidents displays God's sovereign influence and choice.

But Saul's kingship is on probation. Samuel encourages him to "do whatever your hand finds to do, for God is with you" (1 Sam 10:7), a note of delegation appropriate for one exercising divine authority as king, but then tells him to "wait seven days until I come to you and tell you what you are to do" at Gilgal (1 Sam 10:8).

This test is apparently deferred because Saul deals with the immediate crisis, inflicting a crushing victory over the Ammonites (1 Sam 11:1–11; 12:12), and a coronation ceremony is held at Gilgal (1 Sam 11:14–15), but the Philistine hegemony remains. They even have outposts in Israel (1 Sam 10:5) and Saul's son Jonathan attacks one of them (1 Sam 13:3–4), which amounts to a declaration of rebellion and provokes a massive Philistine army to assemble to put the rebellion down (1 Sam 13:5). The small force of Israelites feels completely intimidated and Saul feels he cannot wait for Samuel to arrive before making offerings to God for success (1 Sam 13:6–10). Thus he fails his first test and Samuel lets him know that his kingdom will not be confirmed and his successor has already been appointed (1 Sam 13:13–14).

Israel wins this particular battle, largely through the efforts of Jonathan (1 Sam 14), but then Saul fails a second test by not carrying out all the instructions related to a campaign against the Amalekites (1 Sam 15). This time the Lord himself says, "I regret that I have made Saul king, because he has turned away from me and has not carried out my instructions" (1 Sam 15:11). And this time, His rejection is final; in fact, Samuel says, "He who is the glory of Israel does not lie or change his mind, for he is not a human being, that he should change his mind" (1 Sam 15:29). God *has* changed his mind about Saul. Saul's position would have been confirmed if he had obeyed God's direction through Samuel (1 Sam 13:13). But having failed two tests of obedience, Saul forfeits his authority and there is no longer any chance that God will alter this sentence; Samuel has apparently prayed for this all night but been denied (1 Sam 15:11b). And God sends Samuel to anoint Saul's successor shortly afterwards (1 Sam 16).

How sovereign is God in this narrative? Unquestionably God is in charge, calling the shots, free to choose the king, and guiding events to confirm His choice. But God is also responding to human decisions: in this case, the Israelite demand for a king and Saul's foolish decisions. Did God not know Saul would be like this? The author of 1 Samuel never says. But he shows that God's declared appointments are conditional, and God's sovereign actions are flexible, responding to the situations as they develop.

JOB THE PARADIGMATIC TESTING

Perhaps the greatest text on testing in the Old Testament is the Book of Job. It opens by presenting Job as someone who "was blameless and upright; he feared God and shunned evil" (Job 1:1). He was living under God's blessing in terms of prosperity and indeed was "the greatest man among all the people of the East" (Job 1:3). His family led an idyllic life, but Job was aware of the danger of sin and offered sacrifices for his sons just in case they "have sinned and cursed God in their hearts" (Job 1:5), a prescient action as it turned out, since Job himself would be pressured to do exactly that. Job was clearly a favorite of God, one of God's 'elect.' And this is why he attracted severe testing.

The narrative then introduces Satan, apparently an angelic being and companion of the angels of God (Job 1:6). While the author of Job does not equate him with the serpent of Genesis 3, he is destined to play a similar role and such an equation is made by Revelation (Rev 12:9; 20:2). Satan tells God he has been "roaming throughout the earth, going back and forth on it" (Job 1:7), in response to which God draws Satan's attention to Job, his servant, bragging, "There is no one on earth like him; he is blameless and upright, a man who fears God and shuns evil" (Job 1:8).

Satan retorts, "Does Job fear God for nothing?" insinuating that Job only serves God because of the prosperity he is enjoying, and challenges God to "stretch out your hand and strike everything he has, and he will surely curse you to your face" (Job 1:9–11). God accepts the challenge with one proviso: "everything he has is in your power, but on the man himself do not lay a finger" (Job 1:12).

As a result, Job loses all his oxen, donkeys, sheep, camels, and finally his sons and daughters, through a combination of enemy attacks and natural disasters (Job 1:13–19). But Job responds with worship, acknowledging that everything he had came from God, and "did not sin by charging God with wrongdoing" (Job 1:22). In other words, Job (who apparently knows nothing about Satan's role in all this) respects and submits to God's sovereign will. He (rightly) sees God as finally responsible for what has happened to him.[26]

In the next chapter, God boasts again to Satan of Job's response: "he still maintains his integrity, though *you incited me* against him to ruin him without any reason" (Job 2:3, emphasis added). Satan demands that the testing be ramped up: "stretch out your hand and strike his flesh and bones, and he will surely curse you to your face" (Job 2:5). God consents to this, demanding only that Job's life is spared (Job 2:6), and Satan "afflicted Job with painful sores from the soles of his feet to the crown of his head" (Job 2:7). The impoverished and humiliated man is reduced to scraping his skin with broken pottery as he sits among the ashes of a fire (Job 2:8) and his wife urges him to "Curse God and die!" (Job 2:9). However, Job maintains his faith in God, saying "Shall we accept good from God, and not trouble?" (Job 2:10).

But next, in apparent response to the sympathy of his three friends, Job's composure cracks and he begins to complain about his fate by cursing the day he was born (Job 2:11–3:19). This launches a long dialogue as the three friends seek to explain what has happened in terms of their own ideas about God and suffering, blaming Job for what has befallen

---

26. Cf. Piper, *Providence*, 353–355.

him and rejecting his protestations of innocence. Job cries out to God for an audience even as they all confess God's sovereignty over all events (Job 3–31). A younger man, Elihu, tries to bring a Spirit-led perspective but his mindset is not fundamentally different to the others' (Job 32–37).

Finally, God himself speaks directly to Job, affirming His power over all creation and challenging Job's limited perspective on things (Job 38–41). As a result, Job gives up his protest with a ringing reaffirmation of God's sovereignty:

> I know that you can do all things;
> no purpose of yours can be thwarted.
> You asked, 'Who is this that obscures my plans without
>   knowledge?'
> Surely I spoke of things I did not understand,
> things too wonderful for me to know

(Job 42:2–3).

God then vindicates Job against his accusers because they "have not spoken the truth about me, as my servant Job has" (Job 42:7,8). After Job, in effect, forgives them and prays for them, "The LORD restored his fortunes and gave him twice as much as he had before" (Job 42:10).

So what can we learn from this book about the sovereignty of God? First, and most obviously, God is in control here. He makes the final determination about what happens to Job and others in the story. As Piper rightly says, God ultimately has the power over life and death.[27] Satan can only act within boundaries set by God. God is not compelled to act according to the demands of other actors. As Calvin comments, "whatever men or Satan himself may instigate, God nevertheless holds the key."[28]

Second, God's power and rights as Creator are affirmed. Job declares, "the Lord gave and the Lord has taken away" (Job 1:21) and God gives Job a kind of object lesson in His creative power in His long speech near the end of the book.

But third, Satan seems to be able to appeal to something in God that prompts God to allow him to attack Job; a kind of constitution based on God's character that seems to require God to test His people. More scandalous, however, it is not Satan but God who initiates all this, by drawing Satan's attention to Job with such fulsome praise, twice (Job 1:8; 2:3). God

---

27. Piper, *Providence*, 305, 355.
28. Calvin, *Institutes*, 230.

thus is finally responsible for testing Job (see Job 1:21; 2:10; 42:11) and this demands an explanation.

No clear explanation is given in the book. Several poor explanations are rejected, particularly those offered by Job's friends who persist in saying that Job's misfortunes are his own fault because of some hidden sin or the like. Several possibilities are suggested by the narrative, perhaps. One is that Job's testing will silence Satan and glorify God, since Satan alleges that no one ever serves God except for what they get out of it in return. The absence of Satan in Job 42 may confirm this line of thinking.

But the other possibility is that God has Job's ultimate best interests in mind. Certainly, Job is blessed with double what he lost at the end. But the other implied development is in Job himself. Job has always been righteous, but he has grown in moral and spiritual stature at the end of the story, as displayed by his vision of God (Job 42:5) and his intercession for his deluded friends (Job 42:8–9). I argued earlier that in the divine constitution, 'everything must be tested' so that God's chosen people may grow in stature and authority and inherit everything God has chosen for them. Job has struggled in his commitment to God and needed to repent (Job 42:6), but ultimately, he has triumphed, spoken truly of God, defeated Satan and been rewarded for his faithfulness. Surely this was the outcome God had in mind from the beginning, and it acts also as a kind of model of the Christian life. Satan tempts to bring us down but God tests to bring out the gold in his friends (1 Pet 1:6–7) and to enhance their development.

THE TESTING OF JESUS

The same principle of probation in relation to calling and authority is exemplified in the life of Jesus, the ultimate human being, "the last Adam," "second man" and "heavenly man" (1 Cor 15:45–49). Jesus was publicly declared by God to be His son at his baptism (Matt 3:16–17; Mark 1:10–11; Luke 3:21–22), but immediately afterwards he was sent into the wilderness to be tempted by the devil.

The devil questioned God's word that Jesus was the son of God (Matt 4:3,6) and tried to derail his mission by offering him political power instead (Matt 4:8–9). Clearly Satan was trying to divert Jesus and undermine his loyalty to God the Father. But equally clearly, the Spirit put Jesus in this predicament (Matt 4:1; Mark 1:12; Luke 4:1) and allowed (even prompted) the devil to put Jesus to the test. The affirmation of Jesus by God reminds us of what God had said about Job. Luke relates that after this testing, when the devil had "finished all this tempting" (Luke 4:13), "Jesus returned to Galilee in the power of the Spirit" (Luke 4:14). He had clearly passed the test, served his probation successfully, and was now in a position to fulfill his mission as God planned, as announced in the synagogue in Nazareth (Luke 4:18–21). He had done what Adam (Gen 3) and Israel (Exodus-Deuteronomy) signally failed to do and recapitulated their history successfully, thus winning the prize of delegated authority that they could have won.

The devil continued to tempt Jesus, even through his own disciples (Matt 16:23), and he suffered many things even before his 'passion.' Hebrews speaks of God making "the pioneer of their salvation perfect through what he suffered" (Heb 2:10) since, "Because he himself suffered when he was tempted, he is able to help those who are being tempted" (Heb 2:18) and thus, "we do not have a high priest who is unable to empathize with our weaknesses, but we have one who has been tempted in every way, just as we are- yet he did not sin" (Heb 4:15). In language reminiscent of the Book of Job, Hebrews states: "Son though he was, he learned obedience from what he suffered, and *once made perfect*, he became the source of eternal salvation for all who obey him" (Heb 5:8-9; emphasis added).

In Jesus' case, the climax of his trials came in the Garden of Gethsemane, where he prayed three times to be released from God's call to the Cross but submitted to God's plan (Matt 26:36–44; Mark 14:32–42; Luke 22:39–46). This was no easy decision. Jesus said, "My soul is overwhelmed with sorrow to the point of death" (Matt 26:38; Mark 14:34) and Luke tells us that "being in anguish, he prayed more earnestly, and his sweat was like drops of blood falling to the ground" (Luke 22:44). Moreover, he could have chosen otherwise: "Do you think that I cannot call on my Father, and he will at once put at my disposal more than twelve legions of angels?" (Matt 26:53). It all came down to God's will (Matt 26:39; Luke 22:42) and fulfilment of Scripture (Matt 26:54,56; Luke 24:7,46). Jesus submitted to the Father's Plan out of his own free choice (John 10:17–18) and this made him "perfect," that is, mature, complete, and totally qualified to be the savior of the world.

God tests His chosen people, beginning with Adam and Eve, and on through the Israelites, Job and others, climaxing with Jesus. It seems that God takes the risk that they might fail the test, especially under pressure from the devil, but trusts His elect to pass the test and qualify for higher authority as originally intended for mankind.

THE TESTING OF THE EARLY CHURCH

It didn't end with Jesus, however. Confirming my view that everything must be tested, we read of the infant church being tested in at least three ways in the early chapters of Acts. They are tested by the fires of opposition and persecution (Acts 4:1–20; 5:17–42; 6:11–8:3) but withstand the opposition courageously in the power of the Holy Spirit (Acts 4:8,31; 7:55).

They are tested in a different way by division over the treatment of needy widows (Acts 6:1–6). However, the wisdom of the apostles brings a pragmatic resolution that not only solves the immediate problem but also makes space for new leaders to be raised up in the church. More seriously, in a related area, the funding of help to the needy, which depends on the generosity of believers (Acts 2:44–45; 4:32–37; 11:27–30), there is a serious challenge caused by a dishonest and covetous couple who restrain their generosity while pretending otherwise (Acts 5:1–2). They at least have failed the test at the behest of Satan (Acts 5:3,9). But Peter exposes their sin and they die as a result, somewhat like some of the rebels in the wilderness in Numbers. Hence the church itself is purified from the likely results of their hypocritical scheme.

God has allowed these things to happen, perhaps to strengthen the church and its leaders as they pass the tests. God in His divine power 'could have' caused all the enemies to be converted (as He did with Saul in Acts 9), 'could have' prevented the complaints about Hellenistic widows (or made them unnecessary) and 'could have' moved Ananias and Sapphira to be more generous or prevented the devil from tempting them. God didn't do that. In His sovereign will, He permits testing and tempting to go on. He seemingly allows human free will to continue as at the beginning and for the devil to use that to advantage. He is more interested in defeating Satan through His chosen people than eliminating Satan altogether (though that will eventually happen). Piper puts it well when he writes, "God aims for the fullness of his beauty and worth to be magnified in the way his people prefer him over what Satan offers."[29]

---

29. Piper, *Providence*, 657. See also 277–283.

Perhaps the clearest explanation of testing is found in the Letter of James. James insists that "trials of many kinds" are occasions for rejoicing (James 1:2) because such experiences bring character development, "so that you may be mature and complete, not lacking anything" (James 1:4). In fact, "the one who perseveres under trial, ... having stood the test . . . will receive the crown of life" (James 1:12). Of course, with trials come temptations. God allows the trials but is not responsible for the temptations, which arise, James teaches, from our own "evil desire" (James 1:13–14). Rather God is looking for a different response: "be quick to listen, slow to speak and slow to become angry" (James 1:19). Take note of Job, James says (James 5:10–11)! Testing is part of God's plan and here God shows respect to our dignity as free human beings. God's sovereignty does not make Him either over-protective or a control-freak!

The Book of Revelation is full of such themes. For example, the prophetic messages to the seven churches (Rev 2–3) read like classical Old Testament oracles which assess the progress of God's people and declare promises and warnings based on such assessments.[30] The first church so addressed, in Ephesus, is first praised for its hard work, perseverance and discernment (Rev 2:2–3), but then condemned for forsaking the love they had at first and called on to repent (Rev 2:4–5). What will happen? "If you do not repent, I will come to you and remove your lampstand from its place" (Rev 2:5). The future of this church 'hangs in the balance' (removal of the lampstand suggests the church might cease to exist) but ultimately lies in the hands of those believers. They are not foreordained to fail. But if they do fail, the consequences are sure: they can't disregard Jesus and avoid the consequences; in fact, Jesus himself will come and deal with them sovereignly.

The second church addressed (in Smyrna) is praised unreservedly, one of only two who receive no rebuke or correction (the other is Philadelphia). This church is under serious external threat from unbelieving Jews and others, a situation who seems to be about to get worse:

> Do not be afraid of what you are about to suffer. I tell you, the devil will put some of you in prison to *test* you, and you will suffer persecution for ten days. Be faithful, even to the point of death, and I will give you life as your victor's crown
>
> (Rev 2:10; emphasis added).

---

30. Cf. Newton, *Pentecostal Commentary on Revelation*, 81–82.

This suffering is attributed first to the Jewish synagogue, probably also to local or Roman authorities who had the power to put them in prison, and, more deeply, to the devil. But ultimately this is a test like Job endured. The best church must endure testing. But if they pass the test, they will be rewarded. The language of these messages portrays a conditional future, in other words. God is sovereign but the future is 'open' to some degree.

DIVINE LAW

All this discussion of testing has an underlying assumption which we need to unpack briefly. To put it as simply as possible, God is the supreme Law-giver of the universe, and particularly of the human world. This flows from God's right as Creator to set the rules for all His creation.

I have no space to pursue a full theology of divine law, but a few comments may help locate this theme within discussion of God's sovereignty.

1. Divine laws come from the divine Law-giver Himself, which means that they need no further justification but express His inherent divine justice. They are non-negotiable.

2. Divine laws are based on implied or explicit covenants or treaties dictated by God to some or all people.[31] This is implied in Genesis 2:16–17 by the command and consequences, but made explicit in the covenants with Noah (Gen 9:1–17), Abraham (Gen 15:18; 17:7–14) and the people of Israel (Exod 19:3–8; 24:1–8). The promises or blessing and warnings of disaster to Israel reflect this covenant basis (Lev 26; Deut 28).

3. Divine laws are designed for specific groups. The laws given through Moses, for example, are directed specifically at the Israelites (Exod 20:2). The first case law is specifically about Hebrew slaves (Exod 21:2). God has the right to make different laws for different people and for different times. Jesus makes this point when teaching on divorce, explaining that the Mosaic divorce laws were given "because your hearts were hard" but "it was not this way from the beginning" (Matt 19:8) and would no longer apply to disciples of Jesus (Matt

---

31. A number of scholars have noted that the structure of the covenant between God and Israel is modelled on ancient suzerainty treaties between more powerful and less powerful nations.

19:3-12). In a parallel way, the Gentile converts to Christ are placed under different rules to the Jewish believers (Acts 15:19-21,28-29). However, there also seems to be a universal law to which all people are accountable (Rom 2:12-16; 13:8-10).

4. New covenants demand revised, or even new, laws. Hence the new covenant makes the old covenant with its rites obsolete (Heb 8:7-13; 10:5-10,18; 2 Cor 3:6-18), introduces a "new commandment" (John 13:34-35), and places stronger demands on the disciples than the laws of Moses (Matt 5:17-48).

5. Divine laws come with penalties for disobedience which will ultimately be enforced by God, though the timing and exact nature of the enforcement may vary depending on circumstances and on the response of the Law-breakers to prophetic warnings (Gal 6:7-8; Ps 37:1-2,9-10; Jer 18:7-10; Jonah; Acts 17:30-31; Rom 1:18-28).[32] A final judgment will settle all claims (Rom 2:5-16; Acts 17:31; Rev 20:11-15).

6. Divine laws may take different forms and require different means of enforcement depending on the nature of the case. The Old Testament law code included basic commandments through which everyone was accountable directly to God, such as the Ten Commandments (Exod 20:1-17), but also instructions about ritual matters that were the responsibility of the priests and Levites (Lev 1-7, 11-17) and civil laws, including case law, that governed human relationships and which would be enforced by family and community leaders. Civil laws are not limited to ancient Israel (Rom 13:1-7) and seem to originate with the covenant with Noah (Gen 9:5-6).

7. Divine laws are legitimated by the sovereign right of God over all His creation, but are ultimately expressions of the love and wisdom of God. They show us the best way to live.

Think for a minute what our world, or even our country, would be like if everyone kept just the Ten Commandments consistently! If

---

32. I came across a fascinating case of this principle recently in W. Randolph Tate, *Biblical Interpretation*, 126-128. After David's adultery and murder of Uriah, the prophet Nathan tells him a story about the theft of a lamb, to which David responds in line with the Mosaic law in Exod 22:1, that the thief must restore fourfold what he had stolen. Tate comments, "What the reader must determine is whether the sentence was carried out or not" (ibid., 126) and argues that the ongoing narrative of 2 *Samuel* shows how David loses four sons, one (the baby) to sickness and the others to violent attacks.

everyone gave allegiance to God alone. If everyone respected and honored their parents and other authority figures. If everyone spent one day a week focused on God and enjoying physical rest. If no one stole from others and no one committed murder or assaulted anyone. If everyone was loyal to their marriage partner and never tried to seduce or force their attentions on anyone else. If everyone told the truth and could be relied on to keep their word. If everyone was content with what they had and refused to want or seek what belonged to someone else.

Now think what it would be like if you did this. As Darlene Zschech writes,

> The Lord loves us and gives us guidelines that will cause events to go well with us and with our children forever. He establishes boundaries in our lives to keep us safe, because of His great love.[33]

---

33. *Extravagant Worship*, 81.

CHAPTER 3

REBELLION AND JUDGMENT

GENESIS 1:26–28 TELLS US that God has given responsibility for the earth to humanity. And humans have, to some extent, brought the earth under their power and made it serve human needs and wants. We have cultivated the earth, cleared it of unwanted plants, planted crops, domesticated many animals, and eradicated many species. We have harnessed the incipient forces of gravity, wind, solar energy, radio waves, electronics, the atom, and others. We live in artificial comfort provided by electric power, piped water supply and modern building materials, transportation and electronic communication. We have built up resistance to, and protection from, raw nature, though occasional storms, floods, earthquakes, tsunamis, droughts, bushfires, volcanic eruptions, and epidemics remind us that we're not in total control of nature. Moreover, we are nervous about forces released by our own ingenuity which may overwhelm us and even destroy the planet: nuclear war, 'anthropogenic' climate change and artificial intelligence are the most obvious threats. Things are not quite right.

When I was seeking for truth as a university student, I began by thinking that human beings were by nature good, and hence the poverty, injustice and wars that we experience were caused by unjust class systems, dominating rulers, lack of education, and the like. But my socialist views were disturbed by the novel *Lord of the Flies* (William Golding) and the original movie of that novel in 1966. In the novel, two groups of British boys are wrecked on an uninhabited tropical island. At first, they start to organize themselves with British-style rules and systems so as to survive, but it all begins to break down and they start fighting and killing each other, until a rescue party arrives. The story is very credible to people who have spent time in all-male institutions like boarding schools, as I had done. But it's a kind of parable of human nature, showing how fragile civilization is and how sinful humans are. This is how the Bible sees it, as is graphically portrayed in Genesis 3–6. It begins with simple disobedience and grows to violence and injustice, to the point where God sends a flood to wipe out humanity.

Things are not what they should be, not what they were originally. Humans are fallen.

THE ORIGINAL FALL

The reason for the great struggle to achieve what God set out as the destiny of humanity lies therefore in the deep past. Any analysis of the Fall drawing on Genesis 3 must take into account the roles of the human actors, the serpent and God, all of whom are in some sense 'responsible' for what happens. But since we are discussing God's sovereignty, we will focus on God's part in this disaster.

The first surprise new readers of Genesis would experience, when getting to Genesis 3, would be the presence of an antagonist to God. So far in the narrative there has been no hint of resistance to God's will, except perhaps in God's command to Adam in Gen 2:17, where disobedience was a hypothetical possibility.[1] But suddenly they read, "Now the serpent was more crafty than any of the wild animals the Lord God had made" (Gen 3:1). Readers are given no hint of why this might be the case or where this "craftiness" has come from.[2] It is implied, however, that the serpent was created by God. So did God create the serpent as crafty?[3] Genesis does not say. But the presence of that serpent in the garden seems to be permitted (even ordained) by God, probably as part of the test He required Adam and Eve to pass.

The serpent clearly had its own agenda, to turn the humans against God, to drive a wedge between them and God, to gain control or influence

---

1. Though Greg Boyd argues that the language of Gen 1:26–28 implies resistance that humans are meant to put down (Boyd, *God At War*, 106–111). However, this is not obvious in Genesis 1.

2. Though ancient readers may have seen potential implications based on similarities with other creation myths.

3. The Hebrew term is ambiguous and could be translated 'shrewd.' It can be a desirable trait, i.e. "prudent" (Prov 12:16; 13:16) but "misused it becomes wiliness and guile" (Wenham, *Genesis 1–15*, 72).

over them, and thus over the world they had been placed in charge of. The serpent's strategy was masterful; it sowed doubt about God's command and warning and induced Eve (and through her, Adam) to disobey God's single clear command.

The humans were culpable in that they disobeyed a clear word from God, apparently motivated by covetousness and ingratitude: the serpent insinuated that God was depriving them of something (v.5) and "the woman saw that the fruit of the tree was good for food and pleasing to the eye, and also desirable for gaining wisdom" (v.6). 'Why not?' she must have thought. 'I'm going to take this in spite of what God said.'

But there is also a sense in which the humans are victims here. As Paul comments (1 Tim 2:14), and as Eve herself claimed (Gen 3:13), the woman was deceived. She had no reason to distrust the serpent, except that what it said contradicted what God had said. She (and Adam to a lesser degree) were a bit like children who are taken advantage of by strangers. According to David Bentley Hart, "the Eastern church fathers. . . . tended to ascribe the cause of the fall to the childlike ignorance of unformed souls, not yet mature enough to resist false notions."[4] Calvin, however, argued that Adam was "not given the constancy to persevere" and therefore "fell so easily."[5]

The result of their sin, however, was immediate: "the eyes of both of them were opened, and they realized they were naked" (v.7). Adam and Eve lost their innocence. They were now only too aware of good and evil "like God" (v.5), but did not have the resources to handle this awareness, as God had warned. Their attempt to cover up their nakedness was almost comical (v.7) and they hid from God (v.8), knowing that they were guilty, vulnerable and in trouble. The story suggests that they were like children who disobey their parents and then try to cover it up, yet in their hearts want to be found out and reconciled.

God then entered onto the scene and proceeded to hold each person accountable. God is not portrayed as an all-knowing Divine Dictator. He had to ask Adam, "Where are you?" (v.9) and deduce what had happened (v.10–11).[6] Of course, Adam, then Eve, and then the serpent, were confronted with their responsibility for the disaster. Adam and Eve tried to

---

4. Hart, *That All Shall Be Saved*, 43.
5. Calvin, *Institutes*, 195.
6. I'm not denying that God knew what was going on, simply trying to follow the narrative in its own terms. Wenham suggests it was a rhetorical question, more of a call to Adam to come forward than a request for information (*Genesis 1–15*, 77).

pass on the blame (vv.12–13); Adam perhaps even tried to blame God by saying "the woman *you put here* with me" (v.12, emphasis added). God, however, after interrogating the human pair, pronounced judgment on the serpent (vv.14–15), the woman (v.16), and Adam (vv.17–19). In particular, Adam was punished by a curse on the ground; that is, his ability to control the earth and eat its fruit was now limited and would require much hard effort and struggle, ironically since his sin consisted in what he ate.[7] Adam was made from the dust of the ground which will now resist his efforts, only for him to return to dust in death (v.19).[8]

We could say that there is now a fallen world due to the fall of its (human) governor, a judgment determined by humanity's divine Governor. God is holding humanity accountable and making their life more difficult, but not apparently withdrawing the original commission to both multiply and subdue the earth (Gen 1:26–28).

Finally, God did two significant things. He made "garments of skin for Adam and his wife and clothed them" (v.21), replacing their inadequate attempts at covering with something that will make them less vulnerable. And next, God evicted them from the garden permanently (vv.23–14) because of the danger that the man would eat of the other significant tree, "the tree of life" and thus "live forever" (v.22). Wenham comments that such an expulsion would be seen as a kind of death, much like those who were later expelled from the camp of Israel.[9] The passage does not provide any further reason for either decision, but they are clearly acts of a sovereign God whose property includes both significant trees in the garden, indeed the whole garden.

So let's review by asking three important questions. First, how is the human situation affected and what does the passage tell us about human nature? We learn that human free will is real: Adam and Eve made their own decisions which have clear consequences, but which were not prevented or overruled by God.[10] Next, we see human nature changing radically as a result of their consumption of the forbidden fruit: they can no longer be innocent but must cope with their newfound awareness of good and evil.

Their relationships are also altered significantly: their relationship with God is marred by distrust (on both sides) and guilt; their relationship

7. Cf. Wenham, *Genesis 1–15*, 82.
8. Cf. Macchia, *Tongues of Fire*, 274.
9. Wenham, *Genesis 1–15*, 74, 83, 90.
10. Cf. Sanders, *God Who Risks*, 236.

with each other is disturbed and unequal ("he will rule over you," v.16);[11] their relationship with the serpent is wary and hostile (v.15); and their relationship with the earth is also disturbed (vv.17–19). But their appointment to rule over the natural world is not apparently annulled; in fact, the apparent killing of an animal (by God) for their clothing may emphasize both their lordship over the animals and the more violent way it will now be exercised.

The earth is seen as disrupted and dysfunctional to some degree as a result of the Fall of its appointed governors and caregivers. It resists the farmer's labor (Gen 3:17) and produces "thorns and thistles" (Gen 3:18). As Paul explains, "the creation was subject to frustration" and "bondage to decay" (Rom 8:20,21), a state which he attributes to "the will of the one who subjected it" (Rom 8:20), which I take to refer to the judgment of God, but which, as Macchia points out, is also a place for hope; it will not always be this way (Rom 8:20–21).[12]

Second, let's think about the serpent: did it succeed? And here the answer is 'yes, and no.' It successfully induced the human pair to disobey God and led God to punish them (a nasty trick we see him playing subsequently), thus alienating them from God to some extent and making them more susceptible to further suggestion and deception. This made them less of a threat to the serpent, if they ever were. But the serpent did not succeed in taking over the earth and it provoked future hostility towards itself on the part of succeeding generations of humans (v.15). More ominously, it brought on itself a significant punishment from God as Judge, a curse and a demotion: "you will crawl on your belly and you will eat dust all the days of your life" (v.14). There was also the threat of a future defeat at the hands of a human being: "he will crush your head, and you will strike his heel" (v.15). The serpent has only a limited time in which to operate.

Finally, what do we learn about God's sovereignty in Genesis 3? God acts as Judge: He asserts His right to set the rules and to punish disobedience, which will be one of the main ways the Old Testament portrays God acting as King from then on. Sinners do not get away with their sin, nor can they hide it. But apparently God's order is disturbed by the actions of the serpent and the humans. Innocence is over (v.22). Human obedience

---

11. See discussion in Wenham, *Genesis 1–15*, 81–82.
12. Macchia, *Tongues of Fire*, 139.

will become rarer, and the world will become so disobedient, defiant and violent that God destroys the human race almost completely (Genesis 6).

So to what extent is God still sovereign? He is still free to act; He owes nothing to humanity or the serpent. God could immediately have destroyed both. He chose not to. In fact, this is the first exhibition of God's grace to human beings. In spite of his warning (Gen 2:17), and at the risk of giving credibility to the serpent (Gen 3:4), God does not kill Adam and Eve; their lives are preserved for centuries to come (Gen 5:5). Nor does He destroy the serpent. And He provides good covering to protect Adam and Eve (v.21).

But God maintains His rights over His creation. As Judge, He places all three guilty parties under the appropriate penalty for their actions (vv.14–19). This implies that all these negative features of the world– hostility, pain, subjugation, frustration, natural difficulties, and death–are part of God's sovereign rule over the human race, at least for now. God also asserts His rights over creation by expelling the humans from the Garden (vv.23–24).

God also has a plan to deal with the catastrophe. Not only does He allocate specific penalties to the three sinners and evict Adam and Eve from the garden, in order to prevent a worse result, but He appears to have a long-term plan to defeat the conspirator whom He holds most responsible for what has happened. "He will crush your head, and you will strike his heel," He warns the serpent (v.15). As Wenham comments, "The curse envisages a long struggle between good and evil, with mankind eventually triumphing."[13]

This story sets up how God's sovereignty will operate from that time on, at least on the earth. God will bring judgment on those who disobey His commands. Second, God will use various negative features of life on earth to restrict the operation of sin and the devil. In both of these strategies, God acts as Creator and Judge. But also God will work towards a more distant goal only hinted at in Gen 3:15. This goal will require the emergence of an offspring of the woman, to crush the serpent once for all. It has to be a human being because God has assigned the rule of the earth to humanity.[14] And there is just a hint that this victory may result in a full restoration of human beings to their original God-given destiny, including access to the tree of life (see Rev 2:7). This is the part of

---

13. Wenham, Genesis 1–15, 80.
14. Ancient Christians saw here a prophecy of Christ (Wenham, Genesis 1–15, 81).

God's operations that is less obvious, but the Bible shows God working in, through and around the sinful decisions of human beings to accomplish His purposes.

DIVINE JUDGMENT: THE EARLY DAYS

As we read on through the Pentateuch, we see God acting as Judge of sinful humanity. He respects their free will in that He does not force them to obey Him, but He holds them accountable for their decisions and ensures there are consequences for what they choose, though not always in the expected way.

This is next displayed in the story of Cain and Abel (Gen 4:1–16), who, unlike their parents, begin life outside the Garden of Eden. It begins with God mysteriously rejecting Cain's offering but accepting that of Abel (vv.3–5). Genesis gives no explanation for this, giving us the impression that God is choosing or favoring one over the other. Explanations offered elsewhere include the need for blood sacrifice, which is clear in the rest of the Pentateuch but is not ever stated in *this* story, and the requirement of faith. The explanation offered by the author of Hebrews (Heb 11:4) suggests that Cain did not relate to God as the giver of salvation, as perhaps his parents' experience should have taught him (Gen 3:21), but either brought an offering reluctantly or expected something in return (a "works" mentality), whereas Abel trusted God as his savior and provider. Wenham suggests another possibility, that Abel brought the "pick of his flock to the Lord,"[15] whereas Cain was less generous.

Whatever the reasons for all this, we read that Cain was angry at God's rejection of his offering (v.5), rather than repenting for his wrong attitude. God sees what is going on and where Cain's reaction will lead if he does not repent. However, God does not protect Abel from his brother. Instead, He reasons with Cain and challenges him to resist the power of sin which "is crouching at your door" and "desires to have you, but you must rule over it" (v.7). A new power, Sin, is operating in the human world, and it will overpower many people (as Paul spells out in Rom 5:12–21), but they are still accountable and able to resist it. Free will is still operating and God is permitting this. Bradley Jersak argues that

---

15. Wenham, *Genesis 1–15*, 103; see also, 104, 117.

"God *consents* to the free (and often catastrophic) play of these secondary causes–he allows *natural law* and *human freedom* to do their thing" [16]

After the murder of Abel, the first 'martyr figure' in Scripture, God interrogates Cain. God seeks a confession because the murder demands restitution (v.10).[17] Cain must be directly cursed and punished with greater resistance from the ground (vv.11–12; compare 3:17) and a wandering lifestyle (v.12), possibly implying expulsion from the nascent community.[18] Cain boldly argues back with God and God limits the penalty by protecting Cain as He had *not* done with Abel (v.15). If God has favored Abel, he (Abel) has paid a high price for that favor, a foreshadowing of what God's people must endure for God's sake (see Rom 8:36; Matt 23:35). In this story then, we see ongoing human accountability to God, God acting 'freely' in His dealings with sinful human beings, and God responding to the protests of a human being, but not in the way we might expect.

The next section of Genesis shows humanity declining into further arrogance and violence, as in the words of Lamech (Gen 4:23–24). Lamech follows Cain, only more so, in his arrogance and self-promotion. Arthur Custance explains that

> It needs only one kind of circumstance to bring this deeply rooted malady in human nature to the surface. That circumstance is the acquisition of power over others.[19]

This seems to be what we see in Lamech's threatening words to his two wives (v.23) and later in the violence that dominates the antediluvian world.

But God gives Adam and Eve a new son, Seth (Gen 4:25) and "people began to call on the name of the Lord" (Gen 4:26), including the unique Enoch (Gen 5:22–24), who is actually removed from the earth in apparent response to his faithfulness to God.[20] There is also the hope, soon to be denied, of some relief from God's judgment on the ground (Gen 5:29). The mysterious story of the "sons of God,"[21] "daughters of humans" and

---

16. *A More Christlike God*, 129–130.

17. As Wenham states, "Because man is made in God's image, homicide must be avenged" (*Genesis 1–15*, 107).

18. Cf. Wenham, *Genesis 1–15*, 108.

19. Custance, *Sovereignty of Grace*, 92.

20. Cf. Wenham, *Genesis 1–15*, 127–128,

21. Or "sons of the gods." They are seen by interpreters as either godlike beings

"Nephilim" (Gen 6:1-4) implies a challenge to God's creation boundaries set in Genesis 1 and a possible interference by outside forces.[22] Humanity is, in a sense, fulfilling God's plans in that they are growing in number (Gen 6:1) and in cultural and technological skills (Gen 4:20-22). But God's only explicit move during this period is to limit the lifespan of human beings, first to a number below 1,000 (Genesis 5) and then to 120 years (Gen 6:3).

This tragic, but complex, story comes to a head in Genesis 6:

> The Lord saw how great the wickedness of the human race had become on the earth, and that every inclination of the thoughts of the human heart was only evil all the time. The Lord regretted that he had made human beings on the earth, and his heart was deeply troubled. So the Lord said, "I will wipe from the face of the earth the human race I have created- and with them the animals, the birds and the creatures that move along the ground- for I regret that I have made them." But Noah found favor in the eyes of the Lord.
>
> (Gen 6:5-8).

Here we see both the state of humanity and God's judgment. God assesses the situation and pronounces His verdict. Human beings are too evil to be spared. More significantly, we read that God regretted creating them. God's bold creation of a creature in the divine image is looking decidedly foolish.[23] We might say that God's worst fears have been realized;[24] certainly, the passage portrays God as distressed, if not frustrated.

(angels or spirits, as in Job 1:6), human rulers or godly men from the line of Seth. Wenham says that the 'angel' view is "the oldest view and that of most modern commentators" (Wenham, *Genesis 1-15*, 139)

22. Other Jewish literature explains this as involving fallen angels having sex with human females, e.g. 1 Enoch 6; Jude 6.

23. Cf. Macchia, *Tongues of Fire*, 139. I'm not calling God foolish; I'm simply trying to follow the narrative. Patrick Richmond protests against the idea that God "repented" because, "Being sorry for what one has decided to do suggests that the previous decision was unwise" and "this seems particularly implausible given that God was able to redeem the situation" ("A Traditional Challenge to Pinnock's Understanding of God;" in Gray and Sinkinson, eds. *Reconstructing Theology*, 100-101).

24. Wenham translates the state of the earth in Gen 6:11 as "ruined" rather than "corrupt" (Wenham, *Genesis 1-15*, 170-171), implying that God's good plans have come to nothing.

God decides to eliminate these rebellious people and with them the creatures they are responsible for.

God's sovereignty is displayed in several ways here: God has permitted this situation to develop; God is exercising His rights as Judge; and God is exercising His freedom by deciding not only to destroy the earth's living creatures, but also not to destroy them *totally* and to give favor to one man, Noah (v.8).

This time the narrative suggests why Noah will be spared: "Noah was a righteous man, blameless among the people of his time, and he walked faithfully with God" (v.9). This language resembles that about Enoch in the previous chapter (Gen 5:22,24). However, the outcome for both is different: Enoch is taken away by God, spared perhaps the judgment to come, whereas Noah must go through it to the other side as God's prophetic leader. He must give detailed obedience to God, in the face of considerable difficulty and probably opposition, in order to save himself, his extended family and the living creatures that human beings are in charge of. For God is not going to wipe them all out after all; He is going to rebuild human society and the living world again. God's original Plan is being rerouted but not abandoned.

What does all this tell us about God? First, God's regret at creating human beings (vv.6,7) implies either that He was unable, or unwilling, to stop this situation developing, or that He did not expect this outcome. As Sanders argues, "if God grieves because it is not as he intends, then God is not determining all events" [25] Second, God is aware of what is happening even down to people's inner thoughts (v.5). Third, God has the power to wipe out all the living creatures on earth (v.7). God's sovereignty is emphasized throughout the Flood story, a point made even more forcefully when Genesis is compared to other ancient Flood stories that include competition and conflict among gods.[26] Fourth, however, God clearly cares about the situation: "his heart was deeply troubled" (v.6).[27] As Terence Fretheim argues, "The sinful response of humankind has indeed touched God; God is not apathetic."[28]

Fifth, in this episode, we see God deliberating and making decisions (v.7) in response to human behavior (vv.13–14). God chooses one man

---

25. *God Who Risks*, 235.

26. Cf. Wenham, *Genesis 1–15*, 205.

27. Wenham translates this as "bitterly indignant" as in Ps 78:40; Isa 63:10. (*Genesis 1–15*, 144–145,147).

28. *Suffering of God*, 112.

as His agent in saving people and animals from the imminent catastrophe, on the basis of that man's proven character and piety or faith (v.9; compare Heb 11:7), and enters into covenant with him (v.18). In fact, it seems that Noah's faithfulness may be the reason why God does not fully carry out His announced intention to destroy everything (see Gen 7:1); no other reason is given in the text, though we may assume that God is unwilling to abandon His bigger Plan as heralded in Genesis 1–3.

Noah obeys God completely (Gen 6:22; 7:5) and God's plan of judgment and salvation is carried out as planned, since God controls the forces of nature (Gen 7:11–12; 8:1–2) and even brings all the animals to the ark (Gen 7:8–9). God's sovereign plan is central to the whole Flood story even down to the details of the dates and the operations of wind and rain. As Wenham comments on Gen 8:1, "to an ordinary observer, the waters appeared to be triumphing throughout this time. In reality, however, the stormy wind was bringing Noah's salvation."[29] After the waters have sufficiently receded and the ark is resting "on the mountains of Ararat" (Gen 8:4), God eventually tells Noah to leave the ark with his family and animals so that life on earth can resume and multiply (Gen 8:15–17).

God then makes an absolute promise that this will never happen again (Gen 8:21–22; 9:8–17) and that the normal cycles of climate and seasons will continue uninterrupted (Gen 8:22) under His providential rule. As James Houston comments,

> It is His faithfulness in His covenant with Adam, Noah, Abraham and Israel that is the basis for the uniformity and consistency apparent in the creation, not the mechanical laws of cause and effect, for God made and upholds these laws.[30]

God also renews the mandate of human repopulation and control of the earth with a more violent edge: "the fear and the dread of you will fall on all the beasts of the earth" (Gen 9:2) because humans are now permitted to kill and eat them, though with some restrictions (Gen 9:3–4). God as the final Sovereign makes and changes the rules (Gen 9:3).

Another big change seems to be related to human relationships. Not only does God say, "from each human being, I will demand an accounting for the life of another human being" (Gen 9:5) –which He has done from the outset, as in the Cain and Abel story–but also "Whoever sheds

---

29. Wenham, *Genesis 1–15*, 184.
30. Houston, *I Believe in the Creator*, 103.

human blood, by *humans* shall their blood be shed" (Gen 9:6, emphasis added). God is licensing the killing of one human by another in response to murder, based on the value of the enduring divine image in all people.[31] He is thus envisaging a situation where violence is now ubiquitous (see Gen 6:11) and can only be restrained (if so) or punished by other human beings. This is a massive change to the way the world will operate under God's decree and probably lays the foundation for civil government in the long run.

> Then Noah built an altar to the Lord and, taking some of all the clean animals and clean birds, he sacrificed burnt offerings on it. The Lord smelled the pleasing aroma and said in his heart: "Never again will I curse the ground because of humans, even though every inclination of the human heart is evil from childhood. And never again will I destroy all living creatures as I have done"

(Gen 8:20–21).

God will provide for, and maintain, his world even though humanity is still intent on sin.[32] That is an amazing undertaking. And it is provoked by Noah's act of worship, "the pleasing aroma" of his sacrifice. Wenham suggests that "Soothing.... sacrifices have a restful, soothing, pacifying effect on God," implying that "God's anger at sin is appeased by sacrifice."[33]

Fretheim adds a different perspective:

> By deciding to endure a wicked world, while continuing to open up the [i.e. His] heart to that world, means that God has decided to take personal suffering upon God's own self.[34]

But this does not mean that God has given up or surrendered His rights and freedom. For when Noah and Ham violate implicit codes of decency and respect (not a specific command of God; Gen 9:20–24),[35] there is a consequence, a judgment. However, in accord with the new

---

31. Cf. Wenham, *Genesis 1–15*, 193–194.

32. Wenham comments, "What previously had been cited as the reason for the extinction of all flesh is now declared to be God's motive for its preservation" (*Genesis 1–15*, 206).

33. *Genesis 1–15*, 189. See also ibid., 190.

34. *Suffering of God*, 112.

35. Cf. Wenham, *Genesis 1–15*, 198–200. The passage focuses on Ham's dishonoring behavior rather than on Noah's drunkenness.

arrangement, the curse on Canaan comes from Noah,[36] not directly from God (Gen 9:24–27). Noah has God-given (that is, delegated) rights over his descendants, a principle that will be reaffirmed repeatedly in Genesis.

This new arrangement for managing sin and violence runs into trouble fairly quickly, as narrated in the tower of Babel story in Genesis 11. The growing capability of the human race is emphasized here, based on their technological and organizational skill (vv.3–4). God Himself affirms that "nothing they plan to do will be impossible for them" (v.6). So what is wrong with that? After all, God explicitly gave humanity governing rights over the earth (Gen 1:26–28; 9:1–6).

The only reason for God's displeasure is suggested in verse 4: "Come, let us build ourselves a city, with a tower that reaches to the heavens, so that we may make a name for ourselves; otherwise we will be scattered over the face of the whole earth." This verse suggests three problems. First, they were disobeying God's instruction to "fill the earth" (Gen 9:1). Second, their motive was selfish and humanistic ("build ourselves," "make a name for ourselves"), reminiscent of the serpent's temptation, "you will be like God" (Gen 3:5). As Macchia comments, this was "a monolithic effort to seize wisdom and power on their own terms."[37] God was ignored, even resisted, here. And third, "a tower that reaches to the heavens" suggests a religious element: either this tower was some kind of attempt to invade heaven or it was some kind of declaration of human religious power, perhaps something like Nebuchadnezzar's golden statue in Daniel 3, or a kind of astrological system.[38]

God is seemingly threatened, but it seems from the narrative that His options are limited. He has promised not to wipe out the human world again. He has delegated authority to humanity over the earth and they are now exercising it. He can only use force at the expense of setting aside His own arrangements and thus violating His own charter and character.

But God's sovereignty does not depend just on force. This story is a paradigmatic illustration of how God manages a recalcitrant human

---

36. This is "the first time a man is recorded as uttering a curse" and it has "divine authority" (Wenham, *Genesis 1–15*, 201), as does the blessing of Shem and Japheth.

37. Macchia, *Tongues of Fire*, 98.

38. Gordon Wenham comments, "The great ziggurats of Mesopotamia were a well known feature of its landscape. In particular *Enuma Elish* celebrates the building of Babylon and its temple tower" (*Genesis 1–15*; 236).

society. As Sanders argues, God is resourceful and "omnicompetent."[39] God outwits the people. He limits their capacity to continue this project by disrupting their human organizational capacity. If their language is confused, if they can't understand each other, they won't be able to complete the tower and their human hubris will be localized and less of a threat to divine government and plans that are ultimately for their good. Thus "the Lord scattered them over the face of the whole earth" (v.9).

This story thus explains the existence of multiple languages, tribes, peoples and nations in the world and makes a powerful case against imperialism, understood as human rule over multiple ethnic groups.[40] God's plan is being accomplished in spite of human resistance. It shows God as a disrupter of human plans. As Wenham comments, "The tower of Babylon stands as a monument to man's impotence before his creator, and the multiplication of human languages is a reminder of divine retribution on human pride."[41]

DIVINE JUDGMENT AND GOD'S ONGOING RULE

So how will God's sovereignty work in this new post-Flood age of sin and violence? Certainly, divine acts of judgment will be part of God's rule. Perhaps the most dramatic example of this in Genesis is the destruction of Sodom and Gomorrah. This story clearly demonstrates God's power over natural forces, in this case perhaps a volcanic eruption (Gen 19:23–28), and His willingness to destroy people who deviate strongly from His moral standards (Gen 18:20–21). Such actions would at least limit the effects of human rebellion while fulfilling God's post-Flood promise to preserve life.

But there are several distinctive, even surprising, features of how God goes about this judgment. First, He sends a reconnaissance mission to find out how bad the situation is (Gen 18:20–21). Does God not know what is going on? Clearly He does, but He acts in response to other agents: the "outcry against Sodom and Gomorrah" (v.20) must have come from either heavenly or earthly sources (angels or people; perhaps people oppressed by these cities)[42] and God checks the facts, seemingly in order

---

39. E.g. Sanders, *God Who Risks*, 206.
40. Cf. Howard-Brook, *"Come Out, My People!"*, 49–51.
41. *Genesis 1–15*, 244.
42. Cf. Wenham, *Genesis 16–50*, 50. One recent suggestion is that it was related to

to satisfy both His own sense of justice and perhaps that of others. We are dealing with some degree of anthropomorphism here–the author is using human categories to describe what God is doing–but the point is clear. God is free to act but He determines to act on the basis of some kind of constitution, an expression of justice that He has originated but now is somehow accountable to, as we saw in the previous chapter. God's judgments are based on facts and laws publicly available to all intelligent beings.

Second, God consults a human being with whom He had entered into covenant (Gen 18). God is showing respect to his human partner who is perhaps in some way appointed over the earth, His appointed prophet.[43] Abraham's position with God is itself derived from God's free sovereign action (Gen 12:1–3) and His decision to make a covenant with His chosen man (Gen 15), decisions that Abraham has responded positively to (Gen 12:4; 15:6). So God's consultation with Abraham is an act of grace, but based on a covenant God had initiated as part of His plan for the world and for Abraham, whom God trusts to do right (Gen 18:16–19).

However we understand this, Abraham has been granted a place on which to stand in relation to God and by faith he proceeds to reason with God on the basis of God's own justice, to which God Himself has just referred (vv.20–21).:

> Far be it from you to do such a thing- to kill the righteous with the wicked, treating the righteous and the wicked alike. Far be it from you! Will not the Judge of all the earth do right? (v.25).

This is a bold approach for a man to take with God, as Abraham realizes (v.27), but God is not displeased; He immediately responds with a fresh proposal and the two of them negotiate until the number of righteous people required to save the doomed city is down to ten (vv.26–32). Fretheim comments,

> For the conversation to have any integrity, it thus seems necessary for the destruction of Sodom to be only a probability or a possibility, waiting on the God/Abraham discussion before the final 'go ahead' in the execution of the decision is given.[44]

---

the city's "oppressive relationship with the countryside around" (Goldingay, *Genesis for Everyone*, Part 2, 28 as quoted in Paul Ede, "River from the Temple," 211).

43. Compare Amos 3:7; Gen 20:7.
44. *Suffering of God*, 50.

Third, both God (definitely) and Abraham (probably) know that the number of righteous people in Sodom will not exceed ten, so the city will be destroyed. However, the two angels have a secondary mission now, to rescue Lot and his family, who are seen as righteous and who are related to Abraham. As the story unfolds, two things stand out: the city is as bad as the "outcry" suggested and only one family has any (tenuous) claim on God. Hence the city will be destroyed, and that family will be saved, although their righteousness is not outstanding (Gen 19:6–8; see also 2 Pet 2:7–8), largely for the sake of God's covenant partner (Gen 19:29).[45] Even then Lot's wife fails to follow the angels' directions and dies (Gen 19:26) and his daughters' fiancés also perish because they fail to respond to Lot's warning (Gen 19:14).

God's sovereignty is revealed in the devastation of Sodom and Gomorrah but God's decision is guided by His righteous character and the input of His covenant partner and others. The role played by prayer in God's decisions is underlined.

This balance between judgment and prayer is reflected in several places in the Old Testament. Moses' intercession for Israel influences God not to wipe them out after the 'golden calf' incident (Exod 32:7–14), when he appeals to God's glory and reputation and His covenant promises. John Sanders comments that Moses "believes it is possible to alter the divine word"[46] and argues that "one of the most remarkable features in the Old Testament is that people can argue with God and win."[47] But this can only happen because God wants it and when they take God's side in the situation concerned. As John Piper argues, God desists from judgment and persists in mercy "for his name's sake," that is, for the sake of His reputation among the nations (Ezek 20:8–10,13–14, 20–21).[48] Later, Israel's doom is sealed when God cannot find an intercessor "to stand before me in the gap on behalf of the land so I would not have to destroy it" (Ezek 22:30–31).

The Bible repeatedly insists that God always acts justly and only punishes people reluctantly when justice, His justice, demands it. As Ezekiel puts it, "Do I take any pleasure in the death of the wicked? declares

---

45. Cf. Wenham, *Genesis 16–50*, 64. Wenham draws attention to parallels between this story and the flood narrative: "two cataclysmic acts of divine judgment on outrageously sinful communities, with the only righteous man and his family spared."

46. *God Who Risks*, 61.

47. *God Who Risks*, 62.

48. Piper, *Providence*, 116–118.

the Sovereign Lord. Rather am I not pleased when they turn from their ways and live?" (Ezek 18:23). God frequently (if not always) sends a warning first in the form of a prophet or intercessor; Ezekiel himself was appointed as such a "watchman" (Ezek 3:16–21). But Ezekiel, and Scripture generally, insist on God's right to judge as Creator, independent of human opinion (Ezek 18:1–32).

As Ezekiel understood, what God is looking for is repentance. God's sovereign work has this goal and responds to human responses. Jeremiah 18 makes this clear using the imagery of the potter and clay. This image speaks first of God's sovereign power: "'Can I not do with you, Israel, as this potter does?' declares the Lord. 'Like clay in the hand of the potter, so are you in my hand, Israel'" (v.6). But the application of this analogy does not portray God as just an all-powerful Potter dominating a passive piece of clay. Rather Jeremiah sees God as a just Judge who deals with nations as they deserve. A nation that deserves destruction, but responds to God's warnings with repentance, will be spared (vv.7–8). Similarly, if a nation receives a positive prophetic promise, but does evil, that bright future will be reconsidered (vv.9–10). It is impossible to evade God's judgments. Jeremiah applies this message to Jerusalem and Judah, warning of imminent disaster and calling for repentance, not a kind of fatalistic resignation (vv.11–12). As Carson says in a different context, "divine activity calls for response, not fatalism."[49]

However, God is able to manage events to execute His judgments. For example, Jeremiah calls on his people and neighboring nations to submit to Nebuchadnezzar king of Babylon, even calling him "my servant" (Jer 27:6) and declaring God's right to do this: "I made the earth and its people and the animals that are on it, and I give it to anyone I please" (Jer 27:5). By any normal standard, Nebuchadnezzar does not qualify as a divine appointment, being authoritarian, violent, idolatrous and self-aggrandizing. But this is not an arbitrary action on God's part. Nebuchadnezzar is being used by God to execute His judgments on disobedient Judah (Jer 25:8–11; compare Hab 1:3–7), even though he doesn't know God or serve Him and will attribute his success to his own gods (Hab 1:15–16). Moreover, Babylon will also face God's judgments after God has used them as His instruments to deal with Judah (Jer 25:12–14).

---

49. *Sovereignty and Responsibility*, 14.

JUDGMENT IN NINEVEH AND BABYLON

These principles by which God operates in His sovereign dealings are well illustrated by two particular stories in Jonah and Daniel. Jonah is the reluctant, even recalcitrant, prophet called to announce judgment on the wicked city of Nineveh, who flees westward but cannot avoid God's hand and control of the elements (Jon 1:1-4). He eventually submits to the sovereign Lord (Jon 1:6-16), who rescues him by a "huge fish" (Jon 1:17) and later recommissions him to his appointed mission (Jon 3:1-2). His message to Nineveh is uncompromising: "Forty more days and Nineveh will be overthrown" (Jon 3:4). But surprisingly, the Ninevites believe the message and repent with fasting and sackcloth (Jon 3:5-9), appealing to God for mercy, and God responds: "When God saw what they did and how they turned from their evil ways, he relented and did not bring on them the destruction he had threatened" (Jon 3:10).

The Ninevites and Jonah both knew that God is just and merciful (Jon 3:9; 4:2). Jonah knew that God could have simply destroyed Nineveh (as He later did) without warning, but God is just and cares for even the wicked- and even their animals (Jon 4:11). This story strongly displays God's sovereignty over the weather and the sea creatures, His capacity and right to bring disaster on nations, but also His justice and care and responsiveness to human repentance, and His desire to warn and spare people if He can. In fact, this story conveys a powerful sense of God's willingness to reach 'pagans' who may be open to Him even through a very stubborn Israelite.[50] The sailors (Jon 1:18) and the Ninevites responded even though Jonah himself resisted God's plan.

Daniel 4 is the story of God's dealings with King Nebuchadnezzar. God used Nebuchadnezzar and his Neo-Babylonian empire to bring down the kingdom of Judah and destroy its temple devoted to God. But now God is going to show Nebuchadnezzar who is God. He begins by giving him uncomfortable, disturbing dreams (vv.5-6), not for the first time (Dan 2); one way God's sovereignty works is through His ability to get into people's unconscious mind in dreams, bypassing the conscious mind and its capacity for resistance. Since the usual dream interpreters could not (or maybe would not)[51] interpret the dream, Nebuchadnezzar

---

50. There are parallels with the story of Cornelius and Peter in Acts 10.

51. Perhaps, as Goldingay argues, they were afraid that the king would hold them responsible for the threatened event (*Daniel*, 94).

turns to his one credible fearless interpreter, the prophet Daniel (vv.7–8).[52] Daniel quickly realizes what this dream means and how dangerous its interpretation will be for him, but he faithfully predicts the king's temporary downfall[53] and calls on him to repent so as possibly to avert that fate (vv.19–27), since he (like Jonah and Jeremiah) sees that is possible. As Goldingay comments, Daniel "encourages the world to assume that judgment is never inevitable."[54]

However, Nebuchadnezzar does not repent and becomes increasingly arrogant and boastful (vv.29–30). He then goes through the distressing experience Daniel had predicted, a kind of insanity (vv.31–33), until he learns his lesson and is restored to power (vv.34–36). The point of all this is clear. Daniel says it all: "Seven times will pass by for you until you acknowledge that the Most High is sovereign over all kingdoms on earth and gives them to anyone he wishes" (v.25).[55] The king finally recognizes this:

> All the peoples of the earth are regarded as nothing. He does as he pleases with the powers of heaven and the peoples of the earth. No one can hold back his hand or say to him: 'What have you done?' (v.35).

This is a classic statement of God's sovereignty as we defined it at the beginning. God is totally free, has the right to deal with creation as He chooses and actually does rule. But He does so in a way that takes the attitudes of people into account. Both Nebuchadnezzar and Jonah were stubborn, both were subjected to God's severe dealings, both became obedient in some respects as a result. And in Nebuchadnezzar's case, the outcome was greatness beyond what he had before (v.36), a bit like Job. In fact, I think God was pursuing Nebuchadnezzar throughout Daniel 1–4 and he was actually converted; Daniel 4 is effectively his testimony.

---

52. Cf. Goldingay, *Daniel*, 91.
53. Cf. Goldingay, *Daniel*, 92–93.
54. *Daniel*, 94.
55. Several commentators point out that God is not opposed to Nebuchadnezzar's rule, or his building of a beautiful city as such, but simply his failure to acknowledge God and rule justly (cf. Goldingay, *Daniel*, 93,95,97; Lennox, *Against the Flow*, 158–161).

SOVEREIGN DISCRETION IN GOD'S JUDGMENTS

One thing you would notice in all the above cases is that God does not judge every case the same. He wipes out Sodom and Gomorrah but leaves other nations intact, at least in terms of devastating direct punishments, although eventually all nations are destroyed or brought down by wars or other calamities.

Study, for example, the cases where God executes someone directly. The first case relates to Judah's first two sons. "Er, Judah's firstborn, was wicked in the LORD's sight; so the LORD put him to death" (Gen 38:7). Then his brother Onan was also put to death because he refused to provide a son for his dead brother (Gen 38:8–10). The next case relates to Aaron's sons Nadab and Abihu, who as newly ordained priests "offered unauthorized fire before the Lord, contrary to his command. So fire came out from the presence of the Lord and consumed them, and they died before the Lord" (Lev 10:1–2).

There were several mass executions during Israel's wilderness journey, such as the plague after the golden calf incident (Exod 32:35), the time when they complained and "fire from the LORD burned among them and consumed some of the outskirts of the camp" (Num 11:1), the deaths of the unfaithful spies (Num 14:37), the case when rebels against Moses were swallowed up by the earth (Num 16:31–33) and some of their followers were consumed by fire (Num 16:35), the snake bites resulting from more complaining (Num 21:6), and the plagues that befell the men who were seduced by the Moabites (Num 25:8–9).

God allowed the Philistines to capture the ark of the covenant, though He executed seventy of them "because they looked into the ark" (2 Sam 6:19). When David first tried to bring the ark of the covenant to Jerusalem, the attempt had to be aborted because Uzzah, who was helping guide the cart with the ark on it, "took hold of the ark of God, because the oxen stumbled" and "The LORD's anger burned against Uzzah because of his irreverent act; therefore God struck him down, and he died there. . ." (2 Sam 6:6–7). Elijah called down fire on the king's soldiers sent to bring him to the king (2 Kings 1:9–12), but had mercy on the third group when their leader begged for mercy and he was told to go by "the angel of the LORD" (2 Kings 1:13–15).

Many people were directly executed by God, usually for irreverence or contempt towards Him. But many others were spared such punishments: Adam and Eve, Cain (who was actually protected by God),

Lamech (Gen 4:23-24), King Saul, David himself and others who were probably as bad as those whom God executed. God acts sovereignly in how He responds to sin. However, those physically closest to God, such as priests and Uzzah, are at the most risk.

In the New Testament, God continues to execute people directly: Ananias and Sapphira for their hypocrisy in relation to giving (Acts 5:1-11); King Herod for receiving worship as a god (Acts 12:22-23). But Pilate, Annas and Caiaphas, various Roman emperors and other Roman officials were spared. And Jesus rebuked disciples who wanted Him to call down fire on his Samaritan critics (Luke 9:52-55).

GOD'S JUDGMENTS ON ISRAEL AND JUDAH

There are many stories of judgment in the Old Testament and they cover many nations. But the most detailed are about Israel and Judah. Here we need to keep in mind a number of theological notes: God's covenant with Israel (part of the election theme which we will survey in Chapter 5), which is the basis for God's specific judgments, and the specific ways God executes judgments on Israel, such as through famines, plagues and invasion by neighboring nations. In all of these, God is asserting His freedom to act as He sees fit, His rights over His creation, Israel's accountability to God as their Ruler, and God's ability to control events.

The Israelites of Moses' generation rebel against God almost as soon as God begins the work of releasing them from Egyptian oppression. After the exodus itself, the Israelites face a challenging journey through the wilderness before they get to the promised land. God's Plan is bigger than they realize. They are mainly concerned about provision of their needs, but God is interested in shaping a new nation that obeys His directions and laws and maintains a holy relationship with Him. God consistently provides their needs and uses each occasion as a teaching opportunity. For example, in the problem of the bitter water at Marah, we see that God has sovereignly led them through a dry desert and then to a place with undrinkable water (Exod 15:22-23). Then when they grumble and cry, "What are to drink?" (v.24), God shows Moses a creative and unexpected solution (v.25). The writer adds,

> There the Lord issued a ruling and instruction for them and put them to the test. He said, "If you listen carefully to the Lord your God and do what is right in his eyes, if you pay attention to his

commands and keep all his decrees, I will not bring on you any of the diseases I brought on the Egyptians, for I am the Lord, who heals you."

(Exod 15:25–26).

God asserts His right to govern the Israelites and the conditional nature of enjoying His blessings. But He is also giving them a promise on which to stand if they meet the conditions, a promised rooted in His nature as God: *YHWH-rapha*. God will always act consistently with His nature and He has just demonstrated His care with the miraculous changing of bitter water into drinkable.

In a similar way, God later provides water at Rephidim, when Moses felt they were about to stone him, through a special action using Moses' special staff (Exod 17:1–7), but the writer notes,

> He called the place Massah and Meribah because the Israelites quarreled and because they tested the Lord, saying, 'Is the Lord among us or not?'(Exod 17:7).

All this comes to a head when Moses is kept up on the mountain receiving the laws of God for a lengthy period and the people break out in a total rejection of God's rule and Moses' appointment as God's leader for them (Exod 32), constructing a golden calf which they acclaim with the lying words, "These are your gods, Israel, who brought you up out of Egypt" (v.4). God knows what is happening, of course, and speaks to Moses on the mountain about it, threatening,

> "I have seen these people," the Lord said to Moses, "and they are a stiff-necked people. Now leave me alone so that my anger may burn against them and that I may destroy them. Then I will make you into a great nation"

(Exod 32:9–10).

God has the right to destroy them and they certainly deserve it. But this is really a test for Moses, who gives God two good reasons for sparing the Israelites: God's reputation in Egypt (v.12) and His covenant promises to the patriarchs (v.13).[56] God does not want to destroy the people, but His own holiness demands punishment, which is executed through a police action by the Levites (vv.26–29) and a plague (v.35), with promise of more to come at the time of God's choosing (v.34). Moses' offer to be

---

56. Cf. Fretheim, *Suffering of God*, 50.

blotted out of God's book is curtly rejected (vv.31-33); God can be appealed to but not manipulated and ultimately all judgment is individually calibrated (v.33).

The rebellion of the Israelites keeps going with incidents involving meat supply (Num 11:4-34), Moses' leadership (Num 12:1-16), the abortive entry into Canaan (Num 13-14), the rebellion of some Levites and Reubenites (Num 16:1-50), the second water shortage crisis (Num 20:2-13), and the complaint about the diet near Edom (Num 21:4-9). God frequently uses plagues as part of His discipline of the nation (Exod 32:35; Num 11:33; 14:37; 16:46-49). These incidents highlight both the stubborn sinfulness of the Israelites and even their leaders and God's use of varying disciplinary methods to rein them in. God's sovereign Plan and His love required Him to somehow persist with Israel but to deal with their recalcitrance. As Paul comments, "What if God, although choosing to show his wrath and make his power known, bore with great patience the objects of his wrath–prepared for destruction?" (Rom 9:22).

This is the ongoing saga of the Old Testament. God expresses His sovereign rights and plans in a way that takes Israel's response into account. God acts consistently with His character as God, His implied constitution and the covenant He had made with Israel. In fact, most of Israel's history is foretold in the two lengthy covenant rewards-and-curses passages in the Torah, found in Leviticus 26 and Deuteronomy 28, and in a song which Moses teaches the people (Deut 31:19-22,30-32:45).

Ultimately it all comes to a disappointing conclusion. The kingdom of Israel is torn in two. The northern kingdom immediately falls into apostasy, rebuilding the golden calf religion of Exodus 32 (1 Kings 12:26-33), flirting with Baal worship (1 Kings 16:31-18:40), and finally losing its independence and being taken captive by the Assyrians (2 Kings 17:7-23 explains it all theologically). Finally, the southern kingdom of Judah, after being miraculously delivered from the Assyrians (2 Kings 18-19), rejects the covenant and, despite a short Torah revival under Josiah, succumbs to the Babylonians (2 Kings 21-25).

This all serves to show that judgment is an integral part of God's dealings with sinful and rebellious humanity as their sovereign Lord. God cannot condone human sin without violating His own nature and constitution and without completely losing control over his creation. God cannot unilaterally change human nature without violating His original intention to create an autonomous partner to share His rule of the earth. God is sovereign but is left with only two choices: to wipe humanity out and abandon his disastrous Plan for them (as nearly happened at the Flood) or to release a whole new life force that humans can tap into and be changed. This would not rule out further judgments but would establish a viable alternative. The Old Testament prophets look forward to such a new sovereign intervention which they see as a new Exodus (Isaiah), a new covenant (Jeremiah 31) or a new heart and spirit (Ezekiel 36–37).

But when it came, this new life was largely rejected by the Jews of Jesus' day. Jesus predicted a fresh and more awful judgment as a result, not so much to punish the Jews for rejecting him and his message specifically as to punish them for their consistent rejection of God's ways over the centuries. Jesus denounced the generation of his day, and especially the Jewish leaders, and prophesied that they would receive the judgment building up for centuries prior:

> Upon *you* will come all the righteous blood that has been shed on earth, from the blood of righteous Abel to the blood of Zechariah son of Berekiah, whom you murdered between the temple and the altar. Truly I tell you, all this will come on *this generation*
>
> (Matt 23:33–36, emphasis added).

This was a reluctant judgment, but Jerusalem could not be spared. Jesus continued,

> "Jerusalem, Jerusalem, you who kill the prophets and stone those sent to you, how often I have *longed* to gather your children together, as a hen gathers her chicks under her wings, and *you were not willing*. Look, your house is left to you desolate."
>
> (Matt 23:37–38; emphasis added).

God is sovereign but He acts in response to people's choices: "I longed to gather. . ." but "you were not willing." At times it really seems like God is frustrated by the lack of response from Israel especially. In an extended discussion of how God suffers because of this rebellion,[57] Terence Fretheim concludes,

> God is revealed as one who is not vindictive, legalistic or exacting as to matters of judgment. The disappointment evident in these responses of God indicates that judgment is not something God wants: "What can I do?" (Jer. 9:7).

---

57. *Suffering of God*, 107–126. Some key passages discussed include Ps 78:40–41; Isa 1:2–3; 65:1–2; Jer 2:2–3:2; 3:19–20; 8:4–7; 18:13–15; Mic 6:3; Hos 11:1–9.

God is genuinely in search of an alternative way into the future. God wants life and not death (e.g. Ezek.18:23-32). Moreover, God's extraordinary patience reveals the lengths to which God will go for the sake of the relationship.[58]

Here too, it could have been otherwise, but they (the Jerusalem people) decided. The crowd said, "His blood is on us and on our children" (Matt 27:25). As a result the glorious temple, still in the process of reconstruction initiated by Herod the Great, would be totally destroyed (Matt 24:2) in a terrible struggle (Matt 24:15-26).

No wonder Jesus spoke to women mourners as he went to the Cross:

> Daughters of Jerusalem, do not weep for me; weep for yourselves and for your children. For the time will come when you will say, 'Blessed are the childless women, the wombs that never bore and the breasts that never nursed!' Then
>
> They will say to the mountains, 'Fall on us!'
> And to the hills, 'Cover us!'
> For if people do these things when the tree is green, what will happen when it is dry?
>
> (Luke 23:28-31).

But first, in keeping with God's justice, the members of that generation were given a fresh opportunity to repent. On the day of Pentecost, Peter proclaimed, "Let all Israel be assured of this: God has made this Jesus, whom you crucified, both Lord and Christ" (Acts 2:36) and urged them to repent and be baptized in Jesus' name in order to be forgiven (Acts 2:38; see also 3:13-26). "With many other words he warned them; and he pleaded with them, 'Save yourselves from this corrupt generation'" (Acts 2:40).

Many responded: three thousand on the day of Pentecost (Acts 2:41), rising to five thousand shortly afterwards (Acts 4:4). Subsequently "the number of disciples in Jerusalem increased rapidly and a large number of priests became obedient to the faith" (Acts 6:7). Years later, James (the leader of the Christians in Jerusalem) could still claim, "You see, brother, how many thousands of Jews have believed" (Acts 21:20b). Moreover, the guilt involved in Jesus' death, while real, was specifically limited to "the people of Jerusalem and their rulers" (Acts 13:27). More importantly, this

---

58. *Suffering of God*, 125.

crime was not outside God's sovereign rule. Through this injustice, God's promised Plan was fulfilled (Acts 2:23; 3:18; 4:28; 13:27,32–33).

However, most of that generation of Jews apparently did not repent but resisted the good news in Jerusalem and in the other cities where the apostles preached. Hence the terrible judgment warned of by Jesus was inflicted through the ruthless Roman forces responding to a Jewish uprising in 66 AD, parallel to the Babylonian invasion 600 years previously (2 Chron 36:13–20). This basically destroyed Israel as a nation for nearly 1900 years, with huge ramifications for their religion as well. It was also God's way of sovereignly shutting down the Mosaic covenant by ending all operations of the second temple in Jerusalem (see Heb 8:13).

God's judgments are just. God does not judge lightly or eagerly; He sends warnings, He waits to see if there is repentance and to ensure judgment is necessary.[59] But His judgments are strong, even harsh when necessary, and they serve His sovereign purpose.

ONGOING REBELLION

Human rebellion against God's rule continues to this day. We read another key passage on rebellion and God's sovereignty in Psalm 2. The psalm begins with open rebellion against God and His anointed (or messiah):

> Why do the nations conspire
> and the people plot in vain?
> The kings of the earth rise up
> and the rulers band together
> against the LORD and against his anointed, saying,
> "Let us break their chains
> and throw off their shackles." (vv.1–3).

This is apparently a situation where God and His anointed have captured and chained up these Gentile rulers, but now they are trying to break free, though from the outset this is seen as "in vain." God's response to this rebellion underlines the futility of their rebellion:

> The One enthroned in heaven laughs;
> The Lord scoffs at them. (v.4)

How can any kings or powers possibly get free from God's rule? However, this is no joke:

---

59. See the extended discussion in Fretheim, *Suffering of God*, 53–57.

> He rebukes them in his anger
> and terrifies them in his wrath, saying,
> "I have installed my King
> on Zion, my holy mountain." (vv.5–6)

God's plans cannot be defeated by any rebellion, and especially God's plans to establish His Anointed as Ruler of the world. The rest of the psalm unpacks the power and privilege of the Messiah as God's son (v.7), heir of the earth and its nations (v.8), and final victor over all resistance (v.9). On this basis the rulers are warned of the consequences if they don't submit to the Messiah (vv.10–12) but promised salvation if they "take refuge in him" (v.12). Rebellion against God is futile.

Finally, Psalm 9 provides a generalized declaration of how God's sovereignty and judgment work in a fallen world. This psalm portrays two kinds of people: those who seek God and praise Him on the one hand (like the author of the psalm) and those who oppose God and His followers on the other. The opponents persecute the righteous (v.13) and plot against them (v.15). The righteous are portrayed as oppressed (v.9), physically afflicted (vv.12,18), persecuted (v.13), and needy (v.18). But the God factor dominates the psalm: God is portrayed as "sitting enthroned as the righteous judge" (v.4), reigning, establishing His throne, ruling and judging (vv.7–8), "enthroned in Zion" (v.11). He exercises His sovereign rule by defeating and destroying the enemies (vv.3,5,6,12,15,16,17,19,20) and by protecting and vindicating His followers (vv.9,10,12,18). This revelation inspires prayer and praise in the author (vv.1,2,11,14,19).

This is not how most people see world events or even the events of their own lives. It doesn't look like God "rules the world in righteousness and judges the peoples with equity" (v.8). Often the wicked seem to be triumphant and followers of God seem to be invisible and impotent. Such passages urge us to look at things with God-focused eyes, eyes of faith, and that is one of the main goals of the Bible as a whole.

However, there is a need for a kind of balance here. God's sovereignty continues in the sinful and fallen world but its operation changes. John Piper contends that:

> God's sovereignty over men's affairs is not compromised even by the reality of sin and evil in the world. It is not limited to the good acts of men or the pleasant events of nature. The wind belongs to God whether it comforts or whether it kills.[60]

---

60. Piper, *Desiring God*, 28.

To that I want to say, "Yes, but . . . ." God continues to rule, but the way this works adapts to new situations and God rarely overrules His free partners.

CHAPTER 4

GUIDANCE AND MANAGEMENT

ONE WAY THAT GOD uses to assert His authority over a fallen world and rebellious people is through chastisements or judgments. Here God's power confronts wayward people directly, forcing them to reconsider their actions and possibly motivating them to repent, and meting out consequences if they don't change their ways.[1] However, this kind of obvious and external pressure is not God's only way of ruling in the midst of a fallen world. He also works more subtly in, through and around human attitudes and actions to fulfill His plans even when the human players don't necessarily change their ways, as in the case of Nebuchadnezzar that we discussed in Chapter 3. Most readers of this book have experienced God working with and in other people, not just Christians, to answer their prayers and to open doors for them to serve Him.

I experienced this as a poor intern in a little Pentecostal church in New Zealand in 1975. I was sharing a house with a mail delivery boy who was almost as poor as I was, partly because of his old car's demands. We were asked to show hospitality to members of a visiting ministry team, but neither of us had the money to feed these guests. However, my faith had been built up through some teaching on covenant and thus I had a new level of confidence in God's ability to provide as I prayed. And that's

---

1. Some authors, such as Bradley Jersak (*A More Christlike God*) resist the idea that God specifically punishes people, seeing this kind of language as a way of describing what happens when we run up against the moral order God has established. I commend their desire to rid our picture of God from human motivations of revenge or anger; however, the danger of their theology is in making God an impersonal and distant Ruler.

what God did; He provided. First, some money that was owed to me was released. Second, a fellow graduate of Faith Bible College sent me a donation; he had no knowledge of my need, he had never done this before and never did it again. And then my grandmother, who knew nothing of my need and had never before given me money, sent me a monetary gift from Australia. Clearly God by His Spirit influenced people to send that money at exactly the time I needed it.

JOSEPH AS A CASE STUDY

The story of Joseph in Genesis illustrates multiple ways that God achieves His purposes, in particular His plans for the emerging nation of Israel. As in the story of Nebuchadnezzar, this story begins with dreams. Before his dreams, we only know two things about Joseph: that he was his father's favorite son (Gen 37:3–4) and that his brothers hated him because of that favoritism and because he'd given "a bad report" on some of them to his father (Gen 37:2). Trouble was certainly brewing among the brothers, and it appears we are looking at another Cain and Abel (or Esau and Jacob) story, but Joseph's two dreams made the situation much worse, because they suggested he would be the family leader and rule over his brothers and even his parents (Gen 37:5–11).

God was showing Joseph part of His plan, but how would it happen? His brothers hatched a plot to ensure it would not. "Come now, let's kill him and throw him into one of those cisterns and say that a ferocious animal devoured him. Then we'll see what comes of his dreams" (Gen 37:20). This was a direct challenge to God's sovereignty. God used the consciences of two older brothers to ensure Joseph was not killed (Gen 37:21–22, 26–27), but they sold him into slavery and maintained a fiction with Jacob that he had been devoured by a wild beast (Gen 37:23–35).[2] The motive of the brothers was clearly evil, and they did not break down even when their father mourned grievously.

Joseph's subsequent career is full of setbacks, none of them his fault. After being sold as a slave, he is betrayed by his master's wife after he resists her sexual advances and spends years in jail even after interpreting dreams for two key Egyptians officials (Gen 39–40). His life is seemingly

---

2. There is a note of irony here. As Wenham explains, "Chap. 37 shows Jacob being deceived by his sons with a kid and their brother's garment, just as Jacob had deceived" his father Isaac in Gen 27 (*Genesis 16–50*, 359). This suggests an element of justice, even retribution, in what happens to Jacob.

'out of control,' in spite of his integrity and capacity to win the favor of his masters, itself the gift of God (Gen 39:2–6,21–23), so that at least he survives till the next episode. His leadership gift is certainly a factor in his success, as is his ability to interpret dreams, which he attributes to God,[3] but what good will come of it?

However, finally dreams again appear: Pharaoh has two disturbing dreams that no one can interpret, and his cupbearer remembers Joseph from his time in jail. Before long, Joseph's two spiritual gifts and God-given wisdom have propelled him to the position of Prime Minister of Egypt (Gen 41), where he can implement his plan to save the nation and its region, for the dreams were not mentioned just to be accepted fatalistically, but rather to prompt action (Gen 41:33–36).[4]

Joseph's position is now comfortable and powerful, but this is only for a bigger Plan. The famine he had predicted from Pharaoh's dreams affects Canaan as well as Egypt. This situation forces his brothers to travel to Egypt where they had learned there was food (the result of Joseph's careful plan to preserve Egypt). After Joseph tests his brothers and Judah shows he is a changed man (another facet of God's work on this situation), Joseph reveals his identity and the whole family comes to Egypt, which was God's plan all along (Gen 42–50).

How did God achieve that result with only one good person to use? As in other biblical cases, many people played their part without any reference to God. God also, we presume, sent the seven years of plenty followed by the seven years of famine and gave Pharaoh the dreams that predicted these events. Both events show divine sovereignty directly.[5] Joseph's own integrity[6] and gifts of interpretation and leadership played their part, though not always as he or others might have expected.

However, Joseph himself gave two inspired interpretations of what was happening. First, immediately after revealing his identity to his brothers, he said,

> And now, do not be distressed and do not be angry with yourselves for selling me here, because it was to save lives that *God sent me* ahead of you. . . . For *God sent me* ahead of you to

---

3. Gen 40:8; 41:16,25,28. Cf. Wenham, *Genesis 16–50*, 382–383,392.
4. Cf. Wenham, *Genesis 16–50*, 394.
5. Wenham, *Genesis 16–50*, 399.
6. And increasing maturity. As Wenham comments, "his character has undergone a remarkable transformation" (*Genesis 16–50*, 399).

> preserve for you a remnant on earth and to save your lives by a great deliverance. So then, it was *not you who sent me here, but God*

(Gen 45:4–8, emphasis added).

Here Joseph forgives his brothers' cruel actions against him by appealing to God's sovereign plan. God sent him to Egypt. God did so to save the incipient nation Israel in keeping with His promises.[7] God's will had been done through, and in spite of, the sinful reactions of the brothers, Potiphar's wife, Potiphar himself, the cupbearer and others.

As we read the story of Joseph and his brothers (especially Judah), we see human beings acting independently for their own self-seeking reasons. The brothers act out of jealousy. Potiphar's wife acts out of lust and maybe boredom, Potiphar acts out of anger and wounded pride, and Pharaoh (and Joseph) seek to protect and preserve Egypt and Pharaoh's power. But in and through their sinful actions, God subtly works to bring His will to pass. If we look more deeply, we may even see God working on the character of the chief characters: Jacob being forced to release his next favorite son (Benjamin) in spite of his fears (Gen 42:33–43:14),[8] Judah offering himself as a slave to Joseph to spare Benjamin and especially his father, thus displaying repentance (Gen 44:18–34),[9] Joseph himself being stretched by misfortune (Gen 40:20–23; Ps 105:17–19).[10] As Joseph says, after the death of his father, to his brothers, "Don't be afraid. Am I in the place of God? You *intended* to harm me, but God *intended* it for good to accomplish what is now being done, the saving of many lives" (Gen 50:19–20, emphasis added). God had a plan, as implied by "intended," and His plans are accomplished, not because He somehow 'forces' people to do things against their will, but because He works within their hearts and around their bad choices with contrary circumstances.[11]

---

7. Cf. Wenham, *Genesis 16–50*, 433.
8. Cf. Wenham, *Genesis 16–50*, 431.
9. Cf. Wenham, *Genesis 16–50*, 427, 431
10. Parallels with Job, and indeed Jacob, are strong, and there are even parallels with the testing, rejection and vindication of Jesus (see Wenham, *Genesis 16–50*, 400).
11. For another interpretation of how God worked in this story, see Ware, *God's Greater Glory*, 125–129.

THE EXODUS NARRATIVE

This complex and subtle interweaving of human intentions and actions with God's intervention and guidance is a feature of the rest of Scripture. The narrative of the Exodus is the next big example. God has already spoken to Abraham of a four-hundred-year period of exile and oppression to be followed by an exodus: "I will punish the nation they serve as slaves, and afterward they will come out with great possessions" (Gen 15:14). The delay in this event is explained by the fact that "the sin of the Amorites has not yet reached its full measure" (Gen 15:16); this is God speaking as Judge, unwilling to punish any people without giving them time to repent. Sure enough, the Israelites go down to Egypt to be preserved, initially as honored guests protected by Joseph, to prosper there and multiply greatly (Exod 1:7).

Then a situation arises that reminds today's readers of Nazi Germany and South African apartheid. Fear of a group that is 'different' and growing leads to oppression and attempted genocide (Exod 1:8–22). Male babies specifically are killed by drowning in the Nile River (Exod 1:22). Pharaoh's motives are very explicit and the only resistance to his injustice comes from some well-placed women: the Israelite midwives (Exod 1:15–21), Moses' mother and sister, and strangely enough, Pharaoh's own daughter (Exod 2:1–10). Baby boys are being thrown into the Nile to drown, but this Israelite boy instead is raised under the protection of Pharaoh and even in the royal palace, apparently due to the princess's pity (Exod 2:6) and influence with her father. This is how God's sovereign guidance of affairs can work.

Moses, of course, tries to intervene on behalf of his fellow Israelites and Pharaoh turns against him, causing him to flee into exile in Midian (Exod 2:11–22). The Israelites have to wait for another forty years before their deliverance can begin. The author of Exodus does not attempt to explain this delay, but perhaps it is due to God's patience as Judge: judgment on the Amorites (Gen 15:16) and on Egypt awaits the timing known best to the all-knowing Judge. Even now, Egypt will be given a chance to repent in a series of trials.

But at last, signaled by the death of the oppressive Pharaoh, the cry of the Israelites for help is heard by God.

> God heard their groaning and he remembered his covenant with Abraham, with Isaac and with Jacob. So God looked on the Israelites and was concerned about them.

(Exod 2:24-25).

God in sovereignty decides when and how to act, but He does so in response to injustice, to prayer and to the covenant He had made and confirmed to the ancestors of Israel (see also Exod 3:7,9,15; 6:4-5). Moses later makes it very clear that this was an act of grace and election, not because God was impressed with the Israelites, but "because the Lord loved you and kept the oath he swore to your ancestors" (Deut 7:7-8). God acts justly and deliberately in accordance with election; He keeps His promises and the covenants He has freely entered into.[12]

God calls Moses to be the mediator of His strategy in spite of his initial resistance (Exod 3-4). Moses learns that God has a clear plan to deliver the Israelites and take them to their promised land (Exod 3:7-9,17), but that He will only act through a man and Moses is appointed to be that man (Exod 3:10). Moreover, God will not take 'No' for an answer, somewhat like Jonah centuries later, though He does concede to allow Aaron to be Moses' spokesman (Exod 4:13-16). In this conversation, God overcomes Moses' resistance by theological reasoning and persistence, overcoming Moses' excuses one by one. He promises that "the elders of Israel will listen to you" (Exod 3:18), partly because of miraculous signs Moses is empowered to perform (Exod 4:1-9). He also promises to "make the Egyptians favorably disposed toward this people, so that when you leave you will not go empty-handed" because they (mainly the women) will donate precious items to the Israelite women on request (Exod 3:21-22; 11:2-3; 12:35-36). The role of women in this story is intriguing.

But the king of Egypt is a different matter:

> "I know that the king of Egypt will not let you go unless a mighty hand compels him. So I will stretch out my hand and strike the Egyptians with all the wonders that I will perform among them. After that, he will let you go" (Exod 3:19-20).

Thus the scene is set for the mighty struggle between Moses and Pharaoh, or rather between God and Egypt, in Exodus 5-14. Without going into detail, we need to note significant features theologically. God could perhaps have shortened the process and made the Egyptians submit instantly, but this is not how God operates with humans.

First, the struggle is necessary because God will not forcibly override Pharaoh's stubbornness and pride. He (and his advisors) must come

---

12. Cf. Cole, *Exodus*, 19.

to a decision of their own will to release the Israelites as a result of the plagues that God sends (Exod 7:13-14; 8:15; 9:13-21,30,34-35; 10:3,27-29; 11:8; 12:31-33). Moreover, as Alec Motyer comments, the process functioned as "a process of probation, at any point of which they could have stepped off the ladder of discipline into the path of obedience and escaped the final penalty."[13] God responds, as we have seen, to human actions and choices.

Second, the struggle is necessary because it allows God to punish Egypt for its unjust treatment of the Israelites (Gen 15:14); this is perhaps why God "hardens Pharaoh's heart" at times when he is about to give way (Exod 7:3-5,13,22-23; 10:20; 11:9-10; 14:17).[14] It also explains why it is only when God kills the first-born males of Egypt (perhaps in vengeance for the male Israelite babies cast into the Nile)[15] that the Israelites are released (Exod 11-12). Something similar may explain why God hardened the Canaanite nations in the days of Joshua (Josh 11:19-20); now their sin had "reached its full measure" (Gen 15:16) and, like Sodom, they must now be eliminated (Gen 18:20-21).[16]

Third, the struggle allows some Egyptians to repent of idolatry and later even join the Israelites in their exodus (Exod 9:19-21; 10:7; 11:3; 12:38). In a similar way, the Joshua narrative includes the decision of Rahab to side with the Israelites (Josh 2:1-21).

Fourth, the struggle allows God to show everyone who is God[17] and to expose the impotence of the spiritual forces in Egypt,[18] a result which strengthens the faith of Israel and leads to conversions of some

---

13. *The Message of Exodus*, 116.

14. Based on an analysis of the Hebrew verbs used here, Christian Ramsey argues that what God did was to "strengthen" Pharaoh's resolve, not to force him to do anything (Ramsey, "The Pharaoh Initiative," 754-755).

15. See Fretheim, *Exodus*, 110-111. "The plagues are *not an arbitrarily chosen response* to Pharaoh's sins . . . the consequences are cosmic because the sins are creational" (ibid, 111; emphasis in original text).

16. Alec Motyer suggests that this is all meant as a kind of spiritual lesson: "The plagues reveal his love of obedience and his revulsion from disobedience" (*The Message of Exodus*, 115).

17. While some of plagues may be explicable by natural causes, the precise timing and the language of the Lord's hand in Exodus militates against pushing this too far (Motyer, *The Message of Exodus*, 119-120). Fretheim, however, sees the plagues as "hypernatural" events where the natural order is out of control (Fretheim, *Exodus*, 109).

18. This is evident in the first plague which "struck at the heart of Egypt's life. . . . sustained by the river they considered to be divine, showing that there is a God greater even than the Nile" (Motyer, *The Message of Exodus*, 117).

Egyptians, especially when plagues strike only the Egyptians and do not affect the Israelites (Exod 6:7; 7:8–12; 8:18–19,22–23; 9:4–7,11,26; 10:1–2,23; 11:7; 12:13,23,24–27; 14:4,8,17–18).

Fifth, the struggle glorifies God by showing that it is not by skillful rhetoric or diplomacy or human violence that liberation is attained (Exod 5:1–6:12; 8:10; 9:16; 10:1–2; 14:31). It also demonstrates God's commitment to Israel.[19]

Sixth, the struggle cannot finish until God has got every last Israelite out of Egypt, and so God has to make both Pharaoh and Moses stubborn in order to prevent any compromise deal between them (Exod 6:1; 8:8–15,25–32; 10:7–11,24–27).

Finally, in this struggle God stands with His man and Moses' own reputation increases (Exod 11:3; 14:31). As Terence Fretheim points out, the plagues are God's actions but "one must speak also of the activity of Moses and Aaron with respect to each. Both God and human beings are agents."[20] God works through human representatives.

In short, this episode is a classic demonstration of God's sovereign strategies in action in a fallen world, using His prophetic words in the mouths of His servants, miraculous signs, devastating judgments and the decisions of saints and sinners whom He steers sovereignly but justly. God does not *force* people, but He does *influence* them through both external events and internal motivations so that their decisions are both theirs and, in a sense, His.

However, God's plans will succeed. God's chosen people will be released from Egypt. God will be glorified in His sovereign guidance. Human strategies will not succeed in resisting or diverting God's will. As God says to Pharaoh through Moses, "But I have raised you up for this very purpose, that I might show you my power and that my name might be proclaimed in all the earth" (Exod 9:16).[21] Pharaoh is not a puppet. The passage goes on to say, "You still set yourself against my people and will not let them go" (Exod 9:17), and threatens a disastrous hailstorm, but explicitly gives Egyptians warning so that those who "feared the Lord" could protect their possessions (Exod 9:18–21). God as Judge allows for human response to avert or lessen the effects of His punishments.

---

19. Cf. Motyer, *The Message of Exodus*, 123.

20. *Exodus*, 106.

21. Ramsey points out that according to Paul, "God raised up Pharaoh for purposes, not perdition" due to His "foreknowledge" of Pharaoh's heart and in order to make Himself known ("The Pharaoh Initiative," 751–753,756).

However, as Paul comments on this passage, "God has mercy on whom he wants to have mercy, and he hardens whom he wants to harden" (Rom 9:18). As we saw, God had good reasons to "harden" Pharaoh.[22]

God then demonstrates His power and sovereignty dramatically at the Red Sea. God sets this encounter up very deliberately according to Exodus. He leads the Israelites out on a longer route toward the Red Sea using the pillar of cloud (Exod 13:17-22). He places them in a compressed location specifically to entice the Egyptians to pursue (Exod 14:1-4), and this works; God knew Pharaoh's heart and was able to lure him to disaster (Exod 14:5-8). Once again God hardens Pharaoh's heart (Exod 14:4,8). God's goal is clear: "I will gain glory for myself through Pharaoh and all his army, and the Egyptians will know that I am the LORD" (Exod 14:4; see also vv.17-18). This is the final punishment of Egypt for their oppression of God's people and attempted genocide. God carefully moves the pieces as in a chess game (though with the difference that the pieces move themselves), and Pharaoh and his army are duly destroyed and the Israelites delivered through the Sea (Exod 14:19-30).[23]

God is glorified in the eyes of the Egyptians who observe that "The LORD is fighting for them against Egypt" (Exod 14:25). The Israelites also learn again how much God can be trusted (Exod 14:31). This faith is expressed in the great song of Exodus 15, which attributes everything that has happened to God's power and redemptive purpose.

Indeed, "The LORD reigns for ever and ever" (Exod 15:18). The same God who "does whatever pleases him" in His creation (Ps 135:6) deals sovereignly with Egypt and other nations (Ps 135:8-12) because He is no idol. As Cole comments,

> Pharaoh stands for the height of human power, ranged against God and the people of God; therefore his fall is a fitting symbol for all time of the impossibility of striving against God, or of thwarting His plans.[24]

---

22. Douglas Moo, who is insistent that this hardening is not a response to anything people do, nonetheless states. "God's hardening is an act directed at human beings who are already in rebellion against God's righteous rule" (Moo, *Romans*, 599). For another valid explanation of the hardening process, that puts more emphasis on Pharaoh's culpability, see Lennox, *Determined to Believe?*, 259-266.

23. It is probably no accident that God dealt this way with the army, not the whole population, and specifically not with the women, who had been more merciful to Israel.

24. Cole, *Exodus*, 29.

GOD AND THE NATIONS

A key theme throughout the Bible is God's dealings, not just with Israel but all the nations of the world. Paul affirms that "in the past, he let all nations go their own way" (Acts 14:16), but this did not mean He neglected or ignored them. As Paul said elsewhere,

> From one man he made all the nations, that they should inhabit the whole earth; and he marked out their appointed times in history and the boundaries of their lands. God did this so that they would seek him and perhaps reach out for him and find him, though he is not far from any one of us. For in him we live and move and have our being

(Acts 17:26–28).

This statement affirms that God made all the nations (likely referring back to Genesis 10–11) as part of His plan for the whole earth to be inhabited. Nations are legitimate because of their divine origin and seem to be a permanent part of God's purpose (Rev 21:24,26).

Paul also claims that God is behind the historical fortunes and geographical boundaries of the nations. Given the way that nations have risen and fallen, appeared and disappeared, expanded and contracted over the course of history, this is a huge claim, though well-grounded in the Old Testament. But the purpose of all this is that God wants all nations to seek Him and that isn't hard, since He is close by, part of the atmosphere in which all people live. However, while God controls the fortunes of the nations, He doesn't apparently compel their allegiance to Him, as implied by "perhaps." As Peterson says, "Paul is describing a potential that was not fulfilled in the Athenian situation"[25] into which he was speaking. Nations choose to seek God or not.

God never abandoned His human creatures but guided their history even when they were largely ignorant of Him. He not only brought Israel out of Egypt but did similar things for other nations (Amos 9:7). He also held them accountable for their sins (Amos 1:3–2:15; Jer 46–51).

A standout example of God guiding and dealing with a Gentile nation occurs in the history of Babylon, specifically the neo-Babylonian empire. Jeremiah's core message began with a warning of disaster from the north (Jer 1:14–15; 4:6). As R.K. Harrison comments, "These conquerors

---

25. Peterson, *The Acts of the Apostles*, 498.

are divine agents carrying out God's sentence upon the Judeans."[26] This northern force is likened to a lion (Jer 4:7), a scorching wind (Jer 4:11), clouds and a whirlwind (Jer 4:13), all forces under God's sovereign control. This is then identified with a specific king, Nebuchadnezzar, whom God has appointed to rule the whole region, not just Judah. As Jeremiah is commissioned to say to the ambassadors who have come from surrounding nations to Zedekiah king of Judah,

> With my great power and outstretched arm I made the earth and its people and the animals that are on it, and *I give it to anyone I please*. Now I will give all your countries into the hands of *my servant* Nebuchadnezzar king of Babylon; I will make even the wild animals subject to him. All nations will serve him and his son and his grandson until the time for his land comes; then many nations and great kings will subjugate him

(Jer 27:5–7, emphasis added; see also 28:14)

This ringing declaration of God's sovereign plan is followed by godly 'advice:' submit to Nebuchadnezzar, and live in peace, or resist and be destroyed or exiled (Jer 27:8–13). Nebuchadnezzar, of course, has no understanding of, or faith in, God. He is motivated by his own love for power and attributes his successes to his own armed power or his own Babylonian gods. Yet God raises him up and uses him in God's sovereign purposes.

But, as described in the previous chapter, the Book of Daniel tells us how God then dealt personally with Nebuchadnezzar and brought him to a place of conversion by showing him 'who was boss.' Daniel and three other noble youths from Judah, who were among those taken into exile in Babylon, had a different mindset to others who were privileged to receive indoctrination and training in Babylonian laws and culture so as to become officials of the empire (Dan 1:3–5). Although the circumstances implied that their God was less powerful than the gods of Babylon (after all they had been defeated and taken captive), to these four young heroes their God was the one true God, and they were determined to serve Him above all else. In the first test of faith, they successfully showed that a 'kosher' diet (which at least did not include meat offered to idols)[27] would keep them healthier than the other students in the Babylonian training

---

26. Harrison, *Jeremiah and Lamentations*, 52.
27. Cf. Goldingay, *Daniel*, 18–19.

program and that God would give them insight beyond the other trainees (Dan 1:8–20). The king was impressed (Dan 1:20), perhaps surprised.

In the second test, God gave Nebuchadnezzar an amazing dream and moved him to demand of his best dream interpreters that they tell him what he had dreamed as well as what it meant (Dan 2:1–13). I wonder if the king was starting to doubt the spiritual powers of his own culture and wanting to test them. Their abject failure opened the door for Daniel to pray and receive the content and interpretation of the dream in a vision (Dan 2:14–23). He was then able to attribute this miracle to God (Dan 2:24–28). The message of the dream was itself a powerful declaration of God's sovereign control of history,[28] including God's promotion of Nebuchadnezzar as regional emperor, as well as an outline of future history as planned by God and a prediction of the coming kingdom of God (Dan 2:31–45). Nebuchadnezzar was suitably impressed and confessed, "Your God is the God of gods and the Lord of kings and a revealer of mysteries" (Dan 2:47), as well as promoting Daniel and his three friends. But he hadn't really got the message yet.

The third test was crucial. In a massive show of authority and hubris, perhaps motivated by his growing doubts and resistance to what God was doing, Nebuchadnezzar set up a huge golden statue and demanded that all his officials bow to it, on pain of being killed by fire if they didn't (Dan 3:1–7). Daniel's friends were exposed to this fate when they refused to bow before the golden statue (Dan 3:8–16), declaring that,

> If we are thrown into the blazing furnace, the God we serve is able to deliver us from it, and he will deliver us from Your Majesty's hand. But even if he does not, we want you to know, Your Majesty, that we will not serve your gods or worship the image of gold you have set up

(Dan 3:17–18).

They thus provoked the king's anger with their stubbornness. The fire was increased sevenfold and even the soldiers who threw them into the furnace were burned to death (Dan 3:19–23). But God intervened and Nebuchadnezzar again was forced to acknowledge God's power, "for no other god can save in this way" (Dan 3:29). Surely now Nebuchadnezzar would realize that God alone is sovereign and he was only an unwitting servant of God's plans. No, a fourth test was needed to drive the point home.

---

28. As Goldingay comments, "History is under the control of God in his freedom. It is thus his secret" (*Daniel*, 56).

Daniel 4 takes the form of Nebuchadnezzar's personal testimony of God's intervention in a way that touches him personally. It begins again with a strange dream and again only Daniel can interpret it (Dan 4:4–19), but the dream is very pointed and dangerous, since it concerns the king himself losing his sanity and his position for a set period (Dan 4:19–26). The goal is for Nebuchadnezzar to learn that "the Most High is sovereign over all kingdoms on earth and gives them to anyone he wishes and sets over them the lowliest of people" (Dan 4:17; see also verses 25,26,32). Daniel pleads with the king to "renounce your sins by doing what is right, and your wickedness by being kind to the oppressed" (Dan 4:27) so as to avert this severe discipline. The king fails to respond to this message and what was threatened happens to him a year later (Dan 4:28–34). Finally, Nebuchadnezzar gets the point and confesses,

> His dominion is an eternal dominion;
> his kingdom endures from generation to generation.
> All the peoples of the earth
> are regarded as nothing.
> He does as he pleases
> with the powers of heaven
> and the peoples of the earth.
> No one can hold back his hand
> or say to him, 'What have you done?'
>
> (Dan 4:34–35).

The message is clear: God is in control. He raises up rulers and nations as He sees fit and even defines their boundaries in time and space. Not only so but "everything he does is right and all his ways are just" (Dan 4:37). God has shown himself capable of pursuing a stubborn ungodly ruler and bringing him to some level of faith in Him.

Isaiah makes similar statements in relation to God's judgments on Assyria and Babylon. For example,

> The LORD Almighty has sworn,
> 'Surely as I have planned, so it will be,
> and as I have purposed, so it will happen.
> I will crush the Assyrian in my land;
> on my mountains I will trample him down...'
>
> (Isa 14:24–25a).

This determination of God to crush the Assyrians is a response to their attitude. God had been using them as "the rod of my anger" (Isa 10:5) against "a godless nation" (Israel). "But this is not what he intends"

(Isa 10:7); the Assyrians are boastful and arrogant and take the full credit for their victories (Isa 10:13–14) and hence, after the LORD has finished using them, He promises, "I will punish the king of Assyria for the willful pride of his heart and the haughty look in his eyes" (Isa 10:12). The Assyrians failed to realize they were being used by God and would suffer a plague as judgment (Isa 10:15–16).[29]

But God's judgment on Assyria is only part of His program, as Isaiah 14 continues:

> "This is the plan determined for *the whole world*;
> this is the hand stretched out over *all nations*.
> For the LORD Almighty has purposed, and who can thwart him?
> His hand is stretched out, and who can turn it back?"
> (Isa 14:26–27, emphasis added)

God's plan is universal in scope and certain to be fulfilled because He is God and no one can stop what He determined to carry out. However, this is not just a negative message but rather one of hope for the Israelites experiencing the wrath of the Assyrians or Babylonians. As Christopher Seitz comments,

> . . .it may appear that God's sending forth of the Chaldeans in judgment over Assyria, Judah or even the whole earth does nothing less than unleash a terrible cycle of senseless violence. But as in Habakkuk, God stands firm on the conviction that all takes place according to a mysterious plan of old and that in the end justice will be done, as violence and destruction finally eliminate all forms of pride and arrogance on earth–including the arrogance of those who themselves wreak the judgment.[30]

The nations need to realize how powerless their gods are and how uniquely powerful the true God is. "Why do the nations say, 'Where is their God?'" asks the psalmist, and replies "Our God is in heaven; he does whatever pleases him" (Ps 115:2–3). Idols are powerless but God is to be praised and trusted. "The LORD remember us and will bless us" (Ps 115:12a) but He cannot be manipulated. And God is interested even in saving the Gentile nations and will bring them to submission to himself (Isa 19:18–25).

---

29. Cf. Seitz, *Isaiah 1–39*, 92.
30. Seitz, *Isaiah 1–39*, 132.

THE DEATH OF JESUS

Perhaps the greatest example of God organizing events for His purpose is seen in the events around Jesus' crucifixion. Peter preaches to his Jerusalem audience,

> "This man was handed over to you *by God's deliberate plan and foreknowledge*; and you, with the help of wicked men, put him to death by nailing him to the cross."
>
> (Acts 2:23, emphasis added).

Later, after blaming the people of Jerusalem for handing Jesus over to be killed and disowning him before Pilate, when he wanted to release him (Acts 3:13–14), Peter concedes that they all acted in ignorance (Acts 3:17) and adds,

> But this is how God *fulfilled* what he had *foretold* through all the prophets, saying that his Messiah would suffer
>
> (Acts 3:18, emphasis added).

In both sermons, God is seen as fulfilling His plans, but the Jerusalem Jews are called on to take responsibility and repent for their actions (Acts 2:36–38; 3:19–20). They can't use the sovereign plan of God to diminish their own responsibility (see also Acts 4:10).

Shortly afterwards, we hear the Christians praying in response to threats from the Jerusalem leaders. In their prayer, building on Psalm 2, they say,

> Indeed Herod and Pontius Pilate met together with the Gentiles and the people of Israel in this city to conspire against your holy servant Jesus, whom you anointed. They did *what your power and will had decided beforehand* should happen
>
> (Acts 4:27–28, emphasis added).

Paul makes a similar point in his sermon in the synagogue of Antioch of Pisidia:

> The people of Jerusalem and their rulers did not recognize Jesus, yet in condemning him they *fulfilled the words of the prophets* that are read every Sabbath. Though they found no proper ground for a death sentence, they asked Pilate to have him executed. When they had carried out *all that was written about him*...

(Acts 13:27–29a, emphasis added).

And John comments on Caiaphas' remark that "it is better for you that one man die for the people than that the whole nation perish" (John 11:50), writing,

> He did not say this on his own, but as high priest that year he prophesied that Jesus would die for the Jewish nation, and not only for that nation but also for the scattered children of God. . .

(John 11:51–52).

In other words, Jesus' death was *both* a crime, which those responsible were accountable for, *and* part of God's sovereign purpose. As Jesus himself says to the two disciples on the road to Emmaus, "Did not the Messiah *have to* suffer these things and then enter his glory?" (Luke 24:26 emphasis added).

When one reads the Gospel accounts of these events with this perspective, we see how the events work together to fulfill God's plan, yet without any kind of heavy-handed divine intervention or direction. Judas, the chief priests, the Sanhedrin, Peter, Pilate (and his wife), the Roman soldiers, and the Jerusalem crowd all act entirely 'naturally' throughout the twenty-four hours involved. The dialogues with Pilate and the Jewish leaders turn on political motivations: fears of repercussions from the Romans (John 11:48–50), demands from the chief priests and the mob (Matt 27:12–18,26–26; Mark 15:6–15; Luke 23:13–25; John 18:39–40; 19:15), Jesus's claims (Matt 26:63–65; Mark 14:61–64; Luke 22:70–71; John 19:7), the rightful jurisdiction of Pontius Pilate and Herod (Luke 23:5–12), and threats of Caesar (John 19:12,15). Only Pilate's wife's bad dream shows any sign of a heavenly communication (Matt 27:19).

Only Jesus really knows what is happening and chooses to cooperate with God in this plan (Matt 26:1–2,24,28,31,45,53–54; Mark 14:21–24, 49; Luke 22:20–22; 23:28–31; John 10:11–18; 12:23–33), though with a very human dread and struggle in Gethsemane (Matt 26:39–44; Mark 14:33–39; Luke 22:41–44). Jesus refuses to let Pilate acquit him by any kind of human defense. In a telling exchange,

> "Do you refuse to speak to me?" Pilate said. "Don't you realize that I have power either to free you or to crucify you?"
>
> Jesus answered, "You would have no power over me if it were not *given to you from above*. Therefore the one who handed me over to you is guilty of a greater sin."

(John 19:10–11 emphasis added).

Jesus has to die but those responsible for this are guilty.

In this narrative, the role of Judas is a special focus. Jesus is very aware that Judas will betray him and tells the group of disciples about it without naming the traitor, perhaps to stop them restraining, or even lynching, Judas. However, he does interact more intimately with Judas himself (Matt 26:21–25; Mark 14:18–21; Luke 22:21–23; John 13:18–27) and accedes to his action: "Do what you came for, friend" (Matt 26:50); "what you are about to do, do quickly" (John 13:27). Judas may seem predestined to play this role (John 17:12) but must also be accountable for his actions:

> The Son of Man will go just as it is written about him. But woe to that man who betrays the Son of Man! It would be better for him if he had not been born

(Matt 26:24; compare Mark 14:21; Luke 22:22).

Judas's own motives, and later remorse and suicide, are portrayed as tragic, but as fulfilling God's plan (Matt 27:3–10; Luke 22:1–6; John 12:4–6; compare Acts 1:16–19). His actions are attributed to his own evil motives (John 12:4–6), to Satan (Luke 22:3; John 13:2,27) and indirectly to God's plan. In view of Jesus' words in Matt 26:24, we might ask, why was Judas born to such a horrendous destiny? Greek readers might see parallels with the story of Oedipus who is fated to kill his father and marry his mother. However, I. Howard Marshall challenges that interpretation, writing, "There is no indication here that Judas was predestined to carry out this act of betrayal."[31] John seems to imply he was, when Jesus calls Judas "a devil" (John 6:70) and "the one doomed to destruction" (John 17:12). But perhaps we are reading too much into these words if we take them to mean that Judas had no choice in the matter. His being "doomed to destruction" is the result of his sinful choices and the comment of Jesus that he would be better off not to be born is really a stark way of stressing the enormity of his crime.

---

31. Marshall, *Kept by the Power*, 88.

THE SOVEREIGNTY OF THE SPIRIT

As we consider how God rules in, through and around sinful humanity, it is important to consider the work of the Spirit and the ability of God to influence people's thinking "from within." As Calvin, drawing on Augustine, writes, "He acts within; he holds their hearts within; he moves their hearts within; and he draws them by their own wills, which he has wrought within them."[32]

We saw earlier how the Spirit was at work in the original creation (Gen 1:2). The Spirit is also at work to "contend with humans" (Gen 6:3) after the Fall. While the Spirit is not frequently mentioned later in the Old Testament, God's capacity to get 'inside' even very stubborn humans, and 'steer' them in a certain direction, is evident. He gives visions (Gen 15:1; 32:24–30; Exod 3:1–2; Judg 13:3; Luke 1:11; Acts 9:3–6,10–12; 10:9–19; 16:9; 18:9; 23:11; 26:13–19; 2 Cor 12:1–4; Rev 1:1–2,10–18) and dreams both to His own servants (Gen 15:12–13; 28:12–15; 31:10–13; 37:5–9; 46:2–4; Matt 1:20; 2:13,19) and to those who have no relationship to God, such as King Abimelek (Gen 20:3–7), Jacob's uncle Laban (Gen 31:29), Pharaoh's imprisoned servants (Gen 40:5), Pharaoh himself (Gen 41:1–7), Nebuchadnezzar (Dan 2;4), and the magi or 'wise men' who sought out Jesus (Matt 2:12). Even a sorcerer like Balaam hears from God and speaks God's word, thus defeating the plans of King Balak to use sorcery against Israel (Num 22:9–12,20; 23:3–5,16; 24:2–4); on the last occasion we read that "the Spirit of God came on him."[33]

The Spirit moved in unpredictable ways in Old Testament times. Sometimes God simply caused potential opponents of His people to be restrained by fear (Gen 35:5; Exod 23:27). God's Spirit stirred up Samson to seek excuses to attack the Philistines (Judg 13:25; 14:4) and the Spirit "came powerfully upon him" (Judg 14:6,19; 15:14) to do amazing exploits of strength. This is related to his dedication as a Nazirite to God, symbolized by uncut hair (Judg 16:17). The Spirit came on early kings such as Saul (1 Sam 10:6,10–11) and David (1 Sam 16:12); the Spirit later departed from Saul (1 Sam 16:14), a fate that David feared might happen to him when he committed a serious sin (Ps 51:11).

More disturbingly, in Saul's case "an evil spirit from the Lord tormented him" (1 Sam 16:14) periodically. Frequently the evil spirit could be relieved or sent off by beautiful music, though sometimes this

---

32. Calvin, *Institutes*, 964, quoting from Augustine, *On Rebuke and Grace*.
33. Levison, *A Boundless God*, 34–37.

accentuated Saul's jealous rages (1 Sam 16:15-16,23; 18:10; 19:9). Later the Spirit came on Saul as he was seeking to kill David and he "prophesied" and stripped himself naked (1 Sam 19:23-24); this is one way God protected David from him.

All these and other Old Testament episodes show that the Spirit is not under any human control and acts freely and unpredictably. Nevertheless, the most common outcome of the Spirit's work is prophesying, whether in an occasional and often obscure way (Num 11:25-27), as with Saul (1 Sam 10:6,10: 19:23), or speaking coherently through God's genuine representative messengers (Mic 3:8). A more consistent, regular and powerful experience of the Spirit is expected in the future through the Messiah or Servant of God (Isa 11:2; 42:1; 61:1), to be enjoyed by all God's people (Isa 44:3; Ezek 36:27; 37;14; Joel 2:28-29).

In the New Testament, these prophetic expectations are fulfilled in Jesus' own life and ministry (Matt 3:16; 4:1; 12:18,28; Mark 1:10,12; Luke 3:22; 4:1,14,18; Acts 10:38) to such a degree that John says, "God gives the Spirit without limit" to him (John 3:34). Moreover, Jesus has the authority to impart the Spirit to others (Matt 3:11; Mark 1:8; Luke 3:16; John 1:33) from the Father (Luke 11:13; 24:49; John 7:37-39; 14:16-17; 15:26; 16:7,15; 20:22; Acts 1:5,8; 2:33,38).

The events of the day of Pentecost show the sovereign hand of the newly-enthroned Messiah and Lord (Acts 2:33-36) and, while they have Old Testament precedent to some extent, and fulfill certain Old Testament prophecies, they display God's sovereign freedom to do it as He chooses, especially seen in the unprecedented phenomenon of tongues. Hence as Wolfgang Vondey says,

> Pentecost as symbol . . . upholds not only that redemption always originates sovereignly with God (and that the future is therefore radically new) but also that the new and better future breaks into the public life with unexpected possibilities for our participation.[34]

God often surprises us!

However, the coming and manifestation of the Spirit at Pentecost is not viewed by the author of Acts as solely the result of God's plan without any role for the humans involved. Jesus prepared his followers for this event and commanded them to wait in Jerusalem for it (Acts 1:4-5). They waited expectantly and prayerfully (Acts 1:14) and were so engaged, it

---

34. Vondey, *Pentecostal Theology*, 224.

would appear, when the Spirit arrived (Acts 2:1). Even the speaking in tongues seemed to involve their cooperation to some degree: "*they* began to speak in other tongues as the Spirit enabled them" (Acts 2:4 emphasis added). Vondey thus speaks of tongues as "a manifestation of divine sovereignty and human responsibility."[35]

The sovereignty of the Spirit is repeatedly reaffirmed in the New Testament.[36] Jesus speaks of the Spirit acting like the wind which "blows wherever it pleases" (John 3:8). The Spirit descends on Jesus' disciples, but not automatically or always in the same way. For example, the Pentecost event is seen as fulfilling the promise of Joel (Acts 2:17–18) but is different in detail and has unique signs like wind and fire (Acts 2:2–3), recalling Sinai; even the tongues seem different to the other cases of a similar phenomenon later in Acts (Acts 2:6–12).

The gift of the Spirit is promised to all newly baptized believers (Acts 2:38–39) but the same signs are not always in evidence. The Spirit fails to come on the new believers in Samaria until the apostles Peter and John lay hands on them (Acts 8:15–17), but He falls on the audience in Cornelius' house before Peter even finishes his message (Acts 10:44–47; 11:15), with something like the same sign of speaking in tongues as occurred at Pentecost (Acts 10:46–47; 11:17). Paul receives the Spirit through the hands of an ordinary believer (Acts 9:17) and later imparts the Spirit with his own hands in Ephesus; here again tongues and prophecy are mentioned as outcomes (Acts 19:6). But there is no mention of hands or tongues when we read that in Antioch of Pisidia, "the disciples were filled with joy and with the Holy Spirit" (Acts 13:52).

However, although no human is in control and each event is distinctive, the Holy Spirit's coming is not completely arbitrary. Peter claims that in the case of Cornelius' people,

> God who knows the heart, showed that he accepted them by giving the Holy Spirit to them, just as he did to us. He did not discriminate between us and then, for he purified their hearts by faith
>
> (Acts 15:8).

In other words, while the coming of the Spirit was unexpected and sovereign, it was in response to seeking hearts, as Acts 10 goes out of its

---

35. *Pentecostal Theology*, , 95–96.
36. Cf. Smail, *The Giving Gift*, 34–35.

way to emphasize (Acts 10:2,22,35), and normally in response to faith and baptism.

The sovereignty of the Spirit is also seen in His direction of events in Acts. The Cornelius household story is such a case, involving angels (Acts 10:3–6,22,30–33; 11:13), visions (Acts 10:9–19; 11:5–10) and the direct voice of the Spirit (Acts 10:19–20; 11:12). Earlier the Spirit directs Philip to the chariot of an Ethiopian seeker (Acts 8:29), so that this man might hear the gospel and be saved (Acts 8:28–38). The Spirit directs the leaders of the Antioch church to release Barnabas and Saul (Acts 13:2) so that they are said to be "sent on their way by the Holy Spirit" (Acts 13:4). Paul and his band are directed to Macedonia by a vision (Acts 16:9–10) after being blocked from other directions by the Spirit (Acts 16:6–7).

Not every move of the apostles is explicitly linked to the direction of the Spirit, however, and Paul speaks of ordinary godly motivations and occasional blockages (even from Satan) to his plans (Rom 15:22–29; 1 Cor 4:19; 2 Cor 1:15–17,23–2:2,12–13; 1 Thess 2:17–18). Prophecies are experienced and help guide decisions by the early believers (Acts 11:27–30; Gal 2:2) but they are not seen as infallible (Acts 21:4,10–14), and Paul follows an inner compulsion of the Spirit as a priority (Acts 20:22–23).

The sovereign work of the Spirit is also evident in the life and worship of local churches. Believers are radically changed by receiving the Holy Spirit (Rom 8:1–17). The Spirit helps and guides their prayers so that they follow God's will (Rom 8:26–27). The Spirit "distributes" spiritual gifts "to each one, *just as he determines*" (1 Cor 12:4,11, emphasis added). As Gordon Fee comments, "the gifts, even though they are 'given' to 'each person,' ultimately express the Spirit's sovereign action in the life of the believer and the community as a whole."[37]

The Spirit enables Christians to pray in tongues such that "they utter mysteries by the Spirit" (1 Cor 14:2). But it appears that believers have a choice about praying in tongues or praying in their usual language or prophesying (1 Cor 14:1–5,13–19,27–32,39). Paul even states that "the spirits of prophets are subject to the control of *prophets*" (1 Cor 14:32; emphasis added), and therefore no one can refuse to follow good protocols, as Paul has been urging, by saying 'The Spirit made me do it.' He urges the Corinthians, "be eager to prophesy and do not forbid speaking in tongues" (1 Cor 14:39). Hence the work of the Spirit in the church to some extent depends on the Christians' eager desire for the spiritual

---

37. Fee, *God's Empowering Presence*, 174.

gifts (1 Cor 12:31; 14:1,39)[38] and their cooperation with the Spirit's priorities (intelligible communication, edification and love).[39] The Spirit's sovereignty is not meant to create an attitude either of passive surrender ('whatever you want, Lord') without seeking for the Spirit to move or one that says 'I'm out of control because the Spirit makes me. . .'.

Can believers withstand the operation or will of the Spirit? Lying to the Spirit brings death to Ananias and Sapphira (Acts 5:3–5,9). But Paul teaches that people can "grieve" the Holy Spirit by "bitterness, rage and anger" among other things (Eph 4:30–31), borrowing language from Isa 63:10. He also warns the Thessalonians, "Do not quench the Spirit. Do not treat prophecies with contempt but test them all; hold on to what is good, reject every kind of evil" (1 Thess 5:19–22). This suggests that the will of the Spirit can be successfully resisted by a church that has no place for prophetic gifts or by a church that has no discernment in things of the Spirit.[40] In either case, however, "the antidote for abuse is proper use."[41]

Christians depend on the Holy Spirit for life and holiness, such as the fruit of the Spirit which cannot be developed by unaided human effort (Gal 5:16–18,22–23), but the Spirit does not always prevail in the conflict between flesh and Spirit (Gal 5:17) and Christians need to "keep in step with the Spirit" (Gal 5:25). So it appears that the Holy Spirit is free, has the right to direct human beings, and can influence people 'from within.' But the Spirit's power to control events is more limited. Or to put this another way, a Spirit-filled church is not a guaranteed result of receiving the Spirit.

Keith Warrington responds to the ongoing tensions within the Pentecostal world over various manifestations supposedly 'from the Spirit' with this wise advice: "Pentecostals are prepared to live with tensions, to accept the inexplicable and to acknowledge mystery." He goes on call for

> a safe framework that would enable the articulation and outworking of a belief that explores the sovereign will of the Spirit

---

38. In each of these verses we find the verb *zēloō* (set one's heart on, be deeply concerned about, show a great interest in) in the 2nd person plural imperative.

39. Cf. Fee, *God's Empowering Presence*, 220.

40. Wesley suggested that the decline in spiritual gifts in the early church was due to a spiritual decline after Constantine: "the Christians were turned heathens again, and had only a dead form left" (Wesley, Sermons, 3:264, as quoted in Randall, *An Open Theist Renewal Theology*, Chapter 2).

41. Fee, *God's Empowering Presence*, 59.

as it is facilitated creatively, dynamically and with flexibility in the Church.[42]

We'll discuss the Spirit's work further in a later chapter.

---

42. Warrington, *Pentecostal Theology*, 25.

CHAPTER 5

ELECTION

When I was a boy in primary school, we would sometimes choose two teams for a game of football or cricket on the school oval. Two captains would choose players from the gathered children in turn. I was nearly always the last one chosen because of my lack of strength and ball skills. It was my first lesson in election and rejection.

Election is perhaps the main issue that arises from discussing the sovereignty of God and therefore this is a longer chapter. Election has to do with choice. In a democracy, we get a choice about who governs us and makes the laws we must obey through periodic elections. But in the Bible, we are talking about God's choices, flowing out of His sovereignty, that is, His freedom to act as He chooses, His discerning judgments, and His rights of ownership of all His creation. Thus, as Mark Lindsay observes, "the doctrine [of election] often seems to presume at its head a God of arbitrary caprice."[1] Let's see if this is true.

The first act of election relates to creation. God chose to focus on this minor planet (in terms of its size and location) and to make human beings (not angels) His regents in governing this planet (Heb 2:5–8, quoting from Psalm 8). As James Houston comments, "It is by election, by the free sovereign grace of God, his Maker, that man is man."[2] And Karl Barth wrote, "He elects creation, man, the human race, as the sphere in which He wills to be gracious."[3] Mark Lindsay comments that each of

---

1. *God Has Chosen*, 13.
2. Houston, *I Believe in the Creator*, 77.
3. *Church Dogmatics* II/2 (in Johnson, *Essential Karl Barth*, 183)

the metaphors of election in the Bible "depicts a God who initiates and then activates a will to have a relationship with others who are outside his own Godhead."[4]

One of the great themes of Genesis, however, is God's deliberate choice of certain individual humans to play a central role in His plans. As Grenz says, "the primary purpose of our election . . . is the chosenness we enjoy as a people in Christ to participate in God's program in history."[5] We already saw this in the case of Noah, chosen to preserve a remnant of humans and animals through the disaster of the great Flood, and previously Abel, whose sacrifice was accepted whereas Cain's was not, and in Enoch, who was taken to heaven by God without dying (Gen 5:24).

GOD'S CHOICE OF ABRAHAM AND HIS SEED

But the election story really gets going after humans are scattered across the earth and distinct languages and nations are born. For the first time, as far as the Genesis narrative is concerned, God ceases to deal directly with humanity as a whole (though see Gen 12:3; Acts 17:26–28)[6] and the focus is largely on just one family that will become the nucleus for a special God-nation. God begins by calling a man from Mesopotamia called Abram, commanding him to "Go from your country, your people and your father's household to the land I will show you" (Gen 12:1), and promising him a great destiny, including ultimately that "all peoples on earth will be blessed through you" (Gen 12:3b). Abram did not argue apparently, but "went, as the Lord had told him" (Gen 12:4).

God's freedom to act, God's rights over His creatures and God's rule over the world are all in action here. God's justice could easily have caused Him to abandon all humanity after the Babel rebellion. But God chose rather to order Abram and his family to relocate to Canaan. And God was clearly working to a Plan that becomes clearer as the story goes on. However, there are at least some hints given as to why Abram was chosen. First, he was chosen not primarily for his own sake but for the sake of God creating "a great nation" (Gen 12:2) and also blessing "all

---

4. Lindsay, *God Has Chosen*, 16.
5. Grenz, *Theology for the Community of God*, 453.
6. We still see Melchizedek, Hagar, Abimelech and others dealing with God in *Genesis*, and later Rahab, Ruth, Naaman and others.

peoples on earth" through him (Gen 12:3). God was still interested in all kinds of people, not just Abram's future descendants.

Second, he was apparently chosen because he would respond to God. Abram obeyed. Abram believed God's incredible promises (Gen 15:6). Abram willingly accepted God's offer of covenant and the strange requirement of circumcision that went with it (Gen 15:7–21; 17). In the terrible test that God later placed on him, Abraham (as he was called by then) even surrendered his promised son (Gen 22:1–18). He made a lot of false steps. But he responded to God by faith (see Heb 11:8–12).

Third, more broadly, God could trust Abraham to "direct his children and his household after him to keep the way of the LORD by doing what is just and right, *so that* the LORD will bring about for Abraham what he has promised him" (Gen 18:19, emphasis added; see also 26:5). God's prophetic promises are conditional, not automatic. They require human cooperation (see Jeremiah 18) in order to be fulfilled. This does not mean that Abraham somehow 'merited' or 'deserved' to be chosen by God. In fact, as Mark Lindsay points out, "it is exactly the deficit of merit, of which Sarai's infertility is a sign, that is the point. God's call is unexplained, precisely because it is unmerited, and rests only on God's free decision."[7] But it does suggest that God's choice of Abraham rather than someone else was not arbitrary.[8] As R.C. Sproul says, "God doesn't do anything without a reason. He is not capricious or whimsical."[9]

The next two generations of Abraham's line demonstrate election more starkly. First of all, after God cuts covenant with Abram (Gen 15) and promises him "a son who is your own flesh and blood" (Gen 15:4), there is a testing, as we discussed earlier. Abram's wife Sarai cannot have children, so the promise looks impossible. But she comes up with a great plan to 'help God out,' since it is obvious that she cannot conceive, a fact she attributes to God (Gen 16:2). It's a plausible plan that involves her servant Hagar as a kind of surrogate mother and it works! Hagar conceives a son to Abram. But the results are not good, and Hagar flees from Sarai's cruel treatment of her (Gen 16:4–6).

God now directly intervenes by His angel, sends Hagar back and promises good things to the infant she is carrying (Gen 16:7–14). In fact,

---

7. Lindsay, *God Has Chosen*, 19.

8. Paul Helm insists, predestination is "motivated by grace and love, and not, as it is sometimes portrayed, the whimsical act of an arbitrary despot" ("Classical Calvinist Doctrine of God," 23).

9. *Chosen By God*, 156.

God and Hagar seem to have a closer relationship than God and Sarai/Sarah, who laughs at God's outrageous promise (Gen 16:7-13; 21:17-21). *Ishmael is not rejected*; his very name means "God hears" and he is promised "descendants so much that they will be too numerous to count" (Gen 16:10). Later the text says, "He will be the father of twelve rulers, and I will make him into a great nation" (Gen 17:20; also 21:13,18). This is a clear precedent in the story-line of election; the 'non-elect' are not thereby rejected or excluded from God's favor, they simply move into a different story.[10]

But God makes it very clear to Abraham that Ishmael is not the chosen son He had promised, the one with whom He would enter into covenant. Rather God is going to give Abraham (as he is now called) a son by his infertile wife Sarah (Gen 17:15-19). This is so impossible, such a joke to both parents (Gen 17:17; 18:12-15), that the new son is given a name that means "He laughs" (Gen 21:1-7). Later, Ishmael is sent away because Isaac is the chosen one: "It is through Isaac that your offspring will be reckoned" (Gen 21:12). God's sovereign choice or election is at work, underlined by the miraculous nature of the chosen son's birth (see also Rom 9:7-9).

Then in the next generation, election is demonstrated in the destiny of twins. After a delay, in response to Isaac's prayers, his wife Rebekah becomes pregnant (Gen 25:21) and "the babies jostled each other within her" (Gen 25:22). When she asks God what was going on, she receives a strange prophecy:

> Two *nations* are in your womb,
> and two *peoples* from within you will be separated;
> one *people* will be stronger than the other,
> and the older will serve the younger
>
> (Gen 25:23; emphasis added).

We note here that Rebekah, not Isaac, seeks God and receives this prophecy. Sure enough, when she gives birth, the second twin comes out grasping the heel of the first, as if to supplant him (Gen 25:26). The prophecy was ambiguous but focused on two coming nations more than the individuals. It didn't necessarily mean that Esau himself was rejected, but he would take an inferior place to Jacob in God's plan, implying that

---

10. Hence Calvin is wrong to say, "Disowning Ishmael, he sets his heart on Isaac" (*Institutes*, 938) if he means that Ishmael is totally rejected.

the covenant would be with Jacob, as with Isaac, not with Esau, in defiance of his father's preferences (Gen 25:28).

Paul later commented,

> Not only that, but Rebekah's children were conceived at the same time by our father Isaac. Yet before the twins were born or had done anything good or bad–in order that God's purpose in election might stand: not by works but by him who calls–she was told, 'The older will serve the younger. Just as it is written, 'Jacob I loved, but Esau I hated.'

(Rom 9:10–13)

Nonetheless this election was outworked in some very definite events in the brothers' lives. The two boys were a study in contrast and their parents had divided loyalties (Gen 25:28). Then Esau "despised his birthright" (Gen 25:34) by selling it to Jacob for a serving of stew (Gen 25:29–34). Clearly Jacob wanted this birthright more than Esau. Later Jacob, at his mother's urging, deceived Isaac into speaking over him the blessing reserved for the elder son (Gen 27:1–29). Rebekah is taking the initiative instead of Isaac. But, as we already noted, such patriarchal blessings were usually backed by God.

Jacob's actions are hard to defend, though in fairness we should note that he was expressing a strong desire for God's calling and blessing and obeying his mother (to whom the original prophecy had been given). Moreover, Isaac is portrayed as somewhat carnal and thus easily deceived (Gen 25:28; 27:2–4,22–40). As the narrative moves on, God proceeds to teach Jacob how to live as His chosen man through several supernatural encounters and a series of tests (Gen 28–50); Jacob does not get an easy life from being God's chosen one. Clearly, however, this story shows that God's choice is not based on superior character or piety and that election leads on to sanctification, not the other way around.

But let's also clarify the nature of this elective saga. Jacob's and Esau's destinies are mainly related to their role as ancestors of the nations Israel and Edom respectively. This is seen in several ways. First, the blessing Isaac speaks over Jacob includes the words

> May *nations* serve you
> and *peoples* bow down to you.
> Be lord over your brothers,
> and may the sons of your mother bow down to you

(Gen 27:29; emphasis added).

This never happens to Jacob and Esau as individuals. In fact, when they meet again after Jacob's many years in exile, it is Jacob who bows down to Esau (Gen 33:3) and they separate as equals. The only sign of God's election is that Esau moves out of Canaan, leaving Jacob in the 'promised land' (Gen 36:6–8). But Esau is not erased from the story, as seen by the list of his descendants and rulers of Edom in Genesis 36 (a whole chapter is given over to this topic).

Much later, however, Israel and Edom are in frequent conflict, the Edomites betray the Israelites (Obad 10–14), and come under God's judgment. This is the context of the verse Paul quotes in Rom 9:13. Here it is in Malachi:

> 'I have loved you,' says the LORD.
>   'But you ask, 'How have you loved us?'
>   'Was not Esau Jacob's brother?' declares the LORD. 'Yet I have loved Jacob, but Esau I have hated, and I have turned his hill country into a wasteland and left his inheritance to the desert jackals'
>
> (Mal 1:2–3).

Clearly, God chose Jacob over Esau as His covenant partner in creating His new nation. But Esau's nation came under God's judgment as a result of their own efforts, as seen in the prophecy of Obadiah (and Jeremiah 49:7–22). And by the way, so did Israel! Election is not a safeguard against God's justice!

THE NATION ISRAEL AND THE GENTILES

We have already noted that God's delegation and probation, originally expressed to the original humans, becomes focused on Israel as God's chosen (elect) nation. As stated in the beginning of the Sinai covenant,

> Now if you obey me fully and keep my covenant, then out of all nations you will be my treasured possession. Although the whole earth is mine, you will be for me a kingdom of priests and a holy nation
>
> (Exod 19:5–6).

This reflects God's original promise to Abraham that "all peoples on earth will be blessed through you" (Gen 12:3; see also 18:18; 22:18; 26:4; 28:14). Election is clear ("out of all nations") but is for the sake of a universal cause, since "the whole earth is mine." The nations are not arbitrarily rejected; rather Israel is to serve them as "a kingdom of priests," mediating God's presence and salvation, and as "a holy nation" modelling God's ways.

Israel is to be a mediator of God's rule and blessing to the world. Moreover, this election is clearly conditional and probationary: "if you obey me fully and keep my covenant" (see Exod 23:20–33). Reflecting God's promises to Abraham and the patriarchs, obedience will bring a victorious entrance to, and possession of, the land God has promised with its divinely defined boundaries (Exod 23:23,27–31, reflecting Gen 12:1,7; 13:14–17; 15:7–21; 17:8; 26:3; 28:13; 35:12).

Otherwise, there will be unpleasant consequences. In fact, later God threatened to destroy the Israelites and start afresh with a new people from Moses in response to the golden calf incident (Exod 32:9–10). This was only averted through Moses' intercession, based in part on his ability to appeal to God's promises to the patriarchs (Exod 32:13), as well as to God's reputation (Exod 32:11–12). Even then, there had to be consequences and three thousand were killed in an act of self-punishment by the nation (Exod 32:25–29). The day ended with two dire warnings: God would not destroy the nation, but also would not forgive them for Moses' sake; in fact, "Whoever has sinned against me I will blot out of my book" (Exod 32:33) and "when the time comes for me to punish, I will punish them for their sin" (Exod 32:34). This speech was followed by a plague in which unnumbered Israelites died (Exod 32:35). Being part of God's elect nation does not exempt people from God's wrath or guarantee final salvation.

Paul picks up this thought in Romans 9 as he contemplates the sad response, or lack of response, to Jesus as the promised Messiah by the Jews of his generation. Like Moses, he wants to be "cut off from Christ" if it would bring his fellow Jews to salvation (Rom 9:3; compare Exod 32:32). After all, their heritage as the chosen people is enormous (Rom 9:3–5), but it doesn't guarantee that they are truly God's children. As the Genesis stories show, and as Exodus 32 demonstrates, ethnic descent does not guarantee salvation (Rom 9:6–9), for God alone is the final judge (Rom 9:16–18; Exod 32:33). Or to use Paul's own language, "not all who are descended from Israel are Israel" (Rom 9:6; see also Rom

2:28-29). Israel is fundamentally a spiritual reality more than an ethnic identity (Rom 9:8).

Paul is not discussing a doctrine of predestination in Romans 9–11; at least, not as that word is often understood. Rather, he is thinking through the ways of God as he has experienced in his own ministry. Continually, as Acts tells us, Paul's gospel is rejected by most (not all) of the Jews in the diaspora synagogues but welcomed more often instead by the 'unchosen' Gentiles (Acts 13:42-47; 14:1-5; 15:12; 17:1-5,10-13; 18:4-11; 19:8-10). Not all of them, by any means; rather "all who were appointed for eternal life believed" (Acts 13:48), so there is election going on, but not how Jews expected it. This is what is bothering Paul as he writes to the predominantly Gentile church in Rome.[11]

Acts clearly illustrates election in its narrative. The story of Philip and the eunuch from Ethiopia illustrates the length that God will go to in order to claim one hungry soul who is seeking real answers (Acts 8:26-39), reflecting perhaps the parable of the lost sheep (Luke 15:3-7). The story of Peter and Cornelius has a similar point. Cornelius may seem an unlikely convert, being a Roman soldier, but he is clearly a seeker and "God-fearing" (Acts 10:2).

The anonymous believers who first preached to Gentiles in Antioch found that "The Lord's hand was with them, and a great number of people believed and turned to the Lord" (Acts 11:21). As a result of Paul's preaching in the synagogue in Antioch of Pisidia, many Jews were very resistant (Acts 13:45) but many Gentiles were glad and believed (Acts 13:48). And while Paul was in Corinth, he had a vision in which he was told, "No one is going to attack and harm you, because I have many people in this city" (Acts 18:10). The surprising openness of Gentiles is a key theme of Acts and shows God's sovereign plan at work, as Jesus anticipated (Acts 1:6-8) and Paul came to see, which he then explained in Eph 2–3 as well as Rom 9–11.

Clearly, God was doing something new. As James had put it, responding to Peter's speech based on his experience with Cornelius as well as Barnabas and Saul's missionary reports, "God first intervened to choose a people for his name from the Gentiles" (Acts 15:14). Similarly, Peter's critics in Judea came to realize that "even to Gentiles God has granted repentance that leads to life" (Acts 11:18b).

---

11. Cf. Macchia, *Tongues of Fire*, 328–334.

Paul recognizes that God as sovereign Lord has the freedom to do this; He does not 'owe' anything to the Jews and every person saved is saved by God's mercy alone (Rom 9:16,18). Paul rebukes the hypothetical listener who presumes to talk back to God and affirms God's rights over His creation with the analogy of the potter and the clay (Rom 9:19–21). But this does not mean that Paul sees all humans as passive objects to be manipulated by God in an arbitrary way. In fact, as Lennox points out, the verse Paul quotes in Rom 9:15 ("I will have mercy on whom I have mercy, and will have compassion on whom I have compassion") in its original context is a striking affirmation of God's mercy towards a people who have just forfeited any claim on God through their idolatry (Exod 33:19), but did not mean that all of them would be saved.[12]

As Paul goes on to explain, the rejected pottery stands for the unbelieving and rebellious Jews "prepared for destruction" (Rom 9:22) and the approved pottery stands for those called by God's mercy from among Jews and Gentiles into the messianic kingdom (or the church; Rom 9:23–26). And their approval by God was not allocated by some kind of lottery. As Paul concludes this section of his discussion, he explains,

> What then shall we say? That the Gentiles, who did not pursue righteousness, have obtained it, a righteousness that is by faith; but the people of Israel, who pursued the law as the way of righteousness, have not obtained their goal. Why not? Because they pursued it not by faith but as if it were by works. They stumbled over the stumbling stone [of the messiah].

(Rom 9:30–32).

Thus Paul is interpreting the potter and clay analogy correctly as it was revealed to Jeremiah. In Jeremiah 18, God gives the prophet a message in the potter's house that emphasizes God's sovereignty: "'Can I not do with you, Israel, as this potter does?' declares the Lord. 'Like clay in the hand of the potter, so are you in my hand, Israel'" (v.6). The point of the analogy is that when a nation changes direction, either towards or away from God, God's plan for them adjusts accordingly from what He may have previously stated, and they can't stop it (Jer 18:5–10). The application is a call on Judah to repent and not to continue fatalistically in their ingrained patterns of behavior (Jer 18:11–12).[13] So too in Ro-

---

12. Lennox, *Determined to Believe?*, 253–255.

13. For a more complete discussion of these verses, see Jason A. Staples, "Vessels of Wrath and God's Pathos: Potter/Clay Imagery in Rom 8:20–23".

mans, Paul is putting the responsibility for the failure of the Jews squarely at their own feet (Rom 10:3–4). The point of the analogy is not that all people are just objects in God's hands, but rather that no one can reject God's will without consequences.[14]

But Paul is not therefore pessimistic, as if Jewish unbelief will have the last word. God is still sovereign, and His plans will succeed, because "God's gifts and his call are irrevocable" (Rom 11:29). God already has a Jewish "remnant chosen by grace" (Rom 11:5), which does not mean chosen arbitrarily, but by the work of God's grace through the gospel rather than by works of the law.[15] Paul is one of those remnant ones (Rom 11:1) and there are many others (Acts 21:20), since "God has exalted [Christ] .... as Prince and Savior that he might bring Israel to repentance and forgive their sins" (Acts 5:31). God has always had a faithful remnant even when most of Israel went astray (Rom 9:29; Mal 3:16–18; 1 Kings 19:18; Isa 10:20–22; 28:5; 8:16–18). Moreover, the stumbling of the majority of Jews over Christ is not irreversible: currently they are hardened, but Paul confidently expects their "full inclusion" and "acceptance" in the future (Rom 11:7–15).

Paul proceeds to his famous analogy of the olive tree (Rom 11:17–24). Gentiles have been "grafted in" to the tree (probably referring to Israel)[16] after Jews were "broken off because of unbelief" (v.20) But both depend on the root[17] of the olive tree for life. Paul uses this analogy to warn his Gentile readers not to be complacent, because they will not be spared if they do not "continue in his kindness" (v.22), but also to express hope for Jews to be reinstated "if they do not persist in unbelief" (v.23). In both cases, their place in the olive tree is conditional, but the olive tree itself speaks of the election of Israel as a nation, which is fundamentally unconditional (Rom 11:28–29). As Paul concludes, "Israel has

14. Pink agrees that "God never *forces* the sinner to sin" but argues that the sinners' wills are controlled by their sinful heart (Pink, *The Sovereignty of God*, 135; emphasis in the original). This is true as far as it goes but it doesn't make room for the possibility that the sinner may or may not repent, especially as a result of the work of the gospel and the Spirit.

15. Calvin argues that when the covenant "was violated by that multitude, he confined to a few that it might not utterly cease" (Calvin, *Institutes*, 931). But this very narrow view of election ("meager," "a few") is contradicted by passages like Rev 7:9 and the conclusion of Paul's argument in Rom 11:32.

16. Referring to "true Israel" according to Colin Kruse, *Paul's Letter to the Romans*, 434,438. See discussion in Ben Witherington III, *Paul's Letter to the Romans*, 270–272

17. Referring to the patriarchs, especially Abraham (Kruse, *Paul's Letter to the Romans*, 435).

experienced a hardening in part until the full number of the Gentiles has come in, and in this way all Israel will be saved" (Rom 11:25-26) and "God has bound everyone over to disobedience so that he may have mercy on them all" (Rom 11:32). God's plan will succeed and will include the salvation of many Jews and Gentiles who trust in Christ, not the Law or their own works.

THE ELECTION OF CHRIST

A key figure in the second part of Isaiah is the servant of the Lord. Many aspects of these prophecies are debated among scholars. However, if we assume that these messages refer to the Messiah and are pointing to the coming of Jesus, they tell us that *the* chosen one above all is Christ.

> Here is my servant, whom I uphold,
> my chosen one in whom I delight;
> I will put my Spirit on him,
> and he will bring justice to the nations
>
> (Isa 42:1).

He is chosen for a purpose that includes, but goes beyond, restoring Israel, God's chosen nation (Isa 41:8-9; 43:1). In the same chapter, God says,

> I will keep you and make you
> to be a covenant for the people
> and a light for the Gentiles
>
> (Isa 42:6).

Originally the servant is both Israel and the messianic figure:

> He said to me, 'You are my servant,
> Israel, in whom I will display my splendor'
>
> (Isa 49:3).

But then:

> And now the Lord says–
> he who formed me in the womb to be his servant
> to bring Jacob back to him,
> and gather Israel to himself....
> 'It is too small a thing for you to be my servant

> to restore the tribes of Jacob and bring back those of Israel I have kept.
> I will also make you a light for the Gentiles
> that my salvation may reach to the ends of the earth'

(Isa 49: 5–6).

These prophecies hark back to the original promise of Gen 12:3; Israel is to be restored in order that God's plan to bless the nations may be fulfilled through the 'seed' of Abraham (Gen 22:18), which is Jesus Christ (Gal 3:16).

Peter certainly applies these prophecies to Jesus whom he describes as "rejected by humans but chosen by God and precious to him" (1 Pet 2:4). Likewise, Matthew quotes from Isaiah 42 which he sees as fulfilled in Jesus' ministry (Matt 12:17–21). Luke refers to the same passage in his account of the Transfiguration (Luke 9:35). And in John's Gospel, John the Baptist calls Jesus, "God's Chosen One" (John 1:34).

Jesus is chosen to be the Prophet of God, "the Lamb of God who takes away the sin of the world" (John 1:29), "the one who will baptize with the Holy Spirit" (John 1:33; see also Matt 3:11; Luke 3:16), the Son of God (Luke 1:35), the Savior of the world (John 4:42; see also Luke 2:11), the bread of life (John 6:48), and many other things besides. Perhaps most importantly, He is chosen as the new head of humanity in place of the fallen Adam. "For as in Adam all die, so in Christ all will be made alive" (1 Cor 15:22). Salvation and restoration of humanity is "through" the one man Jesus Christ (Rom 5:15,17,19,21). Or as Frank Macchia puts it, "Christ as the seed of Abraham is the elect One through whom all nations shall be blessed."[18]

Jesus also plays a role in choosing within God's program. He says to his apostles (at least), "You did not choose me, but *I chose you* and appointed you so that you might go and bear fruit" (John 15:16a, emphasis added). While this perhaps related mainly to the choice of certain followers as apostles (see Mark 3:13–14; Luke 6:13; John 7:70; 13:18), it may apply, at least indirectly, to a broader salvific purpose. After all, Jesus says of the apostles (at least), "I have chosen you out of the world" (John 15:19), suggesting that His choice of them included their becoming disciples in the first place.

---

18. Macchia, *Tongues of Fire*, 325.

John's Gospel especially emphasizes that Jesus was "sent" into the world (John 10:36a). And this mission was for the salvation of the world. But Jesus had to respond in obedience. As Jesus also says,

> The reason my Father loves me is that I lay down my life [for the sheep, v.15]- only to take it up again. No one takes it from me, but I lay it down of my own accord

(John 10:17–18a).

Therefore Robert Shank is not far wrong when he writes, "The decision for death was made, not only in the counsels of eternity before creation; in the *final* deliberation, it was made by Jesus in Gethsemane."[19] Jesus had to choose to play the part the Father allocated to him. Hence, "Jesus became the Savior of the world–The Elect and the Elector–at infinite cost to Himself."[20] Jesus is thus a partner with the Father in the elective and saving process. As Shank says, "the will of the Father is that the Son should be as truly the executor of election as the Father himself, and indeed the more *immediate* executor."[21] He follows Barth, who wrote, "Jesus Christ is the electing God. . . . He is also elected man."[22]

This is a core theme because the election of Christian believers is mediated through Jesus, as we will now see.[23]

ELECTION IN NT LETTERS

God's election does not necessarily imply that He has a small bunch of favorites or is narrow in His mercies. As we saw in the call of Abraham, God intends to bring blessing to all peoples through the elect (Gen 12:3). But it is subject to God's sovereign purpose. One of the most important passages about this is Ephesians 1:3–14. Paul[24] gives praise to God for blessing His people ("us") "in the heavenly realms with every spiritual blessing in Christ" (v.3). This blessing is grounded in an ancient election: "For he chose us in him before the creation of the world" (v.4a) and He

---

19. Shank, *Elect in the Son*, 65 (emphasis in the original).
20. Shank, *Elect in the Son*, 152.
21. Shank, *Elect in the Son*, 41 (emphasis in the original).
22. *Church Dogmatics* II/2 (in Johnson, *Essential Karl Barth*, 192)
23. Cf. Macchia, *Tongues of Fire*, 322–326. .
24. Assuming that Paul wrote Ephesians, which many scholars deny.

"predestined us for adoption to sonship through Jesus Christ" (v.5). Then he makes two important points about this choosing of God.

First, it is grounded in God's own purpose and character: God's love (v.4), "his pleasure and will" (v.5), His "glorious grace" (v.6), "freely given" (v.6), "riches of God's grace" (v.7), "the mystery of his will according to his good pleasure" (v.8), "predestined according to the plan of him who works out everything in conformity with the purpose of his will" (v.11). Thus, as Paul explains later, God's choosing is not based on any individual performance or characteristic for we were all "dead in sins" (Eph 2:1–3), nor is it restricted to any special group, but Gentiles are included with Jews, even though the original election was of Israel (Eph 2:11–13; 3:6). This is all part of God's "eternal purpose" (Eph 3:11).

Second, it is channeled through Christ: His blessing is "in Christ" (v.3), "he chose us in him before the creation of the world" (v.4), "he predestined us . . . through Jesus Christ" (v.5), his grace is given "in the One he loves" (v.6), redemption is "in him through his blood" (v,7), his good pleasure is "purposed in Christ" (v.9), "in him we were also chosen" (v.11), "included in Christ" (v.13), "marked in him with a seal" (v.13). There is therefore no election apart from Christ either as the mediator of election before creation (that is, God targeted specific people to be included in Christ) or as the sphere of election in practice (that is, people are only elect by faith in Christ, as verse 13 might suggest), or both. As Macchia explains, Christ "was the elect and faithful Son who was able to expand the boundary of his election to countless others."[25] The "eternal purpose" is "accomplished in Christ Jesus our Lord" (Eph 3:11). Salvation is received solely by faith in Christ (Eph 2:4–9).

But the fact that election is in and through Christ implies that it is in some sense conditional, or at least not automatic:

> And you also were included in Christ when you heard the message of truth, the gospel of your salvation. *When you believed*, you were marked in him with a seal, the promised Holy Spirit, who is a deposit guaranteeing our inheritance until the redemption of those who are God's possession
>
> (Eph 1:13–14, emphasis added).

The readers were only included in Christ, and thus became part of God's elect people, when they heard and believed the gospel. The promise to Abraham is being fulfilled. As Paul says later, "*through the*

---

25. Macchia, *Tongues of Fire*, 326.

gospel the Gentiles are heirs together with Israel, members together of one body, and sharers together in the promise *in Christ Jesus*" (Eph 3:6, emphasis added). As Shank explains, "The atonement is efficacious for all men potentially, for no man unconditionally, and for the Israel of God efficiently."[26]

All this suggests that election is primarily corporate (Israel, Christ, the church), and for individuals, conditional. God's choice of Israel, of Christ and of the church (and all creation, as Eph 1:10 suggests)[27] is unconditional and His plans for them cannot ultimately be thwarted. But not all who 'belong' to Israel (by genealogical descent or Law observance) or the visible church (by parentage, baptism or some other outward response) are chosen. As Jesus says elsewhere, "many are invited, but few are chosen" (Matt 22:14). Jesus is concluding a parable that emphasizes a narrow call to Jews (or religious Jews), that they rejected, followed by a universal call made to all irrespective of merit ("the bad as well as the good", v.10) alongside a discrimination based on "wedding clothes" (vv.11–13); the rejected guest failed to embrace the conditions for election.

Peter opens his first letter in a similar way to Ephesians:

> Peter, an apostle of Jesus Christ,
>   To God's elect, exiles scattered throughout the provinces of Pontus, Galatia, Cappadocia, Asia and Bithynia, who have been chosen according to the foreknowledge of God the Father, through the sanctifying work of the Spirit, to be obedient to Jesus and sprinkled with his blood

(1 Pet 1:1–2).

His audience is clearly God's chosen ones that God foreknew as individuals and worked on by the Spirit so that they became obedient to Jesus. It was not necessarily that God foreknew they would come to Christ, but He did apparently foreknow them as people and based His choice on something in them or something they did. Moreover, Peter knows who they are and where they live, which suggests a corporate election, not a 'secret' decree; they are "a chosen people" (1 Pet 2:9). Peter celebrates the great things God has given them: "new birth into a living hope" (v.3), a guaranteed inheritance (v.4), a future salvation (v.5). He

---

26. Shank, *Elect in the Son*, 85–86. See also Macchia, *Tongues of Fire*, 326–327. Both Shank and Macchia are influenced strongly by Karl Barth's analysis of election.

27. Cf. Macchia, *Tongues of Fire*, 327.

praises their faith under pressure of trials (vv.6–9), a faith whose "end result" is "the salvation of your souls" (v.9). This salvation has ancient roots in the Hebrew prophets and only became clear through the preaching of the gospel (vv.10–12). Clearly all this is the work of God from long ago and is focused on Jesus who "was chosen before the creation of the world, but was revealed in these last times for your sake" (v.20).

In the next chapter, Peter celebrates how the believers are being built up "into a spiritual house to be a holy priesthood" (1 Pet 2:5) because they have chosen to trust in Christ (v.6). But others have rejected Christ and Peter says, "They stumble because they disobey the message–which is also what they were destined for" (v.8b). Their stumbling is attributed to their own disobedience and perhaps to some form of 'destination.' But does this mean they had no choice but to disobey, or rather that, having disobeyed, stumbling was the inexorable outcome? Actually the NIV is a bit misleading here in translating "destined for;" the Greek is a form of *tithēmi*, which simply means 'to place' or 'to appoint.' There is no note of foreordination as such.

There is a similar thought in 2 Peter 1. This letter begins by emphasizing God's gracious provision in Christ to those who know Him: "To those who through the righteousness of our God and Savior Jesus Christ have received a faith as precious as ours" (v.1). This faith is received, not earned, on the basis of His righteousness, not ours (compare Acts 18:27). As a result, God has "given us everything we need for a godly life through our knowledge of him who called us by his own glory and goodness" (v.3), and specifically "his very great and precious promises" (v.4). All these things are given, not earned.

But Peter then stresses the need for readers to respond by making "every effort" (v.5) to grow in holiness so that they will not be "ineffective and unproductive in your knowledge of our Lord Jesus Christ" (v.8). Those who don't make this effort have forgotten that "they have been cleansed from their past sins" (v.9). Peter goes on to say, "make every effort[28] *to confirm your calling and election*. For if you do these things, you will never stumble, and you will receive a rich welcome into the eternal kingdom of our Lord and Savior Jesus Christ" (vv.10–11; emphasis added). Election is thus conditional; God has opened a door for believers to receive of His grace, but we need to respond, not just once but

---

28. The Greek word here, *spoudasate*, from *spoudazō*, means "do one's best, spare no effort, or work hard" (Newman, "Greek-English Dictionary")

continually, in order to confirm the calling and election that we received when we first trusted in Christ.

Election is thus not some kind of automatic process but is implemented by means. Paul writes to the believers in Thessalonica,

> But we always ought to thank God for you, brothers and sisters loved by the Lord, because God chose you as first fruits to be saved through the sanctifying work of the Spirit and through belief in the truth. He called you to this through our gospel, that you might share in the glory of our Lord Jesus Christ

(2 Thess 2:13–14).

These are not the only ones God loves or will save. They are simply the ones who responded first when the gospel came to their city and the Spirit was moving in people's hearts, and hence were chosen as "first fruits" of a greater harvest. Their response is attributed to God's calling and "the sanctifying work of the Spirit," but also to the work of the gospel and their own choice, "belief in the truth." Even Pink points out,

> It is not true that because God has chosen a certain one to salvation that he will be saved willy-nilly, whether he believes or not; nowhere do the Scriptures so represent it. The same God who predestined the end, also appointed the means.[29]

GRACE AND SALVATION

The concept of grace is vital to understanding this. Paul especially argues that God's grace is the sole basis for our salvation because we deserve only wrath as sinners:

> Like the rest, we were by nature deserving of wrath. But because of his great love for us, God, who is rich in mercy, made us alive with Christ even when we were dead in transgressions- .... For it is by grace you have been saved through faith–and this not from yourselves, it is the gift of God- not by works, so that no one can boast.

(Eph 2:3b-5,8–9).

---

29. Pink, *Sovereignty of God*, 56. This contradicts his assertion that everyone for whom Christ died must automatically be saved (ibid., 62–63). Rather their salvation is conditional on faith.

Using the language of grace, mercy, love and gift, Paul attributes salvation to God's gracious and unmerited favor. As John Sanders states, "In the divine-human relationships grace is always first."[30] The sovereign God, who owes no one anything and is free to condemn all, especially in view of human sinfulness, has graciously saved some because of His great nature as Love. As Karl Barth argues, "We must not seek the ground of this election anywhere but in the love of God, in His free love."[31]

Let's unpack this further. In Romans 1–5, Paul argues that no one has any moral claim on God. Gentiles have turned aside from God and become depraved by God's judgment. "God gave them over," he says three times (Rom 1:24,26,28), because of their rejection of God, to service of idols and increased moral depravity. This proves that "the wrath of God is being revealed from heaven against all the godlessness and wickedness of people . . ." (Rom 1:18). But Paul also condemns 'righteous' people, especially observant Jews, who pass judgment on the Gentiles and yet also practice sin and therefore "because of your stubbornness and your unrepentant heart, you are storing up wrath against yourself for the day of God's wrath, when his righteous judgment will be revealed" (Rom 2:5).

God is consistently just:

> God will repay each person *according to what they have done*. To those who by persistence in doing good seek glory, honor and immortality, he will give eternal life. But for those who are self-seeking and who reject the truth and follow evil, there will be wrath and anger. There will be trouble and distress for every human being who does evil: first for the Jew, then for the Gentile; but glory, honor and peace for everyone who does good; first for the Jew, then for the Gentile. *For God does not show favoritism.*

(Rom 2:6–11, emphasis added).

As we saw earlier, humans are accountable to God as their Creator and Lord, not the other way around. The problem is that humanity, after rebelling in the Garden, has largely chosen to resist God and refuse to repent of their evil ways, so God's judgment is a major threat to us all. Paul insists that "Jews and Gentiles alike are all under the power of sin" (Rom 3:9) and "all have sinned and fall short of the glory of God" (Rom 3:23).

We are all doomed, *except that* "all are justified freely by his grace through the redemption that came by Christ Jesus" (Rom 3:24). On the

---

30. Sanders, *God Who Risks*, 59.
31. *Church Dogmatics* II/2 (in Johnson, *Essential Karl Barth*, 185)

basis of Jesus' death ("the shedding of his blood"), God made justification or salvation available to all "to be received by faith" (Rom 3:25). God thus becomes "the one who justifies those who have faith in Jesus" (Rom 3:26).

This outcome is unequivocally the result of God's sovereign grace:

> He has saved us and called us to a holy life- not because of anything we have done but because of his own purpose and grace. This grace was given us in Christ Jesus before the beginning of time, but it has now been revealed through the appearing of our Savior, Christ Jesus, who has destroyed death and has brought life and immortality to light through the gospel
>
> (2 Tim 1:9–10).

We were "powerless" and "still sinners" and "God's enemies" when God demonstrated His love for us in the atoning work of Jesus (Rom 5:6–10). God's salvation is clearly a free gift (Rom 3:22; 5:15,16; 6:23) which we "receive" (Rom 3:25; 5:17). And as Custance says, "saving grace is not an offer of help. Saving grace is unmerited favor."[32]

Not all receive this gift, however. Many Israelites "pursued the law as the way of righteousness" but "have not attained their goal" because "they pursued it not by faith but as if it were by works" and "stumbled over the stumbling stone" of Christ (Rom 9:31–32). Jesus' parable about the Pharisee and the tax collector in Luke 18 demonstrates this well. It was told "to some who were confident of their own righteousness and looked down on everyone else" (v.9). The Pharisee in the story is one of those since he thanks God for him being such a righteous person (vv.10–11). The tax collector, one of a class much despised and hated by Jewish people for their corruption and collaboration with the Roman Empire, was aware of his sins and simply prayed "God, have mercy on me, a sinner" (v.13). Jesus insists, however, that "this man, rather than the other, went home justified before God" (v.14a). Salvation can only come by grace.

This grace is freely offered to all:

> For there is no difference between Jew and Gentile–the same Lord is Lord of all and richly blesses all who call on him, for, 'Everyone who calls on the name of the Lord will be saved'
>
> (Rom 10:12–13).

God's salvation is offered indiscriminately to everyone. Paul says in Romans, "God has bound everyone over to disobedience so that he may

---

32. Custance, *Sovereignty of Grace*, 32.

have mercy on them *all*" (Rom 11:32) and the gospel "is the power of God to *everyone* who believes" (Rom 1:16). In fact, as Paul states elsewhere, "God our Savior . . . wants *all* people to be saved and to come to a knowledge of the truth" on the basis that Christ "gave himself as a ransom for *all* people" (1 Tim 2:3–6) and "the grace of God has appeared that offers salvation to *all* people" (Tit 2:11). As Paul also says, "For God's love compels us, because we are convinced that one died for *all*, and therefore *all* died. And he died for *all*, that those who live should no longer live for themselves, but for him who died for them and was raised again" (2 Cor 5:14–15) and "God was reconciling *the world* to himself in Christ, not counting people's sins against them" (2 Cor 5:19).[33]

Pink and others argue persuasively that 'all' in the Bible is not always exhaustive: "in some passages it means *all without exception*; in others it means *all without distinction.*"[34] However, which of these is meant has to be determined by the context, and the sheer volume of verses that declare God wants all to come, and Jesus died for all (not just those who believe) must be balanced against the lack of any statement in the Bible that God does *not* want some to come.[35] As Adrio König writes, "the apostles proclaimed reconciliation as something done for 'us' and 'you' on the one hand, while they emphasized its breadth and inclusiveness on the other."[36]

Ezekiel has similar sentiments; God says, "A surely as I live. . . . I take no pleasure in the death of the wicked, but rather that they turn from their ways and live" (Ezek 33:11; see also 18:23,32). Peter also says, "he is patient with you, *not wanting anyone* to perish, but *everyone* to come to repentance" (2 Pet 3:9b; emphasis added). And the apostle John agrees, affirming that Jesus "is the atoning sacrifice for our sins, and *not only for ours* but also for the sins of *the whole world*" (1 John 2:2; emphasis added) and, "This is love: not that we loved God, but that he loved us and sent his Son as an atoning sacrifice for our sins" (1 John 4:10), thus offering

---

33. Emphasis added in each of these quotes.
34. Pink, *Sovereignty of God*, 68; emphasis in the original
35. See I. Howard Marshall, "Universal Grace and Atonement in the Pastoral Epistles," in Pinnock, ed., *The Grace of God and the Will of Man*, 51–70. Marshall provides solid exegetical argument that "all" is "all without exception" in the relevant verses in Paul's pastoral letters. Macchia marshals a string of "whoever" promises in John's Gospel to the same end (Macchia, *Tongues of Fire*, 337). Nowhere in the Bible do we find that God "has barred the door of life to those whom he has given over to damnation," as Calvin asserts (*Institutes*, 931).
36. König, *The Eclipse of Christ*, 89.

eternal life through faith (1 John 5:10–12; John 3:16) to "the world" (John 1:29; 3:16). Jesus also says, "And I, when I am lifted up from the earth [on the Cross], will draw *all* people to myself" (John 12:32 emphasis added). Finally, the author of Hebrews also states that "by the grace of God he might taste death for *everyone*" (Heb 2:9 emphasis added).[37]

Now elsewhere the Bible states that Jesus died specifically for the church (Acts 20:28; Eph 5:25), his sheep (John 10:11,15), his friends (John 15:13–14), God's people (Isa 53:8; John 11:51–52), his people (Matt 1:21), or many (Mark 10:45). This is because they are the elect people who ultimately benefit from His death, and this group doesn't automatically include everyone, because not everyone will finally be saved, but it doesn't contradict the fact that God wants all to be saved and offers this salvation to everyone equally.[38] Jesus guarantees that he will save his people, the church, the elect, his body, but membership of that group depends partly on personal response to the gospel. Perhaps 1 Tim 4:10 puts it best, when it says, "we have put our hope in the living God, who is the Savior of *all* people, and *especially* those who believe" (emphasis added).

A.W. Pink protests that Jesus as our high priest only intercedes for the elect, since Heb 7:25 says "he always lives to intercede for *them*" (emphasis added; compare John 17:9).[39] But who are these people? They are "those who come to God through him." Yes, Jesus only intercedes in this way for those who trust in him as Savior, but that is because Jesus is the only way to God (John 14:6), not because God has pre-ordained them, and only them, to trust in Christ.

FACILITATING SALVATION.

However, it's one thing to be offered salvation by God's grace as a gift. It's another to actually take it. If we are indeed "dead in . . . . transgressions and sins" (Eph 2:1,5), we need more than just the offer of salvation. The

37. Cf. Macchia, *Tongues of Fire*, 414.

38. Building on the preaching of C.H. Spurgeon, who insisted that Scripture affirms both God's universal love to everyone and His decision only to save the (unconditionally predestined) elect, T.J. Campbell makes a "herculean" effort to reconcile these two points using the theological language of Aquinas in *The Wonderful Decree*. John Piper seeks to make sense of these verses from a Calvinist perspective by arguing that God "desires all to be saved at one level, and he grants some to repent and be saved at another level" (*Providence*, 548). To some extent this is obvious- God does not save everyone- but it begs the question on what basis God discriminates in this granting.

39. Pink, *Sovereignty of God*, 63.

ELECTION   109

power of sin over us needs to be broken sufficiently that we can see how great God's offer is and embrace it eagerly. Pink rightly says, "In order for any sinner to see his *need* of a Savior and be willing *to receive* the Savior he needs, the work of the Holy Spirit upon and within him were imperatively required."[40]

We all experience the fact that the gospel of Christ, no matter how powerfully preached, does not affect everyone equally; it is actually rejected by many hearers. Paul, for example, had a great response in Antioch of Pisidia, especially among the Gentiles. But not all Gentiles believed and some, even including "God-fearing women of high standing" (Acts 13:50), "expelled" Paul and Barnabas at the instigation of the unbelieving Jews. There is a note of discrimination here: "When the Gentiles heard this, they were glad and honored the word of the Lord; and *all who were appointed for eternal life* believed" (Acts 13:48, emphasis added). The faith of these Gentiles seemed to depend on them being "appointed for eternal life." And apparently not all the Gentiles in that city were so appointed. However, as Macchia points out, "There is nothing in the word or the context that points to an eternal decree."[41] The verb says nothing about why they were appointed to eternal life; it doesn't use the elective language found elsewhere in the NT.[42]

According to John's Gospel, Jesus proclaimed that all who believed in Him would receive eternal life (John 3:14–18,36; 5:24) but that "no one can see the kingdom of God unless they are born again" (John 3:3). This openness to the kingdom seems to depend on the sovereign work of the Spirit who like the wind "blows wherever it pleases" (John 3:5–8). In fact, Jesus says, "No one can come to me unless the Father who sent me draws them" (John 6:44; see also v.65). On the other hand, "All those the Father gives me will come to me, and whoever comes to me I will never drive away" (John 6:37) and "I, when I am lifted up from the earth [on the Cross], will draw all people to myself" (John 12:32).

But the facilitation or election process implied here is not unconditional or secret. Jesus explains,

---

40. Pink, *Sovereignty of God*, 78 (emphasis in the original text).

41. *Tongues of Fire*, 336

42. The Greek is a bit ambiguous. Lennox argues that the Gentiles "lined up" to believe, that is, they were willing to be given faith (Lennox, *Determined to Believe?*, 121). Shank suggests it should be translated as "those who were disposed for eternal life believed" (*Elect in the Son*, 184–187). However, the verb is a perfect passive participle, which suggests they were recipients of this appointment.

> It is written in the Prophets: 'They will all be taught by God.' Everyone who has heard the Father and learned from him comes to me
>
> (John 6:45)

Jesus is referring to Isa 54:13: "All your children will be taught by the Lord, and great will be their peace." This is part of Isaiah's great prophecies of a restored Jerusalem. What Jesus appears to be saying is that those whose hearts are open to God's teaching will come to him, but those whose hearts are unresponsive to God will be unresponsive to Christ. As Jesus says later, "Anyone who chooses to do the will of God will find out whether my teaching comes from God or whether I speak on my own." (John 7:17) and "If God were your Father, you would love me, for I have come here from God." (John 8:42).

In other words, God does not pick out a few reluctant sinners and compel them to become Christians. He chooses those whose hearts are open to Him. He wins by wooing not by warring. As Luther put it, "the will, being changed and sweetly breathed on by the Spirit, desires and acts not from *compulsion* but *responsively*."[43] Or as Geisler says, "God will woo and court so persuasively that those willing to respond will be overwhelmed by His love."[44]

R.C. Sproul, however, argues from the use of "draw" (Greek *helko*) in John 6:44 and 12:32, that people are more literally "dragged" to Jesus, even against their will, in the same way that Christians are "dragged" into court by rich enemies (James 2:6) as in the case of Paul and Silas in Philippi (Acts 16:19).[45] Thus John 6:44 would literally say, "No one can come to me unless the Father who sent me *drags them forcibly*" and John 12:32 would mean, "And I, when I am lifted up from the earth, will *forcibly drag* all people to myself." Superficially this would support the idea that sinners will only come to Christ when God directly acts on their hearts, and then they are guaranteed to come. But the Greek, taken that literally, would prove too much: Calvinists like Sproul envisage rather

---

43. Luther, *On the Bondage of the Will*, Section XXV (emphasis in the original text), as quoted in Custance, *Sovereignty of Grace*, 55.

44. *Chosen But Free*, 104. In Arminian theology, the concept of 'prevenient grace' means that God works by His Spirit in all people, especially when they hear the gospel, and makes it possible for them to respond, but they can resist the Spirit and remain untouched (cf. Olson, *Arminian Theology*, 35–36). See also Wynkoop, *Wesleyan-Arminian Theology*.

45. Sproul, *Chosen By God*, 69–70.

that God gives life to spiritually dead sinners and then they willingly come; they never come *against* their will.[46]

Those who reject Jesus "do not believe because you are not my sheep" (John 10:26). They were not open to God or Christ because "My sheep listen to my voice . . . and they follow me" (John 10:27). However, John never attributes the unbelief of people fundamentally to God's rejection of them, but rather to their inner hearts (John 2:24–25), to their hatred of the light of truth (John 3:19–20), to their narrow interpretation of the Law (John 5:10–18; 7:21–24), to the extreme claims Jesus was making (John 5:18; 6:41–42,52; 7:40–43; 8:48–59; 10:31–39), to their desire for human approval (John 5:44; 12:43) or fame (John 7:4–5), to their fear of human rejection or persecution (John 9:22; 12:42), to their unbelief towards Moses (John 5:45–47), to their false confidence as children of Abraham (John 8:33–41), to their corruption as leaders in the temple (John 2:16; 10:8), and to fear of the Romans (John 11:47–48).

In John 12:37–41, the unbelief of the Jews *is* attributed to God's judgment in fulfilment of two words from Isaiah, but this is a form of judicial blindness in consequence of their initial resistance to the prophetic word of Isaiah, and then to Jesus. It is similar to God's judgment in relation to the end time deception associated with the "man of lawlessness" in 2 Thessalonians 2:

> They perish because they refused to love the truth and so be saved. *For this reason* God sends them a powerful delusion so that they will believe the lie and so that all will be condemned who have not believed the truth but have delighted in wickedness
>
> (2 Thess 2:10b-12; emphasis added).

Note they first refuse the truth and *because of that* God "sends them a powerful delusion" as His judgment on them. This is a good example of a common occurrence. People who refuse the truth have no one to blame but themselves if they then become incapable of seeing a lie for what it is. As G.K. Chesterton said a century ago, "When men choose not to believe in God, they do not thereafter believe in nothing, they then become capable of believing in anything."[47]

In Romans 8, however, Paul asserts that,

---

46. Cf. Sproul, *Chosen By God*, 71–75.

47. Susan Ratcliffe, ed., *Oxford Essential Quotations* (4 ed.) Oxford University Press; Published online: 2016. Said to be widely attributed, although not traced in his works.

the mind governed by the flesh is hostile to God; it does not submit to God's law, *nor can it* do so. Those who are in the realm of the flesh *cannot* please God (vv.7-8, emphasis added).

This perhaps implies that only those whose minds are enlightened by the Spirit will submit to God (vv,6,9), perhaps reflecting Ezekiel 36, where God promises,

> I will give you a new heart and put a new spirit in you; I will remove from you your heart of stone and give you a heart of flesh. And I will put my Spirit in you and move you to follow my decrees and be careful to keep my laws (Ezek 36:26-27).

Paul and Ezekiel both claim that only by the Spirit can any person obey or please God. They both teach some kind of moral inability on the part of sinners: sinners are physically and mentally capable of repenting but morally incapable, being so steeped in their sin that they are unable to break free.[48] This might be like a bad habit or an addiction. So how does a person come to the spiritual mind spoken of by both authors? Is it purely by an act of God's sovereign choice? Paul speaks earlier of the Holy Spirit being given to believers as a gift when they trust in Christ (Rom 5:1-2,5) and he reaffirms this in chapter 8 when he states,

> You, however, are not in the realm of the flesh but are in the realm of the Spirit, if indeed the Spirit of God lives in you. And if anyone does not have the Spirit of Christ, they do not belong to Christ
>
> (Rom 8:9).

In other words, we receive the Spirit as a gift (not as a reward for good works) when we choose to follow Jesus. But is there an elective, indeed predestining, purpose behind all this? Later in the same chapter, speaking of the Spirit's intercession in and for God's people, Paul goes on to say,

> And we know that in all things God works for the good of those who love him, who have been called according to his purpose. For those God foreknew he also predestined to be conformed to the image of his Son, that he might be the firstborn among many brothers and sisters. And those he predestined, he also

---

48. As Carson says, "This inability to believe is moral, not metaphysical; but it is real inability none the less" (*Divine Sovereignty and Human Responsibility*, 165).

called; those he called, he also justified; those he justified, he also glorified (Rom 8:28-30).

The passage clearly places our individual experience of salvation in the context of God's greater Plan which Paul views as a completed act, putting future events in the past tense. The passage is also clearly discriminatory in that not all people are envisaged as part of this process. The discrimination is also elective: when it speaks of "those God foreknew," it is saying not just that God foreknew that they would respond to Christ but that He had already begun a relationship with them even before their conversion (compare Rom 11:2; Amos 3:2). However, earlier in the chapter, it is clear that this ongoing experience of salvation is conditional: "if indeed we share in his sufferings" (v.17), "if by the Spirit you put to death the misdeeds of the body" (v.13).[49]

This passage also says nothing about the basis of God's decision to initiate that relationship. It does speak about predestination, but the purpose of this is seen as restoration of humanity to (and beyond) what was envisaged in creation: to be conformed to the image of Christ as God's Son and become Christ's siblings.[50] God wants him to have "many brothers and sisters." God's heart is big, as Rev 7:9 pictures the outcome: "a great multitude that no one could count, from every nation, tribe, people and language." Election is not a case of God unilaterally picking out a small percentage of humanity and condemning the rest to doom. God has much bigger plans. "God has bound *everyone* over to disobedience so that he may have mercy on *them all*" (Rom 11:32 emphasis added). As Mark Lindsay puts it, the election passages in Scripture "demonstrate a pattern of God's free willing that is characterized more prominently by an expansive inclusivity that extends even to the most unlikely and alien than by either arbitrary or punitive exclusion."[51]

But did not Jesus say, "*many* are invited but *few* are chosen" (Matt 22:14, emphasis added)? This is the conclusion of the parable of the wedding banquet (Matt 22:1–14). In this story, a king "prepared a wedding banquet for his son" (v.2). He sent out his servants to those invited "but they refused to come" (v.3). Even when he continued to urge them, they "paid no attention" and even mistreated and killed the servants of the

---

49. See Shank, *Elect in the Son*, 154.

50. Grenz argues that Paul "used the idea of predestination to give us assurance that God's purpose will be served, which purpose is nothing less than the eschatological glorification of believers" (Grenz, *Theology for the Community of God*, 454).

51. Lindsay, *God Has Chosen*, 35.

king (vv.4–6), leading the angry king to destroy them and their city (v.7), a fairly obvious allusion to the destruction of Jerusalem in AD70. Now the king sent his servants to the city to gather everyone they could find to come to the banquet, since "those I invited did not deserve to come" (v.8). The servants "gathered all the people they could find, the bad as well as the good, and the wedding hall was filled with guests" (v.10). The point is not that only a few were chosen, but almost the opposite: the chosen few, the original invitees, rejected the invitation (resisted God's will, in other words) and now those originally *unchosen* are brought in. In the context, this would include the sinful Jews and the Gentiles, as *Acts* later demonstrates.

But the final scene makes another important point. One of the new guests "was not wearing wedding clothes" (v.11). Perhaps these would have been provided by the host, but even if not, this guest was showing ingratitude to the host by wearing old or dirty clothes.[52] Marshall points out, "The reason why one man ... was rejected was not because he was not appointed by some secret choice of the king (representing God) but because he had failed to provide himself with a wedding garment."[53] This guest was trying to enjoy the banquet on his own terms,[54] in other words, not responding to the great salvation God is providing in Christ with repentance. That was why he was rejected and hence "many are invited, but few are chosen," that is, only a relatively small number accept the condition for entering the kingdom of God. That's not because God is ungenerous, but because humans reject His generous offer of salvation. And the salvation of the others was not their own doing, but simply because they did not reject the Host's generosity as had the original invitees.

Calvinists are keen to emphasize that sinners contribute nothing to their own salvation. To the extent that sinners "contribute" repentance and faith, these must be gifts from God (see Eph 2:8; Acts 5:31; 11:18). For example, Piper asks rhetorically, "Will he [God] get all the glory for your repentance and faith, or will you preserve the uncomfortable suspicion (or even conviction) that you should take final, decisive credit for your repentance and faith?"[55] But those verses do not say these gifts are

---

52. See discussion in R.T. France, *Matthew*, 313.

53. Marshall, *Kept by the Power*, 71–72.

54. Cf. Sanders, *God Who Risks*, 112–113.

55. *Providence*, 572–573. Elsewhere he asks, "does God's grace put us in a position of having *ultimate self-determination* in our conversion? Or does it overcome all our rebellion and blindness so that we are drawn triumphantly by the beauty of Christ to

given only to a select few individuals; rather they indicate that the door is open for all Jews (Acts 5:31) and Gentiles (Acts 11:18) to repent; they must still *do* that.

But does faith or repentance 'contribute' to, or 'earn,' salvation simply because they are conditions? Various analogies have been proposed; for example, a drowning person being rescued by lifesavers; does the drowning person 'contribute' to the rescue if they raise their hand or cry out for help, even though their rescue depends on them doing that? Or does a poor person 'contribute' to the gift given by a generous donor by stretching out their hand to receive the money or taking a cheque to the bank? T.J. Campbell points out that "faith is the one act humans perform that explicitly recognizes the merit of another. In fact, the act of faith has a transitive property wherein its object does all of the work."[56] And the New Testament contrasts faith and works even while making salvation depend on faith. Shank quotes Calvin as saying, "Faith, then, brings a man empty to God, that he may be filled with the blessings of Christ."[57]

Finally, Paul points out another big factor affecting whether someone responds to the gospel positively or not:

> And even if our gospel is veiled, it is veiled to those who are perishing. The god of this age has blinded the minds of unbelievers, so that they cannot see the light of the gospel that displays the glory of Christ, who is the image of God

(2 Cor 4:3–4).

Not just the will of God and the choice of the individual person is involved. We are also contending with "the rulers, against the authorities, against the powers of this dark world and against the spiritual forces of evil in the heavenly realms" (Eph 6:12b). This is part of the 'warfare worldview' in the Bible. As we will explore further in a later chapter, our sovereign God is allowing the devil to operate within certain boundaries and for a fixed period, but not so that believers just passively put up with it; rather God wants to provoke us to resist the enemy. Hence Paul continues later,

---

embrace what is true?" (*Providence*, 553, emphasis in the original text). I rather think this is a false antithesis

56 *Wonderful Decree*, 61, n.71.

57. Calvin, *Commentaries*, as quoted in Shank, *Elect in the Son*, 110.

> For though we live in the world, we do not *wage war* as the world does. The *weapons* we *fight* with are not the *weapons* of the world. On the contrary, they have divine power to demolish strongholds. We demolish arguments and every pretention that sets itself up against the knowledge of God, and we *take captive* every thought to make it obedient to Christ
>
> (2 Cor 10:3–5, emphasis added).

What are these weapons we fight with so that foolish arguments are demolished and thoughts are taken captive? In context, the gospel itself is the primary focus and this is supported by other statements Paul makes about "the readiness that comes from the gospel of peace" (Eph 6:15) and the gospel being "the power of God that brings salvation to everyone who believes" (Rom 1:16). But to the Ephesians, he also brings another factor to focus:

> And *pray* in the Spirit on all occasions with *all kinds of prayers* and requests. With this is mind, be alert and always *keep on praying* for all the Lord's people. *Pray also for me*, that whenever I speak, words may be given me so that I will fearlessly make known the mystery of the gospel, for which I am an ambassador in chains. *Pray that I may declare it fearlessly*, as I should
>
> (Eph 6:18–20, emphasis added).

If we believe that God really wants all people without exception to be saved, we must be prepared to undergird preachers with prayer and contend for the souls of the lost in prayer and witness. No wonder that Paul says, "I urge then ... that petitions, prayers, intercession and thanksgiving be made for *all* people" (1 Tim 2:1, emphasis added). As Grenz points out, such prayers can succeed because the devil has already been defeated at the cross and the Holy Spirit has been released to convict sinners so that they respond to the gospel.[58]

---

58. Grenz, *Prayer*, 71–72. Perhaps the most striking effort to respond seriously to 1 Timothy 2 was that of Argentinian evangelist Ed Silvoso in *That None Should Perish: How to Reach Entire Cities for Christ through Prayer Evangelism* (Ventura, CA: Regal Press, 1994). Silvoso advocates people literally praying for every individual on earth and shows how this could be feasible.

LEAVING ONE'S SALVATION

If election is "in Christ" as the Elect One (1 Pet 1:20) and is primarily corporate (God's people, the church, etc), it follows that people can choose both to enter *and leave* the chosen people, that is, forfeit their salvation. To put it another way, not all those for whom Jesus died will definitely be saved in the end.

Paul tells the church in Philippi that he was "confident of this, that he who began a good work in you[59] will carry it on to completion until the day of Christ Jesus" (Phil 1:6). He is confident that what God is doing in the church will continue, but not necessarily that every member of that church will persevere to the end. Hence he goes on to exhort them to "continue to work out your salvation with fear and trembling, for it is God who works in you to will and to act in order to fulfill his good purpose" (Phil 2:12b-13). It is their responsibility to persevere, though in dependence on God's working.

Speaking to the elders of the church in Ephesus, Paul speaks of "the church of God, which he bought with his own blood" (Acts 20:28), but then condemns both infiltrators and even current elders who will "distort the truth in order to draw away disciples after them" (Acts 20:29-30). And Peter in a similar way warns of false teachers who are "even denying the sovereign Lord who *bought* them" (2 Peter 2:1; emphasis added), implying that Jesus' redemption extends to many who will ultimately turn away from Him. And Paul speaks of "opponents," apparently in the church, who need repentance so that that they will "escape from the trap of the devil, who has taken them captive to do his will" (2 Tim 2:25-26).

We have to be careful here. God's promises of salvation and eternal life are real. Moreover, they include promises of protection, as Jesus makes clear in John 10:

> "My sheep listen to my voice; I know them, and they follow me. I give them eternal life, and they shall never perish; no one will snatch them out of my hand. My Father, who has given them to me, is greater than all; no one can snatch them out of my Father's hand."
>
> (John 10:27-29).

The thief "comes . . . to steal and kill and destroy" (John 10:10), but the good shepherd protects the flock from "thieves and robbers" and

---

59. The Greek is 2nd person plural.

"wolves," even laying down his own life for them (John 10:8–18). Moreover, Jesus says, "they shall never perish," which logically follows from them having eternal life.

This good shepherd also acts as the high priest, "interceding for us" (Rom 8:34) so that we are never separated from God's love by our sins and weaknesses or by "trouble or hardship or persecution or famine or nakedness or danger or sword" (Rom 8:35) or even demonic forces (Rom 8:38). As Hebrews explains, "he is able to save completely[60] those who come to God through him, because he always lives to intercede for them" (Heb 7:25). And as R.T. Kendall comments, "if Jesus cannot get His prayers answered there is no hope for any of us."[61]

Jude affirms that God "is able to keep you from stumbling and to present you before his glorious presence without fault" (Jude 24). Likewise, Peter insists that believers have received an inheritance "that can never perish, spoil or fade" which "is kept in heaven for you," who "through faith are shielded by God's power until the coming of the salvation that is ready to be revealed in the last time" (1 Pet 1:4–5). So if a Christian departs from the faith, it is not because God's power was inadequate to hold them.

Our salvation was not obtained by our own effort or merit and nor can it be maintained that way. We do not lose our position before God every time we sin, because of Jesus' intercession based on his blood shed for us (1 John 1:7; 2:1–2). God's faithfulness is not negated when we are unfaithful (2 Tim 2:13). But the New Testament warns against complacency based on a false assumption of 'once saved always saved.' The fact is that, apparently, strong Christians can and do walk away from Christ and become lost. Explain that how you will, it is a common event and faced squarely in the New Testament.

John's letters especially warn the readers of false Christians whose lifestyle condemns them: they don't live like Jesus, they are full of hatred, they propagate false doctrine about Jesus (1 John 2:22–23; 4:2–3), making them a kind of antichrist (1 John 2:18,22), and they depart from the community because "they did not really belong to us" (1 John 2:19a). The true believers can see through them, it seems (1 John 2:20,21,26,27) –Jesus *is* guarding his sheep–but they are exhorted, "do not let anyone

---

60. Or "for all time." The Greek can be translated either way.

61. Kendall, *Jonah*, 97. Kendall argues for the doctrine of "eternal security" on the basis of God's promise, the nature of atonement and "Christ's continuing intercession" for us (ibid, 95–97).

lead you astray" (1 John 3:7a), and to maintain a life of holiness and love by the Spirit.

After stating that "Everyone who believes that Jesus is the Christ is born of God" (1 John 5:1a), "everyone born of God overcomes the world" (1 John 5:4a) and "you who believe in the name of the Son of God . . . may *know* that you have eternal life" (1 John 5:13, emphasis added), he makes a clear distinction:

> If you see any brother or sister commit a sin that does not lead to death, you should pray and God will give them life. I refer to those whose sin does not lead to death. There is a sin that leads to death. I am not saying that you should pray about that. All wrongdoing is sin, and there is sin which does not lead to death

(1 John 5:16–17).

While this is hard to understand fully, it seems very clear that a "brother or sister," that is someone who apparently believes and has eternal life, can commit an act or follow a path that "leads to death," that is the loss of eternal life.

The next verse may contradict that assumption, as John says,

> We know that anyone born of God does not continue to sin; the One who was born of God keeps them safe, and the evil one cannot harm them.

(1 John 5:18).

So perhaps those who commit a deadly sin are not truly 'born of God,' but are only nominal Christians, somewhat like those who left the church because "they did not really belong to us" (1 John 2:19a). But either way this implies that the knowing referred to in 1 John 5:13 is not absolute. You can think you are born of God and a true believer but be wrong. So how would you know?

Calvin warns against any attempt to detect whether or not you are elect apart from "those latter signs which are sure attestations of it."[62] John's tests of genuine conversion seems to consist of keeping Jesus' commands and his lifestyle (1 John 2:3–6,29; 3:3,24; 5:2–3), not sinning (1 John 3:4–9; 5:18), loving other believers (1 John 2:9–11; 3:10–18,23; 4:7–12,16–21), not loving the world (1 John 2:15), remaining in the fellowship of believers (1 John 2:19) and in the gospel teaching (1 John

---

62. Calvin, *Institutes*, 968.

2:24,27; 4:15; 5:1,10–13), and by some kind of witness of the Spirit (1 John 3:24; 4:13; compare Rom 8:16).[63] John wants to provide assurance to his readers, but not absolute unconditional assurance that might lead to complacency. As I. Howard Marshall writes,

> On the one hand, the Christian life is a life which is continually sustained by the power of God. . . . On the other hand, the believer is continually faced by temptations which jeopardize his faith. He is thus in a state of tension as he receives the gift of life from God and at the same time faces the forces of temptation which threaten to deprive him of that life.[64]

Ultimately, we can have an assurance of salvation as long as we continue as Christians living a Christian lifestyle in fellowship with the Christian community. As Shank claims, Calvin himself concluded that "valid assurance of election and salvation is impossible apart from conscious, deliberate perseverance in faith."[65] Calvin himself writes,

> If we have been chosen in him, we shall not find assurance of our election in ourselves; and not even in God the Father, if we conceive him as severed from his Son. Christ, then, is the mirror wherein we must, and without self-deception may, contemplate our own election.[66]

And I. Howard Marshall claims, "the only proof offered that faith is real is that it proves itself by endurance to the end."[67] But if we choose to leave the Christian community or its faith, we are in mortal danger.

Hebrews makes this even plainer. The author of Hebrews balances the truth of Jesus' "once for all" death as sacrifice for sin, and his intercession for believers on that basis (Heb 2:17; 4:15; 5:9–10; 6:20; 7:23–8:2; 9:11–14,24–26; 10:10–18,21), with strong warnings against falling away.

Our position is conditional: "we are his house, *if indeed* we hold firmly to our confidence and the hope in which we glory" (Heb 3:6 emphasis added; compare Col 1:23). Therefore, we must learn from the bad example of Israel in the wilderness, Moses' generation, who were chosen

---

63. But even here, Paul makes this assurance conditional: we are children and heirs "if indeed we share in his sufferings" (Rom 8:17).

64. Marshall, *Kept by the Power*, 22.

65. Shank, *Elect in the Son*, 215. Comp Kendall, *Calvin and English Calvinism to 1649*, 14,18,24.

66. Calvin, *Institutes*, 970.

67. Marshall, *Kept by the Power*, 89.

but went astray, tested God, were mired in unbelief, and failed to enter God's rest (Heb 3:7–11):

> See to it, brothers and sisters, that none of you has a sinful, unbelieving heart that turns away from the living God. But encourage one another daily, as long as it is called 'Today,' so that none of you may be hardened by sin's deceitfulness. We have come to share in Christ, *if indeed* we hold our original conviction firm to the very end

(Heb 3:12–14, emphasis added).

Clearly professing Christians can be "hardened by sin's deceitfulness" and fail to hold their "original conviction firm to the very end." The letter assures its readers "we who have believed enter that rest" (Heb 4:3a) but exhorts them to "make every effort to enter that rest, so that no one will perish by following their example of disobedience" (Heb 4:11) and "hold firmly to the faith we profess" (Heb 4:14).

This does not mean self-reliance, however. We look in faith to Jesus our high priest who empathizes with our weakness (Heb 4:15) and are urged to "approach God's throne of grace with confidence, so that we may receive mercy and find grace to help us in our time of need" (Heb 4:16). God is not looking for an excuse to reject us; rather He provides all we need to persevere. However, after urging his readers to move on to maturity from a current state of spiritual immaturity (Heb 5:11–6:3), the author again issues a solemn warning:

> It is impossible for those who have once been enlightened, who have tasted the heavenly gift [salvation?], who have shared in the Holy Spirit, who have tasted the goodness of the word of God and the powers of the coming age and who have fallen away, to be brought back to repentance. To their loss they are crucifying the Son of God all over again and subjecting him to public disgrace (Heb 6:4–6).

It's hard to avoid the implication that he is talking of true 'born again' Christians here. They have shared everything that true believers receive from Christ, including the Holy Spirit, before subsequently falling away. However, this falling away is no light thing (which may help us understand John's mortal sin language). The language is one of deliberate apostasy, turning against Christ. They are like Judas, who sold out Jesus for money, rather than Peter, who denied the Lord but repented and was restored. The author of Hebrews is not suggesting that people lose their salvation easily or every time they commit sin. Hence he hastens to assure his readers,

> Even though we speak like this, dear friends, we are convinced of better things in your case–the things that have to do with salvation. God is not unjust; he will not forget your work and the love you have shown him as you have helped his people and continue to help them

(Heb 6:9–10).

The warning is real, but it is not intended to make them terrified of falling away. Rather:

> We want each of you to show this same diligence to the very end, so that what you hope for may be fully realized. We do not want you to be lazy, but to imitate those who through faith and patience inherit what has been promised (Heb 6:11–12).

In other words, warnings are needed lest we become complacent, but they do not negate God's promises or His ability to guard us (see Heb 6:17–20). Rather they are there to keep us on track in faith, part of what John Piper calls "God's command-and-warning strategy."[68]

In a similar way, Hebrews builds confidence in the reader "to enter the Most Holy Place by the blood of Jesus" (Heb 10:19) and "draw near to God with a sincere heart and with the full assurance that faith brings, having our hearts sprinkled [with Jesus' blood] to cleanse us from a guilty conscience" (Heb 10:22). He then exhorts the reader to "hold unswervingly to the hope we profess, for he who promised is faithful" (Heb 10:23) and to encourage others likewise. Then there is a fresh warning:

> If we deliberately keep on sinning after we have received the knowledge of the truth, no sacrifice for sin is left, but only a fearful expectation of judgment and of raging fire that will consume the enemies of God

(Heb 10:26–27).

Once again, he is not talking about the sins all believers are prone to in their fleshly weakness, as he goes on to make clear:

> How much more severely do you think someone deserves to be punished who has trampled the Son of God underfoot, who has

---

68. Piper, *Providence*, 591–607.

treated as an unholy thing the blood of the covenant that *sanctified* them, and who has insulted the Spirit of grace?

(Heb 10:29, emphasis added).

This is clearly speaking of people who have experienced the sanctifying work of Jesus' blood but have later rejected it and all their inheritance in Christ. The original readers were apparently being tempted to abandon the gospel for a safe traditional Judaism. So once again the author follows the warning with an assurance based on their experience so far and a statement of his goal in giving such severe warnings, to ensure they don't "throw away" their confidence (Heb 10:35) but rather persevere in faith (Heb 10:36–39).

Warnings are real and cannot be glossed over, but they are given to help ensure 'the final perseverance of the saints,' to ensure that their confidence in God's keeping power and promises does not decay into a complacent and comfortable 'once saved, always saved' attitude.[69] Thus Hebrews uses the example of Esau:

> See that no one is sexually immoral, or is godless like Esau, who for a single meal sold his inheritance rights as the oldest son. Afterward, as you know, when he wanted to inherit this blessing, he was rejected. Even though he sought the blessing with tears, he could not change what he had done

(Heb 12:16–17).

Finally let's look at the messages from Christ to the seven churches of Asia in the book of Revelation. All but two of these churches are called on to repent of serious sin. The potential effects of failing to repent are also dire. The church in Ephesus has "forsaken the love you had at first" (Rev 2:4). This amounts to a great fall (Rev 2:4–5a) and Jesus threatens to "remove your lampstand from its place" (Rev 2:5b). The lampstand is the symbol of the church (Rev 1:20), so this seems to mean that the church will either cease to exist or cease to be recognized as a legitimate church by Jesus. The churches in Pergamum and Thyatira are both judged guilty of compromise, of tolerating false teaching and the common sins of the Greco-Roman culture (Rev 2:14–16, 20–23). Jesus threatens to "fight against" those following the false teaching (Rev 2:16) and to inflict

---

69. For a different view of assurance of salvation that affirms the view that a truly regenerate Christians cannot be lost, see Lennox, *Determine to Believe?*, 310–356.

suffering and death on the false prophet Jezebel and her followers (Rev 2:22–23).

The church in Sardis is not experiencing outside pressure (persecution) or false teachers. Nonetheless they are in grave spiritual danger because they have 'gone to sleep' spiritually and are rated as dead by Jesus (Rev 3:1–3). But as in every church, there are those who are shining brightly and overcoming the tests and trials and temptations that they all face. To them Jesus says, "I will never blot out the name of that person from the book of life" (Rev 3:5a).

In view of the central role that the book of life plays in Revelation in terms of identifying faithful followers of Christ (Rev 13:8; 20:12,15), there are two serious implications here: first, that it is possible for someone's name to be blotted out from that book (that is, they lose their salvation), and second, that only victorious Christians are assured that their names will not be blotted out. The rewards promised to the victorious ones confirms this: they have "the right to eat from the tree of life" (Rev 2:7), they are not "hurt at all by the second death" (Rev 2:11), they have "authority over the nations" (Rev 2:26), their names are acknowledged by Jesus before God and the angels (Rev 3:5; compare Matt 10:32–33), they have a permanent place in God's temple and identified with the name of God and Christ (Rev 3:12) and they share Christ's throne (Rev 3:21).

This suggests that many professing Christians will not receive such rewards, will indeed not be saved in the end. This is not because Jesus does not care about them. The final church addressed (Laodicea) is also complacent, becoming lukewarm due to having it easy and enjoying affluence (Rev 3:15–17). They seem to have no need of Christ and have effectively shut him out of their congregation (Rev 3:20). But he still cares:

> Those whom I love I rebuke and discipline. So be earnest and repent. Here I am! I stand at the door and knock. If anyone hears my voice and opens the door, I will come in and eat with that person, and they with me.
>
> (Rev 3:19–20).

It is apparently never too late for the backslidden Christian to repent and invite Christ into their life. But if they don't, the chances are that Jesus will spit (or vomit) them out (Rev 3:16).

CONCLUSIONS

The doctrine of election is a clear part of biblical teaching. It originally applied to Israel as children of Abraham, Isaac and Jacob. Even now it is primarily a corporate concept and individuals are included to the extent that they are "in Christ" as faithful members of the people of God. Election is thus conditional and by no means guarantees final salvation. On the other hand, this means that no one is excluded unilaterally. Moreover, the promises of God are real and can be depended on by all who have faith, whatever their concept of election. To quote Robert Shank again, Election comprehends "all men potentially,. . . . no man unconditionally . . . (and) the Israel of God efficiently."[70]

J.I. Packer retells a famous story about a conversation between John Wesley and Charles Simeon, as recalled by Simeon:

> 'Sir, I understand that you are called an Arminian; and I have sometimes been called a Calvinist; and therefore I suppose we are to draw daggers. But before I consent to begin the combat, with your permission I will ask you a few questions. . . . Pray, Sir, do you feel yourself a depraved creature, so depraved that you would never have thought of turning to God, if God had not first put it into your heart?' 'Yes,' says the veteran, 'I do indeed.' 'And do you utterly despair of recommending yourself to God by anything you can do; and look for salvation solely through the blood and righteousness of Christ?' 'Yes, solely through Christ.' 'But Sir, supposing you were at first saved by Christ, are you somehow to save yourself afterwards by your own works?' 'No, I must be saved by Christ from first to last.' 'Allowing, then, that you were first turned by the grace of God, are you not in some way or other to keep yourself by your own power?' 'No.' 'What, then, are you to be upheld every hour and every moment by God, as much as an infant in its mother's arms?' 'Yes, altogether.' 'And is your hope in the grace and mercy of God to preserve you unto His heavenly kingdom?' 'Yes, I have no hope but in him.' 'Then, Sir, with your leave I will put up my dagger again; for this is all my Calvinism; this is my election, my justification by faith, my final perseverance: it is in substance all that I hold, and as I hold it . . . .'[71]

---

70. Shank, *Elect in the Son*, 152.
71. Packer, *Evangelism and the Sovereignty of God*, 13-14.

CHAPTER 6

VICTORY

Is GOD AT WAR, to quote the title of Gregory Boyd's book?[1] It seems plausible when we consider the world around us. But if so, who is/are His opponent/s, and why is such a war necessary, if He is indeed sovereign over all events? And when will He win the victory? Or has He already done so? And how would this relate to the human wars we see around us?

We noticed previously that God's sovereignty over the world takes a different form after the rebellion of His chosen representatives at the instigation of the serpent in Genesis 3. We can trace the development of conflict and violence from that time. For example, God says to the serpent, "I will put *enmity* between you and the woman, and between your offspring and hers" (Gen 3:15, emphasis added). In the next chapter, we see Adam and Eve's two children in conflict and Cain murdering his brother (Gen 4:4–8) and later Lamech threatening violent revenge on anyone who dares injure him (Gen 4:23–24). This decline comes to a head in Genesis 6 where "the earth was corrupt in God's sight and full of violence" (Gen 6:11, see also verse 13).

It seems that God permits real resistance to His will (as in the Fall) and sets Himself to defeat this resistance over time (as in the rest of the biblical narrative). But having delegated the rule of the earth to humanity, God cannot, or will not, bypass humanity in this war. We will explore further how God relates to human and angelic agents in Chapter 8. But it seems that God really does fight and win many battles and the ultimate

---

1. Boyd, *God At War*.

war.² As Adrio König puts it, "God reaches his goal with his creation only by way of a prolonged historical conflict."³

GOD'S ETERNAL PLAN

Paul writes of God's "eternal purpose that He accomplished in Christ Jesus our Lord" (Eph 3:11). God clearly had a plan when He created the world. The New Testament clearly states that Jesus "was chosen *before the creation of the world*" (1 Pet 1:20, emphasis added) to be our redeemer and hence he is "the Lamb who was slain from the creation of the world" (Rev 13:8). This suggests at least that God anticipated the Fall and sin of humanity and prepared a plan of salvation through Christ. God promised us eternal life "before the beginning of time" (Tit 1:2) because of His grace that "was given us in Christ Jesus before the beginning of time" (2 Tim 1:9). This plan was a mystery (or secret) that "God destined for our glory before time began" (1 Cor 2:7). Hence Paul writes that, "He made known to us the mystery of his will according to his good pleasure, which he *purposed* in Christ, to be put into effect *when the times reach their fulfillment*–to bring unity to all things in heaven and on earth under Christ." (Eph 1:9–10, emphasis added). He declares that we were "predestined *according to the plan* of him *who works out everything* in conformity with the purpose of his will" (Eph 1:11, emphasis added).

This verse certainly suggests that God's sovereign Plan takes priority over everything else, encompasses everything and cannot be frustrated, but does it say that it directly causes or drives everything that happens? Millard Erickson contends, "What is now coming to pass is occurring because it is (and has always been) part of God's plan" because "God has from the beginning, from all eternity, had an inclusive plan encompassing all of reality and extending *even to the minor details* of life."⁴

Erickson also points to verses from Proverbs:

> Many are the plans in a person's heart,
> but it is the Lord's purpose that prevails
> (Prov 19:21).
> The lot is cast into the lap,
> but its every decision is from the Lord

---

2. For a full discussion of this in the Bible, see Longman and Reid, *God Is a Warrior*.
3. König, *Eclipse of Christ*, 247.
4. Erickson, *Christian Theology*, 375, emphasis added.

(Prov 16:33).

These verses certainly show that God's will prevails against all opposition and that human plans depend on Him. But they don't say that every single event that occurs is predetermined by God. Based on the famous words of Paul in Rom 8:29–30, Grenz points out that God's goal is glorification, viewed as an eschatological certainty, and the other events named here "are directed toward it and subservient to it."[5] Hence,

> predestination is not 'God's choice of individuals for eternal life or eternal death,' but his resolute intention to bring believers to the final goal of his saving work (glorification).[6]

Clearly, God has eternal plans and they will be accomplished. But the detailed outcomes and decisions of all individual lives are not usually determined by God. Rather the Bible tells a story of how God accomplishes His plan.

WAR AND GOD'S SOVEREIGNTY

As human beings form themselves into nations based on ethnic and language distinctives after the Babel crisis (Genesis 11), war between different groups of humans becomes an inevitable reality. God is inherently opposed to war, as He condemns violence (Gen 6:11). However, God doesn't watch on as a spectator and even uses human violence to fulfill His own purposes as we saw in the Exodus struggle to release the oppressed Israelites.

The first actual war recounted in the Bible involves a battle between two armies in the Ancient Near East when a group of subservient kings rebel against their overlord Kedorlaomer. Kedorlaomer defeats them and captures many, including Abraham's nephew Lot (Gen 14:1–12). Abraham otherwise had no real interest in this struggle, but he was committed to his nephew's well-being, and he forms a small alliance of his own to rescue Lot, which required him to mobilize "318 trained men born in his household" (Gen 14:14) and chase the enemy forces. Using classical military tactics, "During the night Abram divided his men to attack them and he routed them pursuing theme as far as Hobah" (Gen 14:15).

---

5. Grenz, *Theology for the Community of God*, 458–459.
6. Grenz, *Theology for the Community of God*, 459.

So far this reads like a secular account, but the post-battle intervention of "Melchizedek king of Salem. . . . priest of God Most High" (Gen 14:18) makes it clear that it is God who has "delivered your enemies into your hand" (Gen 14:20), a fact that Abraham acknowledges by giving Melchizedek a tenth of the spoils and refusing to take any of the other nine tenths because of an oath made to God (Gen 14:20-24). God was the author of victory, but military action and tactics were engaged to bring that victory.

The next recorded battle takes place at the Red Sea when the Egyptian army, augmented with 600 chariots, comes to attack the departing Israelites (Exod 14:5-9), who themselves "went out of Egypt ready for battle" (Exod 14:18). Exodus sets this up as a war scenario, though the two armies (Exod 14:20) must have been very unequal and the Israelites themselves expected to be annihilated (Exod 14:10-12). But God Himself is seen here as the ultimate director of the situation as He manipulates Pharaoh's mind towards what will be a disastrous attack (Exod 14:1-4,8; see also 15:9). God then promises victory to Israel (Exod 14:13-14), luring the enemy army into a trap and annihilating their forces (Exod 14:21-28). The language of the song sung after this victory specifically declares, "the LORD is a warrior" (Exod 15:3).

The next battle occurs when the Amalekites attack the Israelites in the desert (Exod 17:8). The strategy that Moses devised in this case clearly implies that he was relying on God for victory over these attackers. Joshua will take a select group to fight while Moses "will stand on top of the hill with the staff of God" (Exod 17:9). Sure enough, this was a winning combination: "As long as Moses held up his hands, the Israelites were winning, but whenever he lowered his hands, the Amalekites were winning" (Exod 17:11). With help from Aaron and Hur to keep Moses' hands upraised, "Joshua overcame the Amalekite army with the sword" (Exod 17:13). The story concludes:

> Moses built and altar and called it The LORD is my Banner. He said, "Because hands were lifted up against [or to] the throne of the LORD, the LORD will be at war against the Amalekites from generation to generation."
>
> (Exod 17:15-16).

The lesson seems to be that God determines the outcome of the battle, but He does so in response to prayer (see Ps 141:2). Does God then determine the outcome of every battle? Perhaps not, but in this case His people and His name are at stake.

Later there is the crisis over entering the promised land in Numbers 13-14. The Israelites have arrived at the borders of this territory and Moses sends out spies on a reconnaissance mission (Num 13:1-25). The spies are impressed with the fertility of the land but intimidated by the inhabitants and their fortifications (Num 13:26-33). The community sides with the majority of the spies, rejecting God's leading (Num 14:3), demanding a change of leadership (Num 14:4) and explicitly denying God's power to give them victory as affirmed by Joshua and Caleb (Num 14:9). As the people speak of stoning Caleb and Joshua as false prophets (Num 14:10), God's glory arrives on the scene and God, as it were, takes over.

God pronounces judgement on the Israelites, initially pledging to destroy them completely (v.12), backing off in response to Moses' intercession (vv.13-22), determining that the guilty generation will never enter the promised land (vv.22-35), and inflicting a plague on the unbelieving spies (vv.36-38). Now the nation must change course and *not* attempt to enter the land (v.25). However, they attempt the impossible in an act of pseudo-repentance and are resoundingly defeated (vv.39-45). There is no victory, even for God's people, outside of God's will or sovereign permission.

How that might work positively is revealed in Numbers 21-25. The new generation of Israelites are moving along the eastern side of the Jordan valley prior to invading the promised land. They successfully defeat and destroy several neighboring countries: (Num 21). The attempt by King Balak of Moab to place a curse on the Israelites through the sorcerer/prophet Balaam fails completely; God turns the situation around and causes Balaam to pronounce blessing instead (Num 23:7-11, 19-24; 24:5-9). Israel is seemingly invincible; but only as long as they obey the LORD. Balaam, a savvy and experienced spiritual operator, comes up with a plan to manipulate the spiritual situation to Moab's advantage (Num 31:16) by enticing the Israelite men to a 'pagan orgy', thereby provoking God to act against them (Num 25:1-3). Balaam has the same craftiness as the serpent in Genesis 3. Only after the intervention of the Lord, pronouncing sentence against the leaders of Israel, did Moses and Phinehas succeed in limiting the resultant plague to 24,000 men (Num 25:4-11). Israelite victory is thus guaranteed only as long as Israel is following God's will. God cannot be manipulated by Israelites or sorcerers for human agendas.

The key war in the earlier part of the Old Testament is, of course, the Israelite invasion of Canaan. This is God-ordained. God had promised Abraham and his descendants to give them this land (Gen 12:1,7; 13:14–17; 15:7–21; 17:8; 26:3; 28:13; 35:12; Exod 3:8,17; 23:23,27–31; 33:1–3). Now the time has come after Moses' death (Josh 1:1–2). God is clearly the Commander-in-Chief, not Joshua. This is made clear to Joshua shortly before the attack on Jericho when he sees "a man standing in front of him with a drawn sword in his hand" (Josh 5:13), and when asked on whose side this mysterious 'man' is, he hears, "Neither . . . but as commander of the army of the LORD I have now come" (Josh 5:14).[7] Clearly, he expects to direct operations and to be obeyed by Joshua and the Israelites, though the actual instructions are given by "the LORD" (Josh 6:2). Possibly he is the commander of a heavenly, angelic army, that will win the 'war behind the war,' a spiritual struggle reminiscent of the Amalekite crisis in which Joshua had played a vital part (Exod 17).

This suggests that the real enemy here is not the Canaanites but a spiritual opponent of God, anticipating Eph 6:12 and Rev 12:7–9. The author of Joshua interprets the invasion of Canaan as a judgment against the iniquitous Canaanites (Josh 6:18; see Gen 15:16), as a means of God fulfilling His promise of the land to Abraham's descendants (Josh 1:2–4; see Gen 15:18–21), *and* as a victory against Satanic anti-God forces. In all three interpretations, God is sovereign but in three different senses. God shows that this invasion is His work in clear ways and gives Joshua a detailed and unusual plan to take the fortified city of Jericho, the gateway to the land, a strategy that focuses on God as Victor and the spiritual war (the war behind the war) by its use of marching, trumpets and a final shout that causes the city walls to fall down (Josh 6:1–20), though this had to be followed up with violent destruction of the city and all its inhabitants (Josh 6:21,24).

Things then came unstuck. "But the Israelites were unfaithful in regard to the devoted things; Achan son of Karmi, the son of Zimri, of the tribe of Judah, took some of them. So the LORD's anger burned against Israel" (Josh 7:1). Israel failed the test of obedience. God had reserved the precious items from Jericho for His treasury (Josh 6:19,24), but Achan saw some lovely items and coveted them (Josh 7:21), just as Adam and Eve had coveted the forbidden fruit in Genesis 3. This brings God's judgement in the form of "trouble" and "destruction" (Josh 6:18) and divine

---

7. He appears to be an angel, at least; some would say this is a theophany or even a Christophany That is, the 'man' was God or Jesus Christ.

anger (Josh 7:1), and thus Israel's defeat by a relatively minor town (Josh 7:2–5). God will not give victory to a disobedient people (Josh 7:11–12). Only after the people consecrate themselves and deal with the offender and his family do we read that God "turned from his fierce anger" (Josh 7:26) and then victory is given over Ai and subsequent targets.

God has chosen Israel as a covenant partner, even an agent of His judgement, but on condition that they are faithful to that covenant and obedient to God's instructions. Ultimately, He is not on their side *against* others but acts as Judge of all (Josh 5:13–14). It's *their* task to take *God's* side against *His* enemies. Moreover, God is willing to accept others into His nation who take their side, or more accurately *His* side, because they recognize that "the LORD your God is God in heaven above and on the earth below" (Josh 2:11), as did the prostitute Rahab, the only person in Jericho whose life, and that of her family, are known to have been saved from destruction (Josh 6:22–23,25).

AMBIGUOUS HEROES

Several centuries later, the book of Judges focuses on the ongoing struggle between the Israelites and the Philistines. In Judg 13:1, we read that "the Israelites did evil in the eyes of the LORD, so that the LORD delivered them into the hands of the Philistines for forty years." But then apparently God determines to release them from this tyranny, though the text says nothing about Israel repenting. The way He usually brings salvation to Israel is through a man (or woman), in this case a 'judge,' that is, a military prophetic leader raised up by the Lord, though His imprint is on this story from the beginning when the 'angel of the LORD' appears to Samson's parents with promise of a miracle child (Judg 13:2–23) who is appointed to "take the lead in delivering Israel from the hands of the Philistines" (Judg 13:5).

The man God chooses is impetuous, troubled, violent, susceptible to manipulation, unstable, sexually adventurous, sometimes naïve, and far from an ideal hero, though he remains faithful to his Nazirite call till late in the story. Yet God's choice is seen in his miraculous birth (Judg 13:24) and the work of the Spirit in his life stirring him to action (Judg 13:25). He seeks a Philistine wife in violation of the Torah (Judg 14:1–3; Exod 34:16; Deut 7:3–4). The text explains, "His parents did not know that *this was from the* LORD, who was seeking an occasion to confront the Philistines; for at that time they were ruling over Israel" (Judg 14:4, emphasis added).

God was apparently using even the sexual desires of His chosen man to stir up trouble and provoke Israelite resistance to the Philistines, a resistance which was perhaps lacking. That God is in this is demonstrated by the power of the Spirit giving Samson enormous strength (Judg 14:6,19). There is a pattern where sexual liaisons between Samson and Philistine women are used to stir up battles with the Philistines, fights which Samson wins with ease (Judg 14:19–16:3), but Samson comes unstuck through such relationships and his own weakness in the case of Delilah and ends up a prisoner of the Philistines (Judg 16:4–22).

However, this final crisis in Samson's life reveals the real source of his strength: his dedication to God as a Nazirite (Judg 16:17–20; see 13:4–5,7,14). The triumph of the Philistines and their god (Judg 16:23–24) is short-lived, because Samson's hair regrows after it had been shaved off (Judg 16:19,22), and his last request for vengeance on the Philistines is answered with a final display of supernatural strength by which "he killed many more when he died than while he lived" (Judg 16:30).

Does God use violent people to accomplish His goals? Does this cast doubt on God's own nature? The text does not really address these questions but perhaps three points can be made. First, Samson is chosen and commissioned as God's representative and only succeeds as long as he is faithful to his call as a Nazirite; when he compromises that, the LORD leaves him in spite of his hubris (Judg 16:20) and surrenders him to the enemy. Second, Samson is an agent of God's justice against the Philistines who have violently oppressed Israel, which in turn was God's judgment. And third, this story also shows that God often works best when His people are weak and apparently helpless, as Samson was at the end.[8]

As Carson comments,

> There is no obvious effort to whitewash Samson; nor is Yahweh's character impugned. In some mysterious way he himself stands behind Samson's unworthy motives, not to promote evil but to punish the Philistines; for without the ensuing exploits Israel could easily have succumbed to Philistine influence.[9]

---

8. The Gideon story has a similar message in that God reduces his army so as to take the credit for the victory (Judg 7:2).

9. Carson, *Sovereignty and Responsibility*, 11.

Struggles between the Israelites and Philistines are central to the biblical narrative until 2 Samuel 5. The only consistently victorious Israelite commander is David, starting with the famous victory over Goliath. Prior to this episode, we know that David was the youngest son of Jesse and as a teenager was managing his father's sheep when he was suddenly called home and anointed as future king (1 Sam 16:1–13). Shortly afterwards, he was summoned to the royal palace to play the lyre for a very disturbed King Saul (1 Sam 16:14–23). However, at first he worked in the court only part-time, continuing to manage his father's flock (1 Sam 17:15), and thus was not immediately involved in the latest flareup in the war with the Philistines. He only came on the scene of battle as a messenger and food delivery boy, to supply his brothers.

Almost immediately, he got into trouble with his brothers for asking very direct questions about the crisis caused by the giant Goliath, who was challenging Israel to one-on-one combat (1 Sam 17:1–31). David had seen something that was not obvious to others: this challenge was not just a human problem; rather Goliath was defying "the armies of the living God" (1 Sam 17:26) and apparently getting away with it, because the Israelites were paralyzed with fear (1 Sam 17:11,24). God's sovereignty did not prevent this situation happening and God's delegated representatives were failing the test. David, however, did not theologize about what God should or could do, nor did he accept the situation passively as 'God's will.' Confident in God's power, he volunteered to fight the Philistine, shaming the soldiers and King Saul. David's faith, developed and proven in the wilds with the flocks, enabled him to pass his first test as the potential future king (1 Sam 17:33–51). His victory proved not what a great warrior he was but rather,

> "All those gathered here will know that it is not by sword or spear that the LORD saves; for the battle is the LORD's, and he will give all of you into our hands."
>
> (1 Sam 17:47).

The sovereignty of God, properly understood, should not inculcate passive 'armchair' theologizing, but an active adventurous willingness to risk all in the situations we find ourselves in.

A slightly parallel story is found in 2 Chronicles 20. A godly reforming king of Judah, Jehoshaphat, was facing a massive challenge with the appearance of a vast enemy alliance on the horizon (2 Chr 20:1–2). Jehoshaphat was alarmed, but as a man of faith, he "resolved to inquire of the LORD, and he proclaimed a fast for all Judah" (2 Chr 20:3). The king prayed at the temple in Jerusalem, affirming God's sovereign power (2 Chr 20:6) and looking to God for a solution (2 Chr 20:12). However, the prophetic challenge that came next would have shaken them all. The Spirit came on a prophet who said,

> "Do not be afraid or discouraged because of this great army. For the battle is not yours, but God's. . . . You will not have to fight in this battle. Take up your positions; stand firm and see the deliverance the LORD will give you . . . Go out to face them tomorrow, and the LORD will be with you."

(2 Chr 20:15–17).

The people responded with faith, joy and praise, and after consultation, Jehoshaphat decided on a very risky strategy, putting a choir in front of his army on the basis of this prophetic promise. The choir sang, "Give thanks to the LORD, for his love endures forever" (2 Chr 20:21). Then, "as they began to sing and praise, the LORD set ambushes against the men of . . . . . who were invading Judah, and they were defeated," partly by the vast army dividing against itself (2 Chr 20:22–23). We aren't told why the various enemy soldiers turned on each other, but we do see that God was behind it. This is a powerful illustration of God's sovereignty in action.

GOD'S INVASION

In Chapter 3, I argued that God's sovereignty over the world was challenged, but not destroyed, by the Fall. At times, it seemed that God had almost been shut out of His world because its human governors had come under the sway of the devil (see Luke 4:6; 1 John 5:19). Behind the wars we have just discussed lies a more fundamental conflict hinted at in significant places. But God's interventions had to respect the role of human beings that He had instituted and were initially limited in effect. And even God's chosen people and their chosen leaders frequently failed.

Isaiah 59 expresses the situation as it had developed, probably in the period after the Jewish exile in Babylon.

> Surely the arm of the LORD is not too short to save,
> nor his ear too dull to hear.
> But your iniquities have separated you from your God;
> your sins have hidden his face from you,

so that he will not hear (vv.1–2).

The prophet goes on to list the evils he sees all around him: bloodshed (v.3), false speech (v.3), injustice (v.4), empty arguments and lies (v.4), evil plans (v.5), violence (vv.6–7), resistance to peace (v.8). This is a sick society where God and His ways are excluded and injustice prevails (vv.9–15a).

God's reaction is then described:

> The LORD looked and was displeased
> that there was no justice.
> He saw that there was no one,
> he was appalled that there was no one to intervene
>   (vv.15b–16a).

Someone (a Moses, a David, a Joshua, an Elijah, even a Samson) should have stood up against this situation, but no one did. This is the problem with the way God has set up the world. If no human being is prepared to take God's side or fight for justice, what can God do? So God himself declares war and enters the battle:

> *His own arm* achieved salvation for him,
> and *his own righteousness* sustained him.
> He put on righteousness as his breastplate,
> and the helmet of salvation on his head;
> he put on the garments of vengeance
> and wrapped himself in zeal as in a cloak (vv.16b–17, emphasis added).

And

> he will come like a pent up flood
> that the breath of the LORD drives along (v19b).[10]

God is thus invading the world, and specifically Israel. But how will this work?

When we read the Gospels, we see how it will happen. The angel Gabriel appears to the young Mary and promises her a son "who will be great" and "The Lord God will give him the throne of his father David, and he will reign over Jacob's descendants forever; his kingdom will never

---

10. Some older translations have "When the enemy comes in like a flood, the Spirit of the LORD will lift up a standard against him" (NKJV). This plays down God's initiative, and implies God is just responding to the work of the devil.

end" (Luke 1:31–33). Mary later speaks prophetically of the revolutionary implications:

> "He has performed mighty deeds with his arm
> he has scattered the proud in their inmost thoughts.
> He has brought down rulers from their thrones,
> but has lifted up the humble."
>
> (Luke 1:51–52).

About thirty years later, John the Baptist launches his mission of calling Israel to repentance in view of what is coming:

> As it is written in the book of the words of Isaiah the prophet:
> "A voice of one calling in the wilderness,
> Prepare the way for the Lord,
> Make straight paths for him.
> Every valley shall be filled in,
> Every mountain and hill made low.
> The crooked roads shall become straight,
> The rough ways smooth."
>
> (Luke 3:4–5).

Here Luke is quoting Isaiah 40:3–5, referring to the return of Israel to its homeland after the years of exile in Babylon. But note the image of roadbuilding, for which the ancient Romans were famous. Smooth straight roads not only made travel and commerce easier; they were there primarily for the armies to get to their destinations and enforce Roman rule. In other words, this is invasion language. Through His Messiah, God was invading that sick society Isaiah had protested against.

It began with a wrestling match against the devil, the ancient serpent who had started this bad situation (Luke 4:1–3; see Rev 12:9). The devil was unsuccessful in diverting Jesus into misusing his powers or compromising. He even offered Jesus his own power over the kingdoms of the world, but Jesus was coming to invade and 'dethrone' them, not to coopt them into some kind of alliance.

Jesus then proclaimed his mission, also in the words of Isaiah:

> "'The Spirit of the Lord is on me,
> because he has anointed me
> to proclaim good news to the poor.
> He has sent me to proclaim freedom for the prisoners
> and recovery of sight for the blind,

> to set the oppressed free,
> to proclaim the year of the Lord's favor.'"

(Luke 4:18–19).

Shortly afterwards, we read of Jesus driving out demons (Luke 4:33–36,41),[11] healing the sick (Luke 4:38–40) and proclaiming "the good news of the kingdom of God" (Luke 4:43). His first targets are the forces of the devil that oppress the Israelites, but the human religious leaders represent the powers that resist God's invasion and finally collude in executing the Messiah.[12] It is part of the Plan, an event that must happen to win the victory. As Jesus himself explains after the resurrection,

> "This is what is written: The Messiah will suffer and rise from the dead on the third day, and repentance for the forgiveness of sins will be preached in his name, beginning at Jerusalem"

(Luke 24:46–47).

God has won a decisive victory through Christ's death and resurrection and now the invasion moves into a new phase.

CHRIST ENTHRONED

The New Testament places a strong focus on the outcome of Jesus' suffering and death in his subsequent promotion. Jesus is now victorious and sovereign, not just as God but as a human being.

Paul makes this point at length:

> And being found in appearance as a man,
> he humbled himself
> by becoming obedient to death—
> even death on a cross!
> Therefore God exalted him to the highest place
> and gave him the name that is above every name,
> that at the name of Jesus every knee should bow,
> in heaven and on earth and under the earth,
> and every tongue acknowledge that Jesus Christ is Lord,

---

11. In Mark's Gospel, the Greek frequently uses the same kind of language of Jesus casting out demons as of the Canaanites being driven out of the promised land (Longman and Reid, *God Is a Warrior*, 108),

12. Thus after casting out demons, Jesus now casts out the merchants from the temple, using the same Greek language (Mark 11:15; Luke 19:45). Cf. Longman and Reid, *God Is a Warrior*, 123.

to the glory of God the Father.
(Phil 2:8-11)

Jesus' exaltation "to the highest place" with the highest name of all, the title of Lord (Greek *Kyrios*), is mentioned several times (Eph 1:20-22; Heb 1:3; Rom 10:9; Mark 16:19; Acts 2:33-36; 7:56). Jesus himself claimed, "All authority in heaven and on earth has been given to me" (Matt 28:18), having testified to the high priest, "From now on you will see the Son of Man sitting at the right hand of the Mighty One and coming on the clouds of heaven" (Matt 26:64).

Acts demonstrates how Jesus exercises this authority from his place on God's throne by pouring out the Holy Spirit (Acts 2:33; 11:15-17; see also Luke 24:49; John 7:37-39; 20:21-23), by healing through his representatives (Acts 4:10; 9:34), by intervening to protect His followers and bring others to faith (Acts 9:3-6), by appearing in visions at strategic times (Acts 9:10-12), and by guiding his apostles (Acts 16:7). All these actions are part of Jesus' promise to build his church (Matt 16:18) and a continuation of "all that Jesus began to do and to teach until the day he was taken up to heaven" (Acts 1:1).

The Holy Spirit leads and empowers the infant church and helps them overcome the resistance of Jewish authorities (Acts 4), the pretense of hypocritical believers (Acts 5:1-11), and incipient divisions (Acts 6:1-7). Even the large-scale persecution that arises over the new leader Stephen, which affects not just leaders, but many Christians (Acts 6:8-8:3), only succeeds in spreading the message more widely according to Plan (Acts 8:4-40; 11:19-21). The apostles are sometimes powerfully guided from above (Acts 10-11; 13:2; 16:6-10), but more often they just do what seems right and find that they are guided anyway by God's sovereign hand. There is fierce resistance which sometimes costs the believers dearly, such as the execution of James and Stephen (Acts 12,7), but it never stops the church advancing (Acts 9:31). The narrative ends with the apostle Paul in the capital city of the empire, Rome, poised to influence even the imperial leaders and ruling class.

The sovereignty of God is clear throughout Acts , but a few specific cases are worth mentioning. The ministry of Philip, one of the seven new leaders who emerge in Acts 6, is significant. He was 'on the run' from the big persecution led by Saul (Acts 8:3-5) when he arrived in a city of Samaria. He did not keep quiet, however, but "proclaimed the Messiah there" (v.5) with great signs and wonders, leading to a great response from the people (vv.6–8). The people turned away from the powerful sorcerer Simon, who even himself professed faith in Christ. The power of the gospel and the sovereign work of the Spirit in the midst of opposition and occult powers were both demonstrated.

But the sovereignty of God is also revealed in two other events in this episode. First, the Holy Spirit did not come on any of Philip's converts until Peter and John came from Jerusalem and laid hands on them (vv.14–17). The author offers no explanation for this but Simon's attempts to purchase apostolic power are rebuffed (vv.16–23); the clear message is that the work of the Spirit is not 'for sale' or available to manipulate. Then, second, Philip was sent away from the scene of his triumph to a lonely desert road to speak to one man, whom he providentially met and was directed by the Spirit to approach (vv.26–29), only to find his mind had been strangely prepared to receive the gospel of Jesus (vv.30–35). And then the Spirit sovereignly snatched Philip away and transported him to another location (vv.39–40).

Another episode worth focusing on relates to Paul's time in Philippi. This is very clearly at the direction of God (Acts 16:6–10) and begins well with the conversion of Lydia who then offers hospitality to the apostolic team (vv.13–15). But when Paul is pestered by a fortune-telling slave and finally evicts the demon behind her ability, things turn nasty. Deprived of this nice little money spinner, her owners seize Paul and Silas and they end up being flogged and thrown in jail (vv.16–24). The mission is in trouble.

But God is at work. First, Luke tells us that "about midnight Saul and Silas were praying and singing hymns to God, and the other prisoners were listening to them" (v.25). God is using this painful situation to reach prisoners; already the atmosphere in that prison is changing for the better. Then there is the earthquake which leads directly to the conversion of the jailer and his household, partly because the prisoners choose not to escape when they could have (vv.26–34). None of this would have happened if Paul and Silas hadn't been imprisoned. God is at work even in the midst of trials and the name of Jesus is more powerful than occult forces, mob violence and even civil authorities.

GOD'S SOVEREIGNTY OVER HISTORY

The book of Revelation demonstrates how God wins over the course of history in the way it picks up the threads of the Big Story from Genesis onwards. The Bible does not tell this Story with total consistency or without many side-tracks and even seemingly contradictory elements; it is not an ideological metanarrative that tries to explain everything by one simple theme like Marxism. Even at the end of Revelation there are loose ends. But Revelation is clearly telling us of a final End to history as we know it; not the end of life or the universe, but the end of the particular Story that began in Genesis.[13] Other New Testament books also refer to, or add to, what Revelation portrays more graphically.

As a result, we can legitimately interpret salvation history as told in Scripture through this lens. Certain themes unfold throughout biblical history viewed as the work of a divine Author, for example the story of the "seed of the woman" (Gen 3:15), the promised deliverer from the serpent, which is referenced in Gal 3:16–19 and Rev 12. And biblical authors specifically interpret Israel's history in the light of God's choice of Israel and His covenant with the nation. In some places this idea of God's direction of nations is extended to Gentile nations too, as in Amos 9:7 and Acts 17:26.

But how strongly can we apply this theme to our own times? British Christians have cherished stories of England's protection from the Spanish Armada and the Dunkirk 'miracle' of 1940. But can we see God's hand in the rise *and fall* of the British Empire, the rise of Nazi Germany and World War II, the Holocaust or Shoah, the infamous African slave trade of sixteenth to nineteenth centuries, and other horrors too many to recount here? Trying to 'second guess' what God is doing in any situation is fraught with difficulty, but neither can we ignore or deny God's work even in the broad sweep of history. I think we should look for signs of God doing what He has promised to do, that is building His church (Matt 16:18), bending history to the good of His church (Rom 8:28), bringing in the harvest of the Gentiles (Rom 11:25), preparing for a restoration of Jews to His kingdom (Rom 11:23,26), making opportunities for all people to be saved (2 Pet 3:9) and bringing judgment on the wicked (Luke 1:51–53).

In the light of the foregoing discussion, however, we should remember that, as Richard Rice contends,

---

13. Cf. Newton, *Revelation Worldview*, 249–253,

the course of history is not the product of divine action alone. God's will is not the ultimate explanation for *everything* that happens; human decisions and actions make an important contribution too.[14]

Both human and angelic or demonic actions play a part in the overall story and there is a real struggle before God wins the final victory, as Revelation displays dramatically.

On the other hand, we insist that history is going somewhere definite, that God will achieve what He has set out to achieve (Rev 11:15b).

Clark Pinnock contends,

> At great cost, God is leading the world forward to the place where it will reflect more perfectly the goodness that God himself enjoys. God does all this without having to do it, without being compelled by anything outside of himself.[15]

He continues, "Evil may have its day, but it will not finally triumph" and yet "God showed his willingness to take risks and to work with a history whose outcome he does not wholly decide."[16] Can both of these claims be true? The Bible seems to envisage a final outcome that is decided by God, "a new heaven and a new earth" (Rev 21:1), where God declares, "I am making everything new!" (Rev 21:5a).

Perhaps Goldingay puts it best in his commentary on Daniel:

> It assumes that human beings makes real decisions that do shape history, yet that human decision-making does not necessarily have the last word. It affirms the sovereignty of God in history, working sometimes via the process of human decision-making, sometimes despite it.[17]

Psalm 22 teaches

> All the ends of the earth
> will remember and turn to the LORD,
> and all the families of the nations
> will bow down before him,

---

14. Richard Rice, "Biblical Support for a New Perspective" (in Pinnock et al, *The Openness of God*), 15–16 (emphasis added).

15. Clark Pinnock, "Systematic Theology" (in Pinnock et al, *The Openness of God*), 110.

16. Clark Pinnock, "Systematic Theology" (in Pinnock et al, *The Openness of God*), 116.

17. Goldingay, *Daniel*, 59.

> for dominion belongs to the LORD
> and he rules over the nations
>
> (Ps 22:27–28).

Here we see two aspects of God's rule: it is already operating, "dominion belongs to the LORD" and "he rules over the nations" (both in present tense) and is roughly equivalent to what I am calling God's sovereignty in the third sense of guidance or 'control.' But there is also a future element- people "will remember and turn to the LORD" and "will bow down to him." They are not bowing down to God right now, but they will then.

Graeme Goldsworthy explains:

> We need to distinguish here between the absolute sovereignty of God [God's kingdom in the first sense] and the Kingdom of God. Neither man nor devil can escape the sovereign power of God, no matter how hard either may fight against it. In the end all who rebel against the Creator will be forced to submit to the undeniable reality of God's lordship. But the Kingdom of God as the Bible reveals it [second sense] is the sphere of God's rule in which his creatures submit willingly to this righteous rule. God's sovereign rule is universal; the Kingdom of God is not.[18]

Grenz rightly states that God's work as Creator is unfinished and is only completed in the End.[19] But the New Testament also reminds us that, in order to complete the Story, there needs to be a final resolution of the conflict which has been at the heart of the narrative since Genesis 3. God must overcome the opposition. All the human and angelic players must be judged and sent on to their final destiny. God's sovereignty is revealed in how He passes judgment on everyone. God asserts His freedom, His rights over His creation and His control over what happens. But He does so in a way that is consistent with His character and justice.

God's "eternal purpose" has already been accomplished according to Eph 3:11. But the Story is not yet finished. The Plan is aiming at nothing less than the salvation of the world.

When John sees Jesus unveiled as the slaughtered Lamb, he also hears,

---

18. Goldsworthy, *Gospel and Kingdom*, 54.
19. Grenz, *Theology for the Community of God*, 110–111.

"you were slain,
and with your blood you purchased for God
persons from every tribe and language and people and nation.
You have made them to be a kingdom and priests to serve our God,
and they will reign on the earth."

(Rev 5:9–10).

Two chapters later he sees this visually: "a great multitude that no one could count, from every nation, tribe, people and language" (Rev 7:9a) who were redeemed by the blood of the Lamb (Rev 7:14). This is apparently a fulfilment of Psalm 2:8 ("Ask me, and I will make the nations your inheritance, the ends of the earth your possession").[20]

And later again, those who had not succumbed to the pressure of the beast declare,

"All nations will come and worship before you,
for your righteous acts have been revealed"
(Rev 15:4b).

Of course, this will finally happen in the new order that John sees after the final judgment, when God now dwells with all people, death is gone, "the old order of things has passed away" (Rev 21:3–4) and even the earth's kings bring their glory to the new Jerusalem (Rev 21:24.26). But it is not just a sudden act of God. In fact, the defeat of the devil, while carried out in heaven by angels led by Michael (Rev 12:7–9), is actually due to the Christians with their faith in Jesus:

"They triumphed over him
by the blood of the Lamb
and by the word of their testimony;
they did not love their lives so much
as to shrink from death."

(Rev 12:11).

Conquest or victory is what Christians are meant to do, but not by force of arms or political campaigning. The faithful witness of His servants, and even their blood, is God's main weapon to defeat the opposition. Such witnesses are the heroes of Revelation, the conquerors of Revelation 2–3, those raised to life to reign with Christ for a thousand

---

20. See also John 3:16; 12:32; Isa 49:6; Matt 28:18–19; and Acts 1:8.

years (Rev 20:4). And church history confirms that such courageous Christians constantly defy the forces of evil, often in the form of totalitarian dictatorships, and 'conquer' the nations, because God's justice is on their side.

Elsewhere Paul writes,

> For God was pleased to have all his fullness dwell in him, and through him to reconcile to himself all things, whether things on earth or things in heaven, by making peace through his blood, shed on the cross

(Col 1:19–20).

And in 2 Peter, the author suggests that the second coming is being delayed for this purpose:

> The Lord is not slow in keeping his promise, as some understand slowness. Instead he is patient with you, not wanting *anyone* to perish, but *everyone* to come to repentance

(2 Pet 3:9, emphasis added).

Writing to the Romans, after discussing the strange turn of events in which the Jews have largely rejected their Messiah, but Gentiles have flooded into the kingdom, Paul concludes,

> Israel has experienced a hardening in part until the full number of the Gentiles has come in, and in this way *all* Israel will be saved . . . .for God's gifts and his call are irrevocable . . . ..God has bound *everyone* over to disobedience so that he may have mercy on them *all*

(Rom 11:25b-26a,29,32, emphasis added).

Many of the English Puritans of the 17th century understood this to mean that there would certainly be a mass conversion of Jews before the End, which would lead in turn to an even greater extension of the Kingdom of God throughout the earth. This hope later motivated the early Protestant missionaries.[21]

Such statements have been interpreted in different ways. Some say that it is God's desire that all people come to faith, but this is conditional, and many will refuse, frustrating God's desire to some extent. Others claim that the people to be saved, the 'all' mentioned in these passages,

---

21. Cf. Murray, *Puritan Hope*, 48–50,154–155.

are the elect, who will indubitably be saved, as God has the power to bring them in. Still others mount a case for an evangelical universalism based on such promises. Universalism would seem to be negated by the many other passages that envisage people being sent to hell in the end (such as Matt 25:41–46; 2 Thess 1:6–9; Rev 14:9–11; 20:15; 21:8; 22:15). But at least these big statements suggest to me that God's final harvest will be much bigger than we often realize. Human resistance is real, as is Satanic opposition, but neither will triumph. Instead, Christ eventually overcomes every enemy: "For he must reign until he has put all his enemies under his feet" (1 Cor 15:25). This is the End guaranteed by the operation of God's sovereign Plan, including "a new heaven and a new earth" (Rev 21:1; Isa 65:17; 2 Pet 3:13) in which "There will be no more death or mourning or crying or pain, for the old order of things has passed away" (Rev 21:4).

God's decision to delegate authority to human beings will finally be vindicated. But none of this happens without an almighty struggle as Revelation describes in powerful, even violent, language. This struggle will include imprisonment and persecution, including death, of God's people (Rev 2:10,13; 6:9–11; 11:7–10; 12:13–13:18; 17:6; 20:4), conflicts within the churches (Rev 2:14–16, 20–23), "great tribulation" (Rev 7:14), extensive disasters (Rev 6;8;9; 11:13; 16;18), specific punishment of God's opponents (Rev 11:18; 14:9–11; 16:5–7; 19:20; 20:10,12–13), political upheavals and wars (Rev 6:3–8; 9:13–19; 13:3; 14:18–20?; 16:12–14; 17:12–16; 18:8–10; 19:17–21; 20:7–10). As in 2 Chr 20, sometimes enemy armies fight each other under the sovereign work of God (Rev 16:13–16; 17:15–18). The devil plays an important role in this war (Rev 2:9,10,13,24; 3:9; 12:3–4,7–17; 13:1–4.11; 20:1–3,7–10; and perhaps 9:11). God's plan will triumph, but it requires the participation of the followers of Jesus who play a central role.[22]

God honors His original Plan by winning through human agents: first the Messiah, then the Messiah's followers. And they win primarily through witness and suffering. God's sovereignty is not overt and oppressive but sacrificial and gracious.

---

22. Cf. Newton, *Revelation Worldview*, 253–255.

DIVINE SOVEREIGNTY AND EVIL

The final outcome of God's sovereign Rule on earth is a wonderful new creation. But the road to that End is not always pleasant. The history of the world is blighted by the evil *actions* of human beings: murder, torture, abuse, cruelty of all kinds, genocide, war, slavery, rape, injustice, oppression, racism, intolerance and more. There are also evil *results* of human sin such as poverty, ignorance, destruction and hunger. And to these we must add *natural disasters* such as earthquakes, volcanic eruptions, tsunamis, wildfires, floods, mudslides, typhoons, hurricanes, cyclones, droughts, diseases, plagues, epidemics, and the like. Some of these are a result of human ignorance or exploitation of the environment, such as anthropogenic climate change, but not all. Millions of people have suffered from these terrible phenomena.

All of these are challenging to Christians who believe in a God who is both all-good and all-powerful but nonetheless ask, 'Why?' The theme of God's sovereignty often accentuates the problem by minimizing the responsibility of other actors like the devil and sinful humanity. Surely God is responsible for all this horror, either because He appointed these events, or at least could have prevented them and failed to do so. The idea of God's providence is especially vulnerable to such arguments. As Castelo explains,

> Does God cause everything to happen that occurs? These questions become especially difficult when one recognizes that a number of disturbing and deplorable things occur in the creation, and so God's role in relation to them becomes a significant matter to consider.[23]

And this is not just an intellectual problem; for most of us it becomes an existential or personal issue at some stage when we (or our families) experience tragedy or disaster.

The project called 'theodicy' attempts to justify God in view of these considerations.[24] Some thinkers play down God's role in order to justify God. According to this line of thinking, God cannot prevent bad things happening because He is limited in power, or unable to foresee their occurrence, or somehow unable to overcome the power of the devil or human actors.

---

23. Castelo, *Theological Theodicy*, 57.
24. For a good survey of this issue and how it has been approached, see Erickson, *Christian Theology*, 437–456.

Two books I read recently are good examples of this line of thinking from an Open Theist perspective. Both highlight the problem by focusing on particular true stories and making them a kind of litmus test for any view of God. Thomas Jay Oord begins with several devastating incidents: an Islamic extremist attack, an accident when a large rock crashed through the windshield of a car killing a mother of two, a baby with a severely debilitating medical condition, and a woman raped by members of a militia in Africa.[25] Greg Boyd begins with a horrific Nazi atrocity inflicted on a young girl in Poland during World War II.[26]

Both authors debunk explanations that such horrors are somehow controlled by God and serve some mysterious good plan. How could such awful events serve any good purpose? Oord's own solution is that God's love implies that He literally *cannot* act to restrain evil in humans or other created beings, or even in the natural world, since the creatures must be allowed to operate naturally as empowered by the Creator.[27] Boyd's solution involves the struggle between God and the devil but also comes down to the assertion that God cannot just overpower the devil by sheer force as this would violate the way God has set up the universe. As Boyd writes,

> The warfare worldview is predicated on the assumption that divine goodness does not completely control or in any sense will evil; rather, good and evil are at war with one another . . . God must work with, and battle against, other created beings.[28]

As he contends elsewhere, "Once God gives the gift of self-determination, he has to, within limits, endure its misuse."[29]

There is much truth in these arguments. God has given some autonomy to his creation and delegated control of the earth to humanity, humanity entered into league with the devil, and God is obliged to honor that decision because of His own constitution.

But this approach raises new problems. Why did God set things up that way? Was He unable to devise a constitution for the earth that involved real free will but limited the consequences of bad choices, for example? If such an outcome seems logically impossible, consider that

25. Oord, *Uncontrolling Love*, 17–25.
26. Boyd, *God At War*, 33–46.
27. Oord, *Uncontrolling Love*, 167–175.
28. *God At War*, 20.
29. *Satan and the Problem of Evil*, 181.

the Bible seems to envisage a future situation, in the new heaven and new earth, where people will still be free but will not sin.[30] Human choice is a given in a world where God desires creatures who can have a genuine love-relationship with Him, but this may not be incompatible with God's will being done consistently by such creatures. I argued earlier that something in the nature of God demands that humans are tested in terms of their allegiance to Him, but is this necessarily so?

Others go the other direction, emphasizing God's control and sovereignty as the ultimate Cause of everything and minimizing the power of other actors. As we saw earlier, God sovereignly oversees human history, including the rise and fall of rulers and empires. Does that make God responsible for all the oppression, injustice and violence that such rulers and empires commit? And if so, can God be justified? Lennox represents the reactions of many when he says,

> No amount of special pleading or theological sophistry can make such a view anything less than grotesque and completely unacceptable to a morally sensitive person.[31]

But we may ask, what alternative explanations for the evil aspects of history are possible other than ones that envisage a God like that in the Bible carrying out His Plan over a long period of history in partnership with free will agents like human beings? Is evil just an illusion, for example?[32] That hardly seems to make sense of human experience of suffering and seems to amount to willful blindness. Is everything explicable just by natural factors such as evolution? That's appealing to unbelievers but seems to result in a meaningless life and world and undermines the very concepts of good and evil we began with.

Are natural disasters simply the outcomes of "the 'wild' features of the earth. . . . the outworking of geological and atmospheric patterns of the earth's development and shaping"?[33] Such 'why?' questions may be inappropriate as these events are purely natural and not in any sense evil, except that sometimes their effects are exacerbated by human actions.[34] Victims of natural disasters may find that hard to accept, however.

---

30. Cf. Macchia, *Tongues of Fire*, 129–130.

31. Lennox, *Determined to Believe?*, 65.

32. Some forms of Hinduism propose that evil is illusory; we simply don't see what is real, that at bottom there is no good or evil.

33. Castelo, *Theological Theodicy*, 66, building on Terence Fretheim..

34. *Theological Theodicy*, 67–68.

Are there two equally powerful forces at work causing this dilemma, as in forms of dualistic philosophy and religion? This resembles some of the arguments of Oord and Boyd, and is somewhat appealing intellectually, but robs us of any hope in an ultimate victory of good over evil, and even raises questions about the meaning of these categories.[35] No, we are stuck with biblical ideas of truth, justice, righteousness, mercy, kindness and love and a sovereign God who speaks this language.

So what does the Bible itself have to say about all this? Isaiah declares,

> "I am the Lord, and there is no others.
> I form light and create darkness,
> I bring prosperity and create disaster;[36]
> I, the Lord, do all these things."

(Isa 45:6b-7).

This is a strong affirmation of God's power, control, and rights over all creation. But the context is God's announced decision to raise up and use Cyrus to bring Israel back out of captivity "with an everlasting salvation" (Isa 45:17). The point is that God deserves the credit for this, not any other god or idol. Possibly also Isaiah is countering any Persian-style dualism here which would see events on earth as caused by struggles between various gods, or especially between the good and evil divinities.[37] Even Isaiah sees that there are such heavenly struggles and that view is supported graphically by Daniel's revelations (Dan 10:12-14, 20-21), but finally God's purpose must prevail. Perhaps if we interpret Isa 45:7 in the light of Jeremiah 18, it simply asserts that God acts sovereignly, but justly, in response to human behavior or in pursuance of His gracious plan.

Moreover, this salvation, as envisaged in Isaiah 45, is not only for Israel:

> "Turn to me and be saved,
> all you ends of the earth;
> for I am God and there is no other. . .
> Before me every knee will bow,
> by me every tongue will swear"

---

35. As Castelo says, "Christians have never held to a thoroughgoing dualism although pressures have existed to do so" (*Theological Theodicy*, 38).

36. The KJV reads, "evil", which has led to unfortunate readings of this verse. As Alec Motyer shows, "trouble" or "calamity" is the best translation in this case (*The Prophecy of Isaiah*, 359).

37. Cf. Paul D. Hanson, *Isaiah 40-66*, 102-103.

(Isa 45:22,23).

God is up to good things. He is intending to save the whole world, not just Israel. And He is shaping history, including the political world of empires and wars, to serve this goal. This does not answer every question about evil and suffering, but it does put it in a broader context.

Habakkuk has a similar view, speaking into an earlier situation than Isaiah 44–45, when the kingdom of Judah was still an independent nation. Habakkuk begins by crying out to God about the injustice, violence, strife and wickedness he sees around him (Hab 1:2–4). But he is stunned by the reply he receives to his prayers (Hab 1:6). God plans to use the cruel Babylonians to punish Judah, even though they are even worse than the Judahites and will attribute their victories to their idolatrous gods (Hab 1:13,15–16).

Habakkuk objects, "Is he to keep on . . . destroying nations without mercy?" (Hab 1:17). But God's response is very consistent: all the wicked (both Judah and Babylon) will receive their just deserts and no idol will save them. The Babylonians who have "plundered many nations" will themselves be plundered (Hab 2:8). Justice will be done and God alone will be exalted in a glorious final outcome (Hab 2:13–14).

Let's revisit Job. Job questions, even challenges, God's actions and appeals for God to justify Himself, refusing to accept the pious reasoning of his friends:

> "He destroys both the blameless and the wicked."
>
> (Job 9:22).
>
> "Does it please you to oppress me,
> to spurn the work of your hands,
> while you smile on the plans of the wicked?"
>
> (Job 10:3).

He not only protests about his own suffering but also the sufferings endured by the innocent and poor at the hands of others (Job 24).

But, as every reader knows, when God speaks, He does not explain Himself as we might expect. He basically challenges Job's limited knowledge of things and affirms His own sovereign actions as Creator (Job 38–41).

And Job's protest caves in:

"Surely I spoke of things I did not understand,
Things too wonderful for me to know."

(Job 42:3b).

It may seem like a crushing defeat or servile submission; one submits to God because He has the power. But this is not how the narrative ends. God implicitly affirms Job's right to protest, declaring that Job has "spoken the truth about me" (Job 42:7,8).

Clearly the main point is that, as humans, we have very limited knowledge of God or the circumstances we find ourselves in, and therefore we cannot draw ultimate or dogmatic conclusions about God or His actions towards His creation. We are also called on to submit to God's rights as Creator to govern His earth as He chooses. But Job warns us against a facile and servile conventional theodicy which is just as much the result of ignorance as Job's protest. In fact, Castelo may not be going too far when he says that, "the book of Job serves not so much as a justification of theodicy today but rather as a biblical witness to confound the theodical endeavor overall."[38] Job is right to raise questions as do the authors of the lament psalms. According to leading Old Testament scholar Walter Brueggemann, protests and laments cannot be ruled out of our conversation with God: "To withhold parts of life from that conversation is in fact to withhold part of life from the sovereignty of God." [39]

The Old Testament suggests that God's purposes end well. God has good intentions when He causes or allows pain, even though we cannot always know what they are and cannot even believe that they exist when faced with horrific events and experiences.

When we move to the New Testament, however, we see more clearly what God has *done* about a world infected by evil and experiencing multiple kinds of suffering. The coming of Jesus as "the Word became flesh" who "made his dwelling among us" (John 1:14) means that we could now see God as He really is, not exhaustively but truly, in human form and in a human context. As John writes, "No one has ever seen God, but the one and only Son . . . has made him known" (John 1:18; see also John 14:7,9; 12:45; and 10:30). And the Father's heart is a heart of love (John 3:16).[40]

---

38. Castelo, *Theological Theodicy*, 30.

39. Brueggemann, *Message of the Psalms*, 52, as quoted in Castelo, *Theological Theodicy*, 78.

40. This is the key truth that Jersak gets right in *A More Christlike God*. And it needs emphasizing, though Jersak fails to account for the full revelation of God in Christ as

The Gospels make a point of contrasting Jesus' nature and status as Son of God with his human disadvantages. He was born not in a palace but a stable (Luke 2:7). His parents, like most Jews, were at the mercy of Roman edicts (Luke 2:1–4) and the violent client king Herod (Matt 2:12–20). They became refugees in Egypt and later settled in Nazareth to keep at a distance from the power centers of Judea (Matt 2:14–23). Jesus grew up in a working-class family (Matt 13:55) and did not have the advantage of a rabbinical education (John 7:15). He owned no house (Luke 9:58) and had no fortune, depending on a group of wealthy women for his material support (Luke 8:3). He died a shameful and invidious death after a farcical trial, betrayed by one of his chief followers, denied by another, and deserted by the rest, at least the men. In many ways, Jesus' life and death sum up all that is wrong with the world. Or as Castelo claims, "in Christ God joins Godself to the hurting and the dying."[41]

And yet, in all this God's love for the world is displayed. Jesus deals directly and with compassion to people suffering sickness, demonic oppression, even death. He speaks words of encouragement and forgiveness even to the most unlikely or undeserving people. And he willingly accepts death rather than abandon his flock (John 10:11–15). It is clearly God's will for him to die, and by crucifixion at that (John 10:18; 12:27,33; 3:14; 8:28; Luke 22:20–22,42; Matt 26:23–28). This death is totally unjustified in any legal sense (John 19:4,6; Luke 23:41,47; Acts 13:28); rather Jesus is a kind of scapegoat sacrificed for political expediency (Matt 27:15–26; John 19:1–16).

But Jesus expects more than vindication from his opponents. He expects that his death will glorify God (John 12:28), that it will bear much fruit, that it will lead to a kind of multiplication of his life (John 12:24,32–33), that it will defeat and drive out "the prince of this world" (John 12:31; compare 14:30; 16:11), that it will act as "a ransom for many" (Matt 20:28; Mark 10:45), and that it will release eternal life to all who believe (John 3:14–15). His death will defeat the evil one and release fullness of life to all who believe (John 10:10).

And that is what the rest of the New Testament claims that his death has accomplished. If the root cause of evil in the world is human sin and rejection of God's rule, the death of Christ brings the solution, at least in principle. The death of Christ is also seen to have dealt a mortal blow

---

well as the Old Testament.

41. *Theological Theodicy*, 86.

to the prince of darkness, the biggest single source of evil in this world. Drawing on Gen 3:15, Paul encourages the Romans that, "The God of peace will soon crush Satan under your feet" (Rom 16:20a; see also Col 2:15). By his death and resurrection, Jesus has defeated the powers of darkness and reconciled fallen humanity to God (2 Cor 5:15,18,19). He initiated the new creation that would be fulfilled at the End (2 Cor 5:17). Jesus' death and resurrection begins the inexorable march of the kingdom of God to a perfect world as portrayed in Revelation 21–22. Evil is defeated and will be eliminated when Jesus returns.

Now, of course, this does not look like happening right now and is hard to reconcile with the particularly horrific events of the twentieth century and since. As the story-line of Revelation shows, and as we have seen from time to time in this book, before the glorious new heaven and earth comes, there is a massive struggle between God, His angels and His people on one side and the devil, his angels and his people on the other. Some of the horrors of human history are reflected in the imagery Revelation uses to tell the story and Greg Boyd is right to attribute much of the evil we experience now to this war. But the outcome of this war is guaranteed because of Christ.

John tells his readers,

> After this I looked and there before me was a great multitude that no one could count, from every nation, tribe, people and language, standing before the throne and before the lamb

(Rev 7:9a).

And this vision is explained as follows:

> "These are they who have come out of the great tribulation;
>   they have washed their robes and made them white in the
>   blood of the Lamb. Therefore
> they are before the throne of God
> and serve him day and night in his temple;
> And he who sits on the throne
> will shelter them with his presence.
> Never again will they hunger;
> never again will they thirst.
> The sun will not beat down on them,
> nor any scorching heat.
> For the Lamb at the center of the throne
> will be their shepherd;
> He will lead them to springs of living water.

And God will wipe away every tear from their eyes."

(Rev 7:14–17).

Here we see all kinds of people who have really suffered. But now they are comforted. And the great number implies that this crowd includes people from all ages and places.[42]

There is a similar thought near the end of Revelation:

> "Look! God's dwelling place is now among the people,[43] and he will dwell with them. They will be his people, and he will dwell with them . . . He will wipe every tear from their eyes. There will be no more death or mourning or crying or pain, for the old order of things has passed away."

(Rev 21:3–4).

Death, mourning, crying and pain are experiences of everyone in the present order. But not only will they be removed; God will comfort us for all we have suffered. And finally, "the leaves of the tree (of life) are for the healing of the nations" (Rev 22:2b). This surely means that all traces of suffering and evil will be removed. Hence a biblical theodicy is eschatological in scope.

The doctrine of God's sovereignty as revealed in Scripture thus has implications for constructing a useful theodicy. We are right to raise the issues of suffering and evil as being in tension with a biblical view of God as almighty and good.[44] Job and some of the Psalms do this too. Devout rationalizations do not glorify God. Moreover, the concepts we use to define the 'problem of evil' are themselves derived from God's revelation in the Bible. We must measure our thinking in proportion to our knowledge and realize that we do not understand enough to pass final judgment. As Castelo says, "one is dealing with an entity who is a radically transcendent Other . . . beyond human words, concepts and aspirations."[45]

The metanarrative of the Bible shows us (in a limited way) what went wrong with God's good creation and how God is working towards a great new heavens and new earth (Revelation 21). This Story also includes a real struggle between Good and Evil (God and Satan) but accepts that

---

42. Cf. Newton, *Pentecostal Commentary*, 168–169.

43. Or "peoples"; the Greek is plural.

44. Though, as Castelo points out, these concepts of omnipotence and goodness are hard to pin down (*Theological Theodicy*, 35).

45. Castelo, *Theological Theodicy*, 21.

this struggle was to some extent set up by God, at least as a possibility. The good news is that God has acted in Christ to redeem humanity from human sin and the rule of the devil and reveal the first fruits of a great new creation in which all the sufferings of mortal humanity will be removed.

But in practice, when confronted with other peoples' suffering and tragedy, we should perhaps follow the earlier model of Job's friends who simply wept, "sat on the ground with him" and "no one said a word to him, because they saw how great his suffering was" (Job 2:12–13). This is not just good pastoral advice, but wise apologetics. Too often, like Job's friends, we rush to God's defense when others speak in protest. Perhaps Daniel Castelo is right when he says, in response to authors like Oord, who claim that God *cannot* intervene in painful situations,

> I would rather remain silent than to say in a speculative manner what God cannot do in relation to healing and making right the world. Obviously, God did not prevent the Shoah or any other massive tragedy that comes to mind; rather than futilely defend God on this score, I sense that no other possibility exists outside of silence: a holy, earnest, restless silence, but a silence nonetheless.[46]

---

46. *Theological Theodicy*, 88, n.2.

CHAPTER 7

THE FINAL GOAL

VICTORY OVER DEATH

When we think of divine victory, the adversary is usually seen as Satan, demons, fallen angels or rebellious humans. But the greatest victory celebrated in the New Testament is the victory over death. While in Genesis 2–3, death is seen as the outcome of disobedience (Gen 2:17; 3:3), the genealogical table of Genesis 5 (where everyone lives very long lives) is simply punctuated with the phrase "and then he died." Most of the Old Testament writers assume that all people die and the only outcome after that is *Sheol* or the grave, not exactly a happy hope (Ps 6:5; 30:9; Ps 102:26a; Eccl 7:2; 6:6; 9:2–6,10; 12:1–7)[1] though not necessarily extinction; after all, Samuel can be brought back to pronounce judgment on Saul (1 Sam 28:11–19) and there are hints of a future judgment (Eccl 3:17; 12:14).

The author of Psalm 90 is both realistic and despondent. The limited lifespan of a human being, 70–80 years (v.10) is contrasted with the permanence and eternity of God (vv.1–2,4). Human experience of death is described as returning to dust (v.3), comparable to sleep (v.5a) and the decay of grass (vv.5b-6). Human life, in the light of death, is noted for God's displeasure and wrath due to sin (vv.7–9,11,15) and is seen as altogether miserable: "we finish our years with a moan" (v.9b), "the best of them are but trouble and sorrow" (v.10). In response, the psalmist seeks

---

1. Thus Katherine Sonderegger claims, "the ordering by God has a natural, ordained and fully benevolent end: creatures die" ("The Doctrine of Providence;" in Murphy and Ziegler, eds, *The Providence of God*, 152).

to gain wisdom in some kind of acceptance of mortality (v.12). But he is not satisfied:

> Relent, LORD! How long will it be?
> Have compassion on your servants.
> Satisfy us in the morning with your unfailing love,
> that we may sing for joy and be glad all our days.
> Make us glad for as many days as you have afflicted us,
> For as many years as we have seen trouble
> (vv.13–15)

He has a hope that death is not the end because God's unfailing love will prevail over His anger. The psalmist cries out, "How long?" but sees the long wait for some kind of relief from death as short in comparison with God's eternal perspective: "A thousand years in your sight are like a day that has just gone by" (v.4).

In other places there are more expressions of hope. David, for example, affirms,

> You will not abandon me to the realm of the dead,
> nor will you let your faithful one see decay . . . . .
> you will fill me with joy in your presence,
> with eternal pleasures at your right hand
>
> (Ps 16:9–11).

And Job confesses,

> "I know that my redeemer lives,
> and at the end he will stand on the earth.
> And after my skin has been destroyed,
> yet in my flesh I will see God"
>
> (Job 19:25–26).

So death is not welcomed and hope emerges that there might be something better. Isaiah prophesies,

> On this mountain he will destroy
> The shroud that enfolds all peoples,
> The sheet that covers all nations;
> *He will swallow up death forever*
> (Isa 25:7–8b, emphasis added).

And Hosea is even more direct:

> I will deliver this people from the power of the grave;

I will redeem them from death.
Where, O death, are your plagues?
Where, O grave, is your destruction?

(Hos 13:14).

But only Daniel speaks explicitly of a future resurrection, when it states, "Multitudes who sleep in the dust of the earth will awake: some to everlasting life, others to shame and everlasting contempt" (Dan 12:2).

Whatever all this means, it's very much still in the future. Death, whether seen as God's sovereign agent of judgment (as in the Passover night)[2] or as part of divine providential order or as an anti-God force, is unstoppable, universal, and invincible.

The New Testament, however, picks up the hopeful strands of the Old Testament and builds a strong hope from them. David's words in Psalm 16 are interpreted as fulfilled in the resurrection of Jesus (Acts 2:25–31; 13:35–37), which is seen as the precursor, guarantee and even commencement of the final bodily resurrection of the saints (Acts 4:2; 17:18; 1 Cor 15:20–21). Hence Death is now viewed unequivocally, not as God's punishment but as God's enemy, defeated by the saving work of Jesus:

> This grace was given us in Christ before the beginning of time, but it has now been revealed through the appearing of our Savior, Christ Jesus, who has *destroyed death* and has brought life and immortality to light through the gospel
>
> (2 Tim 1:9b-10, emphasis added).

By God's grace, Jesus' death on the cross took the full force of God's judgment on sin and made death as penalty no longer necessary (Heb 2:9,17; 9:26,28; 1 Cor 15:3; Rom 3:25; 1 John 2:2; 4:10). This was so that "by his death he might break the power of him who holds the power of death–that is, the devil–and free those who all their lives were held in slavery by their fear of death" (Heb 2:14b-15).

Romans 5 spells it out more fully, going back to the beginning to uncover the root of the problem:

> Therefore, just as sin entered the world through one man, and death through sin, and in this way death came to all people, because all sinned (v.12)

---

2. See Piper, *Providence*, 305,337–381, where Piper multiplies examples that show God has the power of life and death.

and

> Death reigned from the time of Adam to the time of Moses, even over those who did not sin by breaking a command, as did Adam (v.14).

In other words, the root problem is not death as such, but sin- "the sting of death is sin" as Paul says elsewhere (1 Cor 15:56a).

So to deal with death, God must deal with sin and this He has done through Christ, through his "one righteous act" (v.18) and "obedience" (v.19) that brings "justification and life" (v.18) and makes many righteous (v.19). This all happens, in other words, by Christ's death for us "while we were still sinners" (v.8). God does not defeat death by superior force but by dealing with the initial reason why it was necessary (Gen 2:17). This is typical of how God defeats His opponents by constitutional means, by means of the rules He Himself has established.

"The last enemy to be destroyed is death" (1 Cor 15:26) after the full triumph of Christ over all his other enemies (1 Cor 15:24-25; Heb 10:12-13), fulfilling the promise spoken through Hosea (1 Cor 15:54-55).

The Book of Revelation unpacks this more visually. The risen Jesus appears to John and proclaims,

> "I am the Living One; I was dead, and now look, I am alive for ever and ever! And I hold the keys of death and Hades."

(Rev 1:18).

Death and Hades still ride and wreak havoc on the earth (Rev 6:8) and the slain martyrs cry out "How long?" and are told to wait for the appointed time (Rev 6:9-11). As with the author of Psalm 90, the wait may seem long to them, but it is just "a little longer" (Rev 6:11) because God's perspective is different: "With the Lord a day is like a thousand years, and a thousand years like a day" (2 Pet 3:8). But eventually, after the thousand years reign of Christ and the martyrs (Rev 20:4), "death and Hades gave up the dead that were in them" for judgment (Rev 20:13) and "death and Hades were thrown into the lake of fire" (Rev 20:14a). Death as the enemy of God and humanity is defeated and annihilated.

ESCHATOLOGY AND GOD'S SOVEREIGNTY

There has been a great resurgence of interest in Christian eschatology during the past two hundred years. This has been fueled by the expectations created by the end of the second millennium, by globalization (making us more aware of the whole planet), by the spread of Christianity across the globe and by threatening developments in world affairs: worldwide wars, new totalitarian regimes, multinational agencies and corporations, and more recently, the decline of the Euro-American world order. Frequently believers have become too focused on what the devil or bad people might be doing or plotting and not focused enough on what God might be doing.

Stanley Grenz claims that, "Strictly speaking God's sovereignty is an eschatological concept,"[3] since the event of the eschaton "will mark the final display of God's rulership."[4] In other words, God's final victory over all opposing forces proves that He is, and always was, sovereign over the universe.

The Bible declares that Jesus himself will personally return from heaven to earth and 'take over.' The timing of Christ's return is subject to God's sovereign call. Jesus himself confessed,

> "But about that day or hour no one knows, not even the angels in heaven, nor the Son, but only the Father."
>
> (Matt 24:36).

And Peter declared,

> "Heaven must receive him until the time comes for God to restore everything, as he promised long ago through his holy prophets."
>
> (Acts 3:21).

However, while the sovereign God, the Father, controls the timing, it appears that the church has some influence upon it. Responding to his disciples' question, "Lord, are you at this time going to restore the kingdom to Israel?" (Acts 1:6), a legitimate question in view of the Old Testament prophets' promises, Jesus redirected their focus from speculating about the future to the mission God had appointed for them: "But

---

3. Grenz, *Theology for the Community of God*, 106.
4. Grenz, *Theology for the Community of God*, 107.

you will receive power when the Holy Spirit comes on you; and you will be my witnesses . . . to the ends of the earth" (Acts 1:8). We may be right to draw from this that Jesus' return will not happen until the job is done.

This thought is more prominent in 2 Peter 3. Peter is responding to scoffers who decry the idea of a second coming because "everything goes on as it has since the beginning of creation" (v.4). Peter points to past cataclysmic events as precedents for the coming "day of judgment and destruction of the ungodly" (v.7). But then he addresses the issue of the apparent delay in the final end:

> But do not forget this one thing, dear friends: With the Lord a day is like a thousand years, and a thousand years are like a day [alluding to Ps 90:4]. The Lord is not slow in keeping his promise, as some understand slowness. Instead he is patient with you, *not wanting anyone to perish, but everyone to come to repentance* (vv.8–9, emphasis added).

The second coming is therefore 'delayed' in order to give people time to repent. Of course, after two thousand years the number of people who are called to repent is much larger, so God's Plan must be bigger, in terms of numbers, than Peter could have grasped.

But then he exhorts his readers, "You ought to live holy and godly lives, as you look forward to the day of God and *speed* its coming" (v.12a, emphasis added). Putting these thoughts together, we might be justified in concluding that the timing of Jesus' second coming is to some degree dependent on the church fulfilling its commission to "make disciples of all nations" (Matt 28:19a). As Michael Green comments,

> The timing of the advent is to come extent dependent upon the state of the church and of society. What a wonderfully positive conception of the significance of our time on earth. . . . . . It is intended to be a time of active co-operation with God in the redemption of society. Our era between the advents is the age of grace, the age of the Spirit, the age of evangelism.[5]

The End is not perhaps fixed, then, in terms of timing. And there may be other developments that must happen before Jesus returns: the appearance of the "man of lawlessness" (2 Thess 2:1–11), the conversion of "the full number of the Gentiles" (Rom 11:25b; see also Rev 7:9), and the conversion of "all Israel" (Rom 11:26). But the final timing still depends on God's decision.

---

5. Green, *2 Peter and Jude*, 153.

Next, the return of Christ interrupts all human plans and expectations. As Paul says,

> The day of the Lord will come like a thief in the night. While people are saying, "Peace and safety," destruction will come on them suddenly, as labor pains on a pregnant woman, and they will not escape

(1 Thess 5:2–3).

The second coming is a massive and unexpected divine intervention, not a development from previous events, but an Event unparalleled in history, that overturns every human system and the natural order of things. Peter puts it this way,

> But the day of the Lord will come like a thief. The heavens will disappear with a roar; the elements will be destroyed by fire, and the earth and everything in it will be laid bare

(2 Pet 3:10).

Jesus said,

> "As it was in the days of Noah, so it will be at the coming of the Son of Man. For in the days before the flood, people were eating and drinking, marrying and giving in marriage, up to the day Noah entered the ark; and they knew nothing about what would happen until the flood came and took them all away. That is how it will be at the coming of the Son of Man."

(Matt 24:37–39).

God exercises His rights over His creation and intervenes with massive power to interrupt normal life and make way for His new creation.

The second coming completes the plan of God with a final climax. Peter preached that, "Heaven must receive him until the time comes for God to *restore everything*" (Acts 3:21; emphasis added). God completes what He began to do in Genesis and restores everything that was damaged or destroyed as a result of the Fall (see Rev 21–22). I find premillennialism problematic because its outline of future events puts the second coming at least a thousand years *before* the final End. But according to the New Testament, the second coming is virtually the last thing in God's program. Consider this passage from 1 Corinthians 15:

> For as in Adam all die, so in Christ all we be made alive. But each in turn: Christ the first fruits; then, when he comes, those who belong to him. *Then the end will come*, when he hands over the kingdom to God the Father after he has destroyed all dominion, authority and power. For he must reign until he has put all his enemies under his feet. The *last enemy* to be destroyed is death

(1 Cor 15:22–26, emphasis added).

This passage is all about the final resurrection (see verses 12–13, 21–23,29–54) and it happens when Jesus comes again (v.23; compare 1 Thess 4:16). Then the "last enemy," death, is defeated (vv.26,54). Jesus is *now* destroying his enemies as he is already ruling at God's right hand (Ps 110:1; Matt 22:44; Eph 1:20–23). Jesus' reign climaxes in his return and then "the end will come," not a thousand years later.

The second coming leads straight into the final judgment. 1 Thess 5:3 speaks of sudden destruction of the unbelieving world. In his second letter to the Thessalonians, Paul spells it out more fully:

> This will happen when the Lord Jesus is revealed from heaven in blazing fire with his powerful angels. He will punish those who do not know God and do not obey the gospel of our Lord Jesus. They will be punished with everlasting destruction and shut out from the presence of the Lord and from the glory of his might on the day he comes to be glorified in his holy people and to be marveled at among all those who have believed

(2 Thess 1:7b–10a).

Jesus himself said,

> When the Son of Man comes in his glory, and all the angels with him, he will sit on his glorious throne. All the nations [or Gentiles] will be gathered before him, and he will separate the people one from another as a shepherd separates the sheep from the goats

(Matt 25:31–32).

This language is very clearly about individual people and their choices, and the outcome is eternal destiny (Matt 25:46).

The second coming and the last judgment pave the way for the new creation, portrayed in Revelation 21 as a beautiful city, a New Jerusalem, a holy community. As Grenz writes,

The final goal of the work of the triune God in salvation history is the establishment of the eschatological community-a redeemed people dwelling in a renewed earth, enjoying reconciliation with their God, fellowship with each other, and harmony with all creation.[6]

FINAL JUDGMENT

A final judgment of all people is the ultimate expression of God's right and power towards human beings as accountable to Him and the ultimate hope of innocent sufferers.

I begin this study in Romans. After introducing the main gospel theme of the letter, Paul spends around two whole chapters (Rom 1:18–3:20) speaking of God's wrath and proving the guilt of all humans, both Gentiles and Jews, idolaters and monotheists, the obviously lawless and the superficially law-abiding. He begins with God's wrath in the present, especially in the Greco-Roman world of his day, where it is expressed largely in God permitting things to get morally worse as He gives rebellious people over to increasingly lawless behavior (Rom 1:18–32). He then argues that so-called righteous people are in just as much trouble since they are frequently hypocrites (Rom 2:1–4).

This leads into a discussion of the future final judgment:

> But because of your stubbornness and your unrepentant heart, you are storing up wrath against yourself for the day of God's wrath, when his righteous judgment will be revealed

(Rom 2:5. Compare Acts 17:31).

There is, then, a future "day of God's wrath," a specific time when God's justice will be shown clearly in action.

Divine justice will be shown in God meting out rewards and punishments relative to each person's merit: "God 'will repay each person according to what they have done.'" (Rom 2:6), says Paul, drawing on Psalm 62:12 and Prov 24:12. A future final judgment is necessary, as in this life, people do not always receive what they deserve. James the apostle is executed unjustly but Stalin dies in his bed full of earthly power and honors. Hitler avoids accountability by committing suicide while his

---

6. Grenz, *Theology for the Community of God*, 115.

victims die painful and cruel deaths. Paul insists that God's judgment will be totally impartial, comprehensive, and fair.

God judges based on the whole direction of a person's life:

> To those who by persistence in doing good seek glory, honor and immortality, he will give eternal life. But for those who are self-seeking and who reject the truth and follow evil, there will be wrath and anger

(Rom 2:7–8).

As Boyd observes, "for better or worse, *we irreversibly become the decisions we make.*"[7] All are judged by this same principle because "God does not show favoritism" (Rom 2:11). However, the measure of guilt and condemnation (or reward) is calibrated to the context of each person; that is, people are assessed in proportion to their knowledge of what God expects (Rom 2:12). Thus many Jews will be condemned for not keeping the Law that they had received and many Gentiles will be commended for living up to their own conscience (Rom 2:13–15). But no one will be able to hide on that day "when God judges people's secrets" (Rom 2:16).

This event is more graphically portrayed in Rev 20:11–15. John sees God on "a great white throne" (v.11) and all the dead people in the world "standing before the throne" (v.12) to be judged. No one escapes, no matter where they have been buried, or not buried (v.13). As in Romans, people are judged "according to what they had done" (vv.12,13). But John adds two other details. First,

> The dead were judged according to what they had done *as recorded in the books* (v.12, emphasis added).

Obviously, God knows everything that everyone has done, even their secrets, but the judgment is based on public records. No one can appeal or complain because this is not a matter of opinion but of evidence. God acts justly according to His constitution or Law and is seen to do so in the end.

Second, John notes that there is only one fate for the wicked, to be "thrown into the lake of fire" (v.15). Moreover, this is not only based on the record of their deeds but on the advance judgment reflected in "the book of life" (v.12), because,

---

7. Boyd, *Satan and the Problem of Evil*, 189 (emphasis in original text).

Anyone whose name was not found written in the book of life
was thrown into the lake of fire (v.15).

On the surface, this seems to contradict the impartiality of God's judgment. God, it might be argued, has a list of favorites and they are acquitted without reference to their deeds. Everyone else must suffer the consequences of their sin. And these names of God's 'favorites' have been written in the Lamb's book of life from the foundation of the world (Rev 13:8), reflecting the election described in Eph 1:4.

But before we rush to the conclusion that God's judgment here is biased, even arbitrary, let's consider, who are these people whose names are written in the book of life? Revelation 13:8 says,

All inhabitants of the earth will worship the beast—all whose names have not been written in the Lamb's book of life, the Lamb who was slain from the creation of the world.

The Greek here can be translated as meaning that the Lamb was slain from the creation of the world *or* that people's names were written in the Lamb's book of life from the creation of the world. Either way, clearly the people we are talking about are identified with the Lamb; their names are in his book because they belong to him. They are true Christians, in other words. And in this passage, they pay a high price for this identity because they, and they alone, refuse to submit to the beast and worship it. They are conquered by that beast. They endure captivity, execution and financial deprivation (Rev 13:10,17). They overcome the seductions of the world (Rev 3:5). There is no 'easy-believe-ism' here. God is not playing favorites but rather rewarding those who have shown total commitment to God and Christ. But this detail in Revelation 20 also underlines one key point: there are only two destinies for those taking part in the final judgment, the lake of fire or the holy city (Rev 21:7–8,27; 22:14–15).

But perhaps you may ask, 'Why are some people excluded from the holy city and cast into the lake of fire? Could not God just forgive them their sins and let everyone in?' I have three issues with this suggestion. First, God's acts of judgment represent His decisions as Judge, not His own personal feelings. God does not condemn people in a fit of pique or frustration because He is personally offended with them. Rather He upholds law and justice. As Custance puts it, "bland forgiveness is tantamount to throwing away the operating principle which governs the universe."[8]

Second, God is the sovereign God not just by power but because He is consistently just, which means that God does not just compromise and 'go easy' on people who should be condemned. Think of Hitler again: how could a just God 'just forgive' him for his cruel and horrible deeds? Would that be just to his victims, for example?

Third, if God allowed people into heaven whose hearts weren't aligned with His, heaven wouldn't be heaven anymore. What makes it heaven isn't just the absence of death, sorrow and pain, but the presence of love and justice and the absence of sin. No one should be in that kingdom who hasn't chosen the lifestyle demanded by it. This is why there has to be a final judgment, to weed out all those whose behavior would spoil it for the rest if they were allowed in (see Matt 13:40–43).

Finally, consider Jesus' own words in Matthew 25. As in Revelation 20, Matthew envisages a scene with a throne and with everyone gathered before it for judgment (vv.31–32). He also agrees with Revelation by dividing all people, specifically the Gentiles,[9] into just two groups (v.32). And the judgment is based on their works, especially on their treatment of Jesus' own "brothers and sisters" (vv.34–45; compare Matt 10:11–15; Mark 9:37,41; Luke 9:50; 10:8–12; 12:4–5,10).

Interestingly, the reactions of those judged may imply that these are unevangelized people, or at least people who are 'outside' the visible community of faith (that is, non-Jews or non-Christians). This supports the hint of Rom 2:14–16 that some Gentiles may be saved apart from knowledge of the gospel. Whether or not this is a fair deduction from this passage, the principle of judgment is clear (vv.40,45). Finally, the outcome is also binary: either "take your inheritance, the kingdom prepared for you since the creation of the world" (v.34) or "Depart from me . . . into the eternal fire prepared for the devil and his angels" (v.41), that is "eternal punishment" versus "eternal life" (v.46).

Note that the reward was prepared for the righteous–God intended to give them the kingdom as an inheritance from the outset (v.34) –but the punishment was not originally prepared for any humans, only for "the devil and his angels" (v.41). The wicked are sent to "eternal fire" not

---

8. Custance, *Sovereignty of Grace*, 338.

9. The Greek does not suggest that these are nations in the sense of countries, but Gentiles as opposed to Jews.

because God ever wanted humans to go there but because they chose, or were seduced, to follow the devil and his ways.

Finally, let's reconsider the universalist passages noted earlier: the innumerable international company seen by John whose robes were "made . . . white in the blood of the Lamb" and who enjoy the blessings of the final creation (Rev 7:9–17); the hope that in the End, "God may be all in all" (1 Cor 15:28), the promise that "all Israel will be saved" after "the full number of the Gentiles has come in" (Rom 11:25–26) since "God has bound everyone over to disobedience so that he may have mercy on them all" (Rom 11:32), the affirmation that "God was reconciling the world to himself in Christ, not counting people's sins against them" (2 Cor 5:19a), and the promise that,

> At the name of Jesus every knee should bow,
> In heaven and on earth and under the earth,
> And every tongue acknowledge that Jesus Christ is Lord,
> To the glory of God the Father
> (Phil 2:10–11).[10]

Paul writes, "just as one trespass resulted in condemnation for all people, so one righteous act resulted in justification and life for all people" (Rom 5:18). This is qualified in verse 17 with the phrase "those who receive God's abundant provision of grace" but would this not include everyone in view of Paul's overall argument in this passage? A similar parallel is found in 1 Cor 15:22, "as in Adam all die, so in Christ all will be made alive."

Other passages are even more wide-ranging. For example,

> for God was pleased to have all his fullness dwell in him, and through him to reconcile to himself all things, whether things on earth or things in heaven, by making peace through his blood, shed on the cross

(Col 1:19–20).

This suggests that Jesus' blood has made reconciliation possible not only for alienated human beings but also for angelic beings. The ancient theologian Origen thought this might even include the devil.[11] Also Eph 1:9–10 speaks of "God's good pleasure, which he purposed in Christ, to

---

10. Other passages include Rom 5:18–19; 1 Cor 15:52; Tit 2:11; and John 12:32.

11. Cf. Markus Mühling, *T & T Clark Handbook of Christian Eschatology*, 315–316; Macchia, *Tongues of Fire*, 414–423.

be put into effect when the times reach their fulfillment–to bring unity to all things in heaven and on earth under Christ."

Macchia writes, "the question of universalism is on a very fundamental level a question of whether or not God's claim on all of humanity at the cross can ever be decisively and forever rejected by people."[12] In other words, if Christ died for all people (as I argued earlier), shall not that result eventually in all people being saved? 'Ultimate reconciliation' is based on the idea that all created beings must be reconciled for God's purpose and victory to be complete. It is sometimes suggested that those who are unsaved at death must spend a period (in most cases a long period) in the lake of fire under chastening *until they truly repent*, at which time they will be released and enter heaven.

Theses is no Scripture passage that specifically says this, however. The nearest might be Isaiah 57:15–21, but this is likely a promise for the repentant among Israel in the time of post-exilic restoration. It still ends with a warning: "'There is no peace,' says my God, 'for the wicked.'" (Isa 57:21). Another passage appealed to is 1 Cor 3:12–15, which speaks of people being saved "even though only as one escaping through the flames" (v.15) after their inadequate works were tested in the judgment and destroyed by that fire.[13] But in context, this is referring only to servants of Christ, such as apostles, building on the foundation of Christ (vv.10–12) and says nothing about people in general.

Ultimate reconciliation is an attractive idea that would help negate the common objection to eternal punishment, that the punishment exceeds the crime. Custance, for example, suggests that every sentence has its end, as suggested in Matt 5:25–26, which speaks of the danger of being thrown into prison such that "you will not get out *until* you have paid the last penny."[14] We could add the parable of the unforgiving servant, whose master "handed him over to the jailers to be tortured *until* he should pay back all he owed" (Matt 18:34, emphasis added). Jesus also suggests that people will have different levels of punishment in hell (Luke 12:46–38),

---

12. Macchia, *Tongues of Fire*, 414. See also ibid., 419–420.

13. Cf. Hart, *That All Shall Be Saved*, 165.

14. Custance, *Sovereignty of Grace*, 338. Jan Bonda mounts a strong biblical argument for something like Origen's view of 'ultimate reconciliation' in *The One Purpose of God*. He contends that the language of final judgment is real, but not final: sinners can still come out of the 'lake of fire' and enter the holy city with its open gates. A similar argument is found in Hart, *That All Shall Be Saved*.

which logically would imply a shorter sentence, implying that hell is not everlasting for everyone.

However, these examples, if taken too literally, would imply that unsaved sinners could be set free *even if unrepentant*, having 'served their time.' This would pollute heaven. Even our morally decadent society is having to face such issues in the case of child sex abusers, who cannot safely be released at the end of their sentences because they will almost certainly reoffend. This also presents a different basis for salvation than in the Scripture passages above, which all ground such a hope in the atoning work of Christ alone. More likely Jesus is using graphic language to show that such unfaithful servants would *never* get out of prison because they could never repay what they owed.

Against all these hopeful arguments and passages we must also consider the language of "eternal punishment" (Matt 25:46) in many places of the New Testament. Many of these are spoken by Jesus in the Gospels, in which he warns his hearers of the enormity of final punishment:

> "Do not be afraid of those who kill the body but cannot kill the soul. Rather, be afraid of the One who can destroy both soul and body in hell."
>
> (Matt 10:28).

> "The Son of Man will send out his angels, and they will weed out of his kingdom everything that causes sin and all who do evil. They will throw them into the blazing furnace, where there will be weeping and gnashing of teeth." (Matt 13:41–42).

> "If your hand or your foot causes you to stumble, cut it off and throw it away. It is better for you to enter life maimed or crippled than to have two hands or two feet and be thrown into eternal fire. And if your eye causes you to stumble, gouge it out and throw it away. It is better for you to enter life with one eye than to have two eyes and be thrown into the fire of hell."
>
> (Matt 18:8–9).

> "whoever blasphemes against the Holy Spirit will never be forgiven; they are guilty of an eternal sin."
>
> (Mark 3:29).

These sayings and others (for example, Matt 24:48–51; 25:30,41; Mark 9:42–49; Luke 12:20,46–48,59; 13:28; 16:22–31; 17:2) may not be meant totally literally, but clearly Jesus is emphasizing the enormity and fearfulness of eternal punishment, and we have no right to tone down the language.

Paul is also insistent on final punishment for the unrepentant, writing "let no one deceive you with empty words, for because of such things God's wrath comes on those who are disobedient" (Eph 5:6) and warning "destruction will come on them suddenly, as labor pains on a pregnant woman, and they will not escape" (1 Thess 5:3). Perhaps his most graphic warning is found in 2 Thessalonians 1:

> He will punish those who do not know God and do not obey the gospel of our Lord Jesus. They will be punished with *everlasting* destruction and *shut out* from the presence of the Lord and from the glory of his might

(2 Thess 1:6–9; emphasis added).

And Revelation seems happy to end its narrative without ultimate reconciliation. Alongside the glory of the new Jerusalem and its inclusion of all kinds of people, there is set the consignment of the wicked into "the fiery lake of burning sulfur" (Rev 21:8), the exclusion from the holy city of "anyone who does what is shameful or deceitful" (Rev 21:27) and "the dogs, those who practice magic arts, the sexually immoral, the murderers, the idolaters and everyone who loves and practices falsehood" (Rev 22:15). Revelation also contains the clearest warning of everlasting punishment in the New Testament:

> If anyone worships the beast and its image and receives its mark on their forehead or on their hand, they, too, will drink the wine of God's fury, which has been poured full strength into the cup of his wrath. They will be *tormented with burning sulfur* in the presence of the holy angels and of the Lamb. And the smoke of their torment will rise *forever and ever*. There will be *no rest day or night* for those who worship the beast and its image, or for anyone who receives the mark of its name

(Rev 14:9–11; emphasis added).

This might cause resistance in the human mind, but God has the right to judge and will judge justly and determine each person's final destiny on the basis of His law.

The theory of ultimate reconciliation has one positive contribution to make, however, even if it fails to make sense of all Scripture. It helps explain why people in hell will remain there. In C.S. Lewis' novel *The Great Divorce*, Lewis puts forward the idea that people in hell have the opportunity to be reconciled to God and exit the grey existence he portrays;[15] however, they refuse to do so unless they can leave on their own terms. It's a story, not an argument, but it suggests that the reason people stay in hell is that they will still not repent.[16] To use the Exodus language, like Pharaoh, their hearts are hardened, a fate that the Bible warns us against repeatedly (Acts 28:25–27; Heb 3:7–4:2; 2 Thess 2:10–12).

It may seem unimaginable that people could be unrepentant forever even in hell, but this may be part of the punishment. Certainly, the idea of ultimate reconciliation of the devil is undermined by Revelation 20. The devil is bound in the abyss for a thousand years (vv.1–3), after which "he must be set free for a short time" (v.3). Even after a thousand years to contemplate his rebellion and its punishment, he is unreformed and goes out to deceive the nations again (vv.7–9) until he is finally "thrown into the lake of burning sulfur, where the beast and the false prophet had been thrown. They will be tormented day and night for ever and ever" (v.10). And the nations are also easily deceived again by him after a thousand years of living under Christ's rule (vv.7–9).

Eternal punishment then is not because God is stubborn and cruel but because people get to a place of hardened hearts that will not, even cannot, change. As Greg Boyd puts it,

> Those who by God's grace used their irrevocable probational freedom as God intended ultimately become irrevocably aligned with him in love, while those who use their irrevocable probational freedom against God become irrevocably set against him in self-absorbed rebellion.[17]

---

15. This idea seem to be based on an ancient idea of *Refrigerium*, a kind of break from torment for those in hell, adapted by Lewis, perhaps under Origenist influence, to claim that "the damned are only damned in so far as they have damned themselves by not choosing salvation in the *Refrigerium*" (Mühling, *Christian Eschatology*, 318).

16. Cf. Macchia, *Tongues of Fire*, 415. Bentley Hart mounts a strong argument against this possibility, contending that no human could ultimately resist God while suffering the purgative suffering of fire (Hart, *That All Shall Be Saved*, especially 171–179). However, his argument is based more on philosophical argument than Scripture.

17. Boyd, *Satan and the Problem of Evil*, 191.

Boyd's comment has a positive implication as well. We can be sure that the redeemed in heaven will be free but will not fall again, like Adam and Eve, because they have become "irrevocably aligned with him in love."[18] They have responded to the sanctifying testing from God as God intended, or at least are doing so, and therefore they "share in his holiness" (Heb 12:10) without which "no one will see the Lord" (Heb 12:14). As Macchia comments,

> As Augustine argued, in correction of Origen, heavenly or risen souls can be viewed as possessing a 'higher' freedom than that which we possess who occupy history. This higher freedom has already conformed perfectly to the will of Christ through overcoming love and has done so in a way that makes a detour from the love of God in Christ unimaginable.[19]

However it all ends, we can be sure that God will be vindicated and His sovereignty fully acknowledged in the end.

THE DESTINY OF THE CHURCH

Church history, as far as human investigation can judge, is a very mixed story. The church has done some great things by spreading the gospel message all over the world with such great outcomes as the abolition of cruel tortures (such as crucifixion), enhancing the place of women in society, creating hospitals, banishing cannibalism, and laying the foundations for modern science and the modern liberal democracy. Christians were in the forefront of campaigns to end the modern slave trade.[20] But these outcomes have to be balanced by such scandals as the crusades, oppression and murder of Jews, the Inquisition and apartheid, to speak only of evils directly attributable to the church or explicitly defended by Christians.[21] The church has also been plagued by division, heresy, fanaticism, complacency, institutionalization, corruption, doubt and unbelief. The church in the Western world experiences declining numbers

---

18. Ibid.
19. Macchia, *Tongues of Fire*, 129–130.
20. Slavery was defended by some Christians in the 18th and 19th centuries when the transatlantic slave trade was at its height, but it was also Christians like John Wesley, John Newton and William Wilberforce who campaigned against it in Britain. Finney and others did the same in nineteenth century USA.
21. For a recent balanced treatment of the good and bad features of church history, see John Dickson, *Bullies and Saints*.

of adherents, with society adopting beliefs and practices contradictory to church or Bible teaching.

Has the church a future, then? The empirical evidence of trends in Western countries may suggest not. Such forlorn trends led John Nelson Darby, a Church of Ireland (Anglican) minister two hundred years ago, to speak of "the church in ruins."[22] But maybe this is too pessimistic an expectation. The church has had many difficult days because of persecution, corruption, false teaching, political alliances and other factors, but it has always been able to renew itself and come out again, sometimes stronger than before. Christianity exploded into western Europe after the fall of 'Christian' Rome, and from there into the non-western world as it was opened up to Europeans, albeit not always in ways consistent with its professed faith. It remains the world's largest religion numerically and is growing strongly in Africa and other nations of the 'majority world.'

However, I want to focus mainly on the biblical witness. Is God determined that the church will end well and can He guarantee this outcome as the Sovereign Lord?

First, let's define what we mean by 'church.' I'm using this word, faithful to its use in the New Testament as I understand it, to mean, not a building nor an organization such as the Roman Catholic Church or the Church of England, but the body of true believers in Christ who have been born again and maintain an active faith by the work of the Spirit. Nothing in the Bible suggests that God is committed to preserve the buildings and organizational structures associated with the church. This New Testament concept lies behind such phrases as the people of God, the saints and the body of Christ.

However, the church is God's idea and He is committed to it. Jesus said,

> "And I tell you that you are Peter, and on this rock I will build my church, and the gates of Hades will not overcome it."

(Matt 16:18).

It is well known that Roman Catholics see this as a promise especially directed to them as a group submitted to the pope as Peter's successor. While the focus on Peter may suggest such an interpretation, it depends on several assumptions which are not supported elsewhere in the New Testament, such as that Peter is the rock or stone on which the church is

---

22. Cf. *New Dictionary of Theology*, 186.

built, a point contrary to Peter's own teaching (1 Pet 2:4–8), that he had a unique and enduring place of authority among the apostles, and that this was then passed on to successive bishops of Rome.

However, this reservation, or clarification, should not cause us to doubt the rest of what Jesus is saying here. Jesus promises to build his church on "this rock." Mostly likely the rock here is the confession of Jesus as Lord as elsewhere Jesus himself is seen as the rock (1 Pet 2:4; Eph 2:20). This church is *his*, a likely contrast to the old idea of Israel as God's congregation led by Moses (Acts 7:38); Christ is its Head (Eph 1:22–23; 4:15). The church is clearly of divine origin and it will be built, an unqualified promise, in spite of resistance from "the gates of Hades." This is linked to the atoning work of Christ. Paul says to the elders of the church in Ephesus that "the church of God" was "bought with his own blood" (Acts 20:29); he later writes that Christ is the Savior of the church (Eph 5:23), which Christ loved and "gave himself up for her" (Eph 5:25).

Therefore the nature of the church is to grow and overcome all opposition. This is illustrated by the narrative of Acts. Acts begins with a fairly small group (120) of Jesus' followers gathered for prayer after Jesus' resurrection and ascension (Acts 1:12–15), but carrying a mandate to bear witness to Christ all over the world by the power of the Holy Spirit (Acts 1:8). The Holy Spirit comes as promised and by the end of Acts, the church has exceeded its Jewish boundaries and crossed into Gentile territory (Acts 10–11; 13–19), eventually reaching Rome itself (Acts 28:14–31).

In order to expand like this, the church had to overcome much resistance, even organized opposition, as well as internal challenges. The church faced opposition and persecution (including violent actions) from the Jerusalem authorities (Acts 4–5), leading to the first martyrdom (Acts 7) and the large-scale campaign led by Saul (Acts 8:1–3). At the same time, there were financial problems that caused internal tensions (Acts 5:1–11; 6:1). After Saul's conversion, he himself faced death threats (Acts 9:23–25,29–30) and the apostle James was executed by Herod (Acts 12:1–2). The expansion of the church among Gentiles had to overcome Jewish prejudices and traditions (Acts 10:13–15,28; 11:2,18; 15:1,5,9), competing spiritual elements (Acts 8:9–13; 13:6–11; 14:11–13; 16:16–18; 17:16–23; 19:13–19, 23–41), and opposition from local Jewish synagogues and Gentile groups and authorities (Acts 13:45,50; 14:4–6, 19–20; 16:19–24; 17:5–9,13; 18:6,12–17; 19:9,23–31; 20:3,19). But Acts continues to tell of the planting of new congregations, geographical expansion, and growth in numbers (Acts 13:42–44; 14:1,21; 17:4,12; 18:8–10; 19:1–10), even in Jerusalem (Acts 21:20).

Even the taking of the gospel to Rome, partly a result of Paul being arrested in a riot in Jerusalem and appealing to Caesar after a drawn-out process of trial in Caesarea (Acts 21–28), fulfills a prophecy that Paul would be "my chosen instrument to proclaim my name to the Gentiles and their kings and to the people of Israel" (Acts 9:15).

Paul's letters also show us a church growing and overcoming every opposing force (Rom 1:5,8,13,16; 9:23–26; 10:14–15; 11:11,15,25,32; 15:8–12,18–21; 16:20,25–26). This growth is not uniform; for example, few converts are made in Athens (Acts 17:32–34) compared to Ephesus (Acts 19:10). But the note is one of growth and triumph, even at some cost in suffering and violence.

All this suggests that the church thus has a glorious future in this age. Dispensationalists tend to reinterpret Acts, focusing on Jewish rejection, and concentrate on the more gloomy predictions of future backsliding and trouble (Acts 20:29–30; Matt 24:12; 1 Tim 4:1–4; 2 Tim 3:1–8). And many Christians, looking at a church that has been divided, often lukewarm, backward-looking, ineffective, oppressive, intolerant and/or powerless, tend to ignore, or even reject, promises of a great future in this age, or put them off into a glorious future after the second coming. But what does Scripture say?

Clearly the letter to the Ephesians will be significant, since this contains Paul's[23] major vision for the church. This vision is anchored in language of election, predestination and the sovereign power of God (Eph 1:3–12), "who works out everything in conformity with the purpose of his will" (Eph 1:11). That is, what God has planned will happen! On this basis, Paul prays that the believers will have their vision expanded by the Spirit:

> I pray that the eyes of your heart may be enlightened in order that you may know the hope to which he has called you, the riches of his glorious inheritance in his holy people, and his incomparably great power for us who believe

(Eph 1:18–19a).

In other words, what they have come into when they believed is much bigger and more powerful than they have understood. This is all

---

23. Many scholars doubt that *Ephesians* was written by Paul, but I am convinced it conveys his heart.

based on the power of the resurrection and exaltation of Jesus "far above all rule and authority, power and dominion, and every name that is invoked, not only *in the present age* but also in the one to come" (Eph 1:21, emphasis added). Note that the present age is not excluded. Already all things are under Jesus' feet, and this is "for the church, which is his body, the fullness of him who fills everything in every way" (Eph 1:22b-23). This places the church very much at the center of what Jesus is doing in this age as he "fills everything in every way."

In order for the church to become what God has planned and fulfill its role in history, two major obstacles had to be overcome. First, the future members of this church were sinful and alienated from God, under the control of the devil and the ungodly world (Eph 2:1–3). And second, the Gentiles among them were also alienated from Israel, God's chosen people (Eph 2:11–12). Both obstacles have been dealt with by the grace of God through Christ (Eph 2:4–10, 13–18). As a result, the believers are "are no longer foreigners and strangers, but fellow citizens with God's people and also members of his household" (Eph 2:19).

There is then a building process going on. The church is "built on the foundation of the apostles and prophets, with Christ Jesus himself as the chief cornerstone" (Eph 2:20) and is in process of becoming "a holy temple in the Lord . . . a dwelling in which God lives by his Spirit" (Eph 2:21–22). This previously hidden secret makes Gentiles equal sharers with Jews in God's plans (Eph 3:3–6) based in God's "eternal purpose" (Eph 3:8–11). In his second prayer in this letter. Paul therefore again prays for his readers to have both experience of, and insight into, the full dimensions of God's plan:

> to grasp how wide and long and high and deep is the love of Christ, and to know this love that surpasses knowledge–that you may be filled to the measure of all the fullness of God

(Eph 3:18–19).

This Plan calls us to a huge vision:

> Now to him who is able to do immeasurably more than all we ask or imagine, according to the power that *is at work within us* [now], to him be glory in the church and in Christ Jesus throughout all generations, for ever and ever! Amen

(Eph 3:20–21; emphasis added).

This power is already in operation in the church, but the possibilities are beyond our comprehension. How can this be and what will it produce?

First, the church has already received "the unity of the Spirit" through the gospel: "one body.... one Spirit....one hope... one Lord, one faith, one baptism; one God and Father of all" (Eph 4:3-6). The members of the church have already received grace gifts (Eph 4:7). The church has received ministry or leadership gifts (Eph 4:11) from the ascended Lord (Eph 4:10). These are great gifts and form a great foundation. However, the church has not yet arrived at its destiny. There is still impatience, strife, division, immaturity and remnants of the old self, as implied throughout this chapter. This is more like the church we see today!

But that is not where God leaves it. God has not given the five special leadership gifts just for show or for them to perform. Rather they are given

> to equip his people for works of service, so that the body of Christ might be built up until we all reach unity in the faith and in the knowledge of the Son of God and become mature, attaining to the whole measure of the fullness of Christ

(Eph 4:12-13).

Think of that! A church that's mature, united and full of Jesus. That's the church Jesus prayed for in John 17:20-23. That's the church we are called to be part of. This is very different even from the actual church Paul was working with. Hence, he continues:

> Then we will no longer be infants, tossed back and forth by the waves, and blown here and there by every wind of teaching and by the cunning and craftiness of people in their deceitful scheming. Instead, speaking the truth in love, we will grow to become in every respect the mature body of him who is the head, that is, Christ. From him the whole body, joined and held together by every supporting ligament, grows and builds itself up in love, as each part does its work

(Eph 4:14-16).

The vision is of a mature and united body full of truth and love, not shifting around according to the latest teaching. We are all responsible to make this happen. But it's also God's promise. Notice the future tenses here: this will happen!

In the next chapter, while discussing Christian marriage, Paul gets caught up in a great vision again:

> Christ loved the church and gave himself up for her to make her holy, cleansing her by the washing of water through the word, and to present her to himself as a radiant church, without stain or wrinkle or any other blemish, but holy and blameless

(Eph 5:25-27).

Christ is looking forward to a perfect church, in other words! Now often this is seen as a kind of instantaneous transformation at the time of the second coming. The poor, imperfect, unholy, divided, 'ugly little duckling' church suddenly becomes this glorious bride! That doesn't seem like the process Paul was explaining earlier. Instead this outcome is promised by God *in this age*, though not without a struggle, as Eph 6:10-20 portrays.

I see a similar story in Revelation. John begins with Jesus' prophetic words to seven typical churches who are a mixture of good and bad, not only buffeted by outside hostile forces but failing in their responsibilities as Christ's body in many cases, due to complacency, laziness, tolerance of false teaching and compromise (Revelation 2-3). But at the end of the story, we see the beautiful bride of Christ much as Paul saw (Rev 19:7-8; 21:2,9-11). What has happened in between? Amongst other things, this narrative shows the church becoming the bride through almighty struggles with pagan religion and culture and oppressive political and economic forces. The beautiful bride is only seen at the End. But God is working out His purpose even through the hard struggle.

How can this be? How can the church display in practice that it is "one holy, catholic and apostolic church," as the Nicene Creed confesses? Many Christians believe it's based on the correct organization, either by "apostolic succession" (Roman Catholics, Eastern Orthodox and many Anglicans) or by eldership (Presbyterians) or by congregational government or by some newly restored apostolic order as espoused by many Pentecostals (Eph 2:20). Other believers, especially evangelicals, believe correct doctrine is more the key to the church God wants. Most Pentecostals see the work of the Spirit as the most important point. Others consider moral holiness to be the main issue. And the modern ecumenical movement has focused instead on bringing visible unity to the church, seeing division as the main roadblock to God's will (John 17:22-23).

I think all of these are important,[24] but they focus largely on what people should do. And indeed the "fine linen" that is given to the bride "stands for the righteous acts of God's holy people" (Rev 19:8). But we mustn't downplay the work of Christ as the primary Builder (Matt 16:18), the head (Eph 1:22-23), and the "cornerstone" (Eph 2:20).

When we look at the empirical history of the Christian church, it seems messy, confused and lacking direction. So some believers are inclined to start all over, since it was 'obviously done all wrong,' at least after the time of the apostles. Instead, the sovereignty of God and Christ may help us to read things differently and see His hand at work, even when things were at their darkest and most chaotic. It may also lead us to work with the Spirit on the *actual* church with its flaws and divisions. Because one thing seems clear to me: God has not given up on the church, and nor will He. Indeed,

> All things are yours, whether Paul or Apollos or Cephas or *the world* or life or death or the present *or the future*–all are yours, and you are of Christ, and Christ is of God.
>
> (1 Cor 3:21b-23, emphasis added).

As Paul says elsewhere,

> And we know that in all things God works for the good of those who love him, who have been called according to his purpose
>
> (Rom 8:28).

The church is so central to God's purpose that He captures all things to fulfill His plan for His 'called'" ones. As John Webster argues, building on Calvin,

> Because the end of creation which providence protects is the fellowship of God's rational creatures with himself, then general and special providence (i.e. God's care for the world in general and for all humankind) are subordinate to singular providence (God's care for the elect or the Church).[25]

---

24. This debate focuses on the 'marks' of the true church. The Creed speaks of "one holy catholic and apostolic church." Each of these words is loaded and debated among Christians. For a good discussion, see Grenz, *Theology for the Community of God*, 468-472 and Macchia, *Tongues of Fire*, 347-362.

25. "On the Theology of Providence" (in Murphy and Ziegler, eds., *The Providence of God*), 169.

Pentecostals and charismatics are hungry for the visible presence and moving of the Spirit. We are often desperate to see supernatural events occurring and to feel the presence of God. We are convinced that it is far better to have 'false fire' than no fire and the one thing we do not want to become is like the church in Laodicea, those lukewarm, complacent, self-sufficient, half-hearted Christians. But the danger is that we try to *make* it happen. We try to stir up, preach up, manipulate or organize revival and experience. The end is worthy, but the end does not justify the means.

Pentecostals are at their best when they display a hunger and openness to the sovereign Spirit. As Daniel Castelo puts it,

> Pentecostals inhabit their identity with a very important conviction.... that the God of Ancient Israel and the God revealed in Jesus Christ is a God who could appear at any time and at any place... there is no person, experience, or situation that is out of the reach of God's gracious and providential hand. [26]

But we must not identify good vibes and emotions with the Spirit. Belief in the sovereignty of God, in fact a truly biblical view of God, should cause a deeper response. Castelo again:

> There is something inherently beautiful but also quite sacred and terrifying about the divine presence in worship, and no description, either lightly and flippantly suggested or seriously and ponderingly offered, can adequately do it justice. After all, this is the God who not only struck blatant sinners like Ananias and Sapphira (Acts 5); this God also struck Uzzah who, in responding to a potential crisis, was simply 'trying to help' the Ark along (1 Chron. 13.9–10). Most of us would think that the examples of Ananias and Sapphira do not apply to us, but what about the case of Uzzah?[27]

The story of Uzzah certainly emphasizes the sovereignty of God in terms of God's rights to dictate the rules. It also illustrates powerfully the kind of response an experience of God can evoke–"sacred and terrifying."

I still recall a time I came into a Pentecostal service and was suddenly so struck by God's presence that I did not know 'where to put myself' or how to respond. It was not the result of the music or the worship

---

26. Castelo, "An Apologia for Divine Impassibility: Toward Pentecostal Prolegomena"; *Journal of Pentecostal Theology* 19 (2010), 122.

27. Castelo, "Apologia", 123.

leader. It was unexpected and awesome in the original sense of that overworked word. I have felt the presence of God in overwhelming ways in both Pentecostal and non-Pentecostal services and even in non-church settings. But I don't feel Him all the time. The Spirit is truly free and uncontrollable.

The opposite danger is a kind of Reformed passivity. We speak reverently of what God in His sovereignty may do and are not too bothered if He apparently does nothing. This may be based on simple trust but it can be complacency or even traditionalism. Paul encourages us to submit to the Spirit's lordship since "he distributes them [spiritual gifts] to each one, just as he determines" (1 Cor 12:11), but also to "eagerly desire gifts of the Spirit, especially prophecy" (1 Cor 14:1). Surely he would only say that if such gifts were available to us, though, as D. Martyn Lloyd-Jones points out, we need to be discerning of claims and experiences claimed to be of the Spirit.[28]

Pentecostals are also restorationists. They want to restore the church to its original pristine spiritual condition, if not better, especially in terms of the power of the Spirit. Here they are part of a long tradition that goes back at least to Luther and includes the Anabaptists, Puritans, Wesleyans, Churches of Christ and some extreme groups like Jehovah's Witnesses. Many of these streams have focused, at least in part, on church structure. The Puritans wanted to do away with bishops. Wesley brought in Methodist classes and challenged the Anglican parish system. Pentecostals originally were more focused on renewal than reformation, but the Latter Rain movement of 1948 and the earlier Apostolic Church called for a reform of church governance and structures based largely on Eph 4:11, including a recognition of modern apostles.

I have a lot of sympathy with all this. But experience has taught me that you can't humanly restore the church in that way and every attempt to do so usually leads to more division, sectarianism and even cultish control. Self-appointed apostles, for example, can be controlling and damaging, as many churches in Africa are experiencing. The development of the Christian church in history is very messy and complex and even contradictory, but we have to trust the Holy Spirit to persist without giving in to a Uzzah-like temptation to put out our hands to 'steady the ship' and without uncritically accepting every development either.

---

28. Lloyd-Jones, *Prove All Things*, 58–61.

PART TWO

THEOLOGICAL AND PRACTICAL DISCUSSION

IN THIS PART OF the discussion, I want to explore what the biblical truth of God's sovereignty means for us today both in terms of theology and practice. What picture does it give of God in relation to His creation, and especially human beings? How should we act in response to this vital reality?

Let's review what we are asking here.

How is **God's freedom** to act preserved and expressed in the current era in which Christ has come and defeated the enemy, and all people can respond to the gospel, but in which sin, evil, death and Satan still operate?

Second, how are **God's rights** over all His creation asserted and expressed today, and how should they influence our actions as believers?

Third, how far does **God's rule and guidance** of events extend in a world full of anti-God elements?

And fourth, **what kind of sovereignty** does God exercise?

CHAPTER 8

GOD AND OTHER ACTORS

JOHN PIPER STATES THE obvious when he says, "There are other wills in the universe besides God's."[1] In the biblical survey, we have explored how the creation of, and choices made by, non-God actors (angels and humans) affect the sovereignty of God. God's sovereignty operates in a different context after the Fall compared to the pre-Fall situation. The victory of Christ in his death and resurrection, and later in his second coming, also changes everything in a different way.

We need to account for the presence of created intelligent beings with a measure of autonomy or free will. Without them, God's sovereignty could act in an uncomplicated, unimpeded way, as it presumably did before creation (if the language of 'before' makes sense) and before the first rebellion against God's commands.

Christian theologians (at least in the Protestant world) have explained the situation mainly in one of three ways:

1. *Calvinist theologians* have emphasized the sovereignty of God in each of the three senses I identified in the Introduction and subjected all other factors and forces to it in their theology. All things, including sin and the operation of the devil, are ordained (in some sense) by God. God's will and grace are never frustrated. For example, God saves exactly all the human beings He has chosen to save, regardless of their merits, and (implicitly at least) predestines the others to perdition.

---

1. Piper, *Providence*, 255.

2. *Arminian theologians* tend to place almost equal emphasis on God's sovereignty and the freedom of angels and humans to choose their own actions. God has ordained the direction of history but does not override people's free will. While He foresees who will respond to His grace, for example, He does not predetermine their responses, and therefore His love can be frustrated by stubborn resistance on their part.[2]

3. *Open Theists* take the Arminian position a step farther. They emphasize the free will of non-God actors even where this seems to restrict God's sovereign freedom or control or God's ability to foresee their free decisions. God adjusts His plans in line with the acts of non-God actors, who are able to resist and even frustrate God's will, without God completely losing control of events.[3]

Perhaps the simplest way of focusing these differences is around the idea of risk. Does God take risks in how He relates to other actors like humans and angels? Paul Helm, for example, argues for a "no-risk" view of divine providence, in which everything that God wills to happen will certainly happen,[4] whereas Open Theists insist that human and angelic freedom imply that God takes risks with regard to their decisions.[5] Underlying this debate is another issue, the nature of creaturely freedom. Helm argues, as do most Calvinists, that human freedom has to be compatible with God's total sovereign control of events, whereas other argue for a more non-deterministic idea of creaturely freedom which is inconsistent with total divine control, and perhaps even with divine foreknowledge, of human (or angelic) choices.

I think each of these positions has some merit and none completely explains the situation or accounts fully for the biblical material which we have just surveyed. So, here. I explore the issues raised in more detail, revisiting the biblical passages surveyed previously and asking new

---

2. Cf. Mildred Bangs Wynkoop, *Foundations of Wesleyan-Arminian Theology*, on the development of Arminian theology.

3. Process Theology takes this step even farther by arguing that God is always changing, learning and growing and that God has goals that He works towards, not all of which may be successful, even in the non-human creation as in the process of evolution (cf. Michael Lodahl, "Divine Sovereignty in the Process Theological Tradition", in Long and Kalantzis, ed., *Sovereignty Debate*, 75–96). This is too radical a change from the traditional Christian view for me to consider here.

4. Helm, *Providence of God*, 39–55.

5. John Sanders has even written a book with the title *The God Who Risks*.

questions. And we cannot allow strict logic to determine what we think. Strict logic starting from a truth or assumption and building on it may lead us astray in a way that ignores or downplays inconvenient passages of Scripture. For example, Pinnock critiques Calvin as follows: "Calvin's logic was impeccable as usual: God wills whatever happens so if there are to be lost people, God must have willed it. It was as logically necessary as it was morally intolerable."[6] However, Pinnock's use of words like "morally intolerable" betrays his own logical starting point; Arminians and Open Theists are frequently guilty of doing the same thing as Calvinists.

THE NATURE OF GOD

Before we discuss the other players in the scheme of reality, it is worth taking a little time to consider what we have been learning about God Himself from this study. T.F. and J.B. Torrance rightly argue that "In order to understand *how* God acts in salvation, it is necessary to first ask *who* God is."[7] Much of the theological discussion in the past has focused on deductions about God's nature from certain biblical and philosophical/theological principles. I want to base my discussion explicitly on Scripture, not on isolated 'proof texts' but the narratives and overall teaching of the Bible. The study in Part 1 of this book has already taken certain directions that may help you anticipate what I think. But it is appropriate for me to state those thoughts specifically and consider the issues involved.

False antitheses abound in this arena. As we have seen, Clark Pinnock expresses a common thought found in Open Theism when he writes, "Is God the absolute Monarch who always gets his way, or is God rather the loving Parent who is sensitive to our needs even when we disappoint him and frustrate some of his plans?"[8] Parallel in some ways is John Piper, who expresses a common Calvinist understanding, writing, "Does God's grace put us in a position of having ultimate self-determination in our conversion? Or does it overcome all our rebellion and blindness so that we are drawn triumphantly by the beauty of Christ to embrace

---

6. Pinnock, "Introduction" (in Pinnock, ed., *Grace of God and Will of Man*), 19.
7. Radcliff, *Claim of Humanity*, 18, emphasis in the original.
8. Pinnock, "Introduction" (in Pinnock, ed., *Grace of God and Will of Man*), ix. In a similar antithesis, Fretheim speaks of "monarchical" versus "organismic" images of God's relationship with the world (*Suffering of God*, 35).

what is true?"[9] Both of these antitheses, in my view, overstate the case, misrepresent the opposite view, and oversimplify the biblical picture.

Open Theists have challenged what they see as the traditional doctrine of God based on a synthesis of biblical revelation and ancient Greek philosophy. Whether or not you accept their conclusions, they have done the church a favor by raising fresh questions and forcing us to reconsider ideas we may have accepted uncritically. Feminist and liberationist scholars have also challenged traditional theism in other ways that may provoke fresh thinking. So here I want to consider some key questions that relate to our investigation.

To begin with, *is God self-sufficient?* Does God need anything from His creatures, humans in particular? Pagan or polytheistic religion would say a definite 'Yes': the gods require *and need* sacrifices, prayers, liturgies, and the like, if not to exist, certainly to operate fully. Some ancient Greek philosophy would instead affirm that the divinity is self-existent and self-sufficient because any other picture would portray God as less than perfect.

Fretheim argues that, "The world is not only dependent upon God; God is also dependent upon the world,"[10] a view often called 'panentheism'. But Paul in his address to the Athenians, says,

> "The God who made the world and everything in it is the Lord of heaven and earth and does not live in temples built with human hands. And he is not served by human hands, *as if he needed anything*. Rather, he himself gives everyone life and breath and everything else."

(Acts 17:24–25, emphasis added).

In other words, we need God, but God doesn't need us.

A similar note is sounded in Psalm 50. Here God speaks to Israel, whom God had commanded to offer various sacrifices of animals and vegetable products, reminding them,

> "I have no need of a bull from your stall
> or of goats from your pens,
> for every animal of the forest is mine,
> and the cattle on a thousand hills . . . ..
> If I were hungry I would not tell you,

---

9. Piper, *Providence*, 553.

10. *Suffering of God*, 35. This is a form of panentheism which views God as indwelling the universe as his 'house.'

for the world is mine, and all that is in it."

(Ps 50:9,10,12).

However, the psalmist goes on,

"Sacrifice thank offerings to God,
fulfill your vows to the Most High,
and call on me in the day of trouble;
I will deliver you, and you will honor me."

(Ps 50:14–15).

God may require sacrifices for a time, but He doesn't *need* them. Rather the psalm emphasizes thanksgiving and calling on God, both of which actions acknowledge our dependence on God and His faithfulness in providing our needs.

On the other hand, perhaps Ware goes too far when he claims "receive, he cannot do!"[11] Certainly nothing we can do or bring can add anything to God's nature or perfection. As Paul says, "Who has ever given to God, that God should repay them?" (Rom 11:35). And David exclaims regarding the collection for the temple,

"But who am I, and who are my people, that we should be able to give as generously as this? Everything comes from you, and we have given you only what comes from your hand."

(1 Chron 29:14).

But God did *ask* His people for such offerings (Hagg 1). And God does desire worship and praise from humanity and He is therefore willing to 'receive' such offerings as the history of sacrifice in the OT illustrates (e.g. Gen 4:4; 8:21; Lev 1; Ps 51:16–19) and NT teaching confirms (John 4:23; Rom 12:1; Rev 4:11).

We have seen that God delegates authority and agency to angels and human beings and largely works through them rather than ignoring them. Does God therefore *need* their help? Did God need Abraham to start the line of Israel and Christ? Did God need Moses to get His people out of Egypt? Did God need Jonah to go to Nineveh, since He insisted on him going there with the warning of judgment? Does God need our tithes and offerings, or prayers, to keep His kingdom operating today?

---

11. *God's Greater Glory*, 139.

The strict answer to these questions, and others like them, is 'No.' Rather God graciously invites us into partnership with Him. He simply *will not* do some things *unless* we act, in prayer or obedience. God is almighty–He can do anything that is not self-contradictory, illogical or immoral–but He limits Himself frequently (though not always) to working with and through creatures like us. He didn't *need* Moses to be the spokesperson and deliverer of Israel from Egypt. He didn't *need* Jonah to go to Nineveh and shock the people into repentance. But He refused to do it any other way. He wrestled both of them to a place of obedience (Exod 3–4; Jon 1), and in Moses' case God even compromised with the stubborn person He was calling by appointing Aaron as Moses' spokesperson (Exod 4:13–16).[12] And that is how God normally operates in relation to humanity because of how He set things up in the beginning (Gen 1:26–28).

In other words, God wants us involved in His plans even though He doesn't actually need us. As Bruce Ware says,

> *The God of the Bible loves and seeks us out with such eagerness and persistence when he himself stands in no need whatever of the objects of his love.*[13]

Second, is God subject to change? Or is all 'change' ascribed to God an anthropomorphism (a human way of speaking imprecisely about God)?

We need to clarify the question: Does God change His mind? Several statements in the Bible tell us that "God is . . . not a human being, that he should change his mind" (Num 23:19 and 1 Sam 15:29b), and that "the Father of the heavenly lights. . . . does not change like shifting shadows (James 1:17).

But we also read of a prophet telling the high priest Eli, "'I promised that members of your family would minister before me forever.' *But now the Lord declares, 'far be it from me!..... The time is coming when I will cut short your strength. . .*'" (1 Sam 2:30,31, emphasis added). Also that, "The Lord *regretted* that he had made human beings" (Gen 6:6) and "I *regret* that I have made Saul king" (1 Sam 15:11). More positively, "Then the Lord *relented* and did not bring on his people the disaster he had threatened" (Exod 32:14), and "When God saw what they did and how they turned from their evil ways, he *relented* and did not bring on them the

---

12. Clark Pinnock, "Systematic Theology" (in Pinnock et al, *The Openness of God*), 116.

13. "Modified Calvinist," 85 (emphasis in original text).

destruction he had threatened" (Jon 3:10).¹⁴ Clearly God does change His announced intentions in response to changes in people's actions towards Him (see also Jer 18).¹⁵

But He does this *because of* certain *unchanging* features of His nature. Hence Jonah responded to God's change of mind in relation to Nineveh, saying,

> "I knew that you are a gracious and compassionate God, slow to anger and abounding in love, a God who relents from sending calamity."
>
> (Jon 4:2).

R.T. Kendall points out that this is grounds for hope: God may threaten judgment but He may yet grant mercy if we respond rightly.¹⁶ As the Ninevite king said, "Who knows? God may yet relent and with compassion turn from his fierce anger so that we will not perish." (Jon 3:9).

When we hear that God doesn't change his mind in 1 Sam 15:29, the point is He has just done exactly that, declaring that Saul would no longer be king, on the basis of His righteous judgment. God always acts consistently with His unchanging nature as God. Hence God is reliable, faithful, dependable, not fickle or changeable in His moods. As Clark Pinnock puts it,

> God is unchanging in nature and essence but not in experience, knowledge and action. ... not ... subject to change involuntarily, which would make God a contingent being, but. ... God allows the world to touch him, while being transcendent over it.¹⁷

Or as philosopher Ronald Nash says,

> Attributing immutability to God should not be taken to mean that God cannot change in any way. It means only that God cannot change with regard to His first-level properties; God cannot change with respect to His nature or character.¹⁸

---

14. Emphasis added in these verses.

15. Cf. Nathan MacDonald, "From Augustine to Arminius, and Beyond," in Gray and Sinkinson, eds., *Reconstructing Theology*, 34. See also the balanced discussion in Kendall, *Jonah*, 201–210.

16. Kendall, *Jonah*, 204–210.

17. Clark Pinnock, "Systematic Theology" (in Pinnock et al, *The Openness of God*), 118.

18. *Concept of God*, 101.

But when God changes His mind, is this because He learns something new and, in a sense, 'grows'? Such questions can be answered two ways, it seems. God is all-knowing and perhaps cannot learn anything new, but He also changes His operations in response to new situations. However, the kind of growing deity envisaged by Process Theology pushes the envelope too far, in my opinion, and sometimes Open Theists travel close to that boundary, as when Richard Rice writes,

> He [God] affects them [humans], and they, in turn, have an effect on him. As a result, God's life exhibits transition, development and variation.[19]

The Bible offers believers a more stable God than that as the focus of their faith. As Hebrews puts it,

> Remember your leaders, who spoke the word of God to you. Consider the outcome of their way of life and imitate their faith. Jesus Christ is *the same* yesterday and today and forever
>
> (Heb 13:7–8, emphasis added).

And Psalm 102:27 says, "But you remain the same, and your years will never end," giving us a similar assurance that God can be relied upon in a context where everything else is always changing. As Robert Morey writes, "It means that when we pray, we pray to the *same* God twice."[20]

More significantly, however, did God change in the incarnation? Certainly God did not become less divine when Jesus came as "the Word became flesh" (John 1:14a), but He did become, as it were, more human. While Jesus was both God and human, he was and is one person. So it is not inaccurate to suggest that a man has entered the Godhead or even to describe Mary as 'the mother of God.'[21] In some sense, we can even speak of God suffering on the Cross (2 Cor 5:19 NKJV),[22] though strictly this suffering was borne by Jesus the man. Never before had deity been united to humanity in a single Person. It was a huge change, in other words. But

---

19. Richard Rice, "Biblical Support for a New Perspective" (in Pinnock et al, *The Openness of God*), 22.

20. Morey, *Battle of the Gods*, 211.

21. This was a title ascribed to Mary in the ancient post-apostolic church and became the springboard of debates about Christ's nature as God.

22. A theme developed strongly by Jürgen Moltmann in his book *The Crucified God*. cf. Nancy Elizabeth Bedford, "'God's Power is God's Goodness': Some Notes on the Sovereignty of God in Jürgen Moltmann's Theology" (in Long and Kalantzis, ed., *Sovereignty Debate*, 97–110).

it was not that God became better or worse than before, or more or less divine, or somehow different in His nature or ways, because that kind of change would mean that Jesus was not really God. The idea that God might stop being loving or just or immortal or almighty is unthinkable.

Another question is, *does God have real relationships?* Once again, we need to clarify the question. Do 'real' relationships require a measure of 'give and take' between those involved? Can a relationship between fundamentally unequal parties be 'real?' It's clear that there are real relationships within the Godhead: the Father, the Son and the Holy Spirit are One but also Three 'Persons'[23] in mutual love and harmony. It's also clear, surely, that there is real relationship between God and all His creatures, if only the relationship of Creator-to-creature or Provider-to-dependent or Lord-to-subject. [24]

Are there any reciprocal relationships in which the creature affects the Creator in some way? The Bible seems to say, "Yes." For example,

> when the LORD saw how great the wickedness of the human race had become on the earth, and that every inclination of the thoughts of the human heart was only evil all the time, the LORD regretted that he had made human beings on the earth, and *his heart was deeply troubled*
>
> (Gen 6:5–6, emphasis added).[25]

Here we see God being deeply and emotionally affected by the behavior and intentions of human beings, to the point where He decided to wipe them out (Gen 6:7). Contrary to this, after the Flood, we read of Noah making a sacrifice to God and the LORD smelled the pleasing aroma and said in his heart: "Never again will I curse the ground because of humans, even though every inclination of the human heart is evil from childhood" (Gen 8:21). And we have previously noticed God compromising with Moses (Exod 4:13–16) and "bargaining" with Abraham (Gen 18:23–32).

---

23. I put this in quotation marks because the English word 'person' does not do justice to the members of the Trinity or translate accurately the Greek *hypostasis* or the Latin *persona*. The members of the Trinity are not individuals as humans experience individuality.

24. But such relationships are qualitatively different from relationships among humans. Cf. D. Stephen Long, "Aquinas and God's Sovereignty," in Long and Kalantzis, ed., *Sovereignty Debate*, 53–56.

25. Cf. Fretheim, *Suffering of God*, 112.

Clearly then, God can be affected and influenced by what we do. God is not untroubled by our sin; in fact His Spirit can be "grieved" by our rebellion (Isa 63:10). However, we need to be careful here not to envisage God feeling things in the same sense that humans do.[26] Our emotions are related to, and influential on, our physical states. God is a spirit without such physicality or limitations. Our emotions are often fickle and can motivate us to act irrationally. That isn't so with God.

Equally clearly, such relationships between God and humans are not equal. We do not bring much at all to a relationship with God. We depend on God, not the other way around. But relationships between God and His people are often portrayed by analogy with ordinary human relationships with God acting analogously with the senior or 'powerful' partner. Thus God is Israel's husband and Israel His wife (Jer 2:1; Ezek 16:8–14; 23:4–5; Hos 2:7,16,19,20; compare Eph 5:23), their desertion is compared to adultery or prostitution (Jer 2:32–3:3; Ezek 16:15–19; 23:3–8; Hos 1:2; 2:2–5) and God threatens to 'divorce' them (Hos 2:2). In the book of Hosea, we get to feel God's agony over his relationship with Israel.[27]

The most significant term for this relationship is covenant. In the ancient world, this word was used for treaties between nations, marriage (Mal 2:14) and friendship alliances (1 Sam 18:3–4). The book of Deuteronomy is shaped like a treaty between a superior nation and a weaker ally or subject people.[28]

The first specific covenant in the Bible is between God and the earth after the Flood (Gen 8:9–17). But the most important covenant in the Old Testament, if not the whole Bible, is the one God initiated with Abraham. Like all covenants involving God, God takes the initiative; He is sovereign and free to enter or not enter such commitments. In Genesis 15, God makes a unilateral promise to Abraham, an old man whose wife was infertile, of a son and multiple descendants (vv.1–5), and then of a land for those descendants (v.7). Abraham responds in faith and thus gains a new status before God (v.6).

But when Abraham asks how he can be sure of the land promise, God starts the work towards a covenant-making ceremony: bring some

---

26. Cf. Vincent Bacote, "John Calvin on Sovereignty" in Long and Kalantzis, ed., *Sovereignty Debate*, 66–67.

27. Cf. Richard Rice, "Biblical Support for a New Perspective" (in Pinnock et al, *The Openness of God*), 24.

28. Cf. Longman and Reid, *God is a Warrior*, 49.

animals, cut them in two, arrange them in order (vv.9-11). Normally the two covenant parties would walk between the pieces, whose death symbolizes the unbreakable commitment being made, and they would make oaths to one another of loyalty to this relationship. But this would not be an equal covenant. Instead, God puts Abraham to sleep, reiterates the promise with more details (vv.12-16) and walks between the pieces alone:

> "When the sun had set and darkness had fallen, a smoking firepot with a blazing torch appeared and passed between the pieces" (v.17).

Then God alone makes the oath and establishes the covenant (v.18).[29]

God does it all, and freely, and He sets the terms of the covenant unilaterally as God.[30] But once that is done, God is 'bound' by that covenant as much as Abraham and his descendants. As Fretheim says,

> God has exercised divine freedom in the making of such promises in the first place. But, in having freely made such promises, thereafter God's freedom is truly limited by those promises.... God will be faithful to God's own promises....[31]

Hence years later, when the enslaved Israelites "groaned in their slavery and cried out" (Exod 2:23),

> God heard their groaning and he *remembered his covenant* with Abraham, with Isaac and with Jacob, So God looked on the Israelites and was concerned about them
>
> (Exod 2:24-25, emphasis added).

It was a real, but unequal, relationship. To put it another way, God has friends in the human race (Isa 41:8; James 2:23; John 15:13-15), but He is still the only God.

Does God force people to do what He wants or does He limit Himself to wooing or persuasion? The overwhelming testimony of the Bible is that God does not force anyone to do His will. He has created human beings as free and He does not take back the freedom of choice which He gave

---

29. Cf. Wenham, *Genesis 1-15*, 332-335.

30. According to T.F. Torrance, this covenant was unconditional (Radcliff, *Claim of Humanity*, 23-24.)

31. *Suffering of God*, 36.

us at the start.³² So when we looked at election, we saw that God does not compel anyone either to follow Jesus, or not.

Two points arise, however. Doesn't the rich man send his servants out to get more guests to his banquet with the words, "compel them to come in" (Luke 14:23)? This verse has been used by some Calvinists to support the idea of irresistible grace. It has also been used since Augustine's time to support the use of force on unbelievers and heretics as in the Inquisition. Not a good history for a statement that is part of a parable and never reiterated anywhere else. It's fairly clearly not to be taken literally. How would a servant literally force people into a banquet anyway? And clearly the refusal of the original guests to come was respected, as was the decision of the younger son to take his inheritance early and abandon his father in another famous parable (Luke 15:12–13).

But does God not *influence* people to do His will? Clearly He does, and sometimes quite forcefully. God would not accept Jonah's decision to run away and get a ship to the opposite end of the world so as not to have to go to Nineveh. The storm and the great fish come very close to force. But when God speaks a second time to Jonah, the prophet must still decide to obey (Jon 3:1–3).

God has many ways of influencing people in the Bible: prophecies, both genuine and fake (Isa 7:1–9; 1 Kings 22:19–23), dreams (Gen 20:3–9), omens (Ezek 21:18–23), supernatural signs (Isa 7:10–17), healing miracles (Acts 3:1–4:4), reasoning (Acts 18:4), heart conviction (Acts 2:37) and others. In the prophets, we read of God promising to work on the hearts of Israel to cause them to follow His ways (Deut 30:6; Jer 31:31–34; Ezek 11:19–20; 36:26–27).³³

Mostly these interventions 'work' in that the recipients do what God intends, but not always. The people of Lystra, for example, saw a powerful healing, misinterpreted it in terms of their polytheistic worldview, and eventually turned against the people who had brought such a powerful message to them (Acts 14:8–20). The Jerusalem Jews of Jesus' day likewise failed to respond: "Even after Jesus had performed so many signs in

32. Calvinists and Arminians debate about the nature and extent of such freedom, of course, using language such as 'compatibilist' and 'libertarian' to define free will more closely in relation to their idea of God and humanity. I'm not entering this debate here. For more detail, see Ware, ed., *Perspectives on the Doctrine of God*, especially 159–172 and P.W. Gooch, "Sovereignty and Freedom: Some Pauline Compatibilisms" (*Scottish Journal of Theology* 40: 531–542).

33. Cf. Nathan MacDonald, "From Augustine to Arminius, and Beyond" in Gray and Sinkinson, eds. *Reconstructing Theology*,37.

their presence, they still would not believe in him" (John 12:37). This is explained as a kind of judicial punishment in fulfillment of two Isaianic prophecies (John 12:38-40) but the language of v.37 suggests that God (or the author) wanted them to believe.

A similar verdict is given on the towns in Galilee which had seen mighty miracles and not repented (Matt 11:20-24) and on the city of Jerusalem as a whole (Luke 13:34-35). Here Jesus says, "how often I have longed to gather your children together, as a hen gathers her chicks under her wings, and *you were not willing*" (Luke 13:34b, emphasis added). In other words, God calls, woos and influences, but He doesn't compel anyone to respond *against their will*.

But this doesn't leave God somehow dependent on humanity. As Don Richardson explains, with a touch of hyperbole:

> Persuasion, not compulsion, is what even He must rely upon! And persuasion, by its very definition, must be resistible! Yet the God who thus renders Himself resistible is so intelligent that He can overrule every consequence of His own self-limitation with ease! Working around and even through human resistance as easily as through response, He still achieves His own eternal goals![34]

A further question, *does God suffer?* Terence Fretheim argues strongly that God, as portrayed in the Old Testament, does suffer in terms of His relationship with human beings. God suffers when human beings reject Him; He suffers with His people as a sympathetic mourner; and He suffers for His people.[35] To borrow from Jersak's book title, Fretheim tries to portray the Old Testament deity as 'a more Christlike God.'[36]

Fretheim's argument is based on constructing a less domineering, more immanent, model[37] of God than found in some traditional theology, one that he considers more faithful to the Old Testament itself.[38] His discussion considers assumptions about real relationships (as discussed

---

34. Richardson, *Eternity in Their Hearts*, 195.

35. *Suffering of God*, 107-148.

36. Fretheim explains that he is explicitly reading the Old Testament with a similar goal (*Suffering of God*, xv, 2-5).

37. Or metaphor. Fretheim insists that "metaphors matter" (cf. *Suffering of God*, 5-12).

38. Fretheim bases this in part on generalising statements such as Exod 34:6-7 (*Suffering of God*, 24-28).

above),[39] the limitations of divine foreknowledge,[40] the nature of God's presence in the world and humanlike theophanies,[41] and the representation of God by and in His prophets.[42]

More importantly, Fretheim offers a close reading of Old Testament passages (especially in the Prophets) that arguably describe God as suffering because of Israel's unfaithfulness.[43] For example, in Jeremiah 2 the prophet speaks for God:

> This is what the LORD says:
> "I remember the devotion of your youth.
> How as a bride you loved me
> And followed me through the wilderness" (v.2)

But then,

> "What fault did your ancestors find in me,
> that they strayed so far from me?" (v.5a)

And,

> "Why do you bring charges against me?
>
> You have all rebelled against me" (v.29)

And,

> "Have I been like a desert to Israel.
> or a land of great darkness?
> Why do my people say, 'we are free to roam;
> we will come to you no more?'" (v.31)

Fretheim comments, "the lament-accusation cries of 'Why?!' have no answer. His abandonment make no sense, even to God, and never will."[44] He considers passages that show God's compassion for Israel when she is suffering, even because of her sin (e.g. Isa 54:7-8, Jer 31:20; Judg 2:18) and how God adopts the role of mourner (e.g. Amos 5:1-2; Jer 9:10;

---

39. Cf. *Suffering of God*, 34-37. Fretheim extends this discussion into philosophical topics such as the relationship of God to time and space (*Suffering of God*, 37-44).

40. *Suffering of God*, 45-59.

41. *Suffering of God*, 60-106.

42. *Suffering of God*, 149-166.

43. *Suffering of God*, 109-126.

44. *Suffering of God*, 116. Similar passages explored in *Suffering of God* include Isa 1:2-3; 65:1-2; Jer 3:19-20; 18:13-15; Mic 6:3; and Hos 11:1-4.

12:7), even sometimes for Gentile nations (e.g. Jer 48:30–32,35–36).[45] Third, there are passages that show God suffering on behalf of Israel, being 'burdened' by their sin (e.g. Isa 43:23–24; 63:9; Jer 15:6) and yet delaying punishment (e.g. Isa 42:14; 48:9).[46] Here he comments,

> It is clear that human sin has not been without cost for God, and that cost is due in significant part to the fact that God has chosen to bear the people's sins rather than deal with them on strictly legal terms.[47]

Finally, prophets themselves feel God's pain at the rejection and imminent judgment of Israel (e.g. Jer 4:19; 8:18–9:1).[48] Fretheim insists on allowing these passages to speak literally of God's suffering.

Other theologians have taken issue with Fretheim here. Weinandy, for example, spends a whole monograph arguing against the idea of a suffering God. His argument is complex and philosophical, drawing especially on the work of Aquinas. But his position is not as different from Fretheim's as might be thought. Weinandy is willing to allow that God might be said to suffer provided that this is not taken to mean a substantial change in God. "God does not grieve or sorrow because he himself experiences some injury or the loss of some good, nor that he has been affected, within his inner being, by some evil outside cause" but because He knows of human suffering and "embraces them in love."[49]

I find some aspects of Fretheim's argument unconvincing; for example, his embrace of a panentheism that makes God dependent on the world somehow.[50] But, if I understand him correctly, Fretheim is not portraying God as a kind of victim of human perfidy. God suffers voluntarily. He chooses to limit his sovereignty, not abandon it, out of love for his creatures. He creates the world that will cause Him to suffer in the first place. Fretheim speaks of

> . . .a self-limitation with respect to divine sovereignty, because the future of the creation, and, indeed, the future of God is made dependent in important ways upon how the creatures respond

---

45. *Suffering of God*, 127–137.
46. *Suffering of God*, 138–148.
47. *Suffering of God*, 148.
48. *Suffering of God*, 154–166.
49. Weinandy, *Does God Suffer?*, 169.
50. *Suffering of God*, 35.

with the power they have. Therefore, one must speak of divine risk *and* vulnerability, beginning with creation.[51]

This is still controversial but not as extreme as some might think.

Finally, *is there a single 'root metaphor' that should be central to our view of God?* Part of the debate stirred up by Open Theism relates to the idea of a central 'root metaphor,' which Open Theists commonly view as a choice between God as Judge or Monarch and God as loving Father. As Clark Pinnock puts the alternatives,

> Two models of God in particular are the most influential that people commonly carry around in their minds. We may think of God primarily as an aloof monarch, removed from the contingencies of the world . . . or we may understand God as a caring parent with qualities of love and responsiveness, generosity and sensitivity, openness and vulnerability. . .[52]

But perhaps this is a false dichotomy. Clearly Jesus encourages his followers to see and trust God as their heavenly Father. But is a Being who is *just* a loving Parent deserving of worship and obedience? Is such a person God? When John declares that "God is Love" (1 John 4:16), I think he is assuming his readers already know God as the almighty Lord of the Old Testament.[53] And he has previously affirmed that "God is light; in him there is no darkness at all" (1 John 1:5b). Elsewhere we read that "God is a consuming fire" (Heb 12:29, quoting Deut 4:24).

The danger of privileging the Father image or "God is love" at the expense of the full picture of God in Scripture is that we end up with a partial, truncated, and therefore false, view of God. And then we are doomed to disappointment when God does not act as we hoped; for example, when He doesn't intervene to save us from pain. Moreover, when we concentrate on God as Father, we are in danger of bringing in a false concept of fatherhood too, one that owes more to postmodern western culture than ancient or biblical concepts. According to Heb 12:5–11, fatherhood includes discipline and chastening. The Fatherhood of God in

---

51. *Suffering of God*, 74–75; emphasis in the original text.

52. Pinnock, "Systematic Theology," 103. Comp Rice, "Biblical Support for a New Perspective," 18; Oord, *Uncontrolling Love*, 144–149

53. As Castelo contends, "Often, what is suggested or taken from this phrase [God is love] depends on an understanding of 'love'; however, the terms 'God' and 'is' are just as important (if not more so) for this statement's meaningfulness" (*Theological Theodicy*, 45).

the New Testament is not set *against* the concept of God as Sovereign Judge and King.[54]

On the other hand, such images do serve to qualify and clarify what kind of judge and king God is, and Jesus models this clearer picture as the one who has pre-eminently revealed the Father (John 1:18; 14:9). Jesus' concept of God and His kingdom is worlds apart from that of the power-driven society of his day. Thus, intervening in a dispute among his disciples about pre-eminence, he says,

> "The kings of the Gentiles lord it over them; and those who exercise authority over them call themselves Benefactors. But you are not to be like that. Instead, the greatest among you should be like the youngest, and the one who rules like the one who serves. For who is greater, the one who is at the table or the one who serves? Is it not the one who is at the table? But I am among you as one who serves"
>
> (Luke 23:25–27).

The metaphors that portray what God is like need to be held together to get the full picture.[55]

INVISIBLE CREATION: ANGELS AND DEMONS

We have already established that God has delegated authority over the earth to human beings. But this reflects more broadly the way that God rules. To put it very simply, God delegates and governs consultatively: He listens to counsel and appeals from his creatures.

As we will explore later, this is a core aspect of prayer.

But God apparently works with an invisible 'parliament' of spiritual beings, sometimes called "the sons of God" (Job 1:6 mg).[56] Psalm 82 speaks of gods who seem to have authority over human nations: "God presides in the great assembly; he renders judgment among the 'gods'"

---

54. Cf. Nathan MacDonald, "From Augustine to Arminius, and Beyond" in Gray and Sinkinson, eds. *Reconstructing Theology*, 36–48.

55. Bradley Jersak's book *A More Christlike God* is a good case here. Jersak rightly seeks to correct a lot of conventional thinking and emphasize the Fatherhood of God (ibid., 19–22). However, he doesn't interact seriously with portrayals of God as King and Judge in Scripture.

56. The NIV translates "angels" but the Hebrew is literally "sons of God."

(v.1).[57] They are also called "sons of the Most High" (v.6). But these 'gods' seem very human by the end of the psalm: "the 'gods' know nothing, they understand nothing" (v.5a) and "you will die like mere mortals, you will fall like every other ruler" (v.7). The "princes" of nations referred to in Daniel 10–12 are perhaps an example of this.

A story that illustrates the working of this 'council' is found in 1 Kings 22. Ahab, the wicked king of Israel, forms an alliance with Jehoshaphat, the godly king of Judah, to attack the king of Aram (Syria) and recover a lost territory in Ramoth Gilead (vv.2–4). Jehoshaphat, however, calls for them to "seek the counsel of the LORD" (v.5) before they proceed with the attack. So Ahab trots out his court prophets who predictably promise victory (v.6). But Jehoshaphat is not satisfied, and the reader of 1 Kings would also be suspicious, given Ahab's hostility to God and His prophets. Jehoshaphat asks, "Is there no longer a prophet of the LORD here whom we can inquire of?" (v.7). Ahab replies that there is one, but he "never prophesies anything good about me" (v.8).

So they call for Micaiah, who is urged by the messengers to be positive (v.13) and reluctantly gives Ahab an optimistic answer (v.15). This time Ahab is suspicious (v.16) and now Micaiah gives him a significant revelation:

> "I saw the LORD sitting on his throne with all the multitudes of heaven standing around him on his right and on his left. And the LORD said, 'Who will entice Ahab into attacking Ramoth Gilead and going to his death there?'
>
> One suggested this, and another that. Finally, a spirit came forward, stood before the LORD and said, 'I will entice him.'
>
> 'By what means?' the LORD asked.
>
> 'I will go and be a deceiving spirit in the mouths of all his prophets,' he said.
>
> 'You will succeed in enticing him,' said the LORD. 'Go and do it.'
>
> So now the LORD has put a deceiving spirit in the mouths of all these prophets of yours. The LORD has declared disaster for you."
>
> (1 Kings 22:19–23).

Clearly God is using this 'devious' method to execute Ahab. God's sovereignty in the spirit world is also demonstrated here. But look more

---

57. Cf. Meadowcroft, "Sovereign God or Paranoid Universe?", 114. Meadowcroft suggests that this reality lies behind naming God as "the Lord of hosts" (ibid., 115).

closely. When Micaiah exposes the heavenly scheme, he is giving Ahab (or Jehoshaphat) a good excuse to change plans. So in fact, the decision is still Ahab's. Moreover, God's decision that he must die is fully justified by the events of 1 Kings 16–21, especially the judicial murder of Naboth in 1 Kings 21, immediately before the incidents we are reading. So this is in many ways a 'typical' story of God's sovereignty in action in judgment.

In Daniel, we have a glimpse of forces opposed to God. The second half of Daniel consists largely of visions granted to Daniel, often using 'apocalyptic' imagery (Dan 7–8), often as a result of his prayers for the future of Israel (Dan 9–10). Daniel's first long prayer for Israel is prompted by his reading of Jeremiah's prophecy of the exile (Dan 9:2). In it, he takes God's stand against the wickedness of his own people (Dan 9:4–16), before pleading for favor and restoration (Dan 9:17–19). The angel Gabriel brings him a quick response (Dan 9:21–23), but it is not perhaps the answer he wants as the restoration would be longer, more complex and more conflicted than Jeremiah predicted (Dan 9:24–27). This was God's decree (Dan 9:24) and it was necessary because of the inbuilt wickedness of the people. Hence

> "Seventy 'sevens' are decreed for your people and your holy city to finish transgression, to put an end to sin, to atone for wickedness, to bring in everlasting righteousness. . ." (v.24).

But the second prayer leads to a different experience. In both prayer times Daniel resorts to fasting in his appeal (Dan 9:3; 10:3). In both cases an angel is sent to respond to Daniel's prayers (Dan 9:23–25; 10:4–11). In both cases his prayer is immediately heard and an answer dispatched (Dan 9:23; 10:12). But in the second case, Daniel has to keep praying for three weeks before the answer arrives (Dan 10:2). The delay is caused not by any deficiency in Daniel's praying but by a heavenly spiritual conflict. As the angel explains,

> "But the prince of the Persian kingdom resisted me twenty-one days. Then Michael, one of the chief princes, came to help me, because I was detained there with the king of Persia."

(Dan 10:13)

Moreover, there is ongoing conflict:

> "Soon I will return to fight against the prince of Persia, and when I go, the prince of Greece will come. . . . No one supports me against them except Michael, your prince . . . ."

(Dan 10:20–21).

So the resistance to the restoration of Israel comes not only from human forces or God's judgments. There are hostile and powerful spiritual or angelic forces at work who can only be defeated by prayer or superior angelic forces. Michael, "the great prince who protects your people" (Dan 12:1), and the other angel of Daniel 10 (Gabriel again?) fight for Israel against the angelic princes of Persia and Greece. The context implies that the fortunes of Israel depend on the outcomes of such fights. But the note of God's sovereignty is still found in the events predicted and the times indicated for these events (Dan 9:24–27; 10:21; 12:9–12; and previously in Dan 7:23–27; 8:26). It is also implied by the role of Daniel's praying in the narrative, which suggests that the outcomes of these struggles depend finally on *God's* decisions, because Daniel's prayers are directed to God's throne.

There is real spiritual resistance to God's plans but it is grounded, at least partly, in the sinful responses of the humans and can only be overcome when the sin is dealt with (Dan 9:24). The prophecy hints that this will involve the death of the coming Messiah: "the Anointed One will be put to death and will have nothing" (Dan 9:26) and "will put an end to sacrifice and offering" (Dan 9:27).

Paul may well have this background in his mind when he writes to the church in Ephesus,

> For our struggle is not against flesh and blood, but against the rulers, against the authorities, against the powers of this dark world and against the spiritual forces of evil in the heavenly realms

(Eph 6:12).

Christians need to put on the armor of God to protect themselves as they go into battle against these forces (Eph 6:11,13). They must especially be diligent in prayer like Daniel (Eph 6:18–20). But the final outcome of this war is not in doubt because of God's "eternal purpose that he *accomplished in Christ Jesus our Lord*" (Eph 3:11, emphasis added).

Col 1:16 tells us that "in him (Christ) all things were created: things *in heaven* and on earth, visible and *invisible*, whether thrones or powers or rulers or authorities."[58] There are heavenly creatures, invisible to us, who exercise some level of power and authority.

58. Emphasis added.

Not all spirits function as advisers nor are they all evil. Angels are agents of God who serve His purposes. They are "ministering spirits sent to serve those who will inherit salvation" (Heb 1:14). All the way through the Bible we read of angels bringing messages and commissions (Judg 6:11–23; 13:3–21; Matt 1:20–24; 2:13,19–20; 28:2–7; Luke 1:11–20,26–38; 2:8–15; 24:4–7; Acts 27:22–24; Rev 1:1; 10:1–11; 14:6–12; 18:1–3; 19:9; 22:6, 16), rescuing God's people (Gen 19:1–22; Acts 12:6–10), interpreting dreams and visions (Dan 8:15–26; 9:21–27; 10:4–21; Rev 17:1–18; 21:9–22:5), giving support to people in difficult times (Matt 4:11; Luke 22:43), praising God (Luke 2:13–14; Rev 5:11–12; 19:1–3), executing God's judgments (Rev 7:1–3; 8:2–6; 14:14–20; 15:6–16:1; 20:1–3), and fighting against evil forces (Dan 10:13,20–21; Rev 12:7–9). God chooses to work through these spirit beings, including the mysterious cherubim and seraphim and the "living beings" seen in the visions of Ezekiel (Ezek 1:4–24) and John (Rev 4:6–8).

The book of Revelation gives us a more pictorial, though highly imaginative and symbolic, window into the heavenly world. Revelation's "four living creatures" are engaged in ceaseless praise like the seraphim (Rev 4:8–9; Isa 6:3). They also mediate God's program by giving instructions to the four horsemen as the Lamb breaks the seals of the great scroll (Rev 6:1,3,5,7). There are also twenty-four elders who have thrones and crowns of their own (Rev 4:4), though they are constantly falling down in worship and casting down their crowns before God's throne (Rev 4:10–11; 7:11–12; 11:16–18). They also interpret aspects of John's vision (Rev 7:13–14). All these spirit beings, whatever they are precisely, serve God's sovereign plans and worship the sovereign ruler. But clearly there are anti-God spiritual powers at work, and the Bible seems to imply a prehistoric "fall" of angelic beings, though it sees their operations as severely restricted (2 Pet 2:4; Jude 6).

Since the emergence of the charismatic renewal in the 1960s, there has been a lot more attention to spiritual beings among evangelical Christians, provoking two somewhat different views of the spirit realm in relation to God's sovereignty. Tim Meadowcroft is wary of some charismatic teaching and practice about demons; for example, teaching on spiritual warfare and curses, elaborate manuals about demonology and 'deliverance' and the concept of 'territorial spirits.'[59] While not rejecting all such ideas completely, Meadowcroft emphasizes the subordination

---

59. He is probably contesting ideas of C. Peter Wagner, who coined this phrase. See Wagner, *Book of Acts*, 442.

of the spirit realm to God as 'Lord of hosts' and the subjugation of the demonic realm to Christ especially after Calvary.[60] He argues,

> Exorcisms in the Gospels . . . take place as demonstrations of the inauguration of the Kingdom of God, not as part of a spiritual battle on the outcome of which the Kingdom is somehow dependent.[61]

And, drawing on Col 2:10,15, he continues, "Whether loyal or rebellious, all things are under Christ's lordship and subject to the purposes of the Lord of hosts."[62] Therefore Christians should not attribute all issues in believers' lives to demons or feel the need to try and rescue people from evil influences or defeat evil powers by forms of spiritual warfare.[63]

From almost the opposite perspective, Greg Boyd in *God At War* takes the existence and operation of ungodly spirits more seriously and suggests that the operation of such spirits (including the devil) helps explain the presence of evil events in the world. He argues for a biblically derived "warfare worldview" which he defines as,

> that perspective on reality which centers on the conviction that the good and evil, fortunate or unfortunate, aspects of life are to be interpreted largely as the result of good and evil, friendly or hostile, spirits warring against each other and against us.[64]

He argues further,

> For all their emphasis on the radical uniqueness, sole eternality and absolute sovereignty of Yahweh, biblical authors generally assume the existence of intermediary spiritual or cosmic beings. . . . (who) can and do wage war against God, wreak havoc on his creation and bring all manner of evils upon humanity.[65]

And more explicitly,

> God's good creation has in fact been seized by hostile, evil, cosmic forces that are seeking to destroy God's beneficent plan for the cosmos. God wages war against these forces, however, and through the person of Jesus Christ has now secured the

60. "Sovereign God or Paranoid Universe?" 117, 124–127.
61. "Sovereign God or Paranoid Universe?" 121.
62. "Sovereign God or Paranoid Universe?" 122.
63. "Sovereign God or Paranoid Universe?" 125–126.
64. Boyd, *God At War*, 13.
65. Boyd, *God At War*, 18.

overthrow of this evil cosmic army. The church as the body of Christ has been called to be a decisive means by which this final overthrow is to be carried out.[66]

This view challenges one aspect of God's sovereignty as I defined it at the start of this book:

> God is not now exercising exhaustive, meticulous control over the world. . . . God must work with, and battle against, other created beings. While none of these beings can ever match God's own power, each has some degree of genuine influence within the cosmos. . . . There is no single, all-determinative divine will that coercively steers all things . . . .[67]

How far does either Boyd or Meadowcroft reflect the biblical perspective, especially in relation to the sovereignty of God?

Let's consider a powerful story from Acts 19. The apostle Paul has arrived in the city of Ephesus, the largest city in the Roman province of Asia (v.1). Previously he had been "kept by the Holy Spirit from preaching the word in the province of Asia" (Acts 16:6) and had cut short an earlier visit to Ephesus, promising, "I will come back if it is God's will" (Acts 18:21). This implies that his eventual ministry there is being directed by God, especially in terms of its timing.

Paul's return visit begins with ministry to a small group of "disciples" who knew only the baptism of John the Baptist and whom Paul leads to faith in Jesus (vv.1–5). This core group receives the Holy Spirit through the laying on of Paul's hands (v.6). Paul then goes into the Jewish synagogue, as he regularly did, and spends three months there "arguing persuasively about the kingdom of God" (v.8b). After a while, the opposition from those not persuaded by Paul gets too hot and Paul leaves: "He took the disciples with him and had discussions daily in the lecture hall of Tyrannus" (v.9b).

Paul's ministry over a two-year period is singularly powerful: "All the Jews and Greeks who lived in the province of Asia heard the word of the Lord" (v.10) and "God did extraordinary miracles through Paul, so that even handkerchiefs and aprons that had touched him were taken to the sick, and the illnesses were cured and the evil spirits left them" (vv.11–12). Clearly God's power is being released in an extraordinary way subject to God's sovereignty. But the means being used are the same

66. Boyd, *God At War*, 19.
67. Boyd, *God At War*, 20.

as Paul employs everywhere: testifying and preaching about Jesus and praying for people's needs.

Next, there is a confrontation with the powers that dominate the city. Ephesus was known as a center of sorcery as well as the location of the famous temple to the goddess Artemis.[68] Therefore there were many people under demonic influence, even oppression, and seeking relief. The next incident reported in this passage is about some Jewish exorcists who tried to use the seemingly powerful name of Jesus, as preached by Paul, to evict such demons. But they got a shock when,

> One day the evil spirit answered them, "Jesus I know, and Paul I know about, but who are you?" Then the man who had the evil spirit jumped on them and overpowered them all. He gave them such a beating that they ran out of the house naked and bleeding (vv.15–16).

We see here the real destructive power of demons and their subjection to, and respect for, Jesus. But Jesus' name was not available for use as a kind of magic formula in the way sorcery usually works. Only those 'licensed' to speak in His name could do so with authority and protection from the demonic power. But next we see how God uses this situation:

> When this became known to the Jews and Greeks living in Ephesus, they were all seized with fear, and the name of the Lord Jesus was held in high honor (v.17).

Moreover, this led to a deeper work in the new converts to Christ, who now renounced their sorcery and burned their sorcery texts (vv.18–19) and "in this way the word of the Lord spread widely and grew in power" (v.20). Demonic forces are real and will bind people with illnesses and other oppressions. They are no match for Jesus who has "disarmed the powers and authorities . . . triumphing over them by the cross" (Col 2:15). However, the way this is displayed and effective here is unique and guided by the sovereign hand of God.

This story is sometimes described as a 'power encounter,'[69] a confrontation between God and evil powers. Such events have been repeated in various ways over time. They illustrate the fact that evil powers exist and should be confronted and are, in fact, powerless before the work of God in Christ. But this confrontation needs the obedience and boldness

---

68. Cf. Wagner, *Book of Acts*, 429
69. Cf. Wagner, *Book of Acts*, 435

of a servant of Jesus subject to the guidance of the sovereign Spirit. The story also shows us that the ultimate strategy for victory in such situations is 'the word of the Lord,' that is, the gospel message of Christ preached in the power of the Holy Spirit.[70]

Of course, the story does not end with this powerful breakthrough. There is a strong pushback from those involved in the temple of Artemis. The advance of the gospel both geographically and spiritually, a move of the Spirit both wide and deep, threatens the spiritual powers centered on Artemis worship as perhaps they have never been threatened before. The economy of Ephesus is bound up with this cult (vv.24–27) and those who benefit make a very loud and threatening protest (vv.28–34). But God protects His people, not through eloquent speeches (vv.30–34) but through the intervention of the city clerk. Paul has had a major impact on "the officials of the province" (v.31) and God uses that, rather than miracles or preaching, to protect him.

As we saw earlier, God works with, through and around the actions of sinful humans, and even evil spirits, and is able to bring victory, not by eliminating the enemies but by outflanking them and demonstrating the victory of Jesus. Thus Boyd is right to argue that spirits are real and active and perhaps to resist the idea of 'meticulous control,' but Meadowcroft is right to warn against too much emphasis on spiritual warfare and to focus on the sovereignty of God in how we approach such conflict. To understand this better, however, we need to consider the chief opponent of God.

SATAN AS PLAYER

The origins of Satan or the devil are shrouded in mystery. Many orthodox believers see in the Old Testament prophets a story of a fall of Satan from a position in God's intimate court, motivated by his[71] ambition (Isa 14:13–14) or pride (Ezek 28:12–17), an event thought to have happened before God's creation of humanity. This makes sense, even though the biblical passages referred to speak explicitly only of the kings of Babylon and Tyre respectively. Both use language that seems to go beyond what is appropriate for a human ruler. In Isaiah 14, we read of "morning star,

---

70. See discussion in Bock, *Acts*, 602–605.

71. I use masculine pronouns by convention but obviously they only apply in a very approximate way.

son of the dawn" (v.12; traditionally "Lucifer" as in KJV) who plotted to ascend to the heavens and "raise my throne above the stars of God" (v.13) and even "make myself like the Most High" (v.14).

In Ezekiel 28, the king was "full of wisdom and perfect in beauty" (v.12) and "you were in Eden, the garden of God" (v.13), being "anointed as a guardian cherub" (v.14); but "your heart became proud on account of your beauty, and you corrupted your wisdom because of your splendor" (v.17). Depicting the king as a cherub *in Eden* suggests perhaps that he was the original serpent and perhaps *Satan's* fall happened in the garden when he started to question God's word.[72] Paul also writes of conceit as a cause of the devil's judgment (1 Tim 3:6).

In both cases the kings are "brought down to the realm of the dead, to the depths of the pit" (Isa 14:15) or thrown down to earth (Ezek 28:17), doomed to suffer "a horrible end and. . . . be no more" (Ezek 28:19). Both passages are enigmatic but can probably be read as referring to the ambition and pride of human empires, inspired by Satanic spirits. This would be parallel to the heavenly "princes" of Daniel 10:13 and 20, the sea beast of Revelation 13 and the devil's boast of control over the earth's kingdoms (Matt 4:8–9; Luke 4:5–6). Revelation 12 describes a heavenly war leading to the defeat and 'casting out' of the dragon (identified as "that ancient serpent called the devil, or Satan" in verse 9), but it doesn't appear to be a primeval event, as the passage attributes Satan's defeat to "the blood of the Lamb and . . . the word of their [disciples'] testimony" and the witnesses' willingness to die (v.11).

However, Jude writes of "angels who did not keep their positions of authority but abandoned their proper dwelling" and as a result these God "has kept in darkness, bound with everlasting chains for judgment on the great Day" (Jude 6; compare 2 Pet 2:4). It does seem that that there was at some point a 'fall' or rebellion of a group of angels who had been created to serve God. The enigmatic passage about "sons of God" cohabiting with human women and the Nephilim (Gen 6:1–4) may refer to such an event as some ancient Jewish apocalypses suggest. So the idea of a prehistoric fall of Satan makes sense.

The Bible portrays the devil as God's opponent (Gen 3:14–15) and presents the scenario of a struggle between God and the devil that comes

---

72. Eugene Rogers comments that "Adam overreached himself and sought divinity as something to be grasped" (*After the Spirit*, 41), based presumably on Gen 3:5 where the serpent promises Eve, "you will be like God." Thus Adam and Eve imbibe the spirit of the "morning star" of Isa 14:12–14.

to a head with Jesus' death and resurrection, but will only be fully resolved after Jesus' second coming. In this sense we may say that "God is a warrior"[73] and affirm what Greg Boyd calls a "warfare worldview."[74]

But the devil is also seen in Scripture as subject to God's sovereignty, as a kind of (unwitting) tool or servant of God. As Calvin remarked, "the devil and his crew are not only fettered, but also curbed and compelled to do service."[75] The Bible does not support a full-on ontological dualism where evil and good are equally powerful or eternal.

As we saw in the previous section, in the Bible we first meet Satan in his role as the serpent in Genesis 3. Whoever he was, or however he came to be there, he is in the Garden and has access to Adam and Eve. He is also described as "crafty," more so than other animals (v.1). His craftiness is displayed in the way he cleverly deceives the woman and lures the two humans into disobeying God's explicit command. But his presence is not outside God's control; apparently God has permitted him to be there and to tempt Adam and Eve. The devil is playing a God-ordained role, though not with a 'servant spirit'; he has no intention of obeying God but only of disrupting God's plans through questioning, tempting and denying (Gen 3:1–5).

We saw something similar in Job. Satan is part of, or accompanies, the group of God's attendants who "present themselves before the Lord" (Job 1:6). God sets off the drama by drawing Satan's attention to Job; Satan reacts predictably enough, since he cannot concede that anyone could love and serve God without being somehow 'bribed' (Job 1:9–11), and God accedes to his request to try Job's loyalty (Job 1:12). The resultant disasters that befall Job may thus be attributed to God (as the initial speaker or subsequent permission-giver), to Satan (as the challenger) and to the human actors such as the Sabeans and Chaldeans (Job 1:15,17). Contrary to the opinions of Job's friends, the only person *not* responsible is Job himself!

God is *ultimately* responsible and never tries to deflect His role when he addresses Job. The friends who lamely attempt to justify or excuse God are rebuked at the end: "You have not spoken the truth about me, as my servant Job has" (Job 42:8). The conclusion is that God is in charge, though His purposes and motive may not be total clear (Job 38–41). God has challenged, "Who is this that obscures my plans without knowledge?"

---

73. The title of a book by Tremper Longman III and Daniel G. Reid.
74. Boyd, *God At War*, 11.
75. Calvin, *Institutes*, 224.

(Job 42:3), but Job concedes, "No purpose of yours can be thwarted" (Job 42:2) and Job is answerable to God, not the other way around (Job 42:4). Whatever God is up to, He is justified, and Satan is silent, at the end of the story.

Another incident where God 'uses' the devil is found near the end of David's reign over Israel. David's foolish decision to take a census of the nation to ascertain its fighting capacity is motivated, no doubt, by human pride; even Joab (David's pragmatic lieutenant) can see it is wrong (2 Sam 24:2-3; 1 Chr 21:3,6). It is attributed to "the anger of the Lord" which "burned against Israel, and . . . incited David against them," in 2 Sam 24:1.

However, in 1 Chr 21:1 the same decision is attributed to Satan. The writers of these documents offer no other explanations, for example as to why God was angry with Israel, though in both cases David is seen as responsible and sinning (2 Sam 24:10; 1 Chr 21:8). Nor do the writers diminish the results when the prophet Gad offers David three judgment options (2 Sam 24:11-13; 1 Chr 21:9-12). David's choice is granted and the result is a plague in which 70,000 men die (2 Sam 24:15; 1 Chr 21:14) and Jerusalem is about to be destroyed when "the Lord relented concerning the disaster" (2 Sam 24:16; 1 Chr 21:15).

The initiative then goes back to David who rightly protests,

> "Was it not I who ordered the fighting men to be numbered? I, the shepherd, have sinned and done wrong. These are but sheep. What have they done? Lord my God, let your hand fall on me and my family, but do not let this plague remain on your people"
>
> (1 Chr 21:17; compare 2 Sam 24:17).

Then David is directed to purchase a threshing floor from Araunah the Jebusite and build an altar on it (2 Sam 24:18-25; 1 Chr 21:18-26), following which the plague is lifted (1 Chr 21:27; 2 Sam 24:25). In the Chronicles account, this story becomes the rationale for the choice of the site of the temple that Solomon will build (1 Chr 21:28-22:1), since the destroying angel was at that place when God relented about the plague (1 Chr 21:15; 2 Sam 24:16). 1 Chronicles spends several chapters praising David for preparing to set up the temple system and donating huge resources for that purpose (1 Chr 22-29). The lesson seems to be that God's sovereign hand used both Satan and David to somehow punish Israel (for unstated reasons) and also set the process for building the temple in motion.

Something slightly similar occurs earlier when King Saul is warned of his downfall and "the Spirit of the Lord had departed from Saul, and an evil spirit from the Lord tormented him" (1 Sam 16:14) intermittently. The effects of this spirit are alleviated by David's music (1 Sam 16:16,23) but at times it stirs up Saul's jealousy towards David so that he tries to kill him (1 Sam 18:10–11; 19:9–10). Saul's plots against David are not attributed to the evil spirit, however, but to jealousy (1 Sam 18:8–9) and fear (1 Sam 18:12,15,29), and his devious plots are well thought out (as in 1 Sam 18:17–27) and increasingly desperate (as in 1 Sam 19:11–17). The spirit is sent from the Lord but is also 'evil' so it may or may not originate with the devil. However, as in the previous story, God is clearly portrayed as sovereign over spirits of all kinds and uses this spirit to destabilize Saul's rule and keep David in position to take over.

We discussed the various players in the arrest and execution of Jesus earlier. Here we see Satan, Judas, the high priests, Herod, Pontius Pilate and others conspiring to execute Jesus but all ultimately serving God's sovereign purpose. Paul says, "None of the rulers of this age understood it [God's wisdom], for if they had, they would not have crucified the Lord of glory" (1 Cor 2:8). This statement either means that human rulers like Pontius Pilate simply acted ignorantly (compare Acts 3:17) or that they were somehow deceived by God, like Ahab, or that demonic forces are referred to and were deceived (as in Eph 6:12). Some ancient Christians actually believed that God tricked Satan into attacking Jesus since he could not hold Jesus in death and thus his kingdom "self-destructed."[76] Satan is thus used by God in many situations to his own ruin.

But this is not how he is usually portrayed in the Bible. In his various guises (the evil one, the serpent, the dragon, the devil), he is viewed as God's implacable opponent in the New Testament, tempting Jesus to deviate from God's plan (Matt 4:1–11; 16:23; Luke 4:1–13), threatening harm to followers of Jesus (Matt 6:13; 1 John 5:18; Rev 12), causing suffering and illness (Luke 13:16; Acts 10:38; Mark 9:14–29), ruling a horde or 'kingdom' of demons (Matt 9:34; 12:24–26) and people (Matt 13:38–39), ruling over the unbelieving world and all its kingdoms (Luke 4:6; John 12:31; 1 John 5:19; Rev 2:13; 13:1–4), deceiving the world, even believers (Matt 16:23; John 8:44; 2 Cor 4:4; 1 John 4:4; Rev 2:9,24; 3:9), luring believers into sin (Eph 4:27; James 4:7), and stirring up opposition and persecution of Christians (1 Pet 5:8–9; Rev 2:10; 12:3–4,13–17; 13:7–10).

---

76. Cf. James Beilby and Paul R. Eddy, *The Nature of the Atonement*, 12–13.

He is even able to hinder the good plans of Paul to visit the struggling new church in Thessalonica (1 Thess 2:18).

Let's finish this study by returning to Revelation 12. The chapter begins with two great signs in heaven, "a woman clothed with the sun" (v.1) and "an enormous red dragon" (v.3). The dragon is identified as "the ancient serpent called the devil, or Satan, who leads the whole world astray" (v.9). He is clearly very powerful: his seven heads, ten horns and seven crowns (v.3) imply significant political power and when "its tail swept a third of the stars out of the sky [or heaven] and flung them to the earth" (v.4), the reader will see that his power and authority are superhuman, whatever exactly John's language means. Perhaps there is a veiled reference to the triumph of Rome over the Mediterranean world with the stars equivalent to the 'princes' in Daniel 10.

The woman's identity is less clear: is she Israel or Mary or Eve, or perhaps represents all three (see Gen 3:15; Isa 66:7–11; Luke 1:26–38; 2:34–35)? But the issue here is the woman's son, who is about to be born as the story starts (v.2) and whom the dragon is desperate to devour (v.4) because his destiny is to "rule all the nations with an iron scepter" (v.5). His identity is fairly clear: he is male (v.5) and his destiny fulfills Old Testament prophecy (especially Psalm 2). Most likely, he is the promised offspring of the woman who will crush the serpent's head (Gen 3:15), so he is a major threat to the dragon.

The dragon is also a major threat to the male baby (v.4). However, God's superior power intervenes: "her child was snatched up to God and to his throne" (v.5), and even the woman has a place of protection (v.6).

This apocalyptic language is hard to 'translate,' if indeed we should do so; it may be a way of reinterpreting Herod's attempt to kill the baby Jesus (Matt 2:16), but John's Gospel also implies that Jesus' life was constantly under threat. Maybe Revelation is summing up Jesus' whole career from birth to ascension in one image. But the passage depicts a very powerful anti-God agent who poses a major threat to God's people, including His chosen messiah, though God's power is greater and God's plan will prevail.[77]

---

77. As recent commentators have noticed, John is also alluding to a widespread "combat myth" in which a divine or human hero defeats a destructive divine opponent and restores order to a world threatened with chaos (cf. Longman and Reid, *God Is a Warrior*, 183). In the OT the same basic theme is represented in how God fights against the sea and its monsters (ibid., 74–81).

The next passage involves a different scene. The devil is in heaven (v.3) and now war breaks out there between two angelic armies led by Michael (Israel's heavenly champion from Dan 10:13,21 and 12:1) and the dragon respectively. "But he was not strong enough, and they lost their place in heaven. The great dragon was hurled down.... and his angels with him" (vv.8–9). The reader might infer that the dragon has been defeated and "hurled down" because Michael's forces were stronger and God's power is greater than the dragon's. So far the woman and the male baby seem to be somewhat passive. But the reader would also note that God does not defeat the dragon directly: He uses angelic forces under Michael.

But now there is another shift in perspective. A loud voice interprets what has been happening in four ways. First, it is seen as a victory for the kingdom of God and his Messiah (v.10a), whose mission it is to defeat the dragon and take control of the nations (v.3; see also Rev 11:15). Second, this victory brings relief for God's faithful people, "for the accuser of our brothers and sisters, who accuses them before our God day and night, has been hurled down" (v.10b). There is a strong allusion to Job 1–2 and Zech 3:1; in both passages we see Satan accusing human followers of God. He will not stop doing so ("accuses" is present tense), but his ability to do so successfully is now ended.

But next comes a surprise. So far, this victory seems to have been the work of Michael and his angels (vv.7–9). But now we read,

> "They [the brothers and sisters] triumphed over him [the dragon]
> by the blood of the Lamb
> and by the word of their testimony;
> they did not love their lives so much
> as to shrink from death" (v.11).

The victory of God's angels over the forces of the devil is attributed to the "blood of the Lamb" (see Rev 1:5; 5:9; 7:14) and to the testimony of his followers even at the risk of death. And such a threat is portrayed graphically in the rest of the passage and into the next chapter, because the passage suggests that the dragon will be very dangerous now that he has been thrown down to earth; in fact, "he is filled with fury because he knows that his time is short" (v.12).

In this passage and the next chapter, we see that anti-God actors have some freedom to operate and some capacity to harm God's cause and God's people (see also Rev 13:7-10, 15-18). Indeed the dragon can "wage war against the rest of her offspring-those who keep God's commands, and hold fast their testimony about Jesus" (Rev 12:17). Through his surrogates, the two beasts, the devil can exercise control over "every tribe, people, language and nation" (Rev 13:7) and "wage war against God's holy people and conquer them" (Rev 13:7) with captivity and death (Rev 13:10). However, their freedom to act is limited: the male baby is snatched away from the dragon (Rev 12:5), the mother is supernaturally protected from the dragon's attacks (Rev 12:13-16), and the devil's capacity to deceive the world and inflict harm on God's people is restricted to a specific period, "forty-two months" (Rev 13:5; compare 12:6,14). Moreover, God's elect are not deceived or intimidated and will not worship the beast in spite of the consequences (Rev 13:8-10).

In other words, God's sovereignty in this drama is not just seen in His permitting of the devil's actions, as perhaps implied by the phrase, "it was given power" (Rev 13:7) and the boundaries He places on the devil's operations. Nor is it exercised purely by God intervening with superior power, though that does happen (Rev 12:5). God operates through His created beings: through angels (Rev 12:7), through the earth itself which "helped the woman by opening its mouth and swallowing the river that the dragon has spewed out of his mouth" (Rev 12:16), through the death of Christ (Rev 12:11), and significantly, through faithful human beings who testify to Christ and are willing even to die for him (Rev 12:11). God's plan advances not just through God's superior power but through weak human actors. God is not limited to raw power to win his victories.

To understand this more, we need to consider the messianic figure portrayed here first as a baby with a mighty destiny as world ruler (Rev 12:5) and elsewhere as the slain Lamb (Rev 5:6-10; 12:11; 13:8). He is clearly a human being of male gender, born of a woman (Rev 12:4-5). He dies violently (Rev 5:9; 13:8; 12:11), as appointed perhaps from of old, "slain from the creation of the world" (Rev 13:8).[78] But his death is not just a martyrdom, true though that would be. It is the key reason for the eviction of Satan and his angels from heaven. John is thus making a very similar point to other New Testament writers: God wins and the devil loses when Jesus dies on the Cross and as that message is testified to throughout the world. This is how the Messiah fulfills his destiny to rule

78. NIV translation. The Greek may indicate that the Lamb was "slain from the creation of the world" or that people's names have been "written in the Lamb's book of life from the creation of the world."

the nations. As Rev 5:9 affirms, "you were slain and with your blood you purchased for God persons from every tribe and language and people and nation." Though John does not spell it out as clearly as other writers, this power from Jesus' violent death implies that the ultimate issue is spiritual: "he has freed us from our sins by his blood" (Rev 1:5).

Satan's power is grounded in his capacity to accuse people, especially those who want to serve God (Rev 12:10), and thus keep them from successfully defeating him. It is a legal or rhetorical power (as we saw in Genesis 3) as much as a political power, though portrayed both ways in Revelation. Therefore Satan's eviction from heaven is a legal defeat more than a military one. This explains why Satan is so desperate to stop this 'good news' from spreading across the earth. But it also shows the important, indeed vital, role that Christians have to play in 'enforcing' this victory through their testimony to the truth, and the reward they get for doing so: "You have made them to be a kingdom and priests to serve our God, and they will reign on the earth" (Rev 5:10; see also 22:5).

God has appointed human beings as earth's governors (Gen 1:26–28) and His elect servants will fulfill that role in the end. In the immediate future to John's readers, the struggle will be with the Roman Empire specifically, which will be brought down as a result of Christian witness, but we can expect a similar struggle wherever the gospel goes and challenges the powers of darkness who have ruled in that territory till then.

GOD'S FOREKNOWLEDGE AND FOREORDINATION

Divine foreknowledge is a key aspect of our discussion of divine sovereignty and a very tricky, complex concept. It seems that foreknowledge is essential to God if He wants to operate sovereignly, especially in terms of guidance of events. If He doesn't know what will happen next, He can't prevent it or control it. As Duffield and Van Cleave comment, "It would be a confusing world if every act and happening surprised God and required Him to improvise to rescue His program from disaster,"[79] though this is the scenario portrayed by many Open Theists.

But if God does intervene to prevent something happening, does this not imply He knew all along that it wouldn't happen? It's easy to get "tied up in knots" logically here. But we can't ignore this issue.

---

79. Duffield and Van Cleave, *Foundations of Pentecostal Theology*, 80.

One way of looking at divine foreknowledge is well stated by Norman Geisler:

> God knows with certainty everything that will happen in the future, including all free actions. Nothing can change this; it is fixed and immutable. Since God is omniscient, He cannot be wrong about anything. Hence, if He knows what's going to happen—and He knows everything that's going to happen—then it must happen exactly as He foreknew it would happen.[80]

Therefore Calvinists like A.W. Pink, on one hand, argue that divine foreknowledge of people's response to the gospel implies some kind of limited atonement or election. If God creates a person when God definitely knows they will not respond to Christ, He is choosing for that person to be condemned, so the argument goes.[81] We have seen this displayed especially in the case of Judas (Mark 14:21).[82] Moreover, Pink argues that God only foreknows *because* He foreordains and *what* He foreordains, that is, everything that happens.[83] As Calvin said, "all events are governed by God's secret plan."[84]

A similar argument is put forward by Erickson, who says that,

> God knows all of the infinite possibilities. He chooses which of these he will actualize. And by meticulously selecting the very individuals he brings into existence, individuals which will respond to specific stimuli exactly as he intends, and by making sure these specific factors are present, he renders certain the free decisions and actions of those individuals.[85]

Open Theists, on the other hand, making similar assumptions about the meaning of foreknowledge, have argued that God's sovereignty cannot operate fully (meticulously) and directly because He has created beings with free will and cannot infallibly foresee what choices they might make.[86] If God could foreknow their choices, they would not be free at

---

80. Geisler, *Chosen But Free*, 16. This is not necessarily Geisler's own view.

81. Pink, *Sovereignty of God*, 82. Cf. Nash, *Concept of God*, 62–65.

82. But as we saw earlier, I. Howard Marshall argues that Jesus never says that Judas was predestined to betray him. The only thing predetermined in this verse is the death of the Son of Man (cf *Kept by the Power*, 88).

83. Pink, *Sovereignty of God*, 109–111. See also Helm, "Classical Calvinist," 26.

84. Calvin, *Institutes*, 199.

85. Erickson, *Christian Theology*, 385.

86. This argument, of course, depends on a concept of freewill as the power to do otherwise than one does. Greg Boyd writes of "self-determining freedom" (*Satan and*

all but determined, since foreknowledge is only foreknowledge if the events foreknown certainly come to pass. Foreknowledge is thus limited, because otherwise, it is argued, human freedom is restricted or annulled.

God thus has to operate in a relatively restricted way in order to accomplish His sovereign purposes. Scripture passages that talk about God changing His mind (Exod 32:14; 2 Kings 20:1–6; Jer 18:7–10; Amos 7:1–6; Jon 3:10), regretting His decisions (Gen 6:6; 1 Sam 15:11), expressing uncertainty about what human actors will do (Gen 18:21; Jer 26:3; Ezek 12:3),[87] being surprised by what they do (Jer 2:31; 3:7,19–20),[88] making conditional promises (Jer 7:5; 22:4–5),[89] consulting with one of his prophets about a possible action (Gen 18; Exod 32:7–14)[90] or learning about individuals when they act in certain ways (Gen 22:12) are appealed to as part of the argument.

God cannot foreknow all the future because it doesn't exist, it is claimed. As Greg Boyd argues, divine foreknowledge is foreknowledge of "*possibilities*, not of future *certainties*."[91] Sanders speaks of what he calls "dynamic omniscience,"[92] arguing, "God has exhaustive knowledge of the past and the present and knows as possibilities and probabilities those events which might happen in the future."[93] Or as Clark Pinnock puts it, "the future is partly settled and partly unsettled."[94]

Open Theism has made an important contribution to the understanding of God's sovereignty and how it operates in a world of free and fallen creatures. These theologians have rightly criticized aspects

---

the Problem of Evil, 56). Others advance a concept of freewill that is "compatibilist", that is, compatible with being determined by God or by the person's own nature as a sinner, for example. (e.g. Ware, *God's Greater Glory*, 78–95). The danger of such compatibilism is that it weakens the sense of *agency* in human actions. Humans may be *motivated* or *influenced* to do certain things, but they can choose not to, I think.

87. Cf. Fretheim, *Suffering of God*, 45. Fretheim argues that the integrity of God is at stake here: "If God knew in fact what would happen. . . . then the 'perhaps' was an outright deception of the prophet" (ibid., 47).

88. Cf. Fretheim, *Suffering of God*, 46–47.

89. Cf. Fretheim, *Suffering of God*, 47–48.

90. Cf. Fretheim, *Suffering of God*, 49–53.

91. Boyd, *Satan and the Problem of Evil*, 114 (emphasis in original text). Comp Sanders, "Openness of God," 223.

92. Sanders, *God Who Risks*, 15, 79–84, 131–139, 165–171, 199, 205–209.

93. Sanders, *God Who Risks*, 166.

94. "Response to Part 1", in Gray and Sinkinson (eds), *Reconstructing Theology*, 85. See also Boyd, *God of the Possible*, 16; John Sanders, "Divine Providence and the Openness of God," in Ware (ed.), *Perspectives on the Doctrine of God*, 196–240.

of traditional systematic Christian theology for the way it sometimes portrays God as a kind of rigid dictator and 'control freak' who "micromanages the entire universe."[95] Some other theological discussion has privileged God's sovereignty as against human freedom or God's own love.

But have Open Theists 'thrown the baby out with the bathwater?' Is it possible that God foreknows every choice of humans and angels without those choices being predetermined by Him,[96] or by some kind of Fate? Certainly knowledge of the future is different from other kinds of knowledge. But what does the Bible itself say about this?

The Bible does ascribe foreknowledge to God.

For example, in relation to the death of Jesus, Peter declares on the Day of Pentecost,

> "This man was handed over to you by God's deliberate plan and *foreknowledge*" (Acts 2:23, emphasis added).

In relation to election, Peter writes to "God's elect. . . . Who have been chosen according to the *foreknowledge* of God the Father . . . ." (1 Pet 1:1–2, emphasis added).

And Paul writes, "For those God *foreknew* he also predestined to be conformed to the image of his Son" (Rom 8:29, emphasis added) and "God did not reject his people, whom he *foreknew*" (Rom 11:2, emphasis added).

Prediction of future events is also ascribed to God throughout the Bible; for example, the future of Gentile kingdoms (Isa 10:5–19; 13–23,34,47; Dan 2:39–45; 7:23–27; 8:20–25;11:2–45), the future of Israel (Isaiah 1–6,11,22,26–31,35,39–41,44,48,54,60–64; Ezek 36–48; Dan 9:24–27), the future Messiah or Servant of God (Isa 11:1–5; 42:1–7; 49:1–7; 52:13–53:12; see 1 Pet 1:11), the career of King Cyrus (Isa 45), new heavens and new earth (Isa 65:17–25), and many other events, too many to list here.

Isaiah makes divine foreknowledge part of what sets God apart from the idolatrous gods of the nations:

> "Tell us, you idols,
> what is going to happen.
> Tell us what the former things were,

---

95. Lennox, *Determined to Believe?*, 58.

96. This was the teaching of most early Christian theologians prior to Augustine (Sanders, *God Who Risks*, 141–145).

so that we may consider them
and know their final outcome.
Or declare to us the things to come,
tell us what the future holds,
so that we may know you are gods"

(Isa 41:22–23a; compare 44:7; 45:21).

Jesus himself predicted his own crucifixion and resurrection (Matt 16:21; 20:17–19) and the destruction of the Jerusalem temple in AD 70 (Matt 24:1–2; Mark 13:1–2; Luke 21:5–6), events he had no control over.

So the fact of divine foreknowledge is clearly established by Scripture.

What is less obvious is the nature and basis of God's knowledge of the future. Does God foreknow everything that will happen? Does God foreknow the future because He controls it meticulously? Does God foreknow possibilities, including some that will not happen? Is God's foreknowledge based on His extensive knowledge of present circumstances or, does God stand 'outside' time and observe infallibly what is coming to pass, a bit like an observer of a parade standing on a tall building? Does God foreknow every human choice or decision?

When we look at specific narratives in the Bible, certain features stand out.

First, many cases of divine foreknowledge are in fact based on what is sometimes called 'middle knowledge' that is God's knowledge of what will happen if He does not intervene. For example, Genesis 11, the story of the tower of Babel, says that, "The LORD came down to see the city and the tower the people were building" (v.5) and, after investigating, concludes, "If as one people speaking the same language they have begun to do this, then nothing they plan to do will be impossible for them" (v.6). God knows what the people are doing and what the consequences will be, though perhaps this is just an inference from God's extensive knowledge of the situation as it is. God then sovereignly intervenes to prevent the future development that might otherwise occur by confusing their language, thus scattering them across the earth (vv.7–9).

Centuries later, David is on the run from a murderous King Saul. He saves the people of Keilah from the Philistines, but when news comes that Saul's army will besiege that city so as to capture him, David seeks God's guidance through the priest Abiathar using an ephod, which could give a yes/no answer (1 Sam 23:9). He prays to God about the news and asks, "Will the citizens of Keilah surrender me to him [Saul]? Will Saul come down, as your servant has heard?" (v.11). God gives him an affirmative answer to both questions (vv.11–12), so David and his men leave Keilah and escape Saul's clutches (v.13). This is a conditional foreknowledge since the event 'foreknown' didn't actually happen. It was based on God's knowledge of the *intentions* of the people involved, which he revealed to David so that David could avoid the disaster.

A similar kind of knowledge is expressed by Jesus in his denunciation of the Galilean towns where he had done miracles because they had failed to repent:

> "Woe to you, Chorazin! Woe to you, Bethsaida! For if the miracles that were performed in you had been performed in Tyre and Sidon, they would have repented long ago in sackcloth and ashes. . . . And you, Capernaum, will you be lifted to the heavens? No, you will go down to Hades. For if the miracles that were performed in you had been performed in Sodom, it would have remained to this day."
>
> (Matt 11:21–24).

In this case we are dealing with counter-factuals; certain things that God knew would happen didn't occur because God didn't intervene. This, of course, raises lots of questions. Why, for example, did God send Jonah to Nineveh and not to Tyre? Why have miraculous signs in Bethsaida and not in Tyre and Sidon?[97]

Sometimes God foresees *and permits* a future development. For instance, God shows Abram what will happen to his descendants hundreds of years in the future, saying, "Know for certain that for four hundred years your descendants will be strangers in a country not their own and that they will be enslaved and mistreated there" (Gen 15:13). In this case, He is surely foreseeing the free actions of both Abram's descendants and, more importantly, the Egyptians. God will intervene to punish Egypt and release Israel (Gen 15:14), but He will not prevent their enslavement, as we see played out in Exodus 1. And He will hold the Egyptians accountable for their oppression of the Israelites. But there is more than foreknowledge here, since God actively 'sends' the Israelites into Egypt in the first place.

---

97. Custance uses this passage to support 'limited atonement,' i.e. God does not choose for all people to be saved (Custance, *Sovereignty of Grace*, 152). But it could equally be used to deny 'total depravity.' Jesus knew that these evil societies would nonetheless have repented if they had seen his miracles.

More specific foreknowledge is seen in Peter and Jesus' interaction not long before Jesus' arrest. The episode issue begins with a Satanic demand: "Satan has asked to sift all of you as wheat" (Luke 22:31). God has clearly permitted Satan to do this and hence Jesus prays specifically for Peter "that your faith may not fail" (Luke 22:32). An overconfident Peter protests that he would never deny Jesus and would willingly die for him (Matt 26:33; Mark 14:29,31; Luke 22:33; John 13:37). But every Gospel reports Jesus' warning to Peter that he will deny him three times that night (Matt 26:34; Mark 14:30; Luke 22:34; John 13:38) and that happens as Jesus has predicted (Matt 26:69–75; Mark 14:66–72; Luke 22:54–62; John 18:15–18,25–27). The events are narrated in a way that makes it clear that Peter is acting 'naturally,' freely, motivated by fear, and accepts the responsibility when he fails (Matt 26:75; Mark 14:72; Luke 22:61–62). Jesus knows Peter well enough to predict such a response.

However, the details about the number of times Peter will deny Christ and the rooster crowing are not humanly predictable, so this is a case including real divine foreknowledge (though partly grounded in God's sovereignty over the natural world, in this case a rooster).[98] Greg Boyd is probably right to suggest "God wanted to humble this future pillar of the church" and "cure Peter of his pride and false conceptions,"[99] which segues into the next point.

Many cases of divine foreknowledge are simply based on divine determination. As discussed in an earlier chapter, Joseph had two prophetic dreams which were understood as meaning his brothers, and even his parents, would bow down to him (Gen 37:5–10). While this did not literally happen with his father, the core meaning of both dreams was fulfilled. The decisions of the brothers, Jacob, Joseph himself, Potiphar and his wife and other Egyptians were made freely for the most part, judging by the narrative. However, these decisions were used by God in (humanly) unforeseen ways; for example, Joseph needed to be in Egypt in order to save his family, and the brothers' sale of him enabled that to happen. But the will of God was also accomplished through divine interventions: the dreams of Pharaoh and his servants and the long famine in particular. God did not merely foreknow everything; God had a plan and ensured it would be fulfilled.

---

98. Cf. Roy, *How Much?*, 96–101.

99. Boyd, *Satan and the Problem of Evil*, 132. Sanders suggests that this prediction is conditional: Jesus is trying to motivate Peter to be prepared for what is coming (Sanders, *God Who Risks*, 137). This may be right but it doesn't account for the specific details.

Other cases involve long-term predictions. Shortly after the death of Solomon, the kingdom of Israel was split in two with the northern ten tribes rebelling against King Rehoboam and establishing a separate nation under Jeroboam, an event foretold and determined by God (1 Kings 10:29–39; 12:22–24). However, in a tactical move, Jeroboam established a new system of divine worship focused on two golden calves in Bethel and Dan and with other parallels to the divine service in Jerusalem (1 Kings 12:26–33). This provoked a prophetic response from God through a prophet from the southern kingdom. He came to Bethel, one of Jeroboam's new 'sacred sites,' where he found the king "standing by the altar to make an offering" (1 Kings 13:1). Immediately the prophet cried out,

> "Altar, altar! This is what the Lord says: A son named Josiah will be born to the house of David. On you he will sacrifice the priests of the high places who make offerings here, and human bones will be burned on you"

> (1 Kings 13:2).

This prediction was confirmed with two dramatic signs: the splitting of the altar causing its ashes to be poured out and the temporary shriveling of Jeroboam's hand when he attempted to seize the prophet (1 Kings 13:3–6). To be fulfilled subsequently, however, this very specific prophecy required a royal son to be born in the south, to be named Josiah, and to defile this specific altar by burning human bones on it. A complex string of human decisions and events were needed for all this to happen and the timing was very far into the future.

But centuries later, with the northern kingdom in ruins after the Assyrian invasion, an eight-year-old boy called Josiah became king of Judah (2 Kings 22:1). This was a crucial low point in Judah's history, after a series of ungodly reigns, and as he grew older, Josiah introduced new reforms to bring his nation back to allegiance to God. This included removing all traces of idol worship in Judah. But because the northern kingdom had fallen, Josiah was able to extend his influence into its former territory, and we read,

> Even the altar at Bethel, the high place made by Jeroboam son of Nebat, who had caused Israel to sin–even that altar and high place he demolished. He burned the high place and ground it to powder, and burned the Asherah pole also. Then Josiah looked around and when he saw the tombs that were there on the hillside, he had the bones removed from them and burned on the

altar to defile it, in accordance with the word of the Lord proclaimed by the man of God who foretold these things

(2 Kings 23:15–16).

Only then did Josiah see the tomb of that prophet who had foretold his action (2 Kings 13:17). God inspired the original warning and God ensured it was fulfilled by guiding subsequent events. Similar comments can be made with respect to other places where prophets pronounce forthcoming judgments, such as Elijah on Ahab (1 Kings 21:19–24).

The ringing declarations of God's unique foreknowledge in Isaiah are based on what God has determined to do, especially in relation to raising up King Cyrus and releasing the Jews to return home. The true God is raising up a new conqueror, an event that no one foretold (Isa 41:25–26). This passage is not just saying, 'God knew this in advance and others didn't,' but rather God *planned* this in advance and is taking everyone by surprise. In other words, God foreknows what He plans to bring about.

Steven Roy comments here that the prophet is comparing future events to seeds in the ground waiting to sprout; they have real existence even before they happen, as opposed to the Open Theist contention that future events do not exist and therefore cannot be foreknown.[100] But if so, it seems that this is true because those future events are planned by God.

In the midst of the prophecy about King Cyrus who is appointed as God's shepherd and "anointed" (Isa 44:28–45:1), God launches another challenge to idol worshipers:

> "Declare what is to be, present it—
> let them take counsel together.
> Who foretold this long ago,
> who declared it from the distant past?
> Was it not I, the LORD?"
> (Isa 45:21a).

And God goes on to say, "a word that will not be revoked: Before me every knee will bow" (Isa 45:23). God foretells and foreknows *what He will do*, although that obviously means He will either foresee or control the situations into which He will act, such as the existence of Cyrus.[101] But we can say more. God declares people's response: "before me every knee

---

100. Roy, *How Much?*, 47.
101. Cf. Craig, *The Only Wise God*, 44.

will bow." Either God simply foreknows this or He ensures this result, perhaps by acting by His Spirit or by force.

In the next chapter of Isaiah, we have this strong declaration:

> "I make known the end from the beginning,
> from ancient times what is still to come.
> I say, 'My purpose will stand,'
> and I will do all that I please."

(Isa 46:10).

Here God's knowledge encompasses all times, ancient and future alike. It includes events such as past, present and future empires and rulers, as we see in Daniel, for example. But this is not just knowledge. As we saw earlier, "the Most High is sovereign over all kingdoms on earth and gives them to anyone he wishes" (Dan 4:32). Even ungodly empires are raised up and put down by God. In the context of Isaiah 46, straight after the declaration of God's foreknowledge, we read,

> "From the east I summon a bird of prey;
> from a far off land, a man to fulfill my purpose.
> What I have said, that I will bring about;
> what I have planned, that I will do."

(Isa 46:11).

God thus knows 'the end from the beginning' not so much as an infallible observer as an omnipotent Supervisor and Guide.

This ability of God to fulfill His own words is emphasized in another famous passage in Isaiah:

> "As the rain and the snow
> come down from heaven,
> and do not return to it
> without watering the earth
> and making it bud and flourish,
> so that it yields seed for the sower
> and bread for the eater,
> so is my word that goes out from my mouth:
> It will not return to me empty,
> but will accomplish what I desire
> and achieve the purpose for which I sent it."

(Isa 55:10–11).

God does not merely 'foreknow' what will happen, He makes it happen. And yet He does it is a way that doesn't destroy the autonomy of His creation (as in the analogy of rain and vegetation) and the free will of people and other agents.

Other prophecies of distant future events relate to Jesus. For example, Mic 5:2 predicts that the coming Messiah would be born in Bethlehem, the town of David, not Jerusalem (see Matt 2:4-6). It was God's determination that it would be so, appropriately, since the Messiah would be a 'son' of David. But Jesus' family lived in Nazareth, in the northern region of Galilee. Hence God used the Roman emperor Augustus to get Jesus's mother to Bethlehem when Augustus "issued a decree that a census should be taken of the entire Roman world. . . . And everyone went to their own town to register" (Luke 2:1,3), which in Joseph's case meant relocating to Bethlehem (Luke 2:4-5). This all happened as part of God's great Plan. We are not told how God guided Augustus in this decree but we previously showed how something similar happened with King David (2 Sam 24:1-4).

Moreover the coming of Jesus released a great Plan for all the world. As Paul writes,

> Scripture *foresaw* that God would justify the Gentiles by faith, and announced the gospel in advance to Abraham: "All nations shall be blessed in you"
>
> (Gal 3:8, emphasis added; compare Eph 3:4-6,9-11).

The many prophecies of the coming Messiah and the result of his mission were grounded in God's great Plan of salvation.

A different situation applies to Elisha's interaction with the future Syrian king Hazael. Hazael, a leading figure in Aram (Syria), is sent by the current ruler Ben-Hadad (who was sick) to ask the prophet, who is visiting Damascus, if he would recover (2 Kings 8:7-9). Elisha's response is revealing: "Elisha answered, 'Go and say to him, "You will certainly recover."' Nevertheless, the LORD has revealed to me that he will in fact die.'" (2 Kings 8:10). Then Elisha proceeds to tell Hazael that he would be the new king of Aram, an outcome he fulfills by murdering Ben-Hadad and seizing his throne (2 Kings 8:13-15). Elisha also foretells that Hazael would inflict horrible suffering on the Israelites (2 Kings 8:12; see 10:32-33; 12:17; 13:3-7).

The prophet seems to be conniving at a deception of Ben-Hadad, and the prophecies are partly fulfilled by deliberate actions by Hazael, but clearly God's sovereignty is at work in raising up a new king and using him as an agent of judgment on the northern kingdom of Israel. This event, where Elisha effectively 'anointed' Hazael as the new king, was also part of Elisha's mandate from Elijah (1 Kings 19:15). God is not forcing Hazael to murder Ben-Hadad or to oppress Israel, but it seems to be part of His sovereign determination.

Some predictive statements in the Bible are a mixture of God's definite plans and His confidence in human partners. For example, Genesis quotes God as saying,

> "Abraham will surely become a great and powerful nation, and all nations on earth will be blessed through him. For I have chosen him, so that he will direct his children and his household after him to keep the way of the Lord by doing what is right and just, so that the Lord will bring about for Abraham what he has promised him"

(Gen 18:18–19).

There are three steps in this speech. The future history of Abraham's descendants is sure because it is God's plan.ABraham's ability to direct his family in the right paths is anticipated but this seems to be based on what God knows in the present, not the future. Third, God will fulfill His promises to Abraham because of Abraham's obedience and influence on his descendants; this is grounded in God's sure plan and His confidence in Abraham.

But in fact, at least two of the three points are actually uncertain. Abraham's influence on his descendants is actually seen as quite limited in the way the sometimes dysfunctional family life of Isaac and Rebekah, and later Jacob, is narrated in the rest of Genesis. Later the future of Israel is strongly challenged when twice God threatens to wipe them out because they haven't followed Abraham's example (Exod 32:9–10; Num 14:11–12). Of course, God is determined to see Israel through even though He has to ditch a whole generation in the process (Num 14:28–35).

There is a series of prophetic predictions made about some of Abraham's descendants in Genesis. Rebekah is told that "two nations are in your womb. . . . and the older will serve the younger" (Gen 25:23). This seems to be God's determined plan, not just what He sees happening. It establishes in advance the future struggle and enmity between Israel and Edom. But Edom does not always serve Israel (a point foreseen in Isaac's prophecy of Gen 27:40) and conspires against them in the Babylonian exile event (Obad 11–14), though the Edomites are frequently subjugated by Israel (see Num 24:18–19). The prophecy mainly establishes that Israel is the chosen nation to accomplish God's Plan, not Edom. In both cases, Jacob and Esau and their descendants act freely but God's plan is accomplished, including the judgment on Edom for warring against Israel (as prophesied by Obadiah).

Let's return to the events around Jesus' death. As we saw, Peter declares,

> "This man was handed over to you by God's *deliberate plan and foreknowledge*; and you, with the help of wicked men, put him to death by nailing him to the cross"

(Acts 2:23; emphasis added).

Jesus' crucifixion is here attributed to the Jews in Jerusalem ("you") and to "wicked men" (Judas and Roman authorities and soldiers) but also to God who "handed him over." God did not just know this would happen. He planned it, though in such a way that the human actors acted freely, that is, without coercion. Judas' role in all this is also foreknown by Jesus from the outset (John 6:64) and predicted in detail at the last supper (Matt 26:21–25; Mark 14:18–21; John 13:11,21–27). In fact, the fulfilment of this prediction would show the disciples "I am who I am" (John 13:19), though Jesus' focus is not so much on his foreknowledge but rather that his suffering is central to the divine Plan. Jesus refuses to do anything to prevent it from happening and submits to God's Plan by releasing Judas to his choice (John 13:21–30).[102]

Even the details of what happened on the Cross are said to fulfill prophecy, especially in John's Gospel: the dividing and casting lots for Jesus' clothing (John 19:23–24), his thirst (John 19:28), the fact that his bones weren't broken unlike the other two victims (John 19:36),[103] the fact that his side was pierced with a spear (John 19:34,37). Some of these were humanly predictable (e.g. thirst, dividing of clothes), but the others were done 'freely' by the people involved. Clearly the relevant prophets

---

102. Roy explains Jesus's actions in handing a piece of bread to Judas as "a final gesture of love.... One final appeal to Judas to turn away from his planned sin" that failed: "this gesture served to harden Judas in his decision to betray Jesus" (Roy, *How Much?*, 107). But it seems from the narrative that Jesus is handing Judas over to the devil, as this is what happens when Judas takes the bread (John 13:27).

103. As Calvin comments, "his bones were fragile, yet it was impossible to break them" (Calvin, *Institutes*, 210).

of the Old Testament foretold what would happen, though their prophecies weren't precise predictions; for example Psalm 22:18, which speaks of the divisions and lots for the clothing, is originally a prayer of David, although it is commonly seen as a pre-enactment of the Cross.[104]

Another form of divine foreknowledge is grounded in God's intimate knowledge of present circumstances. For example, David prays,

> Before a word is on my tongue
> You, LORD, know it completely
>
> (Ps 139:4).

God knows in advance what he will say. But how? In the Psalm, David begins with God searching and knowing him (v.1), "when I sit and when I rise" and all his thoughts (v.2), actions and ways (v.3). This suggests that the foreknowledge of what he will say comes from God knowing what he is thinking and how he usually acts (his ways).

However, all this is governed by God's plan for his life:

> All the days ordained for me were written in your book
> before one of them came to be (v16).

The events of David's life are a combination of God's plans and his own decisions, but both are superintended and watched over by God. David never escapes God's knowledge or His ability to guide events in his life (vv.1–9) which began in his mother's womb (vv.13–16).

God's sovereignty allows Him to change direction when people's responses and His justice require it. Think of Jonah again: God intervened very forcefully (storm, big fish) to make Jonah willing to obey the commission God gave him, but His overall goal was Nineveh's repentance and the 'false prophecy' of Jonah about Nineveh's overthrow was enough to achieve that so that the threat did not have to be carried out, as the prophet himself foresaw (Jon 4:2). In this story, God's stated plans changed–in response to the repentance of Nineveh, "he relented and did not bring on them the destruction he had threatened" (Jon 3:10). It was always God's plan to save the city and that's why He sent Jonah there, overcoming his opposition, which was a feeble attempt to prevent such an outcome.

Moses' predictions of the future rebellion of Israel and God's consequent judgment is another case. Shortly before Moses dies, the Lord says,

---

104. Cf. Roy, *How Much?*, 57–61.

> "You are going to rest with your ancestors, and these people will soon prostitute themselves to the foreign gods of the land they are entering. They will forsake me and break the covenant I made with them. And in that day I will become angry with them and forsake them; I will hide my face from them, and they will be destroyed. Many disasters and calamities will come on them, and in that day they will ask, 'Have not these disasters come on us because our God is not with us?' And I will certainly hide my face in that day because of all their wickedness in turning to other gods."
>
> (Deut 31:16-18).

On what basis did God say this? This passage does not say but two other passages give us a clue. Later in the same chapter, we find Moses saying,

> "For I know how rebellious and stiff-necked you are. If you have been rebellious against the Lord while I am still alive and with you, how much more will you rebel after I die!"
>
> (Deut 31:27).

In other words, the future rebellion of the Israelites is predictable based on their past and current behavior (see also Deut 9:6) and the results of such rebellion are spelled out in the terms of the covenant (Deut 28).

But as well as that, there is a note of divine sovereignty in this section, as Moses states, "But to this day the Lord has not given you a mind that understands or eyes that see or ears that hear" (Deut 29:4; compare Isa 6:10). Their rebellion partly derives from an incomplete work of God in their hearts. Thus God promises that, after their rebellion and the consequent judgments, He will restore them and "will circumcise your hearts and the hearts of your descendants, so that you may love him with all your heart and with all your soul, and live" (Deut 30:6). This suggests that their rebellion is decreed or permitted by God so that He can later intervene more internally (compare Jer 31:31-34; Ezek 36:25-27); it is a promise of the new covenant. It is the Plan of God operating.

Many other prophecies do not seem to relate clearly to God's Plan, but this does not mean that they were only 'foreknown' by God.[105] God

---

105. For more examples, see Geisler, *Chosen But Free*, 115.

seemed to be guiding the histories of all nations even before the coming of Christ (Acts 17:26).

Let's look now at a specific modern example. Among proto-Pentecostals in Armenia, which was then part of the Ottoman (Turkish) empire, a prophecy was given in the 19th century of a terrible tragedy that would befall the Christians, many of whom would be murdered, and directing the Christians to flee to America. About 1900, the prophet who'd spoken that word warned that the time was drawing near, and they must emigrate immediately. Some Pentecostals did exactly that, while others were skeptical. But in 1914, the Turks launched a fierce pogrom against the Christian Armenians and over one million perished.[106]

Clearly the prophecy represented some kind of foreknowledge, but its purpose was not cognitive. The purpose was to warn people to flee and thus avoid the future events. Those who chose to believe the warning and emigrate avoided the pogrom. Those who disbelieved largely perished, though apparently they didn't fall away or deny the Lord.[107] There is no account that would suggest either that the Turks could have repented as a result of the prophecy or that God somehow decreed the tragedy.

The idea of God as an Observer from 'outside' of time is not warranted by Scripture as far as I can see.[108] It is hard to think of God being 'outside' time in the sense that there would be no chronology or 'before' and 'after'. For example, 2 Tim 1:9 speaks of God's grace being given to us "before the beginning of time," and Tit 1:2 says that God promised eternal life "before the beginning of time." However, in both cases, Paul is contrasting "before the beginning of time" with "now" (2 Tim 1:10; Tit 1:3). What he seems to mean is that God decided and promised our salvation before creation, just as Rev 13:8 speaks of "the Lamb who was slain before the creation of the world" and 1 Peter 1:20 says "he was chosen before the creation of the world, but was revealed in these last times for your sake."

Let me try to bring all this together. God's foreknowledge of events, including people's choices,[109] takes three forms as I understand it:

---

106. This is a summary of the account by Demos Shakarian in *The Happiest People on Earth*, 20–23.

107. Shakarian, *Happiest People*, 23.

108. Ware argues that both are true (*God's Greater Glory*, 133–139. For a more philosophical discussion of 'timelessness' in God, see Alan Padgett, "God and Timelessness," in Craig, ed., *Philosophy of Religion*, 230–245.

109. For an Open Theist interpretation, especially in relation to predictive prophecy, see Sanders, *God Who Risks*, 132–139.

1. *Simple foreknowledge*, as in the case of Jesus' prediction of Peter's denial; here Jesus is not viewed as determining what Peter would 'freely' do, he simply knows it.

2. *Contingent foreknowledge*, as in the case of Jesus' words about Sodom and Tyre (a counterfactual case) or God's warning to David about Saul and Keilah (which was preventable). This is more 'middle knowledge,' a 'what if?' kind of knowledge. It is grounded more in God's knowledge of the people concerned and how they would freely act under certain circumstances.

3. *Volitional or determined foreknowledge*, as in the case of Jesus' crucifixion; here God is viewed as causing the events that He either reveals in advance or describes after they occurred.

How do these thoughts apply to foreknowledge in relation to election and salvation? As we saw earlier, Peter, writing to "God's elect" (1 Pet 1:1), tells them they

> have been chosen according to the *foreknowledge* of God the Father, through the sanctifying work of the Spirit, to be obedient to Jesus Christ and sprinkled with his blood
>
> (1 Pet 1:2; emphasis added).

They were not chosen because God foreknew they would be obedient; rather they were chosen "to be obedient" and "sprinkled with his blood." As Erickson claims, "There is simply nothing in the Bible to suggest that God chooses humans because of what they are going to do *on their own*."[110] Their obedience was a result of "the sanctifying work of the Spirit." But Peter does not say that this work of the Spirit was only operating in a select few nor that the work of the Spirit determined their response. Rather this work of the Spirit was God's plan, and hence 'foreknown,' having been promised in the prophets (such as Ezek 36:26–27). But only some responded to that work of the Spirit and hence became obedient and hence chosen. In this way election is based *indirectly* on God's foreknowledge.

God has determined to save people and form His church by the work of His Spirit grounded in the saving work of Christ. But His election of individuals is grounded more in His middle knowledge of what those

---

110. Erickson, *Christian Theology*, 382, emphasis added.

individuals would do in response to the salvation provided indiscriminately to everyone.[111]

Summing up, while the concept of divine foreknowledge is complex in Scripture and philosophically, we can't dispense with it. As Geisler argues,

> A God who does not know for sure what any future free act will be is severely limited in His logistic ability to do things that a God who knows every decision that will be made can do.[112]

But divine foreknowledge is not portrayed in the Bible in the way many think and is always subordinated to God's sovereign plans.

GOD'S ACTIONS TOWARDS HUMAN CHOICES

Many of the examples just discussed focus on how God deals with human choices, whether 'foreknown' or just 'known.' It seems in general that God in His sovereignty takes one of four actions in relation to the choices of human beings:[113]

1. He supports and empowers some choices as being aligned with His will in some way,
2. He permits some choices to be carried out even though they are sinful, and even uses them to carry out His plans,
3. He frustrates or blocks some choices from being carried out, or
4. He influences the human actors to change their choices.

Let's look at examples of each case.

The most straightforward response God can make is to endorse, support, empower and enable human decisions that are aligned with His purpose or obedient to His revealed will. But in fact, there are at least two distinct situations envisaged here. The simplest case is of a human being or group consciously following God's will in obedience. Obviously, the Bible is full of such cases. We might think of Elijah's challenge to the

---

111. Cf. William L. Craig, "Middle Knowledge: a Calvinist-Arminian Rapprochement?" in Pinnock, ed., *Grace of God, Will of Man* 141–163.

112. Geisler, *Chosen But Free*, 175.

113. Erickson offers this classification, focusing specifically on sin: "God can prevent sin," "God does not always prevent sin. At times he simply wills to permit it," "God can also direct sin," and "God can limit sin" (Erickson, *Christian Theology*, 424–426).

prophets of Baal when he calls down fire from heaven on his sacrifice, to show Israel who is the real God (1 Kings 18). God endorses his action by sending down the fire and the Israelites respond by falling prostrate and declaring "the Lord–he is God!" (1 Kings 18:38–39). Or we might think of Peter's sermon on the Day of Pentecost, interpreting the phenomena of the Spirit, explaining the story of Jesus and its Old Testament prophetic basis, and challenging the audience to repentance (Acts 2:14–41). God's endorsement of the message is implied by the audience being "cut to their heart" (v.37) and three thousand of them being baptized.

The less direct cases are where the human decision is not at all one of intentional obedience to God or to advance God's will, but in fact it will have that effect (and results from divine influence in some form) and therefore God endorses and advances it. God's use of King Cyrus of Persia is a good example. Isaiah prophesies,

> "For the sake of Jacob my servant,
> of Israel my chosen,
> I summon you by name
> and bestow on you a title of honor,
> though you do not acknowledge me."
>
> (Isa 45:4).

This is because it is the Lord's prophetically revealed will for Jerusalem and the towns of Judah to be rebuilt and inhabited (Isa 44:26) and, therefore He

> " . . . . ..says of Cyrus, 'He is my shepherd
> and will accomplish all that I please;'
> he will say of Jerusalem, 'Let it be rebuilt,'
> and of its temple, 'Let its foundations be laid.'"
>
> (Isa 44:28).

As Isaiah states, Cyrus is unaware of God's plans and unwilling to give allegiance to God, but nonetheless God chooses and uses him for the divine plan.

God's use of King Nebuchadnezzar to deal with Judah and conquer the whole region is another case in point. Jeremiah 27 declares to the regional rulers in the name of the Lord,

> "With my great power and outstretched arm I made the earth and its people and the animals that are on it, and I give it to anyone I please. Now I will give all your countries into the hands of

my servant Nebuchadnezzar king of Babylon; I will make even the wild animals subject to him"

(Jer 27:5-6).

Hence every nation is called on to subject itself to Babylon (vv.8-11). Therefore, according to Ezekiel, Nebuchadnezzar's strategic decisions in his campaign against the region are being guided by God's judgment even through his call on idols and use of omens and lots (Ezek 21:18-22). God specifically 'steers' him towards an assault on Jerusalem as opposed to the Ammonite city of Rabbah.

Second, God's permitting of sinful decisions is also a common event in Scripture, too common for us to look at every case. Obviously the first one was the disobedience of Adam and Eve in Genesis 3, though God's involvement in that tragedy was more than just one of 'permission,' as we saw earlier. Arminius saw these as examples of God's 'concurrence' with human sin.[114]

A variation on this theme is when God 'permits' a sinful choice but quickly follows it with a negative or positive consequence. An example is found in Genesis 38. This story is sandwiched between the selling of Joseph and his career in Egypt and will affect that story since Judah plays a central role in the selling of Joseph (Gen 37:26-27) and the later reconciliation (Gen 43:8-10; 44:16-34). Readers of Genesis can read Gen 38 as part of God's dealing with Judah so that he becomes the much greater man we see in Genesis 44.

It begins with Judah marrying a Canaanite woman, an implied sin (see Gen 27:46-28:1), and the first two children of this union are explicitly "wicked in the Lord's sight" and put to death by God (Gen 38:6-10). God has intervened twice but in the rest of the chapter God is not mentioned. It is Judah's Canaanite daughter-in-law who takes the initiative when it becomes clear that Judah will not fulfill his responsibility to her by marrying her to his third son. She out-maneuvers him and bears Judah twins, one of whom becomes David's ancestor (Gen 38:11-30). These events are thus brought into the main story line leading up to Jesus (see Matt 1:3).

Examples where God permits sin and there are no immediate consequences include the actions of Lamech and his family, which include the first mention of polygamy, cultural and technical progress and Lamech's boasts of violence (Gen 4:19-24). A more ambiguous example is the defeat and death of the godly king Josiah who rashly fights against

---

114. Olson, *Arminian Theology*, 122. Compare Calvin, *Institutes*, 228-231.

Egypt and is killed (2 Kings 23:29–30; 2 Chr 35:20–24), though in this case the author of 2 Chronicles explicitly accuses Josiah of failing to listen to God's command spoken through the Pharaoh (2 Chr 35:22).

God using the sinful actions of people to carry out His plans is very common in Scripture. The story of Joseph has already been mentioned, as have the events leading to Jesus' crucifixion. But A.W. Pink's comments on Judas are good here:

> God did not decree that He [Christ] should be sold by one of His creatures and then take a good man, instill an evil desire into his heart and thus *force* him to perform the terrible deed *in order to execute* His decree. . . . God decreed the act and selected the one who was to perform the act, but He did not *make him evil* in order that he *should* perform the deed; on the contrary, the betrayer was a 'devil' at the time the Lord Jesus chose him as one of the twelve (John 6:70), and. . . . God simply *directed* his actions, actions which were . . . . performed with the most wicked *intentions*.[115]

On the other hand, Open Theist Richard Rice argues, "While Judas's behavior fulfilled prophecy (Ps 41:9), it is possible the prophecy in question could have found fulfillment in some other way."[116] But both agree that God never *forced* Judas to betray Jesus.

The third set of cases is where God deliberately frustrates or blocks a person from carrying out a plan, whether a sinful or godly plan. This is a common occurrence. For example, David has a good motive in bringing the ark of the covenant to Jerusalem, but God blocks this plan when Uzzah tries to steady the ark and God executes him on the spot (2 Sam 6:1–7; 1 Chr 13:7–10). The underlying issue is that the ark should be carried by Levites, not pulled on a cart by oxen (1 Chr 15:2,12–13). Only when this was corrected would God allow David's (good) plan to be carried out. A different case is found in 2 Chron 17:10 where God protects a good king, Jehoshaphat: "The fear of the Lord fell on all the kingdoms of the lands surrounding Judah, so that they did not go to war against Jehoshaphat."

God's blocking actions are often designed to lead to a change of mind by the humans involved. God blocked Jonah's plan to sail to Tarshish and imprisoned him in a "huge fish" (Jon 1–2) so that he would listen

---

115. Pink, *Sovereignty of God*, 157 (emphasis in the original).

116. Richard Rice, "Biblical Support for a New Perspective" (in Pinnock et al, *The Openness of God*), 55.

to God's instructions the second time (Jon 3:1-3). Jonah was 'free' to disobey the first time, but God would not accept his decision.

A different combination of events occurs during the apostle Paul's 'second missionary journey.'[117] Paul and his team have been traveling "through Syria and Cilicia, strengthening the churches" that were planted by Paul and Barnabas earlier (Acts 15:41; 16:4-5). Now they want to venture into new territory to preach the gospel, but though this was a good plan, things did not go well:

> Paul and his companions traveled through the region of Phrygia and Galatia, having been kept by the Holy Spirit from preaching the word in the province of Asia. When they came to the border, they tried to enter Bithynia, but the Spirit of Jesus would not allow them to. So they passed by Mysia and went down to Troas
>
> (Acts 16:6-8).

God was frustrating their plans and they came to a kind of 'dead end' at the shores of Troas. But now they were in position for God to show them a different plan:

> During the night Paul had a vision of a man of Macedonia standing and begging him, "Come over to Macedonia and help us." After Paul had seen the vision, we got ready at once to leave for Macedonia, concluding that God had called us to preach the gospel to them
>
> (Acts 16:9-10).

The combination of the Spirit's blocking action and the vision guided Paul and his team to enter Macedonia, and subsequently Achaia. The province of Asia would wait until later (Acts 19).

This segues into the fourth category. *Visions, dreams and prophecies are frequently mentioned in the Bible as means by which God influences the decisions of both godly and ungodly people.* Pharaoh's two dreams, interpreted by Joseph, led him to make decisions he would not otherwise have contemplated, decisions that saved Egypt, exalted Joseph and also saved the clan of Jacob (Genesis 41-50). New Testament Joseph was guided by angels in dreams to accept and protect the baby Jesus (Matt 1:19-24; 2:13-15,19-23). Peter was motivated by a strange vision of unclean animals to listen to the Spirit and cooperate with Cornelius's request to hear

---

117. *Acts* does not use this phrase; it is a useful way commentators have organized the book.

the gospel, which he might not have agreed to otherwise, leading to a Gentile harvest (Acts 10). The church in Antioch was motivated to send help to the church of Jerusalem by a prophecy about a coming famine (Acts 11:27–30).

This does not mean that decisions have to be supernaturally originated or endorsed to be acceptable to God. Look at the 'first missionary journey' of Saul-Paul and Barnabas. It was launched with a prophetic word (Acts 13:2–4) so that they "were sent on their way by the Holy Spirit" (Acts 13:4), but there was apparently no specific word about the direction they were to take, nor was there a dream or vision to guide them. It is likely that they went to Cyprus because that was Barnabas' home (Acts 4:36) and he would know people there. God still blessed their mission there. Next they sailed to Pamphylia and then to Pisidia (Acts 13:13–52). The narrative does not explain why. The rest of this journey shows every indication of divine approval (see Acts 14:26–27).

Godly people do not have to get specific divine directions all the time; God can guide silently through very 'natural' means. Millard Erickson points out one implication of God's sovereignty in ordinary events, commenting on Jesus' encounter with the Samaritan woman in John 4:

> The wise Christian will be . . . alert to the opportunities that come in what seem at first glance to be accidental circumstances. That life is pregnant with divinely sent possibilities gives us a sense of expectancy and excitement.[118]

I'll finish this chapter by examining a specific disaster in Israel's history that brings together the themes of God's decisions, foreknowledge and human actions guided by God. The great king Solomon is declining in his devotion to the Lord, influenced by his foreign wives and their gods (1 Kings 11:1–9). His compromise angers God and God announces, "I will most certainly tear the kingdom away from you and give it to one of your subordinates" (v.11). This is apparently an unchangeable decision, maybe because God knows Solomon will not repent. But it is immediately qualified in two ways: "for the sake of David" and "for the sake of Jerusalem" it wouldn't happen until after Solomon died and the Davidic family would hold on to one tribe and the city of Jerusalem (vv.12–13).

Next the narrative reads, "Then the Lord raised up against Solomon" (v.14) two adversaries, a royal Edomite (v.14) and a leader of a small gang ruling in Damascus (vv.23–25). Both men had their own motives

---

118. Erickson, *Christian Theology*, 427.

for opposing Solomon. But the big threat comes from Jeroboam. He is initially promoted by Solomon (vv.27–28), but he has an encounter with a prophet called Ahijah who tells him of God's impending judgment on Solomon and that he would be the new king, with the promise of a lasting dynasty if he followed God's ways (vv.29–39). As a result of this Jeroboam has to go into exile in Egypt until Solomon dies (v.40).

Solomon's son Rehoboam is now set to become the new king, but as the nation is preparing for the coronation, Jeroboam returns and leads the people in making a simple demand of the new king: "lighten the harsh labor and the heavy yoke" put on them by Solomon "and we will serve you" (1 Kings 12:4). Rehoboam asks for time to consider this (v.5) and consults two groups in the intervening three days. The elders advise him to serve the people and "give them a favorable answer" (v.7), but his younger peers instead advise him to be belligerent, thus provoking rebellion (vv.8–16). The author of 1 Kings comments, "this turn of events was from the Lord, to fulfill the word the Lord had spoken to Jeroboam" (v.15). Jeroboam now becomes king of the majority of Israel (v.20), and Rehoboam's plan to conquer the north is opposed by another prophet who tells the leaders of Judah, "this [rebellion] is my doing" (v.24).

God's decision to split Israel and reduce the power of David's line was not His original intention, since previously He had promised David, "Your house and your kingdom will endure forever before me; your throne will be established forever" (2 Sam 7:16), even if Solomon sinned (2 Sam 7:14). But God acts in response to Solomon's apostasy. Having made this decision, God uses the ambitions of other leaders, the feeling of oppression among the Israelites, the foolishness of young Rehoboam (and his peers) and a prophetic word to shape the situation as He had now determined.

This story strongly affirms God's sovereignty but not in an arbitrary way; God acts in response to human decisions, but He also acts directly through prophets and His judgments stand.

In conclusion, the relationship between God's sovereignty and purposes and the actions and thoughts of other agents is more complex than might be supposed, when we read what the Bible itself says. Angels, demons and human beings are clearly portrayed as autonomous but also dependent. God's sovereignty is not dependent on their decisions, but neither is God portrayed as determining those decisions in detail. God carries out His Plans with or without them and often through them, even when they are unaware of His leading or opposed to it.

CHAPTER 9

DIVINE SOVEREIGNTY IN HUMAN LIVING

IN THE LAST CHAPTER, we considered how God's sovereignty relates to the actions and decisions of other agents, especially angels, the devil and human beings. The existence of multiple wills and agencies in God's world complicates the operation of God's sovereign plans and intentions but it does not annul God's sovereignty. But how does divine sovereignty operate in ordinary human living? Does this truth have any relevance to our sense of identity, our experiences of sickness or disability, our political lives and how we make decisions?

SICKNESS AND HEALING

Jesus' healing power raises new questions about a special arena of human experience and how it relates to God's sovereignty: the experience of sickness, disease, and disability.

Sickness and disease are clearly subject to God's sovereignty in the Old Testament, and sometimes directly attributed to God as a form of punishment. The Egyptians are struck with boils (Exod 9:8–11) and their firstborn sons die in a final plague (Exod 11:4–7; 12:12,29–30), perhaps in revenge for their murder of Israelites male babies (Exod 1:22), and as a final judgment that would release the Israelites (Exod 11:1,8; 12:31–33).

Part of the covenant between God and Israel includes freedom from such sickness: "If you listen carefully to the Lord your God and do what is right in his eyes, . . . I will not bring on you any of the diseases I brought on the Egyptians, for I am the Lord who heals you" (Exod 15:26; see also Lev 26:16,25; Deut 28:21-22,27-28,35,59-61). But plagues do befall the generation led by Moses because of their rebellion and unbelief (Exod 32:35; Num 11:33; 12:10-15; 14:37; 16:46-50; 25:8-9) and on David's generation as a result of his presumptuous census (2 Sam 24:15; 1 Chr 21:14). The kings of Israel and Judah suffer judgments such as withered hands (1 Kings 13:4,6), death of their children (1 Kings 14:1,12,17; 16:34), diseased feet (1 Kings 15:23; 2 Chr 16:12), accidental falls (2 Kings 1:2-4), and leprosy (2 Kings 15:5; 2 Chr 26:19-21).

But God's prophets perform miracles of healing, including two resurrections, through prayer (1 Kings 17:17-22; 2 Kings 4:18-37), and a Gentile military commander is even healed of leprosy (2 Kings 5:1-14), though the greedy servant of Elisha catches leprosy as a punishment (2 Kings 5:27). Elijah is taken up to heaven without dying (2 Kings 2:1-12). Elisha dies of illness (2 Kings 13:14), but his dead bones bring a resurrection (2 Kings 13:21). A special case concerns King Hezekiah, the godly king of Judah. When he becomes seriously ill, the prophet Isaiah warns him that he is about to die, but in response to the king's fervent prayer, he is promised a healing and an extension of fifteen years to his life (2 Kings 20:1-6; Isa 38:1-6).

In the New Testament, God still sometimes punishes people with sickness and death: Ananias and Sapphira are directly executed (Acts 5:5-11); King Herod "was eaten by worms and died" (Acts 12:23) after accepting adulation as a god and striking leaders of the church; and a Jewish sorcerer is temporarily blinded when he tries to influence a Roman proconsul to resist the gospel (Acts 13:8-11). Paul attributes sickness and death among the Corinthian believers to their wrong attitudes in the Lord's Supper, though he sees this as discipline as opposed to judgment (1 Cor 11:29-32). Sometimes there seems to be a link between sickness and sin, as when Jesus forgives a paralytic and demonstrates his authority to do so by healing him (Matt 9:1-8) or in James' call for confession of sin in connection for special healing prayers (James 5:15-16).

But the overwhelming emphasis of the New Testament is on *healing* through prayer and faith. Sickness is viewed as something to be removed rather than explained. Jesus and others attribute sickness to the activity of Satan (Luke 13:16; Acts 10:38); Jesus casts out demons that cause sickness (Matt 12:22; 17:18). Healing is now available because the Kingdom of God has come. In a striking case in John's Gospel, when confronted with a man blind from birth, Jesus refuses to blame either the man or his parents for the blindness (John 9:1–3), cutting across Jewish ideas derived from the covenant curse language of the Old Testament. If anything, he attributes the blindness to God's purpose "so that the works of God might be displayed in him" (John 9:3) and then proceeds to heal him. This suggests that God has sovereignly prepared this man for this encounter with Jesus, though perhaps not that God made him blind.

Jesus draws a strong connection between people's faith in him and their experience of healing. He commends those who have strong faith for such healing (Matt 8:5–10; 9:20–22,29; 15:22–28). He authorizes some of his followers to heal and "drive out impure spirits" (Matt 10:1) and reproves them for their limited faith when they fail to evict a demon from a boy (Matt 17:14–20). But he is limited in his own healing ministry when the people of Nazareth do not respect him but act in unbelief (Matt 13:54–58).

The apostles and others continue to heal the sick and disabled, including the man lame from birth at the temple gate (Acts 3:1–10; 4:22), the man in Lystra who had never walked (Acts 14:8–10) and the paralyzed Aeneas (Acts 9:33–34). These miracles are associated with faith in Jesus (Acts 3:16; 14:9). There are even some resurrections (Acts 9:36–41; 20:9–10). In Ephesus there are also "extraordinary miracles" including some using "handkerchiefs and aprons" (Acts 19:11–12).

However, there are instances where servants of God get sick and natural remedies are prescribed. Paul advises Timothy, "Stop drinking only water, and use a little wine because of your stomach and your frequent illnesses" (1 Tim 5:23). Another associate of Paul, Epaphroditus, nearly dies in Rome while serving Paul. Paul does not offer a theological reason for this and nor does he advocate an appeal for miraculous healing; he simply says, "God had mercy on him, and not on him only, to spare me sorrow upon sorrow" (Phil 2:27). Later Paul matter-of-factly reports, "I left Trophimus sick in Miletus" (2 Tim 4:20b).

What can we conclude? Should we submit to sickness as sent or allowed by God in His sovereign (and perhaps inscrutable) will? Few sick people do that. If they don't pray, they certainly take medicines or submit to surgery or change their diet or lifestyle. The New Testament encourages us to look to Jesus for healing and to minister such healing to others.

I'm reminded of the reaction of John Alexander Dowie, a forerunner of the Pentecostal movement, when an epidemic ravaged his Sydney congregation in 1875. As he earnestly prayed to God for the sick, he felt that God gave him light on healing. Shortly afterwards, he was called to the home of a young woman who was dying. As Dowie recalled,

> The doctor, a good Christian man ... said, "Sir, are not God's ways mysterious" .... "God's way!" I said. ... "How dare you, Dr K---, call that God's way....? No, sir, that is the devil's work, and it is time we called on him who came to "destroy the work of the devil," to slay that deadly and foul destroyer, and to save the child.[1]

The girl recovered.
James commands us:

> Is anyone among you sick? Let them call the elders of the church to pray over them and anoint them with oil in the name of the Lord. And the prayer offered in faith will make the sick person well; the Lord will raise them up. If they have sinned, they will be forgiven

(James 5:14–15).

This promise seems absolute, though even Christians still die. Certainly the Bible encourages people to take action to promote healing and Paul writes of "gifts of healing" that are provided to the church by the Holy Spirit (1 Cor 12:9,28,30).

If our efforts don't 'work,' we may say that God is still sovereign, but perhaps the fault is ours for not having enough faith or not fasting or simply being too passive, or worse still, for rejecting the possibility that God might heal today. However, in many cases, we simply cannot know why someone we pray for is not healed.

Certainly healing in the present is an anticipation of the future in a post-resurrection world in which the kingdom of God is fully realized. As Wolfgang Vondey comments,

> Jesus's healings are not paradigmatic realizations but more anticipations of a new world order not yet fully realized. God's sovereign will offers the hope and potential for the healing of all creation.[2]

Another issue is raised when God apparently heals someone in a way that seems to violate our theology; for example, if He uses a

---

1. G. Lindsay, *The life of John Alexander Dowie*, 26, as quoted in Barry Chant, *The Spirit of Pentecost*, 61.
2. Vondey, *Pentecostal Theology*, 117.

non-Christian, a sinful preacher or an occultist to bring healing. What do I as a Protestant Pentecostal make of healings at Lourdes or healing attributed with good reason to the intercession of a dead 'saint'? I remember reading about one such miracle that formed part of the case for the canonization of St Mary McKillop, Australia's first saint recognized by the Roman Catholic church.[3] While prayer and faith were involved, there was a definite need, and the healing was well substantiated medically, praying to a dead person to intercede with Jesus for you seems quite unbiblical. But God is sovereign and merciful, so why should I object if He chooses to heal someone in a form that seems theologically dangerous and may lead to false conclusions?

DISABILITY AND DIVINE SOVEREIGNTY

Disability, including conditions like cerebral palsy and autism, is another field. Although Jesus and the apostles healed people who were blind and lame, this is rare today and there have been many cases of abusive behavior by over-eager Pentecostals trying to heal people in wheelchairs, for example.[4] If we can confess with David, "I am fearfully and wonderfully made" (Ps 139:14a), we may have to accept God's sovereign will as the ultimate cause of many conditions that resist healing prayer. God has at least 'permitted' this even though the immediate cause may be genetic or in some way resulting from the 'fallen' world.

In Romans 8, Paul affirms God's sovereignty in the sense identified at the outset of this book: God is free to do as God chooses, God has the rights over His own creation and God is ultimately in control of events. So "in all things God works for the good of those who love him, who have been called according to his purpose" (Rom 8:28), but their highest good is not necessarily what we might expect.

As Shane Clifton, who himself is quadriplegic as a result of an accident, writes,

> while charismatic gifts may be initial evidences of the Spirit, it is transformed minds and character that matter over the long

---

3. Cf "A step closer for Mary" (*Catholic Leader* 25 December 2009 - Updated on 16 March 2021; https://catholicleader.com.au/news/a-step-closer-for-mary_54405/ , accessed April 8, 2025); . https://www.sosj.org.au/canonisation-of-st-mary-mackillop/ (2020; accessed April 8, 2025);

4. Cf. Shane Clifton, "The Dark Side of Prayer for Healing," 205–218.

haul, especially if happiness is understood to transcend temporary euphoria and exist in the narrative of a meaningful life.[5]

More deeply, Amos Yong has questioned the common attitude to disability, as if disabled people are somehow 'unwhole' or deficient.[6] He suggests that disabled believers may have a special part to play in the body of Christ. Paul himself suffered, at least intermittently, from a physical infirmity. He says to the Galatians

> As you know, it was because of an illness[7] that I first preached the gospel to you, and even though my illness was a trial to you, you did not treat me with contempt or scorn

(Gal 4:13–14a).

Sometimes this is taken to be an eye disease or partial blindness, based on v.15. Certainly it was something which may have called forth "contempt or scorn."[8] Whatever we make of this, God didn't remove the 'illness.'

Paul also writes, "on the contrary, those parts of the body that seem to be weaker are indispensable" (1 Cor 12:22).[9] As Yong comments,

> Instead, the Spirit distributes gifts liberally and graciously so that people with disabilities are just as capable of contributing to the edification of the community of faith and hence are necessary in that sense.[10]

At the very least, this suggests that God in His sovereignty has 'allowed' the disability for a purpose of His own.

Amos Yong also argues that "some impairments are so identity-constitutive that their removal would involve the obliteration of the person as well,"[11] thus raising questions about the common idea that all signs of disability will be removed in the new creation (or heaven). Rather, using the resurrected body of Jesus, with the marks of the crucifixion still visible, as a paradigm for the future general resurrection, he argues that people with disabilities will still resemble their current selves in the new

---

5. Clifton, "Dark Side," 221.
6. Cf. Yong, *The Bible, Disability and the Church*.
7. The Greek is *astheneian tēs sarkos* (literally "weakness of the flesh").
8. See Yong, *The Bible, Disability and the Church*, 83–85.
9. Cf. Yong, "Disability and the Gifts of the Spirit," 86–87.
10. Yong, "Disability," 87; cf. Yong, *The Bible, Disability and the Church*, 91–96.
11. Yong, *The Bible, Disability and the Church*, 121.

order, though transformed. Their God-given identity is not annulled but enhanced.[12]

ORIGINS AND IDENTITY

"Shall what is formed say to the one who formed it, 'why did you make me like this?'" (Rom 9:20). One thing that we all have no control over is our own original identity. Our parentage, our ethnic origin, our place of birth, our gender, the fact that we were born at all,[13] the circumstances into which we were born, our appearance, many of our strengths and weaknesses, our aptitudes were all given. This is something people struggle with today and some of these circumstances can now be altered owing to modern medical technology. But should we do so? Most people would be comfortable with at least some changes and Paul encourages it: "Were you a slave when you were called? Don't let it trouble you–although if you can gain your freedom, do so" (1 Cor 7:21). But in general, he advises, "each person, as responsible to God, should remain in the condition they were in when God called them" (1 Cor 7:24).

This opens several options. You were born to certain parents in a particular time and place because your father and mother chose to have sexual intercourse (unless rape or IVF was involved). Your conception also was a 'lucky accident' when a sperm connected with an egg in your mother's womb. You inherited certain traits from your parents and ancestors, including a propensity to certain illnesses and disabilities. And yet David says of his own conception,

> I praise you because I am fearfully and wonderfully made;
> your works are wonderful,
> I know that full well.
> Your eyes saw my unformed body;
> all the days ordained for me were written in your book
> before one of them came to be.
>
> (Ps 139:14–16).

David clearly believed he was made by God and that God had ordained the days of his life. God's sovereignty controlled all the details of his identity and his future, in this case at least.

---

12. Yong, *The Bible, Disability and the Church*, 125–135.
13. The Bible implies that procreation is a gift from God (Gen 4:1,25; 18:10–14; 25:21; 30:2; Ruth 4:13; Ps 139:13). Cf Carson, *Sovereignty and Responsibility*, 27.

Can this be generalized to every person who has ever lived? God's sovereignty suggests it can, that God is involved with the birth and life of every person ever conceived, that He has some kind of plan for every life and at least permits the circumstances that everyone faces.

This is also relevant to a theology of disability. As Amos Yong contends,

> People with disabilities are created in the image of God that is measured according to the person of Christ, not by any Mr. Universe or Ms. America. As we know, *God doesn't make mistakes*, and people with disabilities should be appreciated as being uniquely different, even differently-abled.[14]

Scripture suggests that we should draw our sense of identity from God Himself, not from our human origins. As Paul writes, "There is neither Jew nor Gentile, neither slave nor free, nor is there male and female, for you are all one in Christ Jesus" (Gal 3:28). Paul's own sense of identity had been grounded in his Hebrew roots (Phil 3:4–5), but when he became a Christian he considered all such things as "loss because of the surpassing worth of knowing Christ Jesus" (Phil 3:8). God's sovereignty over our origins is not like an absolute fixed destiny. Or to put it another way, our true identity comes from Christ, not Adam.[15]

LIFE AND DEATH ETHICS

Especially in the Western world, there has been a long struggle in every nation for several decades about two major issues of life and death: abortion and euthanasia. Most Western countries have passed legislation legalizing the abortion of unwanted unborn children and the termination of life on request for people suffering incurable and painful sicknesses. The issues involved are much contested and I haven't space to explore them all. But does the doctrine of divine sovereignty have a relevant perspective for these debates, at least among Christians?

A simple, perhaps simplistic, approach would assert that both abortion and euthanasia are an affront to, or rebellion against, God's sovereign rights over human life. If life is the gift of God, and God created each of us in our mother's womb (as Psalm 139:13 suggests), no unborn child should be killed in the womb. Similarly, God is the only Person who

---

14. Yong, *The Bible, Disability and the Church*, 13 (emphasis added).
15. Grenz, *Theology for the Community of God*, 112.

has the right to decide the time of my death. Abortionists, euthanasia practitioners, doctors involved in artificial procedures like IVF, researchers interfering with DNA or stem cells are regularly accused of 'playing God.' Many of them would retort that all medical interventions could be rejected on such grounds.

Rights to life are not absolute in the Bible. While God's rights can be challenged and resisted by human and angelic or demonic agents, God's freedom to act as He sees fit cannot be resisted or limited in any way, except by His divine nature. Natural abortions or 'miscarriages' are a common feature of human experience and so is stillbirth. All such deaths are tragic and a source of grief for the parents. But if God is involved in the processes of conception and birth, as we have suggested earlier, then such events are not outside His control or guidance. In fact, such events can be seen at times as attributable to divine mercy. Who knows what trials and tragedies such unborn children have been spared, especially if they have genetic disabilities or diseases? After all, Job's first cry, when he made his protest against what had happened to him, was "if only I had not been born" (Job 3:1–16). He prefers death like a person who asks for euthanasia (Job 3:20–21).

So the abortionist, or the person who administers a mercy-killing, may be fulfilling divine plans, consciously or otherwise. This does not justify what they do; a murderer, rapist or soldier may also be used by the sovereign hand of God. Invoking God's sovereignty can never excuse or condemn any human action by itself. Abortion and euthanasia are sinful to the extent that they violate specific commands of God in Scripture. But no one can thwart what God is determined to bring about and we know that God permits, and even uses, sinful actions, for His purposes.

DECISION-MAKING AND GOD

Some years ago, I read an interesting book called *Decision-Making and the Will of God*.[16] The author criticized the tendency on some people's part to ask God for specific direction for every decision they wanted to make, instead of exercising wise judgment, staying within the bounds of Bible instruction, and trusting God for sovereign guidance as they make their own responsible decisions. While the author was too skeptical about

---

16. By Garry Friesen.

the possibility of hearing God's voice in ordinary life or the church, his overall counsel was solid.

Proverbs 3:5–6 gives some good advice then:

> Trust in the LORD with all your heart
> and lean not on your own understanding;
> in all your ways submit to him,
> and he will make your paths straight.

If we are surrendered to God in the direction we want to take and trusting His guidance, we can trust Him to lead us, to "make our paths straight." In a similar way, Prov 16:3 says, "Commit to the LORD whatever you do, and he will establish your plans." This is not a fail-safe guarantee of success but wise counsel that depends on God's sovereign ability to "straighten" and "establish" things that are outside our capacity to control. Proverbs 19:21 therefore advises, "Many are the plans in a person's heart, but it is the LORD's purpose that prevails." And Prov 21:30 adds, "There is no wisdom, no insight, no plan that can succeed against the LORD."[17]

Of course, these assurances only encourage us if we are trusting God and surrendering our plans to Him. We see this particularly clearly in the life of the apostle Paul. Paul planned ahead according to the light he had and the calling that was on his life. His plans to minister in Asia and Bithynia were blocked by the Holy Spirit (Acts 16:6–7) before he had a night vision that redirected him to Macedonia (Acts 16:9–10). Later he planned a visit to the Corinthian church, partly with a disciplinary purpose, "if the Lord is willing" (1 Cor 4:19), after his work in Ephesus was completed: "I hope to spend some time with you, if the Lord permits" (1 Cor 16:7–8). Earlier a visit to encourage to infant church in Thessalonica was somehow blocked by Satan (1 Thess 2:17–18).

A major plan involved a visit to Rome: "I pray that now at last by God's will the way may be opened for me to come to you" (Rom 1:10). This desire was so far unrealized (Rom 1:13). He now expected to be able to make such a trip as he planned the next stages of his work: first, delivering his contribution to the church in Jerusalem, then visiting Rome en route to a new field in Spain (Rom 15:23–28). But in making these plans he depended on God and therefore called the Christians in Rome to pray:

> Pray that I may be kept safe from the unbelievers in Judea and that the contribution I take to Jerusalem may be favorably

---

17. See also Prov 16:1,9,33.

received by the Lord's people there, so that I may come to you with joy, by God's will, and in your company be refreshed

(Rom 15:31-32).

Paul was aware of dangers ahead and could not assume things would work out. Reading Acts 20-28, we can see that Paul did get to Rome, but not in the way he may have expected. He was nearly lynched in Jerusalem, spent years in Roman custody in Caesarea, survived several plots to kill him, endured unnecessary and unfair trials, came close to death by shipwreck, and finally arrived in Rome as a prisoner. It was not how he planned it, but God's control was evident, or at least it is to us as readers, and God provided explicit guidance in the midst of a storm that threatened Paul's life and that of others:

> "But now I urge you to keep up your courage, because not one of you will be lost; only the ship will be destroyed. Last night an angel of the God to whom I belong and whom I serve stood beside me and said, 'Do not be afraid, Paul. You must stand trial before Caesar; and God has graciously given you the lives of all who sail with you.' So keep up your courage, men, for I have faith in God that it will happen just as he told me. Nevertheless, we must run aground on some island."

(Acts 27:22-26).

Much can be learned from this speech of Paul's. God had control over the storm and the fate of the sailors, but He did not prevent the storm happening and they must still face shipwreck. God controlled Paul's destiny, but he must stand trial rather than being released (in contrast, say, with Peter in Acts 12). They will all be saved, but must still do the sensible thing and try to run the ship aground on an island (and later Paul intervened to prevent disaster–Acts 27:30-32, 42-43).

We are always tempted to make plans without considering the God factor. James therefore warns us:

> Now listen, you who say, "Today or tomorrow we will go to this or that city, spend a year there, carry on business and make money." Why, you do not even know what will happen tomorrow. What is your life? You are a mist that appears for a little while and then vanishes. Instead, you ought to say, "If it is the Lord's will, we will live and do this or that." As it is, you boast in your arrogant schemes. All such boasting is evil

(James 4:13-16).

I first wrote this in the midst of the coronavirus epidemic that began in 2020. I had to cancel many plans and flights over that period, because of restrictions and lockdowns, and spent fourteen days locked down at home without family over Christmas 2020. James warns us against 'taking God for granted' in our complacency and arrogance, a special temptation for people in Western countries. Not only can we not predict what the future will bring, we can't even guarantee we will live to see it.

Some stories from the Old Testament illustrate good and bad planning and decision-making in relation to God's sovereign will. Genesis 24 is the story of seeking a wife for Abraham's son Isaac. It would, of course, be an arranged marriage. But not just any girl would do. Abraham sends off his servant to find the 'right' one, which first meant someone from Abraham's clan, not the Canaanites (vv.3–4). Then, of course, the girl must be willing to come (vv.5,8). But at that point, Abraham's faith kicks in:

> "The LORD, the God of heaven, who brought me out of my father's household and my native land and who spoke to me and promised me with an oath, saying, 'To your offspring I will give this land'- he will send his angel before you so that you can get a wife for my son from there" (vv.7–8).

Abraham relies on God's previous words and His faithfulness and sovereignty to make it happen. Sure enough, when the servant arrives in Aram Nahanaim and the well outside "the town of Nahor" (vv.10–11), he prays to God for success and asks specifically that the young woman who comes out to the well and is willing to give him and his camels a drink will be the one: "By this I will know that you have shown kindness to my master" (vv.12–14). The text goes on, "Before he had finished praying, Rebekah came out with her jar on her shoulder" (v.15). She meets all the criteria: she comes from the right family, she is a virgin, she gives the servant and the camels a drink, and she welcomes this unknown man as a guest (vv.15–25). The servant responds with worship:

> "Praise be to the LORD, the God of my master Abraham, who has not abandoned his kindness and faithfulness to my master. As for me, the LORD has led me on the journey to the house of my master's relatives" (vv.26–27).

Trust in God is being rewarded. Now this was not a case of mere luck or passivity. The servant had sought the right town and had a clear brief. Moreover, he then had to negotiate the deal with Rebekah and her family (vv.30–60). But clearly, God "had led me on the right road" (v.48). Note that everyone in this story acts freely but the guidance of God makes the servant's path straight.

But not all people make good decisions like this. During the invasion of Canaan by the Israelites, several times things went wrong when Joshua and his team failed to seek God and surrender their plans to Him. Not knowing about Achan's sin, they over confidently planned to take the city of Ai with a reduced force because it was a small town, and they were defeated (Josh 7:3–5). Afterwards, when the Gibeonites deceitfully offered to make a treaty with them, they "did not inquire of the LORD" (Josh 9:14) and made the treaty, only to find that they had been deceived and were now committed to defending the Gibeonites (Josh 9:19–26).

Putting all this together, it would appear that the truth of God's sovereignty should give us strong confidence in following God's leading even in challenging circumstances. He is capable of changing situations and even influencing the decisions of others when He chooses to. When God does not change things as we might expect, we have to trust His wisdom and faithfulness. But on the other hand, a knowledge of God's sovereignty should also lead us to plan submissively without being overconfident or complacent, since God may withstand our actions or simply just not favor them.

DREAMS AND GUIDANCE

God guides events to His own goals and intervenes in the lives of people in differing ways, including by means of dreams, to direct them in ways appropriate to His will. God rescues Sarah from the Philistine king's harem through a dream (Gen 20:3–7). The dreams of Joseph (Genesis 37) prophetically inspire a particular sense of destiny. The dreams of Pharaoh's servants, and of Pharaoh himself, give Joseph opportunity to use his prophetic gift and lead to his destiny being fulfilled. God has a divine conversation with Solomon in a dream with far reaching consequences (1 Kings 3:5–15). Dreams and visions are God's "normal" way of speaking to prophets (Num 12:6; Acts 2:17).

In the New Testament, Joseph in a dream sees an angel who guides him to stay engaged to Mary (Matt 1:20–24) and later urges him to flee to Egypt with Mary and the baby Jesus (Matt 2:13), and later still, to return to Israel and relocate to Nazareth (Matt 2:19–23). The wise men are also directed in a dream not to return to Herod after visiting the holy family (Matt 2:12). Paul is sometimes guided by night visions, probably in dreams (Acts 16:9; 18:9–10).

Clearly then God uses dreams to guide people, especially His own people. Elihu, Job's younger advisor, emphasizes this:

> "For God does speak- now one way, now another-
> though no one perceives it.
> In a dream, in a vision of the night,
> when deep sleep falls on people
> as they slumber in their beds."

(Job 33:14–15).

Divine dreams and visions are given sparingly in the Bible, usually only in crisis or dangerous situations. However, we should be open to the possibility of God speaking to us that way. My wife and I have both had significant dreams that guided us in important ways; in fact, she saw my face in a dream years before we met in response to her prayers for guidance in relation to a different young man. Such dreams and visions are imparted by the Spirit at His discretion; that is, they are subject to God's sovereign will, based on His knowledge of our situation and need. But just as Paul encourages us to "earnestly desire spiritual gifts" (1 Cor 14:1), so we can legitimately ask God to speak to us even in dreams and seek to interpret God-given dreams we may already be having.[18]

FINANCE AND PROSPERITY

We saw in Chapter 1 that God is the ultimate Provider of all needs. While we are expected to work for our living, and indeed, "The one who is unwilling to work shall not eat" (2 Thess 3:10), we look to God as our Provider and show gratitude to Him as the Creator and Owner of all. Giving offerings for God's cause and for God's needy people, and especially the local church and its appointed ministers and leaders, is mainly an expression of gratitude for His provision. It expresses our sense of dependence on the sovereign Creator for whatever we have and our confidence in His ongoing provision (2 Cor 9:8–11).

The financial relationship between the apostle Paul and the church he had planted in Philippi is a case in point. This church had been planted

---

18. For more on this, see Tania Harris, *God Dreams*.

in difficult circumstances, including the arrest and overnight imprisonment of Paul and Silas, precipitated by Paul depriving a master of his income from a psychic female slave (Acts 16:16-24). While a businesswoman called Lydia (Acts 16:14-15) and the jailer (Acts 16:25-34) had become believers, and presumably had some means, this church was known for "extreme poverty" (2 Cor 8:2). However, they had supported Paul financially from the outset (Phil 4:15-16) and their generosity was used by Paul to stir up the less generous Corinthians to contribute to his fundraiser for the church in Jerusalem (2 Cor 8:1-7). Later, when Paul was in prison, they sent several contributions for his support (Phil 4:10,14,18).

However, Paul's eyes were on the Lord. He had learned to be content in situations of plenty and times of need; in fact, "I can do all this through him who gives me strength" (Phil 4:13). He was unable to repay the Philippians for their support but "they are a fragrant offering, an acceptable sacrifice, pleasing to God. And my God will meet all your needs according to the riches of his glory in Christ Jesus" (Phil 4:18b-19).

Clearly Paul expected that God would reward this church for their sacrificial generosity to him and to other churches. However, this does not imply a kind of transactional view of the relationship between giving and receiving. Jesus says, "Give, and it will be given to you. A good measure, pressed down, shaken together and running over will be poured into your lap. For with the measure you use, it will be measured to you" (Luke 6:38). He is commending generosity and assuring his disciples that they will not be disadvantaged by sacrificial giving. In fact, he suggests that generous people will receive more provision from God than those who are reluctant or stingy. But this not intended as a kind of chequebook concept, as if God 'owes' the giver a certain reward. Rather such generosity recognizes God as the Source of all good things we currently enjoy: "Everything comes from you, and we have given you only what comes from your hand" (1 Chr 29:14).

However, as we have seen, God has chosen to use human beings to fulfill His purposes, and that includes providing for the needs of other human beings. So in the infant church of Jerusalem, we read,

> God's grace was so powerfully at work in them all that there were no needy persons among them. For from time to time those who owned land or houses sold them, brought the money from the sales and put it at the apostles' feet, and it was distributed to anyone who had need

(Acts 4:33b-35)

This provision is attributed to the "grace of God," but this works by the Spirit inspiring sacrificial generosity among the believers. The result is provision of every need. Later, the church in Antioch, prompted by a prophecy of a forthcoming famine, "as each was able, decided to provide help for the brothers and sisters living in Judea" (Acts 11:29). And Paul later takes up a similar collection among his Gentile churches for the Christians in Jerusalem. As he writes to the Corinthians, the purpose of this is meeting needs:

> Our desire is not that others might be relieved while you are hard pressed, but that there might be equality. At the present time your plenty will supply what they need, so that in turn their plenty will supply what you need. The goal is equality, as it is written, "The one who gathered much did not have too much, and the one who gathered little did not have too little."

(2 Cor 8:13–15).

This is how God provides for the needs of His people, by blessing them directly and inspiring them to give generously to others (2 Cor 9:8–11). Hence the prosperous Christians must play their part in this divine economy, recognizing the source of their prosperity:

> Command those who are rich in this present world not to be arrogant nor to put their hope in wealth, which is so uncertain, but to put their hope in God, *who richly provides us with everything for our enjoyment.* Command them to do good, to be rich in good deeds, and to be generous and willing to share. In this way they will lay up treasure for themselves as a firm foundation for the coming age, so that they may take hold of the life that is truly life

(1 Tim 6:17–19, emphasis added).

The sovereign God is the Source of prosperity, but human believers are His channels to distribute such blessings fairly.

HUMAN CREATIVITY AND INSPIRATION

Human beings are unique in all of God's creation in being created in God's image (Gen 1:26–27) with a mandate to govern the earth on His behalf. To display this image of the Creator and carry out such a huge mandate required humans to have a high order of intelligence and creativity. This was displayed in Adam's naming of the animals (Gen 2:19–20) and Noah using skills of a high order to build a large boat to God's design (Gen 6:14–16,22). Later God filled Bezazel and Oholiab with wisdom and skill to design the features of the tent that God has designed for His dwelling amongst the Israelites (Exod 35:30–35) and to teach these skills to others (Exod 35:34). Still later, David creatively designed the temple which would be constructed in his successor's reign under the Spirit's inspiration (1 Chr 28:11–19).

Much Hebrew literature, including poetry, reflects God's inspiration and is directed to God. David wrote these words near the end of his life:

> The inspired utterance of David son of Jesse,
> the utterance of the man exalted by the Most High,
> the man anointed by the God of Jacob,
> the hero of Israel's songs:
> The Spirit of the LORD spoke through me;
> his word was on my tongue

(2 Sam 23:1–2).

However, not all creative endeavor is said to be directly inspired by the Holy Spirit. The earliest instrumental music described in the Bible comes from a son of the ungodly Lamech (Gen 4:21) and his brother "forged all kinds of tools our of bronze and iron" (Gen 4:22). Nevertheless both inventions were taken up by God's people and used to create items that glorified God.

But these cases provoke questions about the source of human inspiration in all fields, artistic and technical. Does God's sovereignty superintend such creativity even when the results are secular or even antagonistic to God? Or to put it another way, does creative inspiration originate in the grace of God or the working of His Spirit or just in human nature or even demonic sources?

While unsaved persons are sinful, they still seem capable of inspired creation and heroic actions independently of God, perhaps because of what some theologians call 'common grace'. I am thinking of the writing of a Shakespeare, the music of a Mozart, the art of a Rembrandt, the philosophic musings of a Plato or Descartes, the inventive genius of a James Watt, the inspired leadership of a Churchill, the scientific discoveries of an Isaac Newton or Marie Curie, the just reforms of an Abraham Lincoln, or the struggles of a Mohandas (Mahatma) Gandhi when I ask such questions. Some of their work was 'inspired' to a high degree, displaying real truth and unveiling powerful insights into justice, human nature and the natural world.

Arthur Custance points out that the intelligence and gifts of people are often turned towards evil ends and that even good human creation may be carried out for selfish or devious motives. Hence common grace must be source of good deeds, for it is "a reflection of the benevolent sovereignty of God whereby He maintains in fallen man his ability to *do good.*"[19]

Let's look at some examples in the Bible. Balaam was a complex character with a great interest in the spiritual world and fame in the area of divination or sorcery. He was the kind of person who could discern what was happening in the spirit world and even manipulate spiritual forces in the service of his clients, which is why King Balak sent for him (Num 22:4–7). He did not have a clear allegiance to God, but he had some kind of connection with the deity: he could hear from God and converse with Him in dreams and other means (Num 22:8–13,19–20). Because his heart was not right, God had to hedge him in to keep him on track, as in the famous incident with his donkey (Num 22:21–35). He claimed to be careful to "speak only what God puts in my mouth" (Num 22:38; 23:12). He delivered several inspired prophetic words, especially when he abandoned his normal methods of divination and "the Spirit of God came on him" (Num 24:1–2), leading him to a deeper revelation that was literally inspired (Num 24:3–4,15–16) and included predictive prophecy (Num 24:14, 17–24). And yet his heart was unchanged, and he used his spiritual insights to prepare a devious plan against the Israelites (Num 25:1–3; 31:16). Such a person was clearly unrighteous but still capable of being inspired by God in a prophetic ministry.

In Paul's speech to the Athenian philosophers at the Areopagus, he quoted two Greek poets as well as referring to the altar "to an unknown god" (Acts 17:23,28). The two poets were a Cretan and a Stoic philosopher, praising Zeus or other pagan gods, but Paul saw their insights as worthy of note and true and apparently saw God's grace as the ultimate source since God had been guiding their nation (Acts 17:27).

Certainly, then, human inspiration and creativity owes a lot to our human capacity to reflect God's image and to the quiet work of the Holy Spirit.

---

19. Custance, *Sovereignty of Grace*, 99.

GOD'S SOVEREIGNTY AND THE INSPIRATION OF SCRIPTURE

The inspiration of the Bible provides a good case study of how God's sovereignty can work with human initiative and partnership.

Paul writes to his spiritual son Timothy about,

> . . . how from infancy you have known the Holy Scriptures, which are able to make you wise for salvation through faith in Christ Jesus. All Scripture is God-breathed [or inspired by God] and is useful for teaching, rebuking, correcting and training in righteousness, so that the servant of God may be thoroughly equipped for every good work
>
> (2 Tim 3:15–17).

Paul's main emphasis is the usefulness of the Scriptures both to bring people to salvation and to equip God's servants for their service of God. But the reason they are so useful lies especially in their nature and origin; primarily Scripture has its origin in God and is indeed "God-breathed" as the NIV puts it.

But there were human authors involved in every case. Peter, one of those human authors, wrote,

> Above all, you must understand that no prophecy of Scripture came about by the prophet's own interpretation of things. For prophecy *never had its origin* in the human will, but prophets, though human, spoke from God as they were carried along by the Holy Spirit
>
> (2 Pet 1:20–21; emphasis added).

So Scripture has a divine origin but comes through human channels.

However, there is no sense of prophets just taking dictation from God anywhere in the Bible. Even at their most passive, as in the case of visions, they use their own human language and thought forms to speak of what they have seen and heard. They "spoke from God" as humans, but they were also "carried along by the Holy Spirit." To put it another way, God sovereignly directed or supervised what they said and wrote, but it was still them speaking and writing. The authors themselves were not infallible and could go astray (as in the case of Peter in Galatians 2), but nonetheless even their choice of words as they wrote Scripture was guided by God.[20] God's sovereignty thus included both the preparation of each author and God's directing of their thoughts as they wrote.[21]

Peter gives a crucial example of this in his first letter. Speaking of the salvation his readers were now experiencing, he says,

> Concerning this salvation, the prophets, who spoke of the grace that was to come to you, searched intently and with the greatest care, trying to find out the time and circumstances to which *the Spirit of Christ in them* was pointing when he predicted the sufferings of the Messiah and the glories that would follow

(1 Pet 1:10–11; emphasis added).

The prophets were being guided *from within* by "the Spirit of Christ" as they wrote things that they could not understand fully, but knew they were for a future time. Thus they accurately predicted what now constitutes the Christian gospel.

Sometimes this meant God spoke to them directly and verbally, as in Jeremiah's call narrative. God called him to be a prophet (Jer 1:4–5). Jeremiah objected on the basis of his youth and inability to speak well (v.6). But the Lord rejected the objection and amplified the call (v.7). The dialogue goes on for the rest of the chapter. The rest of the book of Jeremiah largely contains oracles, that is, oral messages given by God for Jeremiah to declare in specific situations or directives for Jeremiah to take certain prophetically significant actions (as in Jer 13:1–11; 18:1–12; and 32:1–44).

However, at times we hear again the prophet's human voice objecting to what he has been told (Jer 4:9; 20:7–18), complaining about his contemporaries (Jer 14:13; 18:19–23; 23:9–32), narrating aspects of his own journey (Jer 11:18–20; 18:18; 20:1–6; 26:1–28:17), and praying to God about aspects of the situation he found himself in (Jer 12:1–4). There are also several predictive prophecies of coming disaster (Jer 1:14–16; 23:1–2; 25:1–11) and subsequent restoration (Jer 21:3–4; 25:12; 30:1–31:40) and some of a messianic nature (as in Jer 23:5). In a revealing episode, we get to see how the book of Jeremiah was compiled from all these oracles, revelations and reminiscences in spite of the king trying to destroy the text (Jer 36:1–32). So the book of Jeremiah was not dictated or 'sent down' from heaven; it was compiled by Jeremiah's secretary

---

20. For a lengthy explanation and defence of this view of inspiration, see Millard J. Erickson, *Christian Theology*, 225–245.

21. Cf. Erickson, *Christian Theology*, 242–243.

Baruch in a very natural way out of oracles delivered by the prophet, his own thoughts about his situation, and his memories of various events, though the contents of these oracles and memories are attributed to, or guided by, God.

Some other Bible books are even more 'indirectly' inspired by God than Jeremiah. The book of Esther, for example, never even mentions God. Other historical books are largely narratives. The Psalms are prayers and expressions of praise, including laments and cries for vengeance. The Old Testament consists of a variety of literary genres, in other words. God's guidance and inspiration are implied or assumed, not explicit, in most cases.

When we turn to the New Testament, the same principle applies. Luke compiles his Gospel through a process of investigation and (apparently) interviews of eyewitnesses (Luke 1:1–3). The Fourth Gospel is built on the eyewitness testimony of a single disciple (John 21:24). Paul, Peter, James and John wrote letters to individuals and churches as needed, depending on the situations they saw or heard of or in response to letters they received (see 1 Cor 1:11; 5:1,9; 7:1; 11:18). At times they claimed direct authority from Christ (1 Cor 7:10; 14:37) but other times they simply advised as trusted leaders (1 Cor 7:12,25). Only John in Revelation claims to be writing an authoritative prophecy that must be treated somewhat like Scripture (Rev 22:18–19). In each case the authors display their characteristic vocabulary and thought forms.

Thus the creation of an authoritative inspired book demonstrates the subtlety of God's sovereignty at work with humans. The Bible is *both* a thoroughly human book, bearing the distinctive flavors of its human authors, *and* a thoroughly divine revelation due to God's sovereign and effective guidance of those authors.

HUMAN GOVERNMENT AND DIVINE GOVERNMENT

The Bible teaches us to pray for our leaders (1 Tim 2:1–2) and to submit to civil government (Rom 13:1). These obligations are theologically grounded and relate strongly to God's sovereign work in the world. I want to affirm three points here.

1. *Civil government is God's idea*

We established in Chapter 2 that God entrusted the government of the earth to human beings (Gen 1:26–28) and God has not rescinded this decision. As a result of the overflowing wickedness and violence of the post-Fall world, God wiped out everyone except Noah's family in the Flood. Subsequently, God initiated the beginnings of human civil government with authority over other human beings, when he ordered:

> "Whoever sheds human blood,
> By *humans* shall their blood be shed;
> For in the image of God
> Has God made mankind."
> (Gen 9:6, emphasis added).

This was perhaps no more than a right of revenge initially, and the sophisticated society implied by the Babel project was rejected by God, but in the Mosaic legislation (Exodus to Deuteronomy) we see a more developed system of civil government in Israel, including provision for a monarchy (Deut 17:14–20).

The New Testament, written in the time of the Roman Empire, makes strong statements about civil government. Paul writes:

> Let everyone be subject to the governing authorities, for there is no authority *except that which God has established*. The authorities that exist have been *established by God*. Consequently, whoever rebels against the authority is rebelling against *what God has instituted*, and those who do so will bring judgment on themselves . . . . . The one in authority is *God's servant* for your good. But if you do wrong, be afraid, for rulers do not bear the sword for no reason. They are *God's servants*, agents of wrath to bring punishment on the wrongdoer. . . . The authorities are *God's servants*, who give their full time to governing
>
> (Rom 13:1–2,4–6, emphasis added).

This passage affirms that all (civil) authority has been established by God with the power of the sword (that is, punishment) to fulfill the role of God's ministers. God thus exercises His sovereignty and dominion through such rulers and expects us to submit to their authority, including paying taxes and the like (Rom 13:7; see also Tit 3:1).

Peter also gives a similar exhortation:

> Submit yourselves for the Lord's sake to every human authority: whether to the emperor, as the supreme authority, or to governors, who are sent by him to punish those who do wrong and

to commend those who do right . . . Show proper respect to everyone . . . honor the emperor

(1 Pet 2:13,14,17).

And Jesus boldly says to Pilate as the Roman governor, "You would have no power over me if it were not given to you from above" (John 19:11a).

2. *God controls who is in power*

This is more contentious and in tension with modern ideas of democracy. Most civil governments in biblical times were monarchies or authoritarian regimes of one kind or another. The Roman empire had a veneer of republican quasi-democratic government forms, but it was largely a facade for the rule of the emperor, whose main source of power was the army. And in all such systems, power is ultimately built on violence, even though there may be other means of legitimating a ruler, such as by descent (as in Judah and most modern monarchies) or divine utterance (as in the case of Jehu, see 1 Kings 19:16–17) or some form of consent at least by the aristocratic elite (such as the Roman senate). Governments were changed by natural succession (death of the father leading to the son's accession), assassination, military coups, rebellions and invasions. In many nations today that is still the case. Peaceful transitions of power in response to popular voting are not universal even now.

But the Bible asserts the sovereignty of God in the midst of these turbulent processes. As we saw earlier with respect to Nebuchadnezzar, this mighty king had to acknowledge that "the Most High is sovereign over all kingdoms on earth and gives them to anyone he wishes" (Dan 4:25,32; see also verse 17), and this was demonstrated in him losing and then regaining his position (Dan 4:28–37). As Jeremiah had earlier declared, "With my great power and outstretched arm I made the earth and its people and the animals that are on it, and I give it to anyone I please" (Jer 27:5). This does not mean that God acts arbitrarily or capriciously, but that He has the final say.

This surely applies to the modern state as well as the ancient world. It implies that, in general, God supports governments that act justly and honor God, but will depose rulers who are cruel and rebellious towards Him. However, this is not what we often see in practice. As I wrote the first draft of this chapter (August 2021), the relatively extreme Islamist Taliban had finally ousted the democratically elected moderate Muslim regime, installed with western aid in Afghanistan, after a twenty-year struggle. Was this God's will? And many other oppressive regimes have maintained themselves in power for many years; perhaps North Korea is the prime example.

Was God behind the communist victory in China in 1949 against a regime that, while corrupt and ineffectual, was tolerant of Christians and missionaries and led by a nominal Christian? The result was a violent suppression of the church, massive starvation, economic disaster and the 'Cultural Revolution' against all conventional authority in the name of Mao. But after that, there was a massive explosion in Christianity to perhaps as much as 10% of the population.[22] Interpreting what God is doing in the political arena is notoriously problematic, but these examples might suggest that God is still sovereign, or at least at work, even there.

The Bible also suggests that God guides the decisions even of ungodly governments. We have seen how God dealt with King Nebuchadnezzar in Daniel 4. In Prov 21:1, we also read, "In the LORD's hand the king's heart is a stream of water that he channels toward all who please him." This verse does not say that God is always controlling what the king decides, only that He can do so. But it does imply that God can and does influence rulers to favor God's own servants. In Ezra 1:1, we read that "in order to fulfill the word of the LORD spoken by Jeremiah, the LORD moved the heart of Cyrus king of Persia to make a proclamation throughout his realm and also to put it in writing" releasing the new exodus of Jews to Israel and the rebuilding of the temple in Jerusalem (Ezra 1:2–3). And later Nehemiah, having received a God-ordained burden to rebuild the walls of Jerusalem and soaked his plans in prayer, gained favor with King Artaxerxes to travel to Jerusalem for this purpose; cheekily he even obtained safe-conduct letters and resources of timber for building (Neh 2:1–8).

3. *Christians need to interact with governments on this basis*

If God is still in ultimate control of governments, does this mean that Christians should passively accept whoever or whatever happens in the political sphere? What role should we play?

The boundaries of human governmental authority are often ambiguous and contested. Such debates lay behind the approach of the Pharisees and Herodians to Jesus to test him with a vexatious question about

---

22. Cf. Sigurd Kaiser, "Church Growth in China," 36–37.

Roman taxes (Matt 22:15–22). Jesus replied, "So give back to Caesar what is Caesar's, and to God what is God's" (v.21). In context, Jesus appears to endorse paying taxes as part of the Roman imperial system but claims the whole human person 'made in God's image' for God. Subsequently, Peter and the apostles declared, "We must obey God rather than human beings!" (Acts 5:29) and refused to submit to the demand by the Jerusalem temple authorities not to speak in the name of Jesus (Acts 5:40–42). In the Old Testament, the prophets of God also stood against ungodly monarchs and criticized godly rulers who went astray in God's name; the famous confrontation of Nathan with David is a case in point (2 Sam 12:1–14).

Such 'civil disobedience' has a long history and Peter would have been aware of the disobedience of Daniel's three friends (Daniel 3) and Daniel himself (Daniel 6). In both stories, the king claimed a greater authority than was his due and laid claim to what belongs to God, by commanding worship of a statue (Nebuchadnezzar) and prohibiting prayer except to himself (Darius). Clearly, when civil or religious authorities order what God prohibits or prohibit what God commands, God's people must resist, with respect and acceptance of the consequences, because God's claims take priority. Revelation 13–14 illustrates this principle starkly. Only the elect resist the claims of the sea beast to worship and refuse to take his mark; they are killed, but those who comply with the beasts are doomed to everlasting punishment (Rev 14:9–11).

But Daniel was also an imperial servant and did not refuse to uphold the government of both empires he worked with. Joseph, too, acted as a loyal minister of Pharaoh in centralizing his power over Egypt (Gen 47:13–26). Paul showed respect to the Roman authorities and took advantage of his rights as a Roman citizen (Acts 22:24–29; 23:12–35; 24:10; 25:8–12; 28:17–19).

I suggest that Christians should do four things, therefore:

a. Pray for our rulers.

b. Participate in government to the extent that we have the opportunity.

c. Submit to civil authority in general.

d. Put God first and refuse to submit to anything that directly violates God's commandments

Paul urges prayer for "kings and all those in authority" (1 Tim 2:2), so that we can live quietly and share the gospel with our neighbors (1 Tim

2:3–7). Such prayers are based on a firm confidence that God is indeed sovereign and can influence what is happening at the government level (Proverbs 21:1).

Our opportunities for action are always limited. Therefore we need to have faith that a sovereign God is working out His purposes for our good even when the government is hostile. As Douglas Knight comments,

> God leaves us under regimes that do not intend to serve us as we hope to be served, and we are not able to say why this is. Yet the church says that even bad governments are the servants of God, sent to do us good, and it is for the Church to assist us in finding out how to discern this non-obvious good. Even when the contradiction between our hopes and their intentions is at its worse, we have to be able to tell our rulers that 'You intended it for harm, but God intended it for good.'[23]

Outright rebellion against authority, or refusal to submit to laws or regulations that we don't like, but that don't require us to disobey God, is not countenanced by God. And conspiracy theories that argue that some people or groups have unlimited power in violation of God's sovereignty should be resisted unless there is strong evidence.

The book of Esther may help us understand how all this can work. The setting is the ancient Persian Empire in the reign of Xerxes (Ahasuerus) (Est 1:1). Like all powerful rulers, he is very conscious of his status and privileges, so when these are challenged by his queen (Vashti), after taking advice from his counselors, he deposes her and looks for a replacement (Est 1:19–2:4). But most monarchies do not give the monarch unfettered and absolute power; there are always traditions to uphold and adhere to and a ruling class to consult and uphold, who are also very conscious of their privileges (Est 1:13–18). In this case, there is a special feature of the Media-Persia constitution, that "the laws of Persia and Media . . . cannot be repealed" (Est 1:19; see also 8:8; Dan 6:8,12).

The politics of this story become quite murky. First, an orphaned Jewish girl, Esther (Hadassah) unexpectedly becomes the queen, as a result of a kind of beauty contest (Est 2:1–18). God is perhaps putting her in a place of authority and influence for some reason. Next, we see that her guardian Mordecai is a courtier of some kind, a political operator, someone 'in the system,' "sitting at the king's gate" (Est 2:23). In this

---

23. "Time and Persons in the Economy of God" (in Murphy and Ziegler, *The Providence of God*), 133.

position, he discovers a plot to assassinate the king and passes the information via Esther to Xerxes, thus defeating the plot (Est 2:21–23). Clearly Mordecai is climbing up the political ladder through his connection to the queen and his name is recorded in the royal annals.

But an even more ambitious courtier now appears, "Haman, son of Hammedatha, the Agagite" (Est 3:1). And here Mordecai makes an outrageous decision. The king has ordered everyone to kneel down and honor Haman, but Mordecai refuses. Moreover, the only reason he gives is that he is a Jew (Est 3:4). The text makes no attempt to explain this: does he have a religious objection or is this an ethnic tradition or some kind of political rivalry? Certainly, the Jews are a known force in the empire (Est 6:13) and have distinctive customs that make them visible and potentially liable to suspicions of disloyalty or conspiracy theories (Est 3:8); perhaps, as later under Rome, they have obtained exemption from some civil religious obligations. Mordecai is clearly challenging Haman, and in an honor-shame culture, that calls for a response (Est 3:4–5). Strangely, no one thinks of simply reporting Mordecai to the king whose orders he has disobeyed. And Haman overreaches by plotting wholesale genocide (Est 3:6–15).

What will Mordecai do in response? Potentially he has caused the annihilation of his own people. He cannot appeal to the king, but he has no intention of backing down before Haman. He begins with an open protest, a display of grieving that the king would probably not get to hear about but might affect Haman's popularity. It's a courageous move (Est 4:1–4; compare Neh 2:1–2). Then when Esther intervenes, he reports the situation to her and asks her via a messenger to "go into the king's presence to beg for mercy and plead with him for her people" (Est 4:8). This is politically dangerous, but Esther is persuaded that there is no alternative; she accepts Mordecai's argument that "who knows but that you have come to your royal position for such a time as this?" (Est 4:14). She resolves on three days of total fasting, clearly appealing to God (whose name is never mentioned directly), and makes a clever plan to get through to the king.

Meanwhile Mordecai refuses to back down, Haman plots to have him executed and Esther gets to first base with her scheme to expose Haman (Est 5:1–14). Now divine intervention seems to occur. The king can't sleep, annals are read to him, he finds that Mordecai was never rewarded for exposing the earlier assassination attempt, and he chooses Haman to parade Mordecai around the city with great honors (Est 6:1–11). Haman's fall from power is now imminent and Esther's scheme can go ahead successfully (Est 6:12–7:10). The Jews are saved, Mordecai becomes prime minister, and the empire is at peace, though only after some significant licensed bloodshed at the hand of the Jews.

We see in this story that Mordecai and Esther operated as God's people in the midst of a very conflicted and dangerous environment. Mordecai stood his ground for his convictions and risked his life and even the lives of a whole people. Esther was compliant but took the risk of challenging the king, when called on to do so, to save the Jews. Both called on the Lord through prayer and fasting. God used them to bring deliverance but intervened at a crucial point when the situation could have gone either way. But notably neither Mordecai nor Esther contemplated an insurrection; both worked within the system and in support of the king.

But Mordecai also shows great faith in God's sovereignty when he says to Esther,

> And who knows but that you have come to your royal position
> for such a time as this?"
>
> (Est 4:14).

God's sovereignty and power are real, but rather than being an excuse for passivity, this should lead us to take action in the sphere of influence He has placed us in, depending on Him with prayer and fasting.

CHAPTER 10

PRAYER AND THE SOVEREIGNTY OF GOD

"God does nothing but in answer to prayer," said John Wesley.[1] I baulked at this saying when I first heard it, but it is not far wrong. As we will see in this chapter, much of what God is doing now is in response to people praying.

The idea that human beings can influence God's will and plans by prayer is astonishing in view of the sovereignty of God. And yet, humans all over the world have always attempted to influence the spirit world in various ways, through sacrifices, sorcery and other religious practices.

Of course, prayer and our stated theology sometimes sit in tension. Pinnock and his friends wisely comment,

> People who believe that God cannot change his mind sometimes pray in ways that would require God to do exactly that. And Christians who make use of the free will defense for the problem of evil sometimes ask God to get them a job or a spouse or to keep them from being harmed, implying that God should overrule the free will of others in order to achieve these ends.[2]

---

1. The full quote is "Give me one hundred preachers who fear nothing but sin and desire nothing but God, and I care not a straw whether they be clergymen or laymen; such alone will shake the gates of hell and set up the kingdom of heaven on earth. God does nothing but in answer to prayer." (accessed from *https://unboring.network/god-does-nothing-but-in-answer-to-prayer/* on 12/02/22).

2. Clark Pinnock, Richard Rice, John Sanders, William Hasker and David Basinger, *The Openness of God*, 8.

There are two basic implications of the sovereignty of God for prayer, it seems to me. First, prayer is only possible because God is sovereign in some way over all circumstances. If God was not sovereign, prayer would be pointless. But His power and rule give us confidence to pray even big prayers. Many prayers I hear, and some I pray, fail, because I limit what I pray for to what *I* think is possible. But as Jeremiah prays,

> "Ah, Sovereign LORD, you have made the heavens and the earth by your great power and outstretched arm. Nothing is too hard for you"
>
> (Jer 32:17; see also Matt 19:26; Gen 18:14; Luke 1:37; 18:27; and Rom 4:21).

As the former slave trader and hymn writer, John Newton, wrote (perhaps based on Eph 3:20)

> Thou art coming to a king
> Large petitions with thee bring
> For His grace and power are such
> None can ever ask too much.[3]

Or as British Pentecostal theologian Keith Warrington, writes,

> Such a God can create the unimaginable, initiate the unexpected, institute unique phenomena, supervise the watcher and resurrect the dead. He makes his own rules, acting in conformity to his nature. Pentecostals accept the inexplicable nature of God and they acknowledge his supremacy in determining possibilities and initiating assumed impossibilities.[4]

D. Martyn Lloyd-Jones states,

> The saints always prayed to God, and our Lord supremely did so, because they believed in God's power, because they believed in God's ability to help, and, above all, because they believed in God's willingness and readiness to help.[5]

And J.I. Packer writes

> When we are on our knees, we know that it is not we who control the world; it is not in our power, therefore, to supply our needs by our own independent efforts; every good thing that we

---

3. From the hymn "Come my soul thy suit prepare" by John Newton.
4. *Pentecostal Theology*, 29.
5. Lloyd-Jones, *The Assurance of Our Salvation*, .34.

desire for ourselves and for others must be sought from God, and will come, if it comes at all, as a gift from His hands.[6]

Second, God's sovereignty means that God has the final say about what happens. This has implications for how we should pray, as we will explore in this chapter. I particularly want to explore the biblical teaching about prayer as interactive communication with God; not just aligning ourselves with God's will but really discussing it with Him in a way that gives the human participant power to affect the outcome.

ABRAHAM THE PRAY-ER

The first prominent intercessor and pray-er in the Bible is Abraham. He had been on the road with God for some time and had just won a decisive battle when Melchizedek the priest blessed him and received a tenth of the spoils (Gen 14:17–20), while Abram refused any share in the booty (Gen 14:22–24). Soon afterwards,

> The word of the LORD came to Abram in a vision:
> 'Do not be afraid, Abram.
> I am your shield,
> your very great reward.'
> (Gen 15:1).

The military overtones here imply that God will protect His man from revenge attacks and reward him for his obedience.[7]

This started a dialogue between Abram and God over succession. Abram asked, "Sovereign LORD, what will you give me since I remain childless . . . ..? You have given me no children; so a servant in my household will be my heir" (vv.2–3). God responded with a promise: "This man will not be your heir, but a son who is your own flesh and blood will be your heir" (v.4). In fact, God then 'ups the ante,' by promising Abram descendants uncountable in number (v.5). And "Abram believed the LORD, and he credited it to him as righteousness" (v.6).

But that is not the end of this episode: God added a promise of land (v.7). To this Abram responded, "Sovereign LORD, how can I know that I will gain possession of it?" (v.8). God answered by initiating a powerful covenant-making ceremony that included a defined promise of the land

---

6. Packer, *Evangelism*, 11.
7. Cf. Wenham, *Genesis 1–15*, 327.

God had in mind for him (vv.9–21). God was listening and responding to Abram. But also, God was stretching him to reach out in faith for more. The dialogue was initiated by God and guided by God. God's plan was being accomplished in and through and with God's human partner.

We next come to the famous 'bargaining prayer' of Genesis 18. As I discussed in Chapter 3, Abraham had been granted a place to stand in relation to God. Moreover, he knew enough about God's nature as a just Judge to appeal to God on that basis: "Will not the Judge of all the earth do right?" (Gen 18:25). This bold response was not displeasing to God, who was willing to negotiate with His covenant partner about the destiny of Sodom and Gomorrah.

In fact, this story shows that God is willing to hear and answer prayer, especially if the pray-er is one of God's men (or women) and grounds their requests in God's own nature and will, what I call God's 'constitution.' God was not threatened here because He will act constitutionally, justly, on the grounds of publicly available facts (vv.20–21). As Wenham notes, "The Lord accepts Abraham's logic."[8] Moreover, God initiated this conversation (vv.17,20–21), inviting Abraham to discuss the matter with Him, though as Wenham points out, God also terminated the conversation (v.33).[9]

God is looking for people He can share His heart with and invite into His counsels. He wants to hear our prayers provided that we are His servants and have His will in view. Often He directly seeks to provoke us to prayer by making a statement of His intentions that is not really what He has planned. A case in point is Moses in Exod 32:10. God reveals the rebellion going on amongst the Israelites and says, "Now leave me alone so that my anger might burn against them and that I may destroy them. Then I will make you into a great nation." But Moses objects and God relents. Such cases show how God's sovereignty works, respecting people as His partners, taking their prayers into account, but pursuing His plan.

SOLOMON'S GREAT PRAYER

In 1 Kings 3, we read a prayer conversation that actually takes place in a dream. The new king of Israel, King Solomon, has offered large-scale sacrifices, and that night, "the Lord appeared to Solomon during the night

8. Wenham, *Genesis 16–50*, 52.
9. Wenham, *Genesis 16–50*, 53.

in a dream, and God said, 'Ask for whatever you want me to give you'" (v.5). What will Solomon ask for? Obviously, it's a kind of test, but there is no reason to doubt God's sincerity here. Solomon passes the test when he asks for "a discerning heart to govern your people and to distinguish between right and wrong" (v.9). God is pleased with this, that Solomon had not requested "long life or wealth for yourself, nor. . . . the death of your enemies but for discernment in administering justice" (v.11). Therefore, his prayer is to be granted: "I will give you a wise and discerning heart, so that there will never have been anyone like you, nor will there ever be" (v.12). And God adds the other blessings–"wealth and honor" (v.13) and "long life" (v.14), subject to his obedience to God.

It was legitimate for Solomon to ask for long life, wealth and victory; God was willing to grant those, though with certain conditions. But the prayer God was looking for, the 'priority prayer' in line with God's will, was that prayer for wisdom. This prayer could be granted unconditionally and abundantly because it was the kind of prayer that God's covenant partner would pray, one who had God's heart and was surrendered to God's will. It was a prayer in line with God's will for Solomon's life, his calling to be the king of Israel, not for the privileges of royalty but for help with its responsibilities.

LEVELS OF PRAYER

It seems to me, therefore, that there are three levels of prayer:

1. *Bad Prayers*: prayers that are selfish, foolish, sinful, and should not be granted. As James writes, "When you ask, you do not receive, because you ask with wrong motives, that you may spend what you get on your pleasures" (James 4:3).

2. *Good or Legitimate Prayers*: prayers for legitimate needs such as food, clothing, shelter, health, and forgiveness, which are usually granted, though not always. James again: "Is anyone among you sick? Let them call the elders of the church to pray over them and anoint them with oil in the name of the Lord. And the prayer offered in faith will make the sick person well; the Lord will raise them up" (James 5:15).

3. *Priority Prayers*: prayers prayed with God's will in view, prayers led by the Spirit, prayers that glorify God, and are sure to be granted.

Solomon's prayer was that kind of prayer and James exhorts us to follow his example: "If any of you lacks wisdom, you should ask God, who gives generously to all without finding fault, and it will be given to you" (James 1:5). But he adds, "When you ask, you must believe and not doubt, because the one who doubts is like a wave of the sea, blown and tossed by the wind. That person should not expect to receive anything from the Lord. Such a person is double-minded and unstable in all they do" (James 1:6–8). See also 1 John 5:14–15.

Most of our prayers as Christians are probably at Level 2. The prayer chains organized by some local churches are filled with requests for healing, for jobs, financial needs, and the like. All legitimate! Nevertheless, God is inviting us to come up higher, but warning us perhaps to 'count the cost,' since the level of faith required is greater.

A great example of this is found in the story of the Evangelical Sisterhood of Mary, founded in Darmstadt, Germany, shortly after World War II. This adventurous group of women boldly prayed for God's financial provision and for God to overrule government decisions that might stand in the way of the property God had guided them to develop for His purposes.[10] God answered their prayers in remarkable ways, though sometimes only after a long time of struggle and sometimes only after dealing with sinful attitudes in the sisters themselves.

ELIJAH AS A POWERFUL PRAY-ER

The example James points to in his discussion of prayer is Elijah:

> The prayer of a righteous person is powerful and effective. Elijah was a human being, even as we are. He prayed earnestly that it would not rain, and it did not rain on the land for three and a half years. Again he prayed, and the heavens gave rain, and the earth produced its crops
>
> (James 5:16b-18).

Let's revisit the story James is referring to. The kingdom of Israel (the northern kingdom with its new capital city of Samaria) was in a terrible state. The new king Ahab "did more evil in the eyes of the LORD than any of those before him" (1 Kings 16:30). He married a pagan princess, embraced the worship of Baal and Asherah and "did more to arouse

---

10. Cf. Basilea Schlink, *Realities: The Miracles of God Experienced Today*.

the anger of the LORD . . . than did all the kings of Israel before him" (1 Kings 16:33). Then Elijah appeared, a seemingly unknown "Tishbite, from Tishbe in Gilead" (1 Kings 17:1). We can only speculate what had been going on in his life before this. But clearly he was a servant of God who cared about what was happening to God's people and, according to James, he was praying earnestly about it.

His prayers were motivated by God's honor and God's concern or anger at the situation. And it appears that he finally got to the point of knowing what God wanted, the priority prayer that God would certainly answer. Thus he was able to say confidently to the king, "As the LORD, the God of Israel, lives, whom I serve, there will be neither dew nor rain in the next few years *except at my word*" (1 Kings 17:1, emphasis added).

Then Elijah had to live out the results of his earnest faith-filled prayer, hiding from the king, seeking food wherever he could find it, until the time came for the drought to end (1 Kings 17:2–18:15). Then he had to confront the opposition with strong faith that God would show Himself faithful and turn the people's hearts around (1 Kings 18:16–40).

Finally, it was time to pray for rain, and again Elijah announced the answer before it came, saying to Ahab, "Go, eat and drink, for there is the sound of a heavy rain" (1 Kings 18:41). It was crunch time and Elijah was back on his knees praying for that rain, even though, seven times, when the servant looked, there was no sign of it (1 Kings 18:41–44).

It's a dramatic story but it illustrates how powerful prayer can be, according to James 5. Elijah's prayers were God-glorifying, motivated by God's purpose and priorities, and therefore full of faith and willing to chance all on God's power and faithfulness. This is praying that submits to, and embraces, God's sovereign plans, seeking them out, earnestly embracing them, with unquestioning faith.

THE PRAYERS OF HEZEKIAH

In contrast, let's revisit the life of King Hezekiah, the righteous king of Judah, who courageously resisted the invading Assyrians who had conquered the northern kingdom of Israel. In the middle of this story there is a kind of propaganda war where the Assyrian commander tries to destroy the morale of the Judahite army (2 Kings 18:19–36). Hezekiah appeals to Isaiah to "pray for the remnant that still survives" to "the LORD your God" (2 Kings 19:4) and receives an encouraging prophetic word in response (2 Kings 19:5–7). But then he receives a letter from the Assyrian commander continuing the propaganda offensive (2 Kings 19:9–13). This time Hezekiah himself takes the letter to God's temple and prays to God (2 Kings 19:15–19), based on the conviction that "you alone are God over all the kingdoms of the earth" (2 Kings 19:15). God's sovereign power is explicitly the grounds for his confidence in praying and Isaiah responds with the assurance that God has heard the prayer (2 Kings 19:20) and a strong prophecy directed at the Assyrians and engendering hope in the Judahites (2 Kings 19:20–31).

The Assyrians were ridiculing God because they had successfully defeated many nations (2 Kings 19:10–13,22) and boasting of their own prowess as conquerors (vv.23–24), but they failed to realize that God was supervising all this:

> "Long ago I ordained it.
> In days of old I planned it;
> now I have brought it to pass,
> that you have turned fortified cities into piles of stone." (v.25).

But now God will act against the hubris of the Assyrians:

> "Because you rage against me
> and because your insolence has reached my ears,
> I will put my hook in your nose
> and my bit in your mouth,
> and I will make you return
> by the way you came" (v.28).

God achieves this result by three means: a report of a new resistance (vv.7–8), some kind of plague among the Assyrian army in Judah (vv.35–36), and the assassination of the Assyrian king (v.37).[11]

Hezekiah has learned a valuable lesson about the power and sovereignty of God and the implications for answered prayer. But now he faces a different challenge.

> In those days Hezekiah became ill and was at the point of death. The prophet Isaiah son of Amoz went to him and said, "This is what the Lord says: Put your house in order, because you are going to die; you will not recover."
>
> (2 Kings 20:1).

---

11. Another example of God capturing a sinful act for His will.

This is the first time Isaiah has brought such a disappointing message. What kind of response was God looking for? The obvious response to God's sovereign will is for Hezekiah to submit and do what the prophecy said, that is, put his affairs in order because of his impending death. But Hezekiah does not do this. Instead, he prays for a different outcome:

> Hezekiah turned his face to the wall and prayed to the LORD, "Remember, LORD, how I have walked before you faithfully and with wholehearted devotion and have done what is good in your eyes." And Hezekiah wept bitterly (v.2–3).

Did God want this response? Was the previous prophecy some kind of test of Hezekiah's faith? Whatever might be the case, God responds to this desperate cry, even though, as T.R. Hobbs comments, "The prayer is rather self-serving and provides a sharp contrast to the image of the king presented so far in the account of his reign."[12] Isaiah is immediately sent back with a new message from God:

> "I have heard your prayer and seen your tears; I will heal you. On the third day from now you will go up to the temple of the LORD. I will add fifteen years to your life" (vv.5–6a).

The healing required a medical dressing (v.7),[13] but more significantly, the promise of the healing was confirmed by an extraordinary miracle with the shadow going backward ten steps on the stairway (vv.8–11).

It's an amazing story but it raises several theological questions. Why did God change His mind and heal the king? After all, there is no sign this was a priority prayer, although the promise of healing was also supplemented by a promise of ongoing protection for Jerusalem.[14] Why was Isaiah sent originally with a different message about imminent death? Why was there a need for such a striking sign of the promised healing? And what was the long-term outcome?

Subsequent events reveal the king's thoughtless response to the envoys from Babylon and his cavalier attitude to the predicted Babylonian invasion, the account of which comes straight after the healing and in response to it (2 Kings 20:12–19). The other notable point was that Manasseh, the successor to Hezekiah, who undid all the good reforms

---

12. T.R. Hobbs, *2 Kings*, 290.

13. Suggesting that it was not completely miraculous as it suggests some kind of 'folk medicine' (Hobbs, *2 Kings*, 291–292).

14. Cf. Hobbs, *2 Kings*, 291.

Hezekiah had made (2 Kings 21:1-9), was just twelve when he became king. In other words, he was born during the extra fifteen years that God added to Hezekiah's life. This suggests that Hezekiah misused the extra years and that possibly, if this extra time had not been granted, Manasseh would not have been born and the reforms annulled.

Of course, this point assumes certain points that the text does not spell out. Did Hezekiah have other sons? Who would have succeeded to the throne if Manasseh had not been born? In fact, was the lack of an obvious successor a factor in Hezekiah's prayer and God's answer? Did God grant the prayer so as to continue the successive line of David in Judah?[15] But if so, why announce Hezekiah's imminent death? None of these questions is answered in the text, but the apparent implication of the story is that Hezekiah's prayer for healing was a foolish prayer, at least from a long-term perspective, or at least that he failed to use the extra time well. And this is not a trivial matter, since Manasseh's evil deeds called forth prophecies of Judah's final downfall (2 Kings 21:10-15), a doom that even King Josiah's radical reforms a century later could not avert (2 Kings 23:26-27).

Clearly these events future to Hezekiah were not unknown to God, who warned Hezekiah of the future invasion of Babylon (2 Kings 20:16-18). So there are two theological conclusions that may be drawn here in relation to the healing in response to Hezekiah's prayer. One possibility is that God granted the healing simply because Hezekiah asked for it passionately; God sometimes responds to prayer even when the answer violates His revealed will, as in the case of the original prophecy of Isaiah, and even when the long-term result is actually bad. God sometimes answers even bad prayers positively.

Another possibility is that God deliberately provoked Hezekiah to pray for healing so that He could extend his life, so that Manasseh would be born and become the next king, so that Manasseh would do evil and justify God's plan to destroy the kingdom of Judah. God had already determined to destroy the kingdom, and the Davidic line, in spite of His earlier strong promises to David, because David's successors were often sinful, syncretistic, oppressive and immoral or because the Judahites were rebellious, even when their kings were good, or even in order to make way for the new covenant.

---

15. Isaiah's words imply that this miracle, including the ongoing promise of protection of Jerusalem, were "for my servant David's sake" (2 Kings 20:6). Cf. Hobbs, *2 Kings*, 296.

At the very least, this chapter demonstrates the fragility or superficiality of Hezekiah's faith and the spiritual condition of Judah which will call for divine judgment. God extends Hezekiah's life and promises protection to Jerusalem, but it will only be temporary unless there is a deep-seated turn to God.[16] Either way, however, this story shows how powerful prayer can be, even in changing the announced intention of God, without damaging God's sovereign purposes.

JESUS AS THE MASTER PRAY-ER

Jesus is the Model par excellence when it comes to prayer, obviously, and the One above all whose prayers would line up with God's will. He was also a master Teacher in this area. As D. Martyn Lloyd-Jones writes, "We can always be quite certain that the right way to pray is the way in which he prayed."[17]

When I look at Jesus' own prayers, I notice, first, that he was always praying. For example, very early in his Galilean ministry, when Jesus was in hot demand, Mark tells us that,

> Very early in the morning, while it was still dark, Jesus got up, left the house and went off to a solitary place, where he prayed.

(Mark 1:35).

Such prayers would keep his relationship with God intimate and would help him align himself with the Father's will, since He tells us elsewhere, "the Son can do nothing by himself; he can do only what he sees his Father doing" (John 5:19).

In a similar way, according to Luke, Jesus spends a whole night in prayer before choosing the twelve apostles (Luke 6:12–13). This suggests that for Jesus, prayer was a dialogue, not a place to put forward 'shopping lists' to God. His priority was to *hear* rather than just *ask*.

Second, I notice that Jesus always prayed within the will of God in any situation. For example, as we saw earlier, when his arrest was imminent, Jesus says to Simon Peter,

> "Simon, Simon, Satan has asked to sift all of you as wheat. But I have prayed for you, Simon, that your faith may not fail. And when you have turned back, strengthen your brothers."

(Luke 22:31).

16. Cf. Hobbs, *2 Kings*, 297.
17. Lloyd-Jones, *The Assurance of Our Salvation*, 15.

Jesus does not pray for the disciples *not* to be sifted, nor that Simon would not deny him (Luke 22:34). He does not contest Satan's right to sift them, probably because of the principle of testing discussed earlier. He simply asks for Simon not to lose his faith in the coming trial and (by implication) that he will turn back after denying Christ and be able to help the others who will also fail the test in varying ways.

Related to this, I notice that Jesus sometimes struggles with God in his prayers. This is most obvious in the garden of Gethsemane, where Jesus prays, "Father, if you are willing, take this cup from me; yet not my will, but yours be done" (Luke 22:42), a struggle that was deadly earnest and anguished to the point of Jesus sweating like drops of blood and needing an angel to help him (Luke 22:43–44). This is the only time when Jesus asks for what he knows he can't have but nonetheless aligns himself totally with the Father's will (compare John 12:27–28).

Jesus prays within the big picture of God's plan for him and the world. The brief prayer in John 12, when Jesus declines to ask "save me from this hour" because "it was for this very reason I came to this hour. Father, glorify your name!" (John 12:27–28a), is explained by Jesus' knowledge that his crucifixion will cast out the devil and "draw all people" to himself (John 12:31–33). In a different setting, Jesus says, "I will ask the Father, and he will give you another advocate to help you and be with you forever–the Spirit of truth" (John 14:16–17a). The granting of the Spirit is all part of the Plan, but note that Jesus still sees the need to *ask* for it.

Finally, I notice that Jesus prays confidently, assured of his relationship with the Father and the validity of what he prays for. And he acts confidently, knowing that his prayers are answered. He does miracles such as healing and eviction of demons because he has already lined up with God in prayer (see John 5:19). See him outside Lazarus's tomb, for example, in John 11. He has arrived on scene late, deliberately, under God's guidance (vv.6–15). He has obtained the certainty that this situation "is for God's glory, that God's Son may be glorified through it" (v.4). He has already declared to Martha, "Your brother will rise again" (v.23) and "I am the resurrection and the life" (v.25). Nevertheless, he enters the emotion of the moment and weeps with the sisters (vv.33–35,38). But he then orders the stone to be removed over Martha's objections (vv.39–41) and prays,

> "Father, I thank you that you have heard me. I know that you always hear me, but I said this for the benefit of the people standing here, that they may believe that you sent me" (vv.41–42).

Jesus is totally confident he has been heard and does not pray any more, but simply commands Lazarus in a loud voice to come out (v.43).

All these aspects come together in the longest prayer we find Jesus praying in the Gospels, John 17. Here we see Jesus praying in the will of God, including that big picture of God's Plan, and desiring above all for God's glory:

> "Father, the hour has come. Glorify your Son, that your Son may glorify you. For you granted him authority over all people that he might give eternal life to all those you have given him."
>
> (John 17:1–2).

Jesus is completely focused on the Plan and what it is designed to accomplish. He has accomplished what God had for him to do (v.4). On this basis, he can also pray to be glorified with his pre-incarnate glory (v.5), he can pray for the protection of his disciples (vv.6–19), and he can pray for the future disciples that they will reach (vv.20–23). We note what he does *not* pray for and whom he does *not* pray for and well as what he *does* ask.

> "I am *not* praying for the world, but for those you have given me, for they are yours" (v.9, emphasis added).
>
> "My prayer is *not* that you take them out of the world but that you protect them from the evil one" (v.15, emphasis added).
>
> "My prayer is *not* for them alone. I pray *also* for those who will believe in me through their message, that all of them may be one, Father, just as you are in me and I am in you" (vv.20–21a, emphasis added).

This last request is huge, but it is grounded in the Plan:

> "May they also be in us so that the world may believe that you have sent me" (v.21b)

This is interesting because Jesus *is* now praying (indirectly) for the world:

> "Then the world will know that you sent me and have loved them even as you have loved me" (v.23b).

The disciples are chosen from the world for the sake of the world, not just for their own benefit. This is in accordance with the Plan, as we saw earlier in John 12:32 ("And I, when I am lifted up from the earth, will draw all people to myself").

JESUS AS THE MASTER TEACHER ON PRAYER

The most extensive teaching from Jesus on prayer is found in Matthew 6. Here Jesus emphasizes the need to focus on the Father and pray out of relationship: God is our Father who cares for us and knows our needs (vv.8,30–32). But it also reflects the need to have confidence in a sovereign God, one who "*knows* what you need *before* you ask him" (v.8, emphasis added; see also Isa 65:24), who sees what is done in secret (vv.6,18), and who shows His care for us by His providential care for birds (v.26) and flowers (vv.28–30). But if we are indeed praying to a God who is *both* the sovereign Lord *and* our Father, then praying to impress others is counterproductive (vv.5–6, 16–18), as is thinking that long prayers necessarily impress God and cause Him to hear us (v.7).

Above all, Jesus' model prayer puts God first: we want Him to be glorified and His will be done in the context of the Big Plan of God's kingdom (vv.9–10). Within that priority, it is then legitimate to pray for earthly needs, forgiveness and spiritual protection (vv.11–13). In fact, Jesus sees prayer as a way of obtaining what we most need from the only One able to supply. He rejects any kind of passivity that blindly 'submits' to whatever we think God wants, but he insists that we submit to God's conditions: praying in secret (vv.5–6), forgiving others (vv.14–15), fasting secretly (vv.17–18), refusing to worry (v.25,34) and seeking first "his kingdom and his righteousness" (v.33).

Jesus also emphasizes faith as a key aspect of prayer. For example, during his final week in Jerusalem and Bethany, Jesus curses a fruitless fig tree in front of the disciples (Mark 11:13–14), a seemingly irrational action, since "it was not the season for figs" (v.13). The next morning, the disciples "saw the fig tree withered from the roots" and drew Jesus' attention to it (vv.20–21). Jesus' response is interesting:

> "Have faith in God," Jesus answered. "Truly I tell you, if anyone says to this mountain, 'Go, throw yourself into the sea,' and does not doubt in their heart but believes that what they say will happen, it will be done for them. Therefore I tell you, whatever you

ask for in prayer, believe that you have received it, and it will be yours. And when you stand praying, if you hold anything against anyone, forgive them, so that your Father in heaven may forgive you your sins."

(Mark 11:22–25).

Here Jesus emphasizes faith and forgiveness as keys to answered prayer. But is this a kind of 'blank cheque' promise? Is it saying that the person who performs some kind of mental effort so as to banish all doubt from their mind can ask whatever they like and receive it? As far as I can tell, this is not how prayer works even among those who affirm that kind of faith teaching. It would mean that the pray-er somehow manipulates God, defying God's sovereignty.

But on the other hand, the passage cannot be simply dismissed on the basis that Jesus' actions were prophetic symbolic actions showing judgment on Jerusalem, even though this may be true. Jesus seems to be stating a general principle of prayer and encouraging his disciples to extend their faith, to believe that all things are possible with God, and thus to boldly ask for bigger things in His name.[18] But the question is, how can one have the kind of faith that metaphorically moves mountains? Surely it can only happen if one is sure that they are praying in the will of God.

Bill Vasilakis, the leader of a significant Pentecostal movement in Australia, comments,

> Jesus' mountain-moving faith is one of the indispensable keys to experiencing the limitless revival power of the Holy Spirit in our lives. Revived Christ-followers aim to express a daring faith- just like Jesus did when He walked this earth. This kind of faith response- to who He is and what He has done on our behalf- undergirds everything we do for Him...
>
> Jesus promises to help us rise above what people think is impossible, as all things are really possible for Him (Matthew 19:26). From Christ's point of view, it is quite obvious that most of us are living far below our God-given potential. Our world is just waiting for spiritually reborn and revived Christ-followers, who by the grace and power of God, lay hold of operating in the Holy Spirit's realm of faith.[19]

---

18. See discussion in Craig A. Evans, *Mark 8:27–16:20*, 188–195.
19. Bill Vasilakis, *Revival is our Middle Name*, 132–133.

I think this captures the emphasis of Jesus' stirring words. If our focus is on the kingdom and will of God and His call on our lives, nothing will be impossible. We submit to God's sovereign will, but we do not adopt a passive posture. Rather we allow the Holy Spirit to lead us to pray in His will and thus serve God's sovereign Plan as laid out in Scripture.

A brilliant example of such an application of this promise is found in a famous sermon by a 19th century missionary statesman, Alexander Duff, who said,

> Oh, what promises are ours, if we had only faith to grasp them ... We go forth amongst the hundreds of millions of the nations, we find gigantic systems of idolatry and superstition consolidated for 3,000 years, heaped up and multiplied for ages upon ages, until they tower as high mountains, mightier than the Himalaya. . . . But what does faith say? Believe and it shall be. And if any Church on earth can realize that faith, to that Church will the honor belong of evangelizing the nations, and bringing down the mountains.[20]

PRAYER IN THE EARLY CHURCH

When we explore the prayers of the disciples of Christ in Acts, we can see clearly how they operate with a strong sense of, and response to, God's sovereign Plan as set out in the opening passage. Before he left the earth, Jesus gave his apostles instructions, proof of his resurrection, and teaching about the kingdom of God (Acts 1:2-3). Specifically, he gave them a promise–the gift of the Spirit (vv.4-5) –and a goal or mandate: "You will receive power when the Holy Spirit comes on you; and you will be my witnesses in Jerusalem, and in all Judea and Samaria, and to the ends of the earth" (v.8). The rest of Acts tells how this promise and mandate were fulfilled, though it is an unfinished story.

The original 120 believers obeyed the instruction to remain in Jerusalem (v.4) and spent the next ten days after Jesus' ascension in constant corporate prayer (v.14) until the promise was received and the mandate began to be carried out (Acts 2). The enlarged group, with its three thousand extra members (Acts 2:41), then "devoted themselves to . . . prayer" (Acts 2:42).

---

20. Speech of the Rev. Dr. Duff on Foreign Missions and America, May 29, 1854, as quoted in Murray, *The Puritan Hope*, 158.

After the new movement was challenged by the Jerusalem authorities, some of the Christians had a spontaneous prayer meeting (Acts 4:23-31) which led to a further infilling with the Holy Spirit and consequent boldness and confidence in speaking the gospel (v.31). As we examine the prayer they prayed, we note how full it is of references to God's sovereignty and His Plan for the Christian era. Starting with confession of God as "sovereign Lord" (v.24), the prayer confesses God as Creator (v.24). As sovereign Lord, God speaks in advance of things to come (vv.25-27), things that include the acts of evil men (v.27) but which achieve "what your power and will had decided beforehand should happen" (v.28). God's plan will prevail, not only because of what they have seen in Jesus' history but also because of what Psalm 2 promises, including the promise to the Messiah,

> *Ask me*
> And I will make the nations your inheritance,
> The ends of the earth your possession
> (Psalm 2:8, emphasis added).

Their prayer is fully grounded in God's sovereign power and plan in a context of opposition. Moreover, what they ask of God flowed out of that confidence in God's sovereignty and plan:

> "Now, Lord, consider their threats and enable your servants to speak your word with great boldness. Stretch out your hand to heal and perform signs and wonders through the name of your holy servant Jesus" (vv.29-30).

They do not ask for protection. They ask what the Spirit and the Plan dictate, that is, power to be bold witnesses while the Spirit is doing great works. This is also a model prayer in line with God's will, somewhat like Solomon's prayer for wisdom, and it is therefore not too surprising that "the place where they were meeting was shaken" (v.30) and "they were all filled with the Holy Spirit and spoke the word of God boldly" (v.31).

Signs and wonders are a feature of the apostles' ministry all through Acts and we might think that the apostles were able to do miracles at will. But clearly, they were being guided, as well as empowered, by the Holy Spirit, about whom to pray for and how to pray. For example, Peter faced a grave situation when he was sent for after the death of Tabitha (Dorcas). He was not always led to raise people from the dead and yet the disciples in Joppa were looking for him to do something (Acts 9:30-38), and there seemed to be some reason to think she had more work to do for

God (vv.36,39). So Peter got alone with the dead woman and "got down on his knees and prayed" (v.40a). Only then did he raise her up to life with amazing results (vv.40b-42). We do not know what he prayed but he seemed to be almost 'forced' into this situation so it must have been in line with God's will. Certainly the impact of this miracle was profound: "This became known all over Joppa, and many people believed in the Lord" (v.42).

This leads into the breakthrough miracle in the household of a Roman centurion. Prayer is a key feature of this narrative. Cornelius is said to have "prayed to God regularly" (Acts 10:2) and what happened is portrayed as an answer to those prayers as well as his generous gifts (Acts 10:30–31); God hears the prayers even of non-Christian Gentiles. Also Peter is praying when he sees the strange vision that prepares him to be part of the next thing God will do (Acts 10:9–10; 11:5). Prayer opens the way for this unexpected series of events which takes the Plan outlined in Acts 1:8 a step farther.

The next big prayer event in Acts shows that the outworking of God's sovereign plans cannot always be understood by humans. King Herod arrests some Christians and executes James the apostle, John's brother (Acts 12:2). There was no time, apparently, for the church to intervene on James' behalf. Next Herod seizes Peter. Will the church lose two of its key leaders? No, this time the church gets time to pray because "Herod intended to bring him out for public trial after the Passover" (v.4). Herod's motives are obviously political; he has some popular support for attacking the church (v.3) and he wants to maximize this. But apparently God is intervening to give the church time: "So Peter was kept in prison, but the church was earnestly praying to God for him" (v.5). God then responds with a miracle, freeing Peter from jail through an angelic intervention (vv.6–11), much to the amazement of the prayer meeting at the house of Mark's mother (vv.12–16).

This story raises many questions. Why didn't God prevent Peter being arrested? Why did He set Peter free and not James? Why did God not act more publicly and why did He not save the 'innocent' guards (Acts 12:19)? Clearly God does not intervene to save every person who is serving him. Stephen was killed (Acts 7:57–60), though his dying prayer, "Lord, do not hold this sin against them" (Acts 7:60) was heard and perhaps led to the conversion of the chief persecutor Saul (Acts 7:58; 9:1–6; see 1 Tim 1:13). Nowhere in the Bible does God promise total protection from trouble, although we would have to conclude that the church in

Acts 12 prayed for Peter not just to be faithful and bold, but also to be set free.

PRAYING IN THE WILL OF GOD

We have already suggested that the key to answered prayer, to praying with great faith, is to pray in the will of God. John tells us this explicitly:

> This is the confidence we have in approaching God: that if we ask anything according to his will, he hears us. And if we know that he hears us- whatever we ask- we know that we have what we asked of him
>
> (1 John 5:14-15).

John goes on to give an example of interceding for a fellow believer who commits a sin. But not all such prayers will be heard (vv.16-17). God is the sovereign Judge and we should ask within the bounds of His will as we know it.

This is what praying in Jesus' name really means. Jesus says to his disciples,

> "I will do whatever you ask in my name, so that the Father may be glorified in the Son. You may ask me for anything in my name, and I will do it"
>
> (John 14:13-14).

Jesus has just told the disciples that believers would do "even greater things" than He had been doing (v.12) and he goes on to assure them he would pray to the Father, and in response they would be given the Holy Spirit (vv.16-17). This suggests that the promise in vv.13-14 is not some kind of 'blank check;' it doesn't mean we can ask for literally anything (a Rolls Royce, say, or a mansion) and if we attach the formula 'in the name of Jesus,' it will be granted to us. Pink is surely right here:

> To apply to God for anything in the name of Christ, it must needs be in keeping with what Christ is! To ask God in the name of Christ is as though Christ Himself were the suppliant. *We can only ask God for what Christ would ask.*[21]

---

21. Pink, *Sovereignty of God*, 176 (emphasis in the original).

So praying for the Holy Spirit is always legitimate, for this is what Jesus has obtained and promised and will accomplish God's Plan on earth (John 7:37-39; Luke 11:13; Acts 1:4-8; 2:33,38). This is what I have called a Priority Prayer.

But how otherwise do we discern what the will of God is in prayer? Can we always know? Apparently not, according to Paul:

> We do not know what we ought to pray for, but the Spirit himself intercedes for us through wordless groans. And he who searches our hearts knows the mind of the Spirit, because the Spirit intercedes for God's people in accordance with the will of God

(Rom 8:26-27).

We, as limited human beings, do not always know how to pray or what to ask for. We thus depend on the Spirit to lead us, and the Spirit does not necessarily do so in a way we can discern but may use "wordless groans" or even foreign tongues (1 Cor 14:14-15).

But we are not totally at a loss. Paul goes on in Romans 8 to show us the "will of God" located in the wellbeing and salvation of God's elect (Rom 8:28-30). In other words, Paul is confirming what we learned from Jesus, to pray according to the great Plan of God, and more specifically, for those who are responding to, and benefiting from, that Plan, for whom the risen Christ is interceding (v.34), defeating every accusation against them and holding them safely before God (vv.31-39), even as he promised, "no one will snatch them out of my hand" (John 10:28). We are thus joining the prayers of Christ and the Spirit.

But the next few chapters of Romans show that this is not always simple. Paul is in anguish about his fellow Jews who are not benefiting from the salvation obtained for them (Rom 9:1-5) and he keeps praying for their salvation (Rom 10:1), even though they are resistant (Rom 10:16), a resistance predicted by the prophets (Rom 10:19-21), and only a minority are currently responding to Christ (Rom 11:1,5,7). Here Paul is forced to submit to the sovereign elective purpose of God (Rom 9:6-29; 11:7-10) and to rejoice in what that means for the Gentiles, who are now unexpectedly chosen (Rom 9:23-25, 30; 10:11-15; 11:11-12), as Paul himself has experienced.

However, Paul is not passively resigning himself to make the most of a bad situation. Rather he is praying for the long term, and he confidently expects a regathering of Jews to the kingdom in the end (Rom 11:11-32).

PRAYER AND THE SOVEREIGNTY OF GOD

Paul is thus struggling in prayer, looking towards an outcome he will never see. As the Puritan Thomas Goodwin once wrote,

> There may be some prayers which you must be content never yourselves to see answered in this world, the accomplishment of them not falling out in your time . . . all which prayers are not yet lost, but will have answers . . . .[22]

This is what praying in the will of God can look like. We do not always know what to pray for, but we do know a few things:

1. *The Holy Spirit will help and guide us*, though not always in a way our minds can grasp. Certainly, however, this means we should respond to the Spirit's prompting and leading in prayer (see Neh 1:4). Such prayers might be bold requests for an impossible situation to change (as in Mark 11:22–24).

2. *It's best to pray in line with the Plan of God*, that is, for the progress of the gospel, for the salvation of sinners, for people to come to faith in Jesus Christ, for the growth of the church worldwide (Matt 16:18), and for our growth in Christ (sanctification; see Rom 8:28–29). This is what I have called 'Priority Prayers.' As Grenz puts it, "For this reason, in every circumstance our primary goal as we pray to discern what it would mean for the kingdom to break into the present."[23]

3. *Prayers that seem to assist this Plan are thus good prayers*, as in 1 Tim 2:1–6, where prayer for governments and for "all people" are for that purpose, though these prayers may not be answered in the way we expect: governments may persecute us, hearers may reject us, and this may be God's way of enabling witness (Acts 9:15–16; 23:11), as in the Philippi story we looked at earlier (Acts 16:16–34).

4. *Prayers for physical needs such as food and clothing and sickness are legitimate*, but will not always be granted as we expect, if God has a better plan, for instance if His priority is an aspect of our sanctification or spiritual growth.

5. *Prayers based on promises of God are well-founded*, though the timing and nature of God's response may not always be predictable. Even things that are clearly part of God's plan and will, such as the

---

22. Goodwin, *The Return of Prayers*, as quoted in Murray, *The Puritan Hope*, 102.
23. Grenz, *Prayer*, 68.

liberation of creation (Rom 8:19-23), are only going to be granted in the End.

Here it might be helpful to go back to the Old Testament and to a powerful prayer of the prophet Daniel. In Daniel 9, Daniel is found at a turning point in history. Daniel "understood from the Scriptures, according to the word of the Lord given to Jeremiah the prophet, that the desolation of Jerusalem would last seventy years" (Dan 9:2). But he did not take this for granted. Rather,

> I turned to the Lord God and pleaded with him in prayer and petition, in fasting, and in sackcloth and ashes (v.3).

Daniel understood that prophecies and promises are there for people to use in prayer as arguments before God. He produces a remarkable prayer, grounded in God's nature as covenant-keeper (v.4), but taking God's side in effect, acknowledging His justice and right to punish Israel (vv.5-14), but pleading for God's mercy and favor based on God's past saving acts (vv.15-16) and God's name that is tied up with Jerusalem and Israel (vv.18-19). It's fundamentally for God's own sake and because of His "great mercy" (vv.17-18) that Daniel asks for God to intervene. Daniel follows Moses and Abraham in praying with God's glory and name in mind and acknowledging God's sovereign rights over all things, yet still arguing their case with Him. As D. Martyn Lloyd-Jones says, "Real prayer means taking hold of God and not letting go. . . . Taking hold of God, laying hold upon him, pleading with him, reasoning, and even beseeching . . . ."[24]

But while Daniel's great prayer was answered, it was not granted in the way he may have expected. While he was still praying, the angel Gabriel came with the answer (Dan 9:22-23). While the ensuing prophecy does not contradict Jeremiah's prophecy, it shows that the restoration to come is only the start of a long process of "seventy 'sevens'" to deal with the underlying issues behind Israel's captivity, which will not happen until the messiah comes and without a huge struggle (vv.25-27).

---

24. Lloyd-Jones, *Revival*, 305.

RESISTANCE TO PRAYER

Continuing the study of Daniel, we find Daniel praying seriously again "in the third year of Cyrus king of Persia" (Dan 10:1), that is, two years after Cyrus' famous decree releasing the Jews to go home (Ezra 1:1).

> At that time I, Daniel, mourned for three weeks. I ate no choice food; no food or wine touched my lips; and I used no lotions at all until the three weeks were over
>
> (Dan 10:2–3).

Again, the result was a fresh prophetic vision given via a heavenly being (vv.5–6). But the message this time was different. The heavenly being said,

> Do not be afraid, Daniel. Since the first day that you set your mind to gain understanding and to humble yourself before your God, your words were heard, and I have come in response to them. But the prince of the Persian kingdom resisted me twenty-one days. Then Michael, one of the chief princes, came to help me, because I was detained there with the king of Persia (vv.12–13).

This revelation shows why Daniel had to fast and pray for three weeks. His prayer was heard immediately, but the answer was delayed for three weeks because of resistance at the heavenly level. The "prince" or "king" of Persia was not the human ruler of the Persian empire but some kind of angelic or demonic personage contesting the purposes of God, especially in relation to Israel and its future, the main issue in Daniel 7–12. Similarly, Michael was the corresponding "prince who protects your people" (Dan 12:1).

This is an example of how Satan's kingdom resists the will of God. Jesus told us to pray, "deliver us from the evil one" (Matt 6:13); we need to take him seriously. But resisting the devil is not just a matter of saying "I resist you, Satan." Our focus in prayer needs to be on God, not the devil, as all the prayers in the Bible show, but we need to be aware that our good prayers, even priority prayers, can be blocked or inhibited by demonic forces, especially in the heavenly realms.

This not always easy for us as modern believers to comprehend. As Greg Boyd asks, "How many of us believers would consider the possibility of angelic interference as an explanation for why *we* sometimes do not see an answer to our particular prayers?"[25]

Hence Paul writes,

> Put on the full armor of God, so that you can take your stand against the devil's schemes. For our struggle is not against flesh and blood, but against the rulers, against the authorities, against the powers of this dark world and against the spiritual forces of evil in the heavenly realms
>
> (Eph 6:11–12)

This is part of a passage that finishes with Paul urging his audience to,

> pray in the Spirit on all occasions with all kinds of prayers and requests. With this in mind, be alert and always keep on praying for all the Lord's people (Eph 6:18).

So our spiritual struggle includes the struggles in prayer that Daniel experienced.

Jesus told a parable that reflects this in Luke 18:

> Then Jesus told his disciples a parable to show them that they should always pray and not give up (v.1).

The story is about a widow who was locked in a legal battle with an adversary. The judge hearing her case was biased and would not help her: he was probably being bribed or intimidated by the widow's powerful adversary. But eventually he gave in, saying, "because this widow keep bothering me, I will see that she gets justice, so that she won't eventually come and attack[26] me!" (v.5).

The point of this story is not that you have to wear down God to get your prayers answered. No, "Will not God bring about justice for his chosen ones, who cry out to him day and night?" (v.7). The point is that you need to persevere because there is an adversary. If your prayer is just, God will answer, but you need to persist in faith like Daniel so as to see your prayer answered.[27]

Of course, unanswered prayer is not always attributable to Satanic or demonic resistance. Sometimes the problem is God. God does not

---

25. Boyd, *God At War*, 10.

26. That's the NIV. The ESV translates "beat me down"; NRSV has "wear me out", which seems more likely. It's unlikely that a widow could attack a judge; more plausible that she could wear him down by her persistence.

27. Cf. Grenz, *Prayer*, 99–101.

answer every prayer favorably, even good prayers. There seem to be three main reasons for this. One has to do with how we treat others; the second has to do with our growth in grace, our spiritual need, or the need of others; and the third has to do with God's decisions about others.

In Isaiah 58, we see the Israelites seemingly seeking God (v.2), even fasting (v.3), but God does not seem to be taking any notice of their prayers. The prophet tells them why: their prayers are not being heard because of their behavior, especially how they are treating those in their power: "You do as you please and exploit all your workers" (v.3b). He exhorts them to act with justice and love towards those in need (vv.6–7.10). The principle seems to be that God treats us as we treat others, especially those in our power or who need our help. Are we hearing their pleas? If not, why should God hear ours?

Peter makes a similar point when he speaks specifically to men:

> Husbands, in the same way be considerate as you live with your wives, and treat them with respect as the weaker partner and as heirs with you of the gracious gift of life, *so that nothing will hinder your prayers*
>
> (1 Pet 3:7, emphasis added).

In a similar way, Proverbs says, "Whoever shuts their ears to the cry of the poor will also cry out and not be answered" (Prov 21:13). God responds to what He sees in us.

The second kind of case where God refuses to grant a person' prayer relates to the good that is served, or the need that demands, such a negative response. For example, Moses prayed to be blotted out of God's book if He would not forgive the Israelites (Exod 32:32), but God reserved the right to punish them and insisted that Moses continue his leadership (Exod 32:33–34). Elijah prayed to die in a moment of despondency as he was running from Jezebel (1 Kings 19:4), but God had more for him to do, so He sustained him through an angel (1 Kings 19:5–8) and recommissioned him (1 Kings 19:15–18). Jonah wanted to die when his prediction of doom for Nineveh was averted (Jon 4:3) and again, when the plant that had shaded him died and he was exposed to a hot sun (Jon 4:8), but God expressed greater concern for the people He had sent Jonah to than the prophet's comfort or reputation (Jon 4:9–11).

One of the most famous negative answers to prayer is the case of Paul's "thorn in the flesh" in 2 Cor 12. Whatever this "thorn" was exactly (sickness? trouble? opposition? temptation?), we know that it was "given" by God, that it was "a messenger of Satan" and it was designed "to torment" him (v.8). As it was hardly a desirable experience, "Three times I pleaded with the Lord to take it away from me" (v.8). This was a legitimate prayer. However, it was not answered favorably: "But he said to me, 'My grace is sufficient for you, for my power is made perfect in weakness'" (v.9). Paul learns to respond appropriately by boasting of his weaknesses and even delighting "in weaknesses, in insults, in hardships, in persecutions, in difficulties" (v.10). He comes to see that the "thorn" was there "to keep me from becoming conceited" as a result of his "surpassingly great revelations" (v.7). In other words, his prayer was not answered favorably because it was in his best interests for him to endure the painful experience.

In several places, the Bible makes the same point, that trials and difficulties come our way to help make us more holy and mature, and instead of asking for these to be removed, we should ask for the capacity and wisdom to respond well (James 1:2–5; Heb 12:5–13; Rom 5:3–4). Here A.W. Pink is right:

> Faith *endures* 'as seeing Him who is invisible' (Heb. 11:27): endures the disappointments, the hardships, and the heart-aches of life, by recognizing that *all* comes from the hand of Him who is too wise to err and too loving to be unkind.[28]

I had a similar experience some years ago. I was facing serious challenges and difficulties in my work and ministry. I was praying for God to intervene. Nothing was changing. One day as I walked in bushland near our home, the Spirit led me to change my prayers. I began to pray, 'Lord, change the situation or change *me* in the situation,' and 'Help me to respond as I should in every situation.' This was the prayer God wanted prayed, and shortly afterwards He answered it, and then even the situation began to change.

Catherine Marshall, originally the wife of Peter Marshall, a famous pastor in the USA seventy years ago,[29] in her book *Beyond Ourselves*[30] tells of an illness she suffered for years, which withstood both medical care and prayer for healing. Nothing changed until she learned 'the Prayer of Relinquishment.' Sometimes, we just have to surrender our lives

---

28. Pink, *The Sovereignty of God*, 16 (emphasis in the original).

29. The book and movie *A Man Called Peter* were about him. He was the chaplain to the US Senate at one point before dying of a heart attack.

30. *Beyond Ourselves*, 52–58, 93–106.

and hopes to God, not expecting a desired result, but just trusting Him to do what is best, and such surrender frequently releases His power to help us, often with the result we were originally hoping for.

An example of the third kind of negative answer from God, related to His decisions about others, has to do with King Saul. After a good initial start, Saul started to compromise and be swayed by events rather than by what God said. The 'final straw' was Saul's disobedience to Samuel's prophetic direction in relation to the Amalekites (1 Sam 15). God spoke to Samuel,

> "I regret that I have made Saul king, because he has turned away from me and has not carried out my instructions." Samuel was angry, and he cried out to the Lord all that night.
>
> (1 Sam 15:11).

The next day, Samuel confronted a very recalcitrant Saul who was slow to admit he'd done anything wrong. Samuel, however, had not been able to change God's mind on this:

> "He who is the Glory of Israel does not lie or change his mind; for he is not a human being, that he should change his mind."
>
> (1 Sam 15:29).

God's judgment here cannot be undone. Samuel's prayer all night to God had failed to change that. And sometimes we too have to bow to God's judgment about others we are praying for; He knows better than we do what is happening in those hearts and lives.

CONCLUSION

God's sovereignty is the ultimate foundation for prayer. This truth also helps us focus on how we should pray. Campbell rightly says,

> Prayer is not the means whereby God serves us, but is the means whereby we serve God–and, amazingly, have the privilege to contribute to the divine plan.[31]

Carson rightly declares that "Man's voice in addressing God is never the pre-programmed recording of the robot" and,

---

31. *Wonderful Decree*, 321.

the idea that men may prevail in prayer with God again presupposes human responsibility, and a significant measure of human freedom; for such language depicts the interplay of personalities, not the determinism of machines.[32]

---

32. *Divine Sovereignty and Human Responsibility*, 22.

CHAPTER 11

OUR PART IN GOD'S PLAN

PREVIOUSLY, WE SAW THAT God has an eternal Plan which He is bringing to pass over a long period of time, climaxing with the return of Jesus Christ, the last judgment and the new heavens and earth. We have also insisted that God works through and with human agents in carrying out this Plan. In chapter 10, we explored how prayer contributes to this. But what other contributions are we as believers expected to make?

Think of William Carey, the English bootmaker, who was stirred with the responsibility of the church to "use means" for the "evangelization of the heathen."[1] Not everyone in his particular (Calvinist) Baptist church was convinced. The famous story tells of an older minister rebuking Carey with these words, "Young man, sit down; when God is pleased to convert the heathen world, He will do it without your help or mine."[2] Thankfully, Carey did not accept that misplaced counsel and established a missionary society. He then went to India as a missionary, leaving a legacy that still continues today.

---

1. Carey's 1792 book on this was entitled, *An Enquiry into the Obligations of Christians to Use Means for the Conversion of the Heathens; in which the Religious State of the Different Nations of the World, the Success of Former Undertakings, and the Practicability of Further Undertakings are Considered.*

2. Cf. Packer, *Evangelism*, 33. See also https://www.wholesomewords.org/missions/bcarey10.html (accessed August 30, 2021).

THE EVANGELISM MANDATE

Having died on our behalf and risen from the dead, Jesus then commissioned human beings to work with Him to carry out the program of God by proclaiming the good news worldwide (Matt 28:18–20a; Mark 16:15–16; Luke 24:46–47; John 20:21; Acts 1:8).

As Adrio König writes,

> It is our glorious, God-given privilege to be his fellow workers and thus to have a share in salvation history. . . . No mere onlookers but rather covenant partners, we reap with him a harvest produced by the seed of the cross.[3]

There are no conditions or limits in Jesus' words, except the command to wait for the coming of the Spirit before beginning (Luke 24:49; Acts 1:4). Otherwise, the disciples do not have to wait for special instructions in order to carry out this mandate, which is grounded in the OT prophets (Acts 13:47). The sovereign hand of God is clearly evident in Acts, not only in the special directions He gives but also in the outcomes which are described, first in Jerusalem (Acts 2:41; 4:4; 5:12; 6:1; 6:7) and then beyond (Acts 8:12; 9:31,35,42; 10:44,46; 13:43,44,49; 14:1,21; 16:5; 17:4,12; 18:8,10; 19:10.20.26). It is stated explicitly in places where God's agency is emphasized, for example: "when God raised up his servant, he sent him first to you to bless you by turning each of you from your wicked ways" (Acts 3:26), "So then, even to Gentiles God has granted repentance that leads to life" (Acts 11:18), "the Lord's hand was with them, and a great number of people believed and turned to the Lord" (Acts 11:2), and "God first intervened to choose a people for his name from the Gentiles" (Acts 15:14).

More broadly, in Acts individual conversions are attributed to the skillful preaching of the messengers (Acts 14:1,21; 17:2–4; 19:8), the witness of signs and wonders confirming the message (Acts 5:12–16; 8:6–13; 13:8–12; 14:3; 19:11–12), other powerful events (Acts 2:5–12; 16:26–30; 19:13–20), the maneuvers of the Spirit bringing seeking people in touch with witnesses (Acts 8:26–35; 10:1–33; 11:4–14), the heart attitude of the hearers or seekers (Acts 10:2,22,35; 13:7; 17:11–12), and the work of the Lord or the Spirit in their minds or hearts (Acts 2:37, 10:44; 11:15–18; 16:14). It's a mixture of divine movement and human response.

---

3. König, *Eclipse of Christ*, 100.

Evangelism is the mandated means for communicating the good news of salvation and inviting people to respond with repentance and faith (Rom 10:14). The Spirit has the sovereign ability to set up unlikely encounters to make such communication possible and credible (e.g. Peter and Cornelius) and will also perform 'signs and wonders' to confirm the message (Heb 2:4). The results of evangelism are not exclusively the responsibility of the evangelist, but evangelists should use all means to communicate effectively, as seen in Paul's different messages to Jewish and Gentile audiences and his attempts to persuade his hearers (Acts 17:2,17; 18:4; 19:9; 1 Cor 9:20–22). Persuasive communication is not relied on but not rejected either.

The response of any individual to the good news is their choice but also influenced by, and dependent on, the work of the Spirit. God's great foreordained Plan ultimately cannot fail, but the results of evangelism will vary from place to place depending on cultural, political and religious factors. The church's task is to proclaim the gospel. God's task is to guide and empower them and work in the hearers.

REVIVAL

Matthew Henry once wrote, "Whenever God is about to do something truly great, He first sets His people a praying!"[4] However, the idea that prayer is the main cause of revival has been challenged by Barry Chant who calls it "part of evangelical folklore" that "cannot be established either biblically or historically."[5]

> To believe that revival is impossible unless we engage in serious prayer places an intolerable burden upon us and boils down to the fact that we can somehow limit the sovereign purpose of God. What if we don't pray? What if we pray almost enough but not quite enough?.... What if we are responsible for thwarting God's will?[6]

However, he concedes that, "without prayer there can be no ongoing revival. For revival without prayer is simply not revival."[7]

---

4. Cf. https://seapc.org/blog/he-first-sets-his-people-praying/ accessed on 12/02/22; Mahlburg and Marsh, *Great Southland Revival*, 270.

5. Chant, *This is Revival*, 40.

6. Chant, *This is Revival*, 41.

7. Chant, *This is Revival*, 41.

Revival has been a prominent theme of evangelical and Pentecostal language for several hundred years, especially since the great awakening events of the 18th century in Britain and America associated with people like John Wesley, George Whitefield and Jonathan Edwards. Revivalists in the 19th and 20th centuries often used means to stir up revival–Finney was the most famous for doing this–and there was a backlash against human efforts which led to an emphasis on revival as a sovereign work of God.[8] In some cases, such as the Welsh revival of 1904–1905, Evan Roberts withdrew from preaching lest he gain glory at God's expense, but the result was that the revival stopped.[9]

Chant claims that, "Biblically a leaderless revival is an anomaly."[10] One of the reasons why the Methodist movement had the most lasting results of the eighteenth century awakenings lay in Wesley's gift for organization and discipline. Historian Stuart Piggin comments, "At its best, revivalism insists that revival is a work of God's Spirit . . . Human might cannot produce revival, revivalism asserts, but it can organize for it, and it can block it."[11]

The Pentecost event itself has several features relevant to the study of revival. And D. Martyn Lloyd-Jones argues, "every revival of religion that the Church has ever known has been, in a sense, a kind of repetition of what happened on the day of Pentecost" [12] First, it was clearly a work of God, not something organized or stirred up by preachers, and came at God's chosen timing.[13] However, it was preceded by a season of waiting and intensive community prayer (Acts 1:14) in obedience to Jesus' instructions.

Second, the Pentecost event was something that happened first to the 120 waiting disciples. (Acts 2:1). "All of them were filled with the Holy

---

8. Lloyd-Jones asserts, "many and many a time have men tried to produce a revival. . . . They have done their utmost with all their techniques and methods, but there has been no revival" (*Revival*, 138).

9 See Chant, *This is Revival*, 97 and Lloyd-Jones, *Prove All Things*, 93.

10. Chant, *This is Revival*, 94.

11. Piggin. *Firestorm of the Lord*, 81. See also Mahlburg and Marsh, *Great Southland Revival*, 285. A new book by Robert J, Nyhuis tells of a highly organized mission in Melbourne in 1902 which was undergirded by multiple prayer circles and resulted in profound effects on churches and society (Nyhuis, *Global Revival*)

12. *Revival*, 199.

13. As Lloyd-Jones argues, "A revival is a miracle . . . a miraculous, exceptional phenomenon . . . something that can only be explained as the direct action and intervention of God" (*Revival*, 111–112).

Spirit and began to speak in other tongues as the Spirit enabled them" (v.4). Revival likewise is something that happens in and to the church.

Third, this experience attracted the attention of others, in this case "God-fearing Jews from every nation under heaven" (v.5) who had come to Jerusalem for the Pentecost festival and were amazed at what they heard (vv.6–12), though some were skeptical and looked for a natural explanation (v.13).

Fourth, these strange events gave Peter a platform to preach Jesus to the crowd (v.14). He began by explaining the phenomena of the understood tongues in the context of "the last days" (v.17) but moved on to an explanation of the story of Jesus with a strong conclusion: "Therefore let all Israel be assured of this: God has made this Jesus, whom you crucified, both Lord and Messiah" (v.36).

Fifth, there was a strong response brought about, we conclude, by the Holy Spirit: "When the people heard this, they were cut to the heart and said to Peter and the other apostles, 'Brothers, what shall we do?'" (v.37). History confirms that strong preaching of the clear word of God under the power of the Spirit, leading to powerful responses, is a constant feature of revivals. And as Barry Chant comments, "Where there is a sound biblical basis for revival, it is likely to be sustained."[14]

Peter then called for a specific response of repentance and baptism "in the name of Jesus Christ for the forgiveness of your sins" (v.38), with the promise of receiving the Holy Spirit. And it is not just a 'take it or leave it' call, because the passage continues, "With *many other words* he warned them; and he *pleaded* with them, "Save yourselves from this corrupt generation" (v.40; emphasis added). It sounds like an extended 'altar call' from a modern evangelist.

The response was strong, with three thousand converts being baptized (v.41). And the new congregation was highly committed and enthusiastic (vv.42–47). This description reads like a revived or renewed or pioneering church: hunger for more of God, commitment to prayer, generosity to others, awe towards God because He is so real,[15] intense joy, and ongoing numerical growth through multiplied conversions.

Of course, another feature of this move, both in Jerusalem and elsewhere, was strong opposition and persecution (Acts 4–8). Revival

---

14. Chant, *This is Revival*, 115.

15. Jonathan Edwards famously said that revival is "waking up to reality, which is God's perspective on his own character and that of sinners" (Piggin. *Firestorm of the Lord*, 10; see also, 22).

praying and preaching is an act of war against the powers of darkness[16] and revivals can only persist if the leaders persevere against all criticism and opposition. Lloyd-Jones points out that

> No revival that has ever been experienced in the long history of the Church has ever been an official movement in the Church. ... It was always unofficial, and the officials did not like it.[17]

Was this a repeatable phenomenon? Peter suggests so when he quotes Joel: "In the last days, God says, I will pour out my Spirit on all people" (Acts 2:17,18) and the Spirit is promised to converts into the future (Acts 2:38–39) because God's intention is for people to call on the name of the Lord and be saved (Acts 2:21) and "times of refreshing" will be granted to those who repent (Acts 3:19).

In every move of God narrated in Acts, the story begins with the Spirit coming on a group of new converts or seekers and only then spreads to the wider population as they see what is going on. This move brings non-Christian people into right relationship with God and as a result, their lives are changed (see Acts 2:42–47; 4:32–37; 8:39; 11:22–30; 13:52; and most strikingly 19:17–20). In Ephesus the effects were not only wide but deep, with new converts abandoning lingering connections with sorcery (Acts 19:18–19) and the local religion and economy being affected (Acts 19:24–27). This change spreads across the general population: "all the Jews and Greeks who lived in the province of Asia heard the word of the Lord" (Acts 19:10) and "the word of the Lord spread widely and grew in power" (Acts 19:20), so that Demetrius claimed, "this fellow Paul has convinced and led stray large numbers of people here in Ephesus and in practically the whole of Asia" (Acts 19:26).

It seems that this is meant to be 'normal,' though it does not happen uniformly everywhere. Acts challenges the church to seek for a revival of their experience of God and a renewed move of the Spirit among us. Such revival depends, of course, on the Spirit and cannot be 'worked up,' but it can be sought by prayer (especially corporate prayer) and facilitated by people who obey the voice of the Spirit, preach the unadulterated word of God and are willing to face the cost of opposition. A passive attitude, that God will do something when He chooses to, and we can do nothing about it, is *not* what is called for. As Stuart Piggin argues, we must not try to "take revival production out of the hands of the sovereign God"

---

16. Cf. Piggin. *Firestorm of the Lord*, 15.
17. Lloyd-Jones, *Revival*, 166.

but we can "foster legitimate longing and heartfelt prayer for spiritual awakening."[18]

Finney defined revival as "a new beginning of obedience to God."[19] While I would see that as part of revival, or something leading to revival, it's an important ingredient. David Wilkerson says,

> A true revival, as I see it, is a restoration of this kind of intense love for Jesus. This love is marked by a new desire to obey His every word, a heart attitude that says, 'whatever He says, I will do.'[20]

Revivals are 'messy' events that may include heresies, fanaticism, extremes, scandals and fleshly manifestations as well as the pure work of the Spirit bringing salvation, sanctification, spiritual life, power and gifts.[21] This should not surprise us as the devil will do what he can to stop or divert a true revival. Moreover, such a 'mixture' can be seen in the early church, as Paul's letters to the Corinthians make clear. But God may well sovereignly tolerate this to test His people (as we saw earlier) and train them in discernment and holiness. As Jonathan Edwards, perhaps the greatest theologian of revival, once wrote,

> For it will be very likely to be of excellent benefit to his church, in the continuance and progress of the work afterwards: their experience in the first setting out of the mischievous consequences of these errors, and smarting for them in the beginning, may be an happy defense to them afterwards, from these errors, which otherwise they might continually be exposed to.[22]

D. Martyn Lloyd-Jones urges that,

> There is nothing that is really going to touch the world as it is today except a mighty revival of the Spirit of God. . . . If only men and women would put all the energy that they are ready to put into organizations, into seeking God and living in his

---

18. Piggin. *Firestorm of the Lord*, 1.

19. Charles G. Finney, *Lectures on Revivals of Religion* (1835). Delhi, India: Grapevine India, 2024. Also at https://www.ccel.org/ccel/finney/revivals.iii.i.html (accessed April 8, 2025).

20. Wilkerson, *Hungry for More*, 108.

21. Cf. DeArteaga, *Quenching the Spirit*, 55.

22. Edwards, "Some Thoughts Concerning Revival," as quoted in DeArteaga, *Quenching the Spirit*, 54.

presence and becoming truly sanctified, then revival would come at once.[23]

In other words, pray for revival and be open to revival in your own life for the glory of God and the advancement of His kingdom, bearing in mind that revival is just one means God uses to build his church.

WHAT ABOUT THE UNEVANGELIZED AND OTHER RELIGIONS?

Some years ago I took part in a Pentecostal-style outreach in the Melbourne (Australia) 'Mind Body Spirit' Festival, a four day event that functions as a kind of spiritual 'supermarket.' Here different groups promote their ideas and products (anything from health foods to transcendental meditation) from rented stalls in one of Melbourne's huge exhibition centers. Several other Christian groups were operating using low-key apologetics and contextual approaches. This outreach, 'The School of the Prophets,' would instead offer prayer and prophetic words to all comers. Other Christians warned us against trespassing onto Satan's territory, and indeed every year team members came under intense attack in the form of sickness, accidents and other bad things. But the first year we operated, our stand was swamped with seekers. It was challenging to depend on the Spirit for a 'word' for someone who wasn't a professing Christian, but we could think of good Old Testament precedent especially in Daniel's ministry to Nebuchadnezzar.

I discovered that more people are seeking spiritual reality than I had realized. In fact, it seemed to me that the festival was functioning to bring together lots of spiritual seekers for us to connect with. I also found that the Holy Spirit is indeed omnipresent and active all over the world, not just among Christians. I was regularly surprised at what the Spirit was doing in the lives of people with little or no Christian background. God has provided salvation for all people through Christ and wants everyone to believe and be saved. And the New Testament assures us that God's Plan will triumph. But what does that mean for the millions who have not heard the gospel, both in past ages before Jesus and in many parts of the world since then, and even today?

Pink argues that God could have saved them all, or at least given them the opportunity to be saved, but He didn't, and this goes to show it

23. Lloyd-Jones, *The Assurance of Our Salvation*, 372–373.

was never His will. God has decreed that many people are to be lost, in other words.[24] But is this biblical?

We noted earlier that after Babel, God apparently stopped dealing directly with the whole of humanity and mainly concentrated on Abraham and his descendants until the coming of Christ. Fundamentally this act of judgment governed the nations (Gentiles) until Christ came. On the other hand, the restriction of God's work largely to Israel is explicitly with a view to a universal outcome: "all peoples on earth will be blessed through you" (Gen 12:3).

Paul says to the Lystrans, "in the past, he let all nations go their own way" (Acts 14:16). Until Jesus died for the sins of the whole world and commissioned his preachers to take this good news everywhere, most people had little access to the truth about God.

But Paul goes on to say,

> "Yet, he has not left himself without testimony. He has shown kindness by giving you rain from heaven and crops in their seasons; he provides you with plenty of food and fills your hearts with joy."
>
> (Acts 14:17).

Paul points out that God did not just ignore the Gentile world. And in Romans, he makes this point more sharply:

> what may be known about God is plain to them, because God has made it plain to them. For since the creation of the world God's invisible qualities- his eternal power and divine nature- have been clearly seen, being understood from what has been made, so that people are without excuse
>
> (Rom 1:19-20).

And his argument is supported by the conclusion of some Greek philosophers who came to some understanding of God by rational thought.[25] But generally, the ancient world "exchanged the glory of the immortal God for images" (Rom 1:22) and came under God's judgment in the form of moral and social decline (Rom 1:24-32).

Paul also points to another source of light for the Gentiles when he contends that "they know God's righteous decree that those who do

---

24. Pink, *Sovereignty of God*, 82–84.
25. E.g. Aristotle. Cf. Richard Tarnas, *The Passion of the Western Mind* (London: Pimlico, 1996), 63.

such things deserve death" (Rom 1:32). He is pointing to the fact that all cultures share at least some common knowledge of morality and it is this common morality that will be the basis for judgment of those who do not have the greater light of God's law (Rom 2:12).

He even envisages the possibility of this revelation in the human conscience of some Gentiles having a major consequence:

> (Indeed, when Gentiles, who do not have the law, do by nature things required by the law, they are a law for themselves, even though they do not have the law. They show that the requirements of the law are written on their hearts, their conscience also bearing witness, and their thoughts sometimes accusing them and at other times *even defending them*)

(Rom 2:14–15, emphasis added).

Paul at least opens the *possibility* that Gentiles could be justified by their response to this light.

In his speech to the Athenian Areopagus, Paul argues that God has guided and wooed all the nations:

> "he marked out their appointed times in history and the boundaries of their lands. God did this so that they would seek him and perhaps reach out for him and find him, though he is not far from any one of us. For in him we live and move and have our being"

(Acts 17:26–28).

God was there with them all the time, close and available. He had not just consigned them to perdition. And Paul adds, "As some of your own poets have said, 'We are his offspring.'" (Acts 17:28b); some of them had grasped at least the rudiments of true revelation, so they should have deduced that God is not like an idol (Acts 17:29).

Paul says, "In the past God overlooked such ignorance, but now he commands all people everywhere to repent" (Acts 17:30). This also suggests that the Gentiles of old were not judged by a light they did not have; their ignorance was "overlooked" or "disregarded."[26] In a similar way, Jesus' 'middle knowledge,' about how some ancient nations might have responded if they had seen miracles like his, leads him to expect a milder judgment on them than on the Jews of his day (Matt 11:20–24).

Speaking of the pre-incarnate Word of God, John writes,

26. Greek *huperoraō*, overlook, disregard, pass over.

In him was life, and that life was the light of all mankind. The
light shines in the darkness, and the darkness has not overcome
it

(John 1:4–5).

I think this means that the light of the Word was available in some form to all mankind; even in the midst of their gross darkness and idolatry, this light was not put out. Ancient people had more light than we give credit for; they were never completely cut off from God.

If we look at the Old Testament, we can see that God speaks to Gentile rulers in dreams and they respond to some degree (Gen 20:3–7; Dan 2,4). He speaks to Ahasuerus in a sleepless night through the written annals of his reign (Est 6). There are wise men or prophets in Gentile nations: Melchizedek king of Salem, "priest of God Most High" (Gen 14:18–20), Balaam the prophet/diviner (Num 22–24), Moses' father-in-law (Exod 18), Job, "the greatest man among all the people of the East" (Job 1:3), and supremely the wise men who followed the star to Bethlehem (Matt 2:1–12).

God guided other nations apart from Israel (Amos 9:7). He sent prophetic words of warning and judgment to neighboring nations (e.g. Isa 10:5–19; 14:3–27; 31; 34; 37:21–35; 45:1–14; 46–47; Jer 27:1–11; 46–51; Amos 1:3–2:3; 3:9). In at least one case, a Gentile city was saved from destruction because of their response to such a prophetic warning from an Israelite prophet (Jonah 3). When the prophet complained, God replied,

> "And should I not have concern for the great city of Nineveh, in which are more than a hundred and twenty thousand people who cannot tell their right hand from their left- and also many animals."

(Jon 4:11).

Reliable sources today tell frequent cases of Muslims having dreams or visions of Jesus and subsequently becoming Christians.[27] Whatever the case, we can be sure that God's judgment is impartial and reasonable

---

27. One remarkable case is told in Ripken, *The Insanity of God*, 267, of a desperate man whose life was in a mess and as he sought divine help in response to an imam's guidance, "a voice without a body came to me after midnight. That voice said, 'Find Jesus, find the gospel.'"

(Rom 2:9-16). We can also depend on God to honor His promises to be found by all who actually seek Him (Isa 55:6-7; Matt 7:7-8; Heb 11:6).

Calvinists like R.C. Sproul may retort,

> God revealed himself to Moses in a manner he did not grant to Pharaoh. God gave Saul of Tarsus a blessed revelation of the majesty of Christ that he did not give to Pilate or Caiaphas.[28]

Yes, God doesn't deal with everyone in exactly the same way. Obviously, God's will for Pharaoh was not the same as the call He placed on Moses' life; but Pharaoh did have the opportunity to learn from Moses! We are only guessing about what God did or didn't do to many Gentile figures. We do know what God did with Nebuchadnezzar (Daniel 2-4), with Naaman (2 Kings 5), with Nineveh (Jonah 3), with Darius and other Persians (Daniel 6),[29] with the others on the boat with Jonah (Jon 1:16), with Pilate's wife (Matt 27:19), with Pilate himself (John 18:28-19:16) and various other Roman officials (Acts 18:12-17; 24:10-26; 26:1-32), and even the emperor Nero (2 Tim 4:16-17). The difference between Paul and Pilate is clearer in the NT, but while Jesus' intervention with Paul was more forceful, Pilate had the advantage of seeing and talking with Jesus in person, as did Caiaphas. All we can be sure of, is that God responds strongly to seeking hearts as in the case of Ruth the Moabite widow, the Ethiopian official (Acts 8:26-39) and Cornelius the Roman officer (Acts 10).

Researchers have discovered a rich lode of authentic spirituality within 'pagan' cultures waiting for missionaries to unearth and use in evangelism. Don Richardson is one missionary who came to realize this through his own attempts to evangelize a particularly stubborn tribe in West Papua. As told in *Peace Child*, Richardson struggled to communicate with the Sawi people for whom treachery was a virtue and whose hero, when they heard the Jesus story, was Judas. It was only when he discovered the 'peace child' practice, by which two warring tribes made peace by adopting a child from the other, the one person who could not be betrayed without consequences, that he found a road into their hearts.[30] In his later book *Eternity in Their Hearts*, Richardson describes how similar elements may be found in the mythology and religion of

---

28. R.C. Sproul, *What Is Reformed Theology?* (Grand Rapids: Baker Books, 1997), 151.

29. See also Esther, Ezra and Nehemiah.

30. See also Richardson, *Eternity*, 111-112.

many non-Christian cultures and concludes, "God has indeed prepared the Gentile world to receive the gospel."[31]

Clearly Jesus is the only Savior and Lord. Clearly God "commands all people everywhere to repent" (Acts 17:30b). But just as strongly, we cannot restrict the work of the Spirit or minimize the sovereign hand of God over all nations, including their religious life. Nor can we play down the vision of "a great multitude that no one could count, from every nation, tribe, people and language standing before the throne and before the Lamb" (Rev 7:9). God's Plan will not be defeated, not even by false religions.

---

31. Richardson, *Eternity*, 33.

CONCLUSIONS

IN THIS FINAL CHAPTER, I want to sum up some of the themes we've been exploring and suggest how we should respond to the truth of God's sovereignty as we now understand it.

Let's return to the definition of divine sovereignty I proposed in the Introduction.

GOD'S FREEDOM.

God is totally free. God is not obligated to any other person or force. He is not dependent on any other person or force. His will is only subject to His own character as God. We have seen that this is true: God always makes His own decisions about how He will act in any situation and does not owe us, or anyone, an explanation. "God is conditioned by nothing but God," as Chris Green says.[1] However, God's character means that we can depend on God to act in certain ways; He will never lie (Tit 1:2) or act unjustly. His nature as Love (1 John 4:16) is unchangeable. There is a kind of 'moral constitution' flowing out of God's character that guides God to require certain things (for example, that all things must be tested) and that gives His free creatures (even the devil) a basis for prayer or argument with God.

GOD'S OWNERSHIP.

God has absolute rights over His creation. He has the moral and legal right to interact with His creation and dispose of His creation as He sees fit. In the case of humanity, God is the absolute Judge; He has the right to judge

---

1. *Surprised by God*, 17.

us and we are totally accountable to Him (not the other way around). This has been seen as totally correct according to the Bible. However, it does not mean that God treats His free creatures (such as human beings) as puppets, since God always acts justly. As Abraham protested, "Will not the Judge of all the earth do right?" (Gen 18:25). And that means that sometimes God's friends *do* have the right to hold Him accountable, as Job attempted, but only to His own nature and constitution.

GOD'S RULE.

God rules over the universe He has created. All created things depend on Him. Nothing happens without His permission. His purposes prevail and are fulfilled. To put it another way, God is never frustrated. This has been established from Scripture as largely true. But the freedom God granted to human beings and angelic beings relativizes God's control.[2] God does not (usually) coerce humans and His permissive will is broad. Hence, God *is* often 'frustrated' in the sense of being disappointed with outcomes, as in His regret at having created humans in Genesis 6. However, He will do what is needed for His plans and promises to be fulfilled, including putting strong influence, even pressure, on people from outside and within, thereby ensuring that His overall Plan is not finally frustrated. In the End, God succeeds in His endeavors and creates a new heaven and new earth where all resistance to His will is ended.

Next I want to make some final comments on the application of this truth to our lives and thinking as Christians.

First, the truth of the sovereign God of the Bible, the almighty Ruler of all, should serve *to enlarge our concept of God and lead us to a profound reverence and trust towards Him* and surrender to His will. As Bible translator J.B. Phillips said years ago, too often 'your God is too small.'[3] If our idea of God doesn't sometimes cause us to be overwhelmed with His greatness and 'bigness,' if we don't experience the fear of the Lord, not because we are afraid of punishment but because we are up against a Reality far too big for us to contain or understand, far too pure for us to compromise with, we need to ask questions about what God we

---

2. "Control" is perhaps not the best word anyway given the domineering overtones in that word these days. (cf. Chris Green, *Surprised by God*, 41).

3. This was the title of a book he wrote published in 1962 in London by Wyvern.

are serving.[4] We must also respect God's rights and freedom, not try to manipulate God (as if we could!), and learn to take God's side in any controversy

But in this we need to be careful not to be the kind of friends Job had; in other words, not to assume *we know* what God wants or is doing in such a situation. And we should never assume God *needs* our help. As John Piper says, "the one who actually sets himself above God is the person who presumes to come to God to give rather than to get."[5] We should become teachable before God, which is the first expression of "the fear of the Lord" (Prov 1:7), and highly dependent on Him, aware of our own weakness and limitations. As Psalm 127 says, "Unless the LORD builds the house, the builders labor in vain" (Ps 127:1). And as Jesus said, "apart from me you can do nothing" (John 15:5b).

But this truth should not create a picture of God as somehow distant, unknowable, arbitrary or unpredictable. God is not totally predictable or knowable, but He does reveal enough of His nature in the Bible for us to relate to Him with confidence. We know that God cannot lie (Heb 6:18; Tit 1:2) and therefore we can depend on His promises. We know that "God is light; in him there is no darkness at all" (1 John 1:5)–God has no dark side and cannot sin. We know that God "cannot be tempted by evil, not does he tempt anyone" (James 1:13); wherever temptation comes from, it's not from God. We know that God is love and has expressed that love to us by sending Jesus into the world "as an atoning sacrifice for our sins" (1 John 4:8–10). We know that God does not "change like shifting shadows" (James 1:17). We know that God shows no favoritism but is totally impartial as Judge (Col 3:25; Rom 2:11). While we don't always know how these attributes of God will be expressed in specific situations, mainly because we do not know all the aspects of any situation as God does, we can trust Him to act as Himself.

Second, we need to respect the fact that *God's sovereignty makes room for other forces and persons to exist and operate*. He doesn't operate as a kind of 'puppet master,' pulling strings and playing with His creatures. He has established certain 'laws' that operate with a measure of autonomy in the natural realm, and He has created beings with free will, who can even disobey what He commands them and who also have freedom to

---

4. As Chris Green, quoting Edith Stein says, "'God is always ever greater'. . . . than our affirmations . . . Greater than what we can say or think" (*Surprised by God*, 14). See also Kendall, *Out of the Comfort Zone*, 73.

5. *Desiring God*, 74.

make their own choices in most situations. We need to respect the autonomy of God's creation and not expect it to behave as we think fit. We need to respect the freedom of other human beings and not demand that they conform to our ideas of righteousness or try to manipulate or coerce them to do what we think is best.

Third, *we need to face life with wisdom*. The problems and situations we face can be caused by natural forces, human decisions, the devil and God Himself. We don't always know which cause is the one we should focus on, though we can be sure that God's sovereign rule is over all and ultimately nothing happens without His (general or specific) permission. So when faced with, say, sickness, we may need to take natural remedies (e.g. medicine) or consider any foolish things we've done and change our habits (e.g. diet, alcohol) or resist the devil or simply pray to God for relief and healing and call for others to pray for us (James 5:14–16). Perhaps we need to do all of these. Ultimately, however, we face all such issues with an attitude of trust in, and surrender to, Almighty God. As Calvin wrote,

> Gratitude of mind for the favorable outcome of things, patience in adversity, and also incredible freedom from worry about the future all necessarily follow upon this knowledge.[6]

Fourth, a conviction of God's sovereignty should help us *be content with our lot in life*. We are all placed in different situations and created with different attributes. We had no say in our gender, our parents, our racial or ethnic identity, our size and shape (within limits), our genetic makeup, the time period in which we were born, our abilities and intelligence, even perhaps our temperament. While modern science now offers us the choice to change some aspects of this heritage and we can adapt some aspects by education and training (such as weight and strength), certain things just have to be accepted. But many people go through life wishing they were someone else. The conviction that God chose that I should be as I am, then, motivates me to a sense of contentment and even thankfulness.

Paul encourages slaves to take their freedom if possible (1 Cor 7:21) but otherwise to "remain in the situation they were in when God called them" (1 Cor 7:24). Paul himself experienced both good and bad circumstances and wrote to the Philippian Christians from prison,

---

6. Calvin, *Institutes*, 219. See also ibid., 223–224.

> I have learned to be content whatever the circumstances. I know what it is to be in need, and I know what it is to have plenty. I have learned the secret of being content in any and every situation, whether well fed or hungry. I can do all this through him who gives me strength
>
> (Phil 4:11–13).

Fifth, therefore, knowing God is sovereign should help us to *interpret what happens to us in that light*. Even though afflictions may come from the devil or from other people, they may well be directed by God our loving Father to help us mature as His sons. As the writer to the Hebrews exhorts us,

> And have you completely forgotten this word of encouragement that addresses you as a father addresses his son? It says,
>
> "My son, do not make light of the Lord's discipline,
> and do not lose heart when he rebukes you,
> because the Lord disciplines the one he loves,
> and he chastens everyone he accepts as his son."
>
> Endure hardship as discipline; God is treating you as his children. For what children are not disciplined by their father? If you are not disciplined- and everyone undergoes discipline- then you are not legitimate, not true sons and daughters at all...
>
> God disciplines us for our good, in order that we nay share in his holiness. No discipline seems pleasant at the time, but painful. Later on, however, it produces a harvest of righteousness and pace for those who have been trained by it
>
> (Heb 12:5-8,10b-11).

D. Martyn Lloyd-Jones comments,

> If you are God's child, then God is going to perfect you. If you will not listen to positive teaching, he will chastise you, he will lay his hand upon you. Perhaps your health will suffer or the health of a dear one; there may be an accident, a calamity, a death.... My sanctification is in his hands and thank God it is ....[7]

---

7. Lloyd-Jones, *The Assurance of Our Salvation*, 396.

Just before I went to Papua New Guinea as a young schoolteacher, I read a book[8] by the Chinese pastor Watchman Nee that prepared me for God's 'dealings' in life and it helped me immensely to respond to the troubles and challenges I faced there away from family and friends. Seeing the Lord's hand in what happens to you adds meaning to your life and helps you respond as God wants. This is what Joseph learned (Gen 50:20) and it is a great implication of divine sovereignty. As Pink says, perhaps with a measure of hyperbole, "there is no real rest for your poor heart until you learn to see the hand of God in everything."[9]

This insight helps us keep a balanced focus towards not just what happens to us but also what we ourselves achieve. Custance wisely observes,

> We are so accustomed to reading success stories, and even *Christian* success stories, that we imagine God's purposes are fulfilled only, or at least *best*, during those times when our lives are "successful." But for most of us such successes are few and far between.... the dangers to our spiritual welfare from success are far greater than the dangers from failure.[10]

God often uses other people in our lives–bosses, friends, teachers and others–to chasten and mature us, not because they deliberately set out to do so, but because they react in what may be ungodly and unkind ways to us.[11] God our Father sovereignly shapes situations and steers events for our good, to make us more like Jesus (Rom 8:28–29).

Greg Boyd strongly objects to this line of thinking, pointing out that nowhere in Scripture does God promise us protection from harm, and that undeserved, irrational and gratuitous evil may happen to us all. He suggests that we interpret such events instead as war injuries, the results of the struggle between God and Satan, and not attribute them to God.

> This world is a spiritual war zone under the control of Satan (1 Jn 5:19), the "god of this world" (2 Cor 4:4) .... The good news of the gospel is not that we will never suffer, get raped, be maimed or die an early death. The good news is rather that the

---

8. Nee, *The Release of the Spirit*.
9. Pink, *Sovereignty of God*, 187.
10. Custance, *Sovereignty of Grace*, 241; emphasis in the original.
11. Custance, *Sovereignty of Grace*, 257.

Lord has given us something so marvelous that even if we suffer or die, our loss is ultimately insignificant.[12]

This is certainly true and a salutary lesson to us all, especially perhaps to Pentecostals who are influenced by prosperity theology. But it is also one-sided. I think Joseph (in Genesis), who spent years suffering slavery, imprisonment and undeserved treatment, would want to say that God's sovereign hand was in all this. "It was not you who sent me here, but God" (Gen 45:8a). "You intended to harm me, but *God intended it for good*" (Gen 50:20a, emphasis added; see also Ps 105:17–19). Job also suffered at the instigation of Satan, but it was ultimately God's doing (at least by God's specific permission) with a good intention and outcome.

Paul's "thorn in the flesh," while it was "a messenger of Satan", was "given" (apparently by God) for a sanctifying purpose, "to keep me from becoming conceited" (2 Cor 12:7) and God declined to remove it, not because of Satan, but because "my power is made perfect in weakness" (2 Cor 12:9a). Boyd suggests that Paul's case is exceptional and that "unless we have direction from God to think otherwise, we should in faith oppose the illness as something that is contrary to God's will."[13] Again, he is right but one-sided. Leaving God's sovereignty out of consideration is more likely to cause confusion and frustration, especially when the illness or other contrary circumstance resists our prayers for its removal.

But the problem, as Erickson points out, is that mostly we do not know what God is up to: "He alone determines his plan and knows the significance of each of his actions. It is not necessary for us to know where he is leading."[14] Faith comes in here; I trust Him even though I don't understand what is going on.

Sixth, therefore, the truth of God's sovereignty, that God is 'on the throne,' gives us *great encouragement in trying times*. The forces of evil are not going to win or overpower us. God has the last word. He will prevail and His Plan will succeed. Jesus will build his church. Wild beasts might rise up and oppress the church (Rev 13), as has happened many times and is happening today, but ultimately they will not succeed. The mighty Roman Empire could not defeat the gospel and had to sue for peace under Constantine. The Soviet Union and the whole Eastern communist bloc fell down partly because they were unable to crush the church in Poland

---

12. Boyd, *Satan and the Problem of Evil*, 160.
13. Boyd, *Satan and the Problem of Evil*, 370.
14. Erickson, *Christian Theology*, 429.

and Romania and Russia. God is at work even in the minds and hearts of wicked politicians and rulers, as in Rev 17:17, which declares, "God has put it into their hearts to accomplish his purpose by agreeing to hand over to the beast their royal authority, until God's words are fulfilled."

This is not just applicable to large-scale events. Our personal trials are also important and Paul affirms,

> No temptation [or testing/trial] has overtaken you except what is common to mankind. And God is faithful; *he will not let you be tempted* [or tested/tried] *beyond what you can bear. But when you are tempted* [or tested/tried], *he will also provide a way out so that you can endure it*
>
> (1 Cor 10:13, emphasis added).

God's sovereign control prevents us being tempted, tested or tried (the Greek verb *peirazō* can mean all of these) more than we can bear. He intervenes, if necessary, or he directs events (including the actions of others), in order to protect us. This is an amazing promise to hang onto in trying times.

Seventh, however, *God's sovereignty should never lead us to a passive 'que sera sera' attitude*. We trust that God is sovereign and that nothing we face has surprised Him or escaped His rule. But that may not mean we should accept every situation as we find it. God often wants us to change it with His help or at least pray that He will act for change. As we saw in the chapters on prayer and evangelism, God is not committed to the 'status quo.' He is a God of change and wants to use us as partners in changing unjust situations. Pious resignation to evil or injustice can be no more than a 'cop out.' As Greg Boyd puts it,

> Jesus and the New Testament authors instruct us to revolt against evil as coming from the enemies of God rather than trying to find security and consolation in the hope that God is somehow secretly behind it.[15]

I would want to qualify this assertion, as I said earlier. If we are only talking about inconvenience, hardship or personal suffering, there might well be a place for submission to the 'dealings' of God for our sanctification. But if we are facing gross injustice, corruption or Satanic plots, we need to consider that God may be calling us to fight. "Submit yourselves, then to God. Resist the devil, and he will flee from you" (James 4:7).

15. Boyd, *Satan and the Problem of Evil*, 162.

Consider Elijah. Consider the story of David and Goliath. As far as we know, God never 'told' David to fight Goliath. David stumbled into the crisis as a messenger bringing supplies to his older brothers and started asking some rather pointed questions, for which impudence he was rebuked by his oldest brother (1 Sam 17:26–30). Then he volunteered to take on the giant (v.32). David had a history of killing wild beasts that attacked his father's sheep (vv.33–36). But more importantly, he saw the crisis for what it was, a brazen challenge to the living God (vv.36,45–47). His faith in that God prompted and empowered him to resist the Philistine challenge and defeat it.

God is looking for such heroes and uses them to carry out His plans. The Bible is full of such cases and Hebrews 11 surveys them: for example, Noah building a ridiculous big boat (Heb 11:7), Moses' parents hiding their baby son in spite of "the king's edict" (Heb 11:23), or Rahab hiding the Israelite spies (Heb 11:31). Elijah pronounces a long drought and calls down fire from heaven (1 Kings 17–18), Jehoshaphat calls a fast and sends out the choir in front of his army (2 Chr 20). Cheeky Jonathan challenges a Philistine garrison, one of my favorite stories (1 Sam 14:1–14). Jesus refuses to debate about the causes of a man's blindness and just heals him (John 9:1–11) and stays away for two more days when he hears of Lazarus' illness so that he could be raised to life to God's glory (John 11:1–44). Think of Peter and John healing a random lame man (Acts 3:1–10) or Paul starting provocative conversations in the Athens marketplace (Acts 17:16–18). Few of these cases involve a direct word from God. The heroes just had faith in a big sovereign God who can do anything, who was out to right wrongs, and whose honor and cause they were committed to. As William Carey famously preached, "Expect great things from God; attempt great things for God."[16]

Rory Randall suggests that "An open theist renewal theology in praxis takes risks and, as led by the Holy Spirit, takes initiative."[17] But in practice, other theological views have had a similar result: Calvinist George Whitefield led the charge into open air preaching in the English evangelical revival of the 18th century and the Arminian Wesley followed later. But Wesley led the way in opposing slavery and Whitefield never followed.[18]

---

16. Based on a sermon he preached on Isaiah 54.

17. Rory Randall, *An Open Theist Renewal Theology: God's Love, The Spirit's Power, and Human Freedom* (SacraSage Press, 2021 Kindle version), Chapter 5 (loc.4,233).

18. Randall, *An Open Theist Renewal Theology*, Chapter 5 (loc. 4,292–4,298).

As Chris Green suggests, "we're called to live fearlessly" and for that to happen, "we have to allow ourselves to be shown a reality truer than our experience."[19] What is the Lord stirring you to do for Him? What situations are you burdened about because they are unacceptable to God? Respond to that gentle pressure from the Holy Spirit. Trust God that, if He is calling you to pray or act, this is somehow part of His sovereign plan for you and for the world. Hence He will 'open doors' and touch hearts so that your mission succeeds. But even if it does not succeed, or at least not in the way you expected, know that God's plan is bigger than you could imagine and He will work it out.

---

19. Green, *Surprised by God*, 1–2.

BIBLIOGRAPHY

Althouse, Peter. *Spirit of the Last Days*. London: T & T Clark, 2003.
Barrett, Matthew. *None Greater: The Undomesticated Attributes of God*. Grand Rapids: Baker, 2019.
Baudin, Frédéric. *Ecology and the Bible*. Translated by Damon Dimauro. Peabody: Hendrickson, 2020.
Beilby, James and Paul R. Eddy, eds. *The Nature of the Atonement: Four Views*. Downers Grove: IVP Academic, 2006.
Bock, Darrell L. *Acts*. Baker Exegetical Commentary on the New Testament. Grand Rapids: Baker Academic, 2007.
Bonda, Jan. *The One Purpose of God: An Answer to the Doctrine of Eternal Punishment*. Grand Rapids: Eerdmans, 1998.
Boyd, Gregory A. *God of the Possible: A Biblical Introduction to the Open View of God*. Grand Rapids: Baker, 2000.
———. *God At War: The Bible and Spiritual Conflict*. Downers Grove: IVP, 1997.
———. *Satan and the Problem of Evil: Constructing a Trinitarian Warfare Theodicy*. Downers Grove: IVP Academic, 2001.
Byerly, T. Ryan. *The Mechanics of Divine Foreknowledge and Providence: A Time-Ordering Account*. New York: Bloomsbury Academic, 2014.
Calvin, John. *Institutes of the Christian Religion*. Edited by John T. McNeill; translated by Ford Lewis Battles. 2 vols. Philadelphia: Westminster, 1960.
Carey, William. *An Enquiry into the Obligations of Christians to Use Means for the Conversion of the Heathens; in which the Religious State of the Different Nations of the World, the Success of Former Undertakings, and the Practicability of Further Undertakings are Considered*. Pantianos Classics, 1792.
Campbell, Travis James. *The Wonderful Decree: Reconciling Sovereign Election and Universal Benevolence*. Bellingham: Lexham, 2020.
Carson, D.A. *Divine Sovereignty and Human Responsibility: Biblical Perspectives in Tension*. London: Marshall Pickering, 1994.
Castelo, Daniel. "An Apologia for Divine Impassibility: Toward Pentecostal Prolegomena." *Journal of Pentecostal Theology* 19 (2010) 118-126.
———. *Theological Theodicy*. Eugene: Cascade, 2012.
Chant, Barry. *The Spirit of Pentecost: The Origins and Development of the Pentecostal Movement in Australia 1870-1939*. Emeth, 2011.
———. *This Is Revival*. Adelaide: Tabor, 2013.

Clifton, Shane. "The Dark Side of Prayer for Healing: Toward a Theology of Well Being." *Pneuma* 36.2 (2014) 204-225.
Cole, Alan. *Exodus*. Tyndale Old Testament Commentaries. Leicester: Inter-Varsity Press, 1973.
Craig, William Lane. "Is God's Moral Perfection Reducible to His Love?" *Religions* 14 (2023).
———. *The Only Wise God: The Compatibility of Divine Foreknowledge and Human Freedom*. Grand Rapids: Baker, 1987.
———. ed. *Philosophy of Religion: A Reader and Guide*. Edinburgh: Edinburgh University Press, 2002.
Custance, Arthur C. *The Sovereignty of Grace*. Phillipsburg: Presbyterian and Reformed, 1979.
DeArteaga, William. *Quenching the Spirit: Examining Centuries of Opposition to the Moving of the Holy Spirit*. Lake Mary: Creation House, 1992.
Dickson, John. *Bullies and Saints: An Honest Look at the Good and Evil of Christian History*. Grand Rapids: Zondervan Reflective, 2021.
Duffield, Guy P. and Nathaniel M. Van Cleave, *Foundations of Pentecostal Theology*. Los Angeles: L.I.F.E. Bible College, 1987.
Ede, Paul. "River from the Temple: The Spirit, City Earthkeeping and Healing Urban Land." In *Blood Cries Out: Pentecostals, Ecology and the Groans of Creation*, edited by A.J. Swoboda and Steven Bouma-Prediger, 207-226. Eugene: Pickwick Publications, 2014.
Erickson, Millard J. *Christian Theology*, 2nd edition. Grand Rapids: Baker, 1998.
Evans, Craig A. *Mark 8:27-16:20*, Word Biblical Commentary 34B. Nashville: Thomas Nelson, 2001.
Fee, Gordon D. *God's Empowering Presence: The Holy Spirit in the Letters of Paul*. Peabody: Hendrickson, 1994.
Ferguson, Sinclair B. and David F. Wright, ed. *New Dictionary of Theology*. Leicester: Inter-Varsity, 1989.
Finney, Charles G. *Lectures on Revivals of Religion* (1835). Delhi, India: Grapevine India, 2024.
France, R.T. *Matthew*. Tyndale New Testament Commentaries. Leicester: Inter-Varsity, 1985.
Fretheim, Terence E. *Exodus*. Interpretation. Louisville: John Knox, 1991.
———. *The Suffering of God: An Old Testament Perspective*. Philadelphia: Fortress, 1984.
Friesen, Garry with J. Robin Maxson. *Decision Making and the Will of God*. Homebush West: Lancer, 1980.
Geisler, Norman L. *Chosen But Free: A Balanced View of God's Sovereignty and Free Will*. 3rd edition. Minneapolis: Bethany House, 2010.
Goldingay, John E. *Daniel*. Word Biblical Commentary 30. Dallas: Word Publishing, 1987.
Goldsworthy, Graeme. *Gospel and Kingdom: A Christian Interpretation of the Old Testament*. Exeter: Paternoster, 1981.
Gooch, P.W. "Sovereignty and Freedom: Some Pauline Compatibilisms." *Scottish Journal of Theology* 40.4 (1987) 531-542.
Gray, Tony and Christopher Sinkinson, eds. *Reconstructing Theology: A Critical Assessment of the Theology of Clark Pinnock*. Carlisle: Paternoster, 2000.

Green, Chris E.W. *Surprised by God: How and Why What We Think about the Divine Matters*. Eugene: Cascade, 2018.

Green, Michael. *2 Peter and Jude*. TNTC. Leicester: Inter-Varsity, 1987.

Grenz, Stanley J. *Prayer: The Cry for the Kingdom*. Revised edition. Grand Rapids: Eerdmans, 2005.

———. *Theology for the Community of God*. Grand Rapids: Eerdmans, 2000.

Hall, Christopher A. and John Sanders. *Does God Have a Future? A Debate on Divine Providence*. Grand Rapids: Baker Academic, 2003.

Hanson, Paul D. *Isaiah 40-66*. Interpretation. Louisville: John Knox Press, 1995.

Harris, Tania M. *God Dreams: How to Hear God's Voice in Dreams and Visions*. Milton Keynes: Authentic, 2024.

Harrison, R.K. *Jeremiah and Lamentations*. Tyndale Old Testament Commentaries. Leicester: Inter-Varsity Press, 1973.

Hart, David Bentley. *That All Shall Be Saved: Heaven, Hell and Universal Salvation*. New Haven: Yale University Press, 2019.

Helm, Paul. *The Providence of God: Contours of Christian Theology*. Downers Grove: IVP, 1993.

Hobbs, T.R. *2 Kings*. Word Biblical Commentary Vol.13. Waco: Word Books, 1985.

Houston, James M. *I Believe in the Creator*. Grand Rapids: Eerdmans, 1980.

Howard-Brook, Wes. *"Come Out, My People!" God's Call out of Empire in the Bible and Beyond*. Maryknoll: Orbis, 2010.

Hughes, Philip. *Putting Life Together: Findings from Australian Youth Spirituality Research*. Nunawading: Christian Research Association, 2007.

Jersak, Bradley. *A More Christlike God*. Pasadena: Plain Truth Ministries, 2015.

Johnson, Keith L. *The Essential Karl Barth: A Reader and Commentary*. Grand Rapids: Baker Academic, 2019.

Kaiser, Sigurd. "Church Growth in China: Some Observations from an Ecumenical Perspective." *The Ecumenical Review* 67.1 (2015) 35-47.

Kendall, R.T. *Calvin and English Calvinism to 1649*. Carlisle: Paternoster, 1997.

———. *Jonah: An Exposition*. Carlisle: Paternoster, 1995.

———. *Out of the Comfort Zone: Is Your God Too Nice?* London: Hodder and Stoughton, 2005.

König, Adrio. *The Eclipse of Christ in Eschatology: Toward a Christ-Centred Approach*. Blackwood: New Creation Publications, 2007.

Kruse, Colin G. *Paul's Letter to the Romans*. The Pillar New Testament Commentary. Grand Rapids: Eerdmans, 2012.

Lennox, John C. *Against the Flow: The Inspiration of Daniel in an Age of Relativism*. Oxford: Monarch Books, 2015

———. *Determined to Believe? The Sovereignty of God, Freedom, Faith, and Human Responsibility*. Oxford: Monarch Books, 2017.

Levison, Jack. *A Boundless God: The Spirit according to the Old Testament*. Grand Rapids: Baker Academic, 2020.

Lewis, C.S. *The Great Divorce*. London: Collins, 1972.

———. *Surprised by Joy*. London: Collins, 1959.

Lindsay, Mark. *God Has Chosen: The Doctrine of Election Though Church History*. Downers Grove: IVP Academic, 2020.

Lloyd-Jones, D. Martyn. *The Assurance of Our Salvation; Exploring the Depth of Prayer for His Own*. Wheaton: Crossway, 2000.

———. *Prove All Things: The Sovereign Work of the Holy Spirit*. Eastbourne: Kingsway Publications, 1985.

———. *Revival: can we make it happen?* Basingstoke: Marshall Pickering, 1986.

Long, G. Stephen and George Kalantzis, ed. *The Sovereignty of God Debate*. Cambridge: James Clake & Co., 2009.

Longman, Tremper III and Daniel G. Reid. *God Is A Warrior*. Carlisle: Paternoster, 1995.

Macchia, Frank D. *Tongues of Fire: A Systematic Theology of the Christian Faith*. Eugene: Cascade Books, 2023.

Mahlburg, Kurt and Warwick Marsh. *Great Southland Revival: Tracing the Spirit's Flame from Acts to Australia*. Unanderra: Australian Heart Publishing, 2022.

Marshall, Catherine. *Beyond Ourselves: a woman's pilgrimage in faith*. London: Peter Davies, 1961.

Marshall, I. Howard. *Kept by the Power of God*. Revised Edition. Carlisle: Paternoster, 1995.

Meadowcroft, Tim. "Sovereign God or Paranoid Universe? The Lord of Hosts is His Name." *Evangelical Review of Theology* 27.2 (2003) 113-127.

Moltmann, Jürgen. *The Crucified God*. London: SCM Press, 1974.

Moo, Douglas. *The Epistle to the Romans*. New International Commentary on the New Testament. Grand Rapids: Eerdmans, 1996.

Morey, Robert A. *Battle of the Gods*. Southbridge: Crown Publications, 1989.

Motyer, Alec. *The Message of Exodus*. Bible Speaks Today. Leicester: Inter-Varsity Press, 2005.

———. *The Prophecy of Isaiah*. Leicester: Inter-Varsity Press, 1993.

Mühling, Markus. *T & T Clark Handbook of Christian Eschatology*. London: Bloomsbury T & T Clark, 2015.

Murphy, Francesa Aran and Philip G. Ziegler, eds. *The Providence of God*. London: T & T Clark, 2009.

Murray, Iain H. *The Puritan Hope: Revival and the Interpretation of Prophecy*. Edinburgh: Banner of Truth, 1971.

Nash, Ronald H. *The Concept of God*. Grand Rapids: Zondervan Academie Books, 1983.

Nee, Watchman. *The Release of the Spirit*. New York: Christian Fellowship Publishers, 2000.

Newman, Barclay M., Jr. "A Concise Greek-English Dictionary of the New Testament." In Kurt Aland et al, ed., *The Greek New Testament*. Germany: United Bible Societies, 1983.

Newton, Jon K. *A Pentecostal Commentary on Revelation*. Eugene: Wipf and Stock, 2021.

———. *The Revelation Worldview*. Eugene: Wipf and Stock, 2015.

Nyhuis, Robert J. *Global Revival: How a City's Mission Catalyzed a Worldwide Awakening*. Eugene: Resource Publications, 2025.

Olson, Roger E. *Arminian Theology: Myths and Realities*. Downers Grove: IVP Academic, 2006.

Oord, Thomas Jay. *The Uncontrolling Love of God: An Open and Relational Account of Providence*. Downers Grove: IVP Academic, 2015.

Packer, J.I. *Evangelism and the Sovereignty of God*. Downers Grove: IVP, 1961.

Peterson, David G. *The Acts of the Apostles*. The Pillar New Testament Commentary. Grand Rapids: Eerdmans, 2009.

Phillips, J.B. *Your God is Too Small*. London: Wyvern, 1962.
Piggin, Stuart. *Firestorm of the Lord*. Carlisle: Paternoster, 2000.
Pink, Arthur W. *The Sovereignty of God*. Grand Rapids: Baker, 1976.
Pinnock, Clark H., ed. *The Grace of God and the Will of Man: A Case for Arminianism*. Grand Rapids: Academie Books, Zondervan, 1989.
Pinnock, Clark, Richard Rice, John Sanders, William Hasker and David Basinger, *The Openness of God*. Downers Grove: IVP, 1994.
Piper, John. *Desiring God*. Leicester: Inter-Varsity Press, 1989.
———. *Providence*. Wheaton: Crossway, 2020.
Radcliff, Alexandra S. *The Claim of Humanity in Christ: Salvation and Sanctification in the Theology of T.F. and J.B. Torrance*. Eugene OR: Pickwick Publications, 2016.
Ramsey, Christian L. "The Pharaoh Initiative: God's Middle Knowledge in Action Through a Pauline Perspective." *Journal of the Evangelical Theological Society* 62.4 (2019) 749-758.
Randall, Rory. *An Open Theist Renewal Theology: God's Love, The Spirit's Power, and Human Freedom* SacraSage Press, 2021 Kindle version.
Ratcliffe, Susan, ed. *Oxford Essential Quotations* (4th edition) Oxford University Press; Published online:2016.
Richardson, Don. *Eternity in Their Hearts*. Revised. Ventura: Regal Books, 1984.
———. *Peace Child*. Ventura: Regal Books, 2005.
Ripken, Nik. *The Insanity of God: A True Story of Faith Resurrected*. Nashville: B&H Publishing, 2013.
Rogers, Eugene F., Jr. *After the Spirit: A Constructive Pneumatology from Resources outside the Modern West*. Grand Rapids: Eerdmans, 2005.
Roy, Steven C. *How Much Does God Foreknow? A Comprehensive Biblical Study*. Downers Grove: IVP Academic, 2006.
Sanders, John. *The God Who Risks: A Theology of Divine Providence*. Revised Edition. Downers Grove: IVP Academic, 2007.
Schlink, Basilea. *Realities: The Miracles of God Experienced Today*. Translated by Larry Christenson and William Castell. London: Lakeland, 1967.
Seitz, Christopher R. *Isaiah 1-39*. Interpretation. Louisville: John Knox Press, 1993.
Shank, Robert. *Elect in the Son: A Study of the Doctrine of Election*. Minneapolis: Bethany House, 1989.
Shakarian, Demos, with John and Elizabeth Sherrill. *The Happiest People on Earth*. London: Hodder and Stoughton, 1977.
Silvoso, Ed. *That None Should Perish: How to Reach Entire Cities for Christ through Prayer Evangelism*. Ventura, CA: Regal Press, 1994.
Smail, Thomas Allan. *The Giving Gift: The Holy Spirit in Person*. London: Darton, Longman and Todd, 1994.
Sproul, R.C. *Chosen by God*. Amersham-on-the-Hill: Scripture Press, 1986.
———. *What Is Reformed Theology? Understanding the Basics*. Grand Rapids: Baker Books, 1997.
Staples, Jason A. "Vessels of Wrath and God's Pathos: Potter/Clay Imagery in Rom 9:20–23." *Harvard Theological Review* 115:2 (2022) 197–218
Studebaker, Steven M. "The Mode of Divine Knowledge in Reformation Arminianism and Open Theism." *Journal of the Evangelical Theological Society* 47.3 (2004) 469-480.
Tarnas, Richard. *The Passion of the Western Mind*. London: Pimlico, 1996.

Tate, W. Randolph. *Biblical Interpretation*. 3rd edition. Grand Rapids: Baker, 2014.
Thompson, Matthew K. *Kingdom Come: Revisioning Pentecostal Eschatology*. Blandford Forum: Deo, 2010.
Vasilakis, Bill. *Revival is our Middle Name*. Seaton: CRC Churches International, 2020.
Vondey, Wolfgang. "The Holy Spirit and the Physical Universe: The Impact of Scientific Paradigm Shifts on Contemporary Pneumatology." *Theological Studies* 70.1 (2009) 3-36.
———. *Pentecostal Theology: Living the Full Gospel*. London: T & T Clark, 2017.
Wagner, C. Peter. *The Book of Acts: A Commentary*. Ventura: Regal, 1994.
Walton, John H. *Ancient Near Eastern Thought and the Old Testament*. 2nd edition. Grand Rapids: Baker Academic, 2018.
Ware, Bruce A. *God's Greater Glory: The Exalted God of Scripture and the Christian Faith*. Wheaton: Crossway Books, 2004.
———. ed. *Perspectives on the Doctrine of God: 4 Views*. Nashville: B&H Academic, 2008.
Warrington, Keith. *Pentecostal Theology: A Theology of Encounter*. London: T & T Clark, 2008.
Weinandy, Thomas G. *Does God Suffer?* Edinburgh: T &T Clark, 2000.
Wenham, Gordon J. *Genesis 1-15*. Word Biblical Commentary 1. Waco: Word Books, 1987.
———. *Genesis 16-50*. Word Biblical Commentary 2. Dallas: Word Books, 1994.
Wilkerson, David. *Hungry for More of Jesus*. Eastbourne: Kingsway Publications, 1993.
Witherington III, Ben. *Paul's Letter to the Romans: A Socio-Rhetorical Commentary*. Grand Rapids: Eerdmans, 2004.
Wright, N.T. *Colossians and Philemon*. Tyndale New Testament Commentaries. Leicester: Inter-Varsity Press, 1986.
Wynkoop, Mildred Bangs. *Foundations of Wesleyan-Arminian Theology*. Kansas City: Beacon Hill Press, 1967.
Yong, Amos. *The Bible, Disability, and the Church*. Grand Rapids, Eerdmans, 2011.
———. "Disability and the Gifts of the Spirit: Pentecost and the Renewal of the Church." *Journal of Pentecostal Theology* 19.1 (2020) 76-93.
Zschech, Darlene. *Extravagant Worship*. Minneapolis: Bethany House, 2002.

Subject Index

Aaron, 70, 72, 192
Abel, see Cain and Abel
Abiathar, 223
Abimelek, King, 82
Abortion, 250-251
Abraham, 34, 51-52, 69, 89-90, 91, 94, 99, 100, 101, 111, 125, 128, 129, 131, 191, 196, 197, 224, 229, 230, 254, 273-274, 292, 307, 313
Achaia Roman province, 240
Achan, 131, 255
Accountability, xvi, xvii, xix,18, 35, 39-40, 43, 47, 57, 81, 105, 165, 214, 224, 313
Accusation/s, 28-29, 217, 219, 290
Acts, Book of, 176, 286, 287, 300, 304
Adam and Eve, 18, 21, 23, 30, 31, 38-42, 56, 131, 160, 164, 169, 174, 213, 238, 250, 259
Afghanistan, 265-266
Africa, 175, 183
Ahab, King, 204-205, 215, 227, 276-277
Ahasuerus (Xerxes), 268-270, 309
Ahijah, 242
Ai, 132, 255
All, 105-108, 145-146, 169, 170, 283
Amalekites, 129, 130
America, 234, 302
Amorites, 69
Anabaptists, 183
Ananias and Sapphira, 57, 86, 182
Angel/s, xviii, 27, 50, 52, 56, 85, 90, 132, 136, 142, 143, 144, 154, 157, 164, 168, 171, 172, 187, 188, 191, 206, 207, 212, 217, 218, 222, 242, 243, 251, 253, 254, 282, 288, 292, 293, 295, 313
Anglicans, 180, 183
Animals, 4-5, 6-7, 9-10, 11, 54, 75, 309
Annas, high priest, 57
Antioch (Syria), 85, 95, 241, 258
Antioch of Pisidia, 79, 84, 95, 109, 241
Apollos, 181
Apostle/s, 62, 85, 107, 139, 170, 176, 178, 181, 183, 245, 247, 257, 267, 286, 287
    Modern apostles 183
Apostolic Church, 183
Aquinas, 201
Aram (Syria), 229
Ararat, 47
Areopagus: see Athens
Ark of the covenant: see covenant
Armenia, 234
Arminian, xiii, xxii, 110n, 125, 188, 189, 320
Arminius, 238
Armor of God, 206, 294
Artaxerxes, 266
Artemis, 210, 211
Asherah, 276
Asia, Roman province, 209, 240, 252, 304
Assurance, 120, 122, 123
Assyria, Assyrians, 59, 77, 78, 226, 277, 278

Astrology, 49
Athens (ancient), 10, 177, 260, 308, 320
Augustine (of Hippo), 82, 174, 198
Augustus, emperor, 229
Autonomy of creatures, 6, 21, 59, 148, 187, 229, 242, 314, 315

Baal, 59, 237, 276
Babel, 49-50, 58, 89, 128, 223, 264, 307
Babylon, Babylonians, 50, 53-54, 59, 62, 74-77, 78, 135, 137, 151, 211, 237-238, 279
Balaam, 82, 130, 260, 309
Balak, King, 82, 130, 260
Baptism, 85, 102, 179, 209, 237, 303
Baptist, 299
Barnabas, 10, 85, 95, 109, 240, 241
Barth, Karl, xix, 88, 100, 105
Baruch, 263
Baudin, Frederic, 17
Beasts, 218
Beginning, 3
Ben-Hadad, King, 229-230
Benjamin (patriarch), 68
Benjamin (tribe), 26
Bethany, 284
Bethel, 226
Bethlehem, 229
Bethsaida, 224
Bezazel, 259
Biblical theology, xviii, xxii
Big bang, 3
Birthright, 92
Bithynia Roman province, 240, 252
Blessing/s, 6, 13, 78, 92, 94, 99, 100, 115, 130, 229, 230, 275
Blood of Jesus, 43, 61, 102, 106, 117, 122, 123, 144, 145, 169, 176, 212, 217, 219, 235
Bonda, Jan, 170n
Book of life, 59, 94, 124, 166-167, 295
Boyd, Gregory, 4n, 38, 126, 148, 150, 154, 166, 173, 208-211, 213, 221, 225, 293-294, 317-318, 319
Britain, British, 141, 302

Brueggemann, Walter, 152

Caesar, Roman Emperor 80, 177, 253, 265 267
Caesarea, 253
Cain and Abel, 43-44, 47, 56, 60, 66, 89, 126
Caiaphas, high priest, 57, 80, 310
Caleb, 130
Call, calling, 92, 97, 104, 112-113, 181, 252, 262, 286
Calvin, John, xiii, xix, 8, 13n, 39, 82, 91n, 97n, 107n, 115, 119, 120, 181, 189, 213, 220, 231n, 315
Calvinism, Calvinists, xiii, xvii, xxii, 23n, 108, 110, 114, 125, 187, 189, 198, 310, 320
Campbell, T.J., xix, 108, 115, 297
Canaan, Canaanite, 49, 59, 67, 71, 89, 93, 131, 255
Capernaum, 224
Carey, William, 299, 320
Carson, D.A., xviii, xx, 53, 112n, 133, 297-298
Castelo, Daniel, 4, 147, 150n, 152, 153, 155, 156, 182, 202n
Chant, Barry, 301, 302, 303
Charismatic renewal, 207
Cherubim, 207, 212
Chesterton, G.K., 111
China, 266
Chorazin, 224
Chosen, see Election
Church, 32-34, 85, 86, 96, 102, 108, 117, 119, 123, 139, 141, 145, 161, 162, 174-183, 209, 235, 244, 246, 252, 257, 258, 266, 268, 276, 286, 288, 299, 301, 302, 303, 304, 305, 306, 318
  Church growth, 61, 176-177, 266, 291, 303
Church of Christ, 183
Churchill, Winston, 259
Cilicia Roman province, 240
Circumcision, 90
Civil government, 35, 48, 263-270, 276, 291
Clifton, Shane, 247-248

Climate change, xv, 17, 37, 147
Cole, Alan, 73
Combat myth, 216
Comfort, 155
Communists, 318
Conspiracy theories, 268, 269
Constantine, Emperor, 318
Contentment, 257, 315–316
Control, divine, xv, xvii, xx, 11 18, 23, 29, 57, 59, 74, 76, 77, 86, 143, 148, 149, 150, 188, 209, 213, 219, 222, 223, 227, 247, 251, 252, 253, 265, 266, 272, 313
   Meticulous, xx, 209, 211, 220, 223
Conversion, 55, 71, 75–77, 113, 162, 300, 304
Coronavirus, 254
Corinth, Corinthians, 95, 244, 252, 258, 305
Cornelius, 84, 85, 95, 240, 288, 301, 310
Covenant, 24–25, 34, 47, 51, 52, 57, 58, 59, 60, 62, 65, 69, 70, 90, 93, 98, 123, 132, 141, 196–199, 233, 243, 245, 273, 275, 292
   Ark of, 22, 56, 182, 239
   New, 35, 60, 280
Creation, xvii, xix, 3–14, 17, 29, 41, 45, 88, 100, 101, 102, 103, 113, 127, 148, 150, 152, 155, 162, 163, 165, 167, 181, 185, 187, 206, 208, 229, 234, 246, 248, 292, 307, 312
   Ex nihilo, 3
   Of humans, 5, 18, 185, 211, 249, 258
   New, 142, 146, 147, 149, 154, 163, 164, 222, 248, 313
Creation care, 17
Cross, Crucifixion of Jesus, 31, 61, 79–81, 100, 116, 138, 153–154, 159, 170, 187, 194, 206, 208, 210, 213, 215, 218, 223, 231, 232, 235, 239, 300, 303, 307
Crusades, 174
Curie, Marie, 259
Curses, 48, 245

Custance, Arthur, 44, 106, 167–168, 170, 224n, 260, 317
Cyprus, 241
Cyrus, King, 150, 222, 227, 237, 266, 293

Damascus, 229, 241
Daniel, 55, 75–77, 150, 205, 228, 267, 292, 293, 294, 306
Darby, John Nelson, 175
Darius, King, 267, 310
Darmstadt, 276
David, King, 35n, 56, 57, 83, 134, 136, 158, 159, 191, 214, 215, 223–224, 226, 229, 232, 235, 238, 239, 241, 242, 244, 247, 259, 267, 280, 320
Death, 20, 42, 56, 106, 108, 119, 124, 144, 146, 153, 154, 155, 157–160, 164, 166, 168, 169, 170, 181, 185, 197, 215, 217, 218, 250–251, 278, 279, 280, 308, 317
   Second death, 124
Deception, 39, 41, 111, 121, 215, 218, 229
Deism, 8
Delegation, 7, 16–25, 26, 31, 49, 93, 126, 134, 146, 148, 191, 203, 264
Delilah, 133
Deliverance, deliverer, 141, 207–208
Demetrius, 304
Demons, see Evil powers
Dependence, x, xix, 10, 12, 191, 196, 242, 256, 313, 314
Descartes, Rene, 259
Deuteronomy, 196
Devil, Satan, xviii, xxi, 27–32, 34, 85, 115, 116, 131, 135, 136n, 137, 138, 143, 146, 147, 148, 154, 155, 156, 157, 159, 161, 168, 169, 173, 178, 185, 187, 208, 211–219, 225, 243, 244, 246, 281, 282, 283, 293, 294, 296, 305, 306, 312, 315, 316, 317, 318
Diet, 5, 75
Disability, 243, 245, 247–250, 251
Dispensationalism, 177

Diversity, 11
Divorce, 34
Dowie, John Alexander, 245–246
Dragon: see also devil, 212, 216–217
Dreams, 54, 66–67, 76, 77, 82, 198, 207, 225, 240, 241, 255–256, 260, 274–275, 309
Dualism, 150, 213
Duff, Alexander, 286
Duffield and Van Cleave, 9, 219

Earth, 10, 37, 40, 41, 47, 46, 72, 94, 147, 169, 196, 212, 218
Earthquake, 140
Eastern Orthodox, 180
Edom, Edomites, 59, 92, 93, 230–231, 241
Edwards, Jonathan, 302, 303n, 305
Egypt, 10, 13, 25, 57, 58, 66–68, 69–73, 129, 153, 191, 192, 224, 225, 239, 240, 242, 243, 244, 255
Elders, 70, 117, 242, 246
Elect, election, xxi, 24, 27, 32, 46–47, 51, 57, 70, 88–125, 167, 235
  Signs of election 119–120
  Jesus as Elector, 99–100
    Conditional, 94, 97, 102, 103–104, 117–125, 145, 235
    Corporate, 102, 117, 125
    In Christ, 101–102, 103, 117, 125
Elijah, 10, 13, 56, 136, 227, 230, 236–237, 244, 276, 277, 295, 320
Elisha, 229–230. 244
Elihu, 256
Emmaus, 80
Emperor: see Caesar
End (of history), 141, 143, 145, 146, 147, 154, 162, 163, 164, 169, 174, 180, 292, 313
England, 141
Enoch, 44–46, 89
Epaphroditus, 245
Ephesus, 33, 84, 117, 123, 176, 206, 209–210, 245, 252, 304
Er and Onan, 56
Erickson, Millard, 12, 127, 220, 235, 236n, 241, 262n, 318

Esau, 66, 91–93, 123, 231
Eschatology, xix, 161–174
Esther (Hadassah), 263, 268–270
Eternal life, 40, 95, 105, 109, 119, 127, 159, 166, 168, 171, 283
Ethiopian, 85, 95, 140, 310
Euthanasia, 250–251
Evangelical Sisterhood of Mary 276
Evangelicals, 180, 302
Evangelism, xxii, 162, 286, 299–301, 303
Evil, 105, 142, 147–156, 185, 239, 287, 294, 318, 319
Evil powers/spirits/demons, 14, 82, 115, 138, 140, 142, 145, 153, 206, 207, 208, 209- 211, 215, 242, 244, 245, 251, 259, 293, 294, 304
Evolution, 5, 11n, 149
Executions, divine, 56, 57, 238
Exile, 137
Exodus, 57, 69–73, 128, 129, 173
  New exodus, 60, 266
Eyewitnesses, 263
Ezekiel, 52–53, 107, 112, 207

Faith, 9, 20, 21, 43, 51, 61, 63, 65, 71, 73, 75, 77, 85, 90, 96, 101, 103, 104, 106, 109, 114, 115, 118, 120, 121, 134, 135, 139, 140, 144, 145, 179, 196, 209, 244–245, 246, 247, 253, 254, 273, 274, 276, 277, 279, 281–282, 284–285, 286, 289, 294, 296, 301, 318, 320
Fall of humanity, 38–43, 82, 126, 127, 135. 163, 187, 213
Fallen world, 63, 65, 221, 247, 264
Fall of angels, 207, 212
Famine, 241, 258
Fasting, 13, 135, 246, 269, 270, 284, 292, 293, 295
Favor, 46, 47, 91, 105, 138, 205, 266, 292
Fee, Gordon, 85
Feminism, 190
Feuerbach, xvi
Finance, 32, 256–258, 276

SUBJECT INDEX

Finney, Charles, 302, 305
Flood, 46–47, 60, 89, 195, 196, 264
Forgiveness, 20, 94, 97, 167, 284, 285, 295
Free will, human, xviii, xix, xx, 18–19, 20–21, 32, 40, 43, 44, 60, 63, 64, 71, 148, 149, 173, 174, 187–188, 197, 198, 198n, 199, 200, 217, 220, 221, 222, 229, 236, 240, 271, 298, 312, 313, 314, 315
Fretheim, Terence, 46, 48, 51, 60, 71n, 72, 189n, 190, 197, 199–202
Friesen, Gary, 251n

Gabriel, 136, 205–206, 292
Gad, 214
Galatia Roman province, 240, 248
Galilee, 199, 224, 229, 281
Gandhi, Mohandas, 259
Gap theory, 4n
Garden, of Eden, 19, 42, 43, 105, 212, 213
Geisler, Norman, 21, 110, 220, 236
Gender, 5
Generosity, 19, 32, 43, 114, 115, 257, 258, 276, 288, 303
Genesis, 3, 141, 163, 230, 318
Genocide, 69, 73, 147, 269
Gethsemane, 31, 100, 282
Genres, 263
Gentiles, 35, 95, 98, 99, 101, 102, 105, 109, 114, 115, 141, 145, 162, 164, 165, 166, 168, 169, 176, 177, 178, 201, 203, 229, 241, 244, 258, 288, 290, 300, 301, 307, 308, 309, 310, 311
Gibeonites, 255
Gift, 105, 106, 112, 120, 273
Gifts, spiritual, 67, 68, 85, 86, 179, 183, 246, 247, 248, 305
Globalization, 161
Glorification, 128
God
    As Creator, 3, 4, 6, 8, 10, 34, 53, 143, 148, 152, 195, 201, 256, 287,
    As Father, 9, 83, 109–110, 189, 202–203, 281, 284, 316, 317
    As Judge, xvi, xix, 41, 42, 46, 52, 53, 69, 72, 105, 132, 165–174, 202, 203, 274, 289, 312, 313, 314
    Authority of, xviii
    Change of mind/plans, xxi, 27, 45, 46, 52, 53, 58–59, 94, 192–193, 221, 232, 241–242, 271, 274, 279, 280, 281, 297
    Constitution of, 22, 29, 49–51, 59, 148, 160, 166, 274, 312, 313
    Consultative, 51, 203, 221, 274
    Dealings of, 317, 319
    Eternity of, 157, 158
    Faithfulness of, 47, 118, 122, 191, 193, 254, 277, 292, 310, 319
    Foreknowledge of, xviii, 79, 102, 113, 147, 188, 200, 219–236, 241, 280, 287
    Freedom of, xvii, xix, 3–4, 5, 19, 21, 23, 27, 29, 42, 44, 46, 48, 55, 57, 83, 84, 86, 88, 89, 90, 96, 101, 105, 113, 127, 142, 143, 185, 197, 228, 247, 251, 312, 314
    Grieving, 45, 46, 86, 195, 196, 201
    Glory of, 14, 138
    Holiness of, 58, 174, 314
    Immanence of, 6, 12, 82, 199
    Immutability, 27, 192–195, 220, 312, 314
    Infinity of, 10, 313
    Influence of, 66, 72, 82, 86, 129, 197–198, 199, 236, 237, 240, 255, 266, 268, 313, 319
    Justice of, 51, 52, 53, 54, 61, 62, 63, 78, 93, 133, 143, 145, 150, 151, 165, 167, 168, 195, 232, 292, 293, 313
    Knowledge of, xvii, 10, 40, 46, 50, 58, 194, 232, 256, 314
    Law of, 25, 34–36, 47, 57, 58, 98, 102, 106, 111, 112, 166, 308
    Love of, 36, 59, 70, 105, 106, 107, 110, 148, 152, 153, 158, 174, 178, 188, 192, 193, 195, 201, 202, 222, 283, 312, 314

(God continued)
  Nature of, xix, 21, 49, 58, 59, 101, 103, 147, 149, 189–203, 251, 274, 292, 307, 312, 313, 314
  Patience of, 59, 61, 69
  Permissive will of, 238–239, 251, 313, 318
  Persuasion by: see Influence of
  Plan/s of, xvi, xx, 3 4, 8, 31, 42, 46, 47, 51, 54, 57, 59, 60, 62, 63, 65, 66–68, 70, 72, 73, 76, 78, 79, 80, 81, 89, 96, 97, 98, 99, 101, 113, 127–128, 138, 143, 146, 148, 149, 150, 162, 163, 178, 206, 207, 208, 213, 215, 225, 227, 228, 229, 230, 231, 232, 233, 235, 236, 239, 242, 243, 250, 251, 274, 277, 278, 280, 282, 283, 284, 286, 287, 288, 290, 291, 297, 299, 301, 306, 311, 313, 318, 319, 321
  Power of, 11, 29, 46, 50, 65, 72, 79, 147, 192, 195, 202, 209, 216, 272, 278, 285, 286, 287, 297, 305, 307, 320
  Responsiveness of, xx, 53, 54, 59, 60, 96, 150, 195–199, 232, 242
  Revelation of, 12, 76, 105, 150, 155, 229, 263, 307, 308, 309, 310, 314
  Righteousness of, 103, 136
  Rights of, xviii, xix, 5, 7, 20, 25, 29, 34, 35, 41–42, 48, 55, 57, 58, 59, 88, 89, 96, 143, 150, 163, 172, 182, 185, 247, 250, 251, 292, 312–313, 314
  Rule of, xx, 5–6, 23, 23, 24, 42, 50, 55, 58, 61, 62, 63, 65–68, 69, 72, 75, 77, 89, 94, 143, 147, 153, 161, 185, 189, 203, 228, 229, 230, 236, 237–238, 240, 242, 247, 265, 272, 313, 315, 319
  Self-sufficiency of, 190–192, 314
  Suffering of, 199–202
  Transcendence of, 6
  Wrath of, 105, 165, 166, 172
God overruling plans, 239, 240, 255, 276

God and time, 7, 106, 127, 158, 159, 167, 187, 221, 223, 228, 234
Golden calf/ calves, 25, 52, 56, 58, 59, 94, 226
Goldingay, John E., 54, 142
Goldsworthy, Graeme, 143
Goliath, 134, 320
Goodwin, Thomas, 291
Gospel, 62, 95, 97, 101, 102, 103, 104, 106, 109, 115, 116, 123, 137, 138, 140, 156, 159, 164, 165, 168, 172, 174, 177, 179, 185, 211, 219, 229, 240, 241, 248, 262, 267, 287, 291, 300, 301, 306, 307, 311, 317
Gospels, 80, 136, 153, 171, 263, 283
Grace, 46, 57, 70, 97, 101, 103, 104–108, 121, 125, 159, 162, 169, 173, 178, 187, 188, 198, 257–258, 272, 285, 292, 296
  Common grace, 259, 260
Grave, 157, 158–159
Greece, 205
Greeks, 209–210, 260, 304
Green, Chris, 312, 314n, 321
Green, Michael, 162
Grenz, Stanley, xvii, xviii, xix, xx, 4, 89, 113n, 116, 128, 143, 161, 164–165, 181n, 291
Guidance, 26, 69, 72, 241, 251–256, 262, 263, 266, 282, 287, 309
Guilt, 21, 40, 61, 81, 165

Habakkuk, 151
Hades, 160, 176, 224
Hagar, 90–91
Ham, 48
Haman, 269
Hamlet, 15
Hardening, 97, 98, 173
Harris, Tania, 256n
Harrison, R.K., 74
Hart, David Bentley, 39, 170n, 173n
Harvest, 104, 146
Hazael, King, 229–230
Healing, 20, 58, 138, 139, 155, 209, 243–247, 275, 279, 280, 282, 287, 315, 320

SUBJECT INDEX 335

Hearing God, 252, 260
Heaven, holy city, 167–168, 170, 171,174, 218, 248
, Heavenly realm/s 206, 212, 216, 217, 219, 293, 294
Hell, lake of fire, 146, 160, 164, 166, 167, 168, 170, 171, 172, 173, 267
Helm, Paul, xx
Henry, Matthew, 301
Herod, 57, 61, 79, 80, 176, 215, 216, 244, 256, 288
Herodians, 266
Hezekiah, King, 244, 277–281
History, xvii, xx, 14, 59, 74, 76, 141–142, 145, 149, 151, 163, 178, 188, 218, 230, 234, 292, 303–304, 308
    Salvation history 141, 164, 300
Hitler, 165, 168
Hobbs, T.R., 279
Holiness, 86, 103
Holocaust/Shoah, 141, 156
Holy Spirit, Spirit of God, 6, 9, 12, 29, 30, 31, 66, 82–87, 98, 99, 101, 102, 104, 109, 110, 112, 116, 121, 132–133, 135, 136n, 137, 139, 140, 162, 171, 175, 176, 177, 179, 180, 181, 182, 183, 196, 209, 211, 215, 228, 235, 237, 240, 241, 256, 259, 260, 261, 262, 282, 285, 286, 287, 289, 290, 291, 293, 296, 300, 301, 302, 303, 304, 305, 306, 320, 321
Hope, 177, 193
Hosea, 158–160, 196
Houston, James, 11, 12, 47, 88
Human freedom, see free will, human
Human religious leaders, 138
Humanity, xviii, xix, 5, 6, 12, 14, 15, 18, 21, 44, 82, 99, 105, 113, 126, 135, 136, 142, 148, 149, 152, 157, 185, 187, 191, 194, 213, 218, 242, 243, 250, 251, 257, 258, 290, 313
    Human choices, xxii, 27, 81, 142, 236, 242, 251–256, 315

Human partners with God 13, 51, 52, 64, 72, 90, 92, 132, 192, 218, 221, 274, 299, 300, 302, 319, 321
Human plans, xx, 72, 82, 127–128, 252, 253–254
Human creativity and inspiration, 258–260
Human limitations xix, 19, 45, 152, 251, 314
Human multiplication, 5, 7
Human sinfulness, 82, 146
Human restoration, 113
Rule of, 7, 16–20, 37, 40–42, 47, 49, 59, 88, 126, 144, 146, 148, 203, 219, 258, 264

Identity, personal, 248, 249–250, 315
Idols, idolatry, 53, 71, 75, 78, 105, 150, 151, 165, 172, 210, 222, 226, 227, 238, 286, 307, 308, 309
Image of God, 5, 16, 45, 48, 113, 115, 250, 258, 260, 267
Imperialism, 50, 149, 212, 228, 267, 270
Incarnation, 194–195
Innocence, 39, 41
Inquisition, 174, 198
Inspiration, human, 259–260
Inspiration of Scripture, 261
Intercessor, 52, 53, 108, 112, 118, 120, 130, 136, 273, 290
Invasion by God, 135–138
Invisible powers, 8, 206
Isaac, 91–92, 125, 197, 230, 254
Isaiah, 14, 98, 110, 111, 137, 150, 222, 227, 237, 244, 277, 278, 279, 280
Ishmael, 91
Israel, Israelites, 13, 14, 24–25, 34, 40, 54, 57–60, 62, 66, 68, 69, 70, 71–72, 73, 74, 77, 78, 82, 93, 94, 97, 98, 101, 102, 120, 125, 128, 129, 130, 131, 132, 133, 134, 137, 138, 141, 145, 150, 151, 162, 169, 176, 177, 178, 182, 191, 192, 196, 198, 200, 201, 205- 206, 214, 216, 222, 224, 226, 229, 230, 231, 232, 233,

SUBJECT INDEX

(Israel, Israelites, continued)
237, 241, 242, 255, 259264, 266, 275, 278, 292, 293, 307
  Spiritual reality, 95, 178
  Restoration of, 141, 145, 150, 161, 170, 205–206, 233, 237, 262, 292, 293

Jacob, 66, 68, 91–93, 98, 125, 136, 197, 225, 230–231, 237, 240, 259
James, apostle, 139, 165, 176, 288
James, author of letter, 33, 61, 95, 244, 246, 254, 263, 276, 277
Jehoshaphat, King, 134–135, 204–205, 239, 320
Jehovah's Witnesses, 183
Jehu, King, 265
Jeremiah, 53, 75, 205, 262, 265, 266, 272, 292
Jeremiah, Book of, 262–263
Jeroboam, King, 226, 242
Jericho, 131
Jersak, Bradley, 43, 65, 152n, 199
Jerusalem, 53, 60, 61, 62, 79, 80, 110, 114, 138, 144, 172, 176, 177, 198, 199, 214, 229, 231, 237, 238, 239, 241, 252, 253, 257, 258, 266, 267, 279, 281, 284, 285, 286, 287, 292, 300, 303
  New Jerusalem 164
Jesus, 9, 11, 13, 20, 30–32, 57, 60, 61, 79, 80, 81, 83, 84, 98, 99, 100, 102, 106, 107, 108, 109, 110, 111, 112, 113, 117, 118, 119, 123, 124, 131n, 137, 138, 139, 140, 143, 146, 152, 153, 159, 160, 171, 175, 176, 178, 182, 194, 202, 203, 210, 215, 216, 218, 224, 225, 231, 235, 237, 239, 245, 247, 281–286, 287, 290, 293, 299, 302, 303, 305, 306, 307, 309, 310, 311, 318, 320
  Heir of creation, 8
  Lamb of God, 99, 143–144, 167, 172, 212, 218, 234
  Name of, 138, 140, 169, 210, 267, 285, 289
  Second coming of, 145, 154, 161–165, 177, 180, 187, 213, 299
Jews, 60, 61, 62, 79, 95, 96, 97, 98, 101, 102, 105, 109, 115, 141, 145, 153, 163, 165, 166, 168n, 174, 176, 178, 198, 209–210, 227, 231, 266, 269, 270, 290, 293, 301, 303, 304
  Jewish (temple) leaders, 60, 80, 138, 139, 176, 215, 231, 267
Jezebel, 124
Job, 27–30, 33, 52, 55, 151–152, 155, 156, 213–214, 251, 256, 309, 313, 314, 318
Joel, 304
John (apostle), 80, 83, 140, 143, 160, 207, 216, 263, 289, 320
John the Baptist, 137, 209
Jonah, 12, 54, 55, 70, 191, 192, 193, 198, 224, 232, 239, 295, 309
Jonathan, 320
Joppa, 287–288
Joseph (OT), 66–68, 69, 225, 238, 239, 240, 255, 267, 318
Joseph (NT), 229, 240, 255
Joshua, 71, 129, 130, 131, 136, 255
Josiah, King, 59, 226–227, 238–239, 280
Judah (patriarch), 56, 67, 68, 238
Judah (nation), 53, 57, 59, 75, 78, 96, 134, 151, 226, 237, 265, 277, 278, 280, 281
Judas, 80, 81, 121, 215, 220, 231, 239, 310
Jude, 118
Judges, 132
Judgment, 35, 41, 42–63, 65, 78, 93, 105, 111, 132, 133, 141, 143, 144, 157, 159, 164, 166, 170, 191, 193, 201, 204, 205, 206, 207, 212, 227, 230, 232, 233, 242, 243 281, 285, 297, 307, 308, 309
  Final, 35, 105, 162, 165–174, 299
Justice, 51, 136, 265
Justification, 105–106, 160, 169, 229, 308

SUBJECT INDEX 337

Kedorlaomer, 128
Keilah, 223, 224, 235
Kendall, R.T., 118, 193
Kingdom of God, 20, 76, 77, 96, 109,
    114, 138, 143, 144, 145, 154,
    164, 168, 171, 191, 203, 208,
    209, 217, 244, 246, 284, 286,
    290, 291, 306
Knight, Douglas, 268
König, Adrio, 107, 127, 300

Lamech, 44, 57, 126, 238
Laments, 152, 263
Land, promised, 57, 94, 130, 196,
    254, 273–274
Language, 50, 89, 154, 223
Laodicea, 124, 182
Latter Rain, 183
Laws of nature, 7, 8, 13, 44, 47, 314
Lazarus, 282, 320
Leadership, 59, 67, 130, 179, 288,
    295, 302, 304
Levites, 35, 58, 59
Lewis, C.S., xix, 173
Lennox, John, 18, 20, 96, 109n, 149
Leprosy, 244
Liberationist theology, 190
Light, 4, 309
Lincoln, Abraham, 259
Lindsay, Mark, 88, 90, 113
Lloyd-Jones, D. Martyn, xvi, 183, 272,
    281, 292, 302, 304, 305–306, 316
Lord, lordship of God/Christ, 61,
    106, 138, 139, 169, 176, 178,
    202, 208, 311
Lord of the Flies, 37
Lot, 52, 128
Lourdes, 247
Luke, 140, 263
Luther, Martin, 110, 183
Lydia, 140, 257
Lystra, 10, 198, 307, 245

Macchia, Frank, 45n, 49, 99, 101,
    107n, 109, 170, 174, 181n
Macedonia Roman province, 85, 240,
    252
Manasseh, King, 279–280
Mao Ze Dong, 266

Marshall, Catherine, 296
Marshall, I. Howard, 81, 107n, 114,
    120, 220n
Martha, 282
Marxism, 141
Mary (mother of Jesus), 136, 137,
    194, 216, 255
Matthew, 168
Maturity, 23, 30, 31, 39, 121, 179,
    296, 316, 317
McKillop, Mary, 247
Meadowcroft, Tim, 204n, 207–211
Media-Persia, 268
Medical procedures, 251
Melbourne, Australia, 306
Melchizedek, 129, 273, 309
Mercy, 52, 54, 56, 73, 96, 98, 100,
    104, 105, 107, 113, 121, 125,
    193, 245, 251, 292
Messiah, 63, 79, 80, 83, 98, 119, 137,
    138, 145, 146, 206, 216, 217,
    218, 222, 229, 262, 287, 292
Metaphors, 202, 203
Metanarrative, 141, 155
Methodist, 302
Micaiah, 204–205
Michael, archangel, 144, 205–206,
    217, 293
Middle knowledge, 223, 235, 236,
    308
Midian, 69
Millennium: see Thousand Years
Miracles, 13, 91. See also signs
Missions, missionaries, 145, 299, 310
Moltmann, Jürgen, 194n
Moo, Douglas, 73 n
Monarchy, 264, 265
Morality, 21, 22, 50, 180, 308
Mordecai, 268–270
Morey, Robert, 194
Moses, 34, 52, 57, 58, 59, 69–73, 94,
    111, 129, 130, 131, 136, 160,
    176, 191, 192, 232, 233, 244,
    264, 274, 292, 295, 310, 320
Motyer, Alec, 71, 150n
Mozart, 259
Music, 82, 182, 215
Muslims, xvi, 309

Naaman, 310
Naboth, 205
Nadab and Abihu, 56
Narrative/s, 49, 92, 95, 263
Nash, Ronald, 193
Nathan, 267
Nations, 50, 52, 53, 56, 63, 73, 74–78, 90, 91, 92, 93, 94, 98, 99, 100, 128, 141, 142, 143, 144, 145, 151, 155, 164, 173, 196, 201, 216, 228, 229, 230, 233, 234, 286, 287, 307, 308, 311
Natural disasters, 12, 13, 17, 28, 146, 147, 149, 241, 253, 258
Natural forces, 5, 10, 14, 43, 47, 50, 54, 63, 253, 315
Nazareth, 153, 229, 245, 255
Nazirite, 82, 132, 133
Nazis, 141, 148
Nebuchadnezzar, 49, 53, 54–55, 65, 66, 75–77, 82, 237–238, 265, 267, 306, 310
Nee, Watchman, 317
Nehemiah, 266
Nephilim, 45
New exodus, 60, 266
New life/ birth, 60, 102, 112
Newton, Isaac, xvii, 259
Newton, John, 272
Nicene Creed, 180, 181n
Nineveh, 12, 54, 191, 192, 193, 198, 224, 232, 309, 310
Noah, 34, 45–49, 89, 163, 195, 259, 264, 320
North Korea, 266
Nyhuis, Robert, 302n

Obedience, 236
Occult, 140, 247
Oedipus, 81
Offerings, financial, 191, 256, 258
Oholiab, 259
Olson, Roger, xx, 110n
Omens, 198, 238
Oord, Thomas Jay, 8, 11n, 148, 150
Open Theism, xiii, xxii, 148, 188, 189, 190, 194, 202, 219, 220–222, 227, 239, 320

Origen, 169, 174
Origins, 249–250
Others, 295, 316, 317, 319
Ottoman empire, 234

Packer, J.I., 125, 272–273
Padgett, Alan, 234n
Pamphylia Roman province 241
Panentheism, 190, 201
Papua New Guinea, 317
Parable of wedding banquet 102, 113–114, 198
Parents, 39, 43, 66, 92, 132, 249, 251
Parliament, divine, 203–204
Passivity, 86, 96, 115, 183, 217, 266, 270, 286, 290, 304, 319
Passover, 159, 288
Patience, 122
Paul, apostle, 7, 10, 59, 73, 74, 79, 84, 85, 86, 92, 93, 94, 95, 96, 97, 100, 101, 104, 109, 112, 113, 115, 116, 117, 138, 140, 145, 164, 166, 172, 176, 177, 178, 181, 190, 206, 209, 210, 215, 216, 222, 229, 240, 241, 248, 252, 253, 257, 258, 260, 261, 263, 290, 294, 304, 305, 307, 310, 315, 318, 320
Peace Child, 310
Pentateuch, 3, 25, 43, 264
Pentecost, 61, 83, 237, 302, 304
Pentecostal, Pentecostalism, xiii, xvii, 65, 86, 180, 181, 182, 183, 234, 245, 247, 272, 285, 302, 306, 318
Pergamum, 123
Persecution, 32, 33, 63, 139, 146, 175, 176, 215, 303
Perseverance, 117–124
Persia, Persian, 150, 205, 293
Persuasion, 301
Peter, Simon, apostle, Cephas, 61, 79, 80, 84, 95, 99, 102, 103, 117, 121, 140, 162, 163, 175, 176, 181, 222, 225, 231, 235, 237, 240, 261, 262, 263, 267, 281, 287, 288, 289, 295, 301, 303, 320
Peterson, David, 74

SUBJECT INDEX

Pharaoh, 67–68, 69–73, 82, 129, 173, 225, 239, 240, 255, 267, 310
Pharisees, 106, 266
Philadelphia, 33
Philip, 85, 95, 139–140
Philippi,, Philippians, 117, 140, 256–257, 291
Philistines, 26, 82, 132, 133, 134, 223, 320
Phillips, J.B., 313
Philosophy, philosopher/s 190, 260, 307
Phinehas, 130
Phrygia Roman province 240
Piggin, Stuart, 302, 304–305
Pilate, 57, 79, 80, 215, 265, 310
Pink, A.W., xvii, xix, 97n, 104, 108, 109, 220, 239, 289, 296, 306–307, 317
Pinnock, Clark, 142, 189, 193, 202, 221, 271
Piper, John, xxn, 8, 10, 12, 29, 32, 42, 63, 108n, 114, 122, 159n, 187, 189, 314
Pisidia Roman province, 241
Plagues, 13, 56, 57–59, 71–72, 78, 94, 130, 147, 214, 243, 244, 278
Plato, 259
Polygamy, 238
Polytheism, 53, 75, 190, 198, 260
Potiphar, 68, 225
Power, powers, 30, 80, 138, 162, 178, 210, 211, 216, 217, 218, 219, 295
  Power encounter 210,
Praise, 63, 263
Prayer, xxi, xxii, 13, 52–53, 63, 65–66, 70, 76, 79, 83, 85, 116, 129, 130, 135, 151, 178, 191, 192, 203, 205, 206, 210, 244, 246, 247, 252–253, 254, 262, 263, 266, 267–268, 270, 271–298, 301, 302, 303, 304, 306, 318
  Priority prayers 275, 277, 279, 282, 284, 287, 290, 291, 293, 296
Preaching, 103, 109, 210, 211, 240, 248, 300, 301, 303, 304
Predestination, 95, 101, 103, 104, 112, 113, 127–128, 177, 187

Premillennialism, 163
Presbyterians, 180
Prince/s (over nations), 203–206, 212, 216, 293
Prison, 33, 34, 66, 140, 146, 170, 253, 257, 288, 315, 318
Probation, 20, 24, 25, 26, 30, 71, 93, 94
Process Theology, 188n, 194
Promises of God, 33, 34, 47, 58, 68, 70, 90, 91, 94, 103, 112, 117, 122, 123, 125, 130, 141, 161, 179, 196, 197, 230, 254, 273, 286, 291, 292, 310, 313, 314 319
  Conditional, 25, 27, 58, 90, 94, 221, 230
  Promised land: see Land
Property, 276
Prophesying, 26, 83, 85, 86, 255, 306
Prophecy, 26, 72, 80, 84, 85, 86, 91, 92, 93, 99, 135, 161, 180, 183, 198, 199, 229, 230–232, 234, 235, 237, 241, 242. 258, 260, 261, 277, 278, 279, 280, 285, 292, 297, 306, 309
  Fulfillment of, 79, 83, 84, 111, 199, 216, 228, 229, 231–232, 237, 239, 242, 266, 292
Prophet, /s, 51, 53, 54, 55, 99, 103, 110, 135, 178, 192, 200, 201, 204, 221, 226, 227, 234, 235, 261, 262, 267, 309
Prosperity, 28, 150, 318
Protection, 63, 117–118, 216, 283, 287, 288, 317
Protest, 152
Providence, provision, 7–14, 57, 65–66, 147, 181, 182, 195, 256, 258, 284, 307
Psalms, 155, 263
Puritan, Puritanism, xvi, 145, 183, 291

Rabbah, 238
Rahab, 71, 132, 320
Ramsey, Christian, 71n
Randall, Rory, 320
Rebekah, 91–92, 230, 254

Rebellion, 25, 26, 45–46, 57, 59, 60, 62–63, 89, 126, 148, 165, 173, 187, 189, 200, 233, 242, 250, 265, 268, 274
Reconciliation, 8, 39, 107, 145, 154, 165, 169, 170
 Ultimate reconciliation: see universalism
Red Sea, 14, 73, 129
Redeemer, 158
Redemption, 83, 105, 117, 156, 162, 165
Refrigerium, 173n
Regularity in creation, 9, 10, 13, 47
Rehoboam, King, 226, 242
Relationships, 40–41, 47, 61, 89
Rembrandt, 259
Repentance, 13, 43, 53, 54, 55, 61, 62, 65, 69, 71, 77, 79, 96, 97n, 105, 107, 114, 115, 121, 123, 124, 130, 132, 137, 138, 162, 170, 171, 173, 192, 224, 232, 234, 237 241, 281, 300, 301, 303, 304, 308, 311
Rephidim, 58
Resistance, 76, 267–270
Restoration, Restorationism, 163, 183
Resurrection of Christ, 138, 154, 159, 178, 187, 213, 223, 248, 286
Resurrection, general, 159, 164, 248, 282
Resurrections in this life, 244, 245, 282–283, 288, 320
Revelation, Book of, 123, 141, 142, 144–146, 154, 160, 168, 180, 207, 216, 219, 263, 308
Revival, 59, 182, 285, 301–306
Reward/s, 124, 167, 168, 219, 254, 273
Rice, Richard, 141–142, 194, 239
Richardson, Don, 199, 310
Right to life, 251
Righteous, Righteousness 63, 96, 106, 136, 165, 181
Risks, divine, 142, 202
Roberts, Evan, 302
Rogers, Eugene, 212n,
Romania, 319

Rome, Romans, 34, 57, 62, 80, 95, 106, 111, 123, 137, 139, 145, 153, 175, 176, 177, 209, 216, 219, 229, 231, 244, 252–253, 265, 267, 269, 288, 310, 318
Roman Catholic, /s, 175, 180, 247
Roy, Steven, 227, 231n
Russia, 319
Ruth, 310

Sabbath, 7
Sacrifice, 27, 43, 48, 107, 190–191, 195, 206, 226, 257, 271
Salvation, 14, 31, 46, 47, 52, 63, 94, 96, 98, 99, 100, 102–103, 104–124, 127, 132, 136, 150, 151, 170, 171, 189, 229, 235, 236, 261, 262, 290, 291, 300, 301, 305, 306
 Leaving salvation 117–124
Samaria, Samaritan, 57, 84, 139–140, 241, 276, 286
Samson, 82, 132–133
Samuel, 26, 136, 297
Sanctification, 92, 103, 104, 123, 174, 235, 291, 305, 316, 318, 319
Sanders, John, 22, 46, 50, 52, 105, 221, 225n, 234n
Sarah, 90–91, 255
Sardis, 124
Satan, see Devil
Saul, King, 26, 57, 83, 134, 193, 215, 223–224, 235, 297
Schlink, Basilea, 276n
Scripture, 261–263
Seas, 4, 7
Seeing God's hand, 317–318
Seitz, Christopher, 78
Seraphim, 207
Sermon on the Mount, 9
Serpent, 21, 28, 38–43, 49, 126, 130, 141, 212, 213, 216
 See also devil, dragon
Seth, 44
Shakespeare, William, 15, 259
Shame, 21
Shank, Robert, xvi, 100, 102, 109n, 115, 120, 125

SUBJECT INDEX

Sickness, 153, 215, 229, 243–247, 275, 278–279, 296, 306, 315, 318
Sidon, 224, 235
Signs (miraculous), 70, 72, 84, 139, 198, 209, 216, 226, 279, 287, 288, 300, 301
Silas, 140, 257
Silvoso, Ed, 116n
Simeon, Charles, 125
Simon the sorcerer, 140
Sin, 30, 45, 43, 48, 59, 63, 68, 71, 80, 81, 94, 101, 103, 105, 106, 107, 109, 112, 118, 119, 122, 127, 135, 147, 149, 153, 156, 159–160, 167, 168, 185, 187, 196, 200, 201, 205–206, 214, 215, 219, 236, 238, 239, 244, 251, 255, 259, 307
Sinai, 84, 93
Slavery, slave trade, 34, 66, 68, 69, 141, 147, 174, 224, 249, 315, 318, 320
Smyrna, 33
Sodom and Gomorrah, 50–52, 71, 224, 235, 274
Solomon, King, 9, 26, 214, 226, 241–242, 255, 274–276
Sonderegger, Katherine, 157n
Songs, 59, 73, 129
Sorcery, sorcerer/s, 130, 140, 210, 244, 260, 271, 304
Sovereignty of God defined, xvii–xx, 185
Soviet Union, 318
Spain, 252
Spies, 130
Spiritual warfare, 116, 205, 207–211
Spirituality, 260, 306, 310
Spirits, 8, 71, 204, 207, 208, 215, 260, 271
Spurgeon, C.H., 108
Sproul, R.C., xviii, 24, 90, 110, 310
Stalin, 165
Stars, 4, 212, 309
Stephen, 139, 288
Stoics, 260
Storm, 12, 253
Story, Biblical, 141, 143

Struggle, 30, 42, 61, 70–72, 115, 131, 134, 142, 146, 148, 150, 154, 155–156, 180, 206, 212, 266, 276, 282, 291, 292, 294, 317
Suffering, 34, 48, 149, 151, 152, 155, 156, 165, 194
Sun, 7, 11
Sydney, 245–246
Syria Roman province, 240

Tabitha (Dorcas), 287–288
Tate, J. Randolph, 35n
Taxes, 264, 267
Technology, xv, 45, 49, 238
Temple, 54, 61, 124, 135, 214, 259, 266, 267, 278, 279
Testimony, 77, 217, 219, 263, 286, 307
Testing, 20–34, 58, 67, 90, 92, 149, 174, 275, 279, 282, 296, 305, 312, 319
Theodicy, 17, 147–152, 155, 156
Theophanies, 200
Thessalonica, 104, 216, 252
Thousand years, millennium, 144–145, 158, 160, 162, 164
Thyatira, 123
Timothy, 245, 261
Tongues, speaking in, 84, 85, 290, 303
Torah, 3, 59, 132
Torrance, T.F. and J.B., 189
Traditionalism, 183
Tragedy, 147
Transfiguration, 99
Tree, forbidden, 20–21, 39, 40, 131
Tree of life, 40, 42, 124
Trinity, 12, 195
Troas, 240
Trophimus, 245
Turks, 234
Tyre, 211, 224, 235

Unevangelized people, 168, 306–311
Unity, 179, 180, 283
Universalism, 108, 146, 169–173, 311
Uzzah, 56, 182, 183, 239

Vasilakis, Bill, 285

Victory, 126, 129, 130, 132, 142, 150, 157, 161, 211, 219
Visions, 82, 85, 139, 205, 207, 240, 241, 256, 261, 288, 293, 309
Violence, 11, 42, 44, 47, 48, 49, 50, 53, 54, 72, 78, 126, 128, 131, 133, 146, 149, 177, 218, 264, 265, 266
    See also War
Vondey, Wolfgang, 83–84, 246

War, 26, 56, 115–116, 126–135, 146, 147, 148, 154, 161, 208, 212, 217, 218, 277, 304, 317
Ware, Bruce, 191, 192, 234n
Warnings, 120–123
Warrington, Keith, 86, 272
Watt, James, 259
Weather, xxi, 9, 12, 13, 47, 54
Webster, John, 8, 181
Weinandy, Thomas, 6, 201
Welsh revival, 302
Wenham, Gordon, 5, 6, 40, 42, 43, 47, 48, 50, 52, 66, 67, 274

Wesley, John, 86n, 125, 271, 302, 320
Western world, 174, 175, 250, 254
Whitefield, George, 302, 320
Wilkerson, David, 305
Wisdom, 67, 274–276, 315
Wise men (magi), 255–256, 309
Witness, 146, 286, 291, 300
Women, 10, 19, 40, 61, 69, 70, 73 n., 153, 174
Worldview/s, 12, 16, 115, 148, 198, 208, 213
Worship, 8, 28, 48, 57, 59, 144, 167, 172, 182, 191, 202, 207, 211, 254, 267

Yong, Amos, 248=249, 250

Zechariah, 60
Zedekiah, King, 75
Zion, 63
Zschech, Darlene, 36

Scripture Index

GENESIS

1–3	47
1	4–7
1:1	3
1:2	4 n6,6, 82
1:5–8,10	19
1:14	7
1:18	7n23
1:21	4 n10
1:22	6
1:26–27	258
1:26–28	6, 16, 37, 40, 49, 192, 219, 264
1:26–30	5–7
1:28	6
2–3	157
2	18–21
2:2–3	7
2:7	42
2:10–14	23
2:16–17	19, 20, 34
2:17	38, 42, 157, 160
2:19–20	23, 259
2:25	21
3–6	38
3	31, 38–43, 126, 130, 131, 143, 213, 219, 238
3:1–5	313
3:1	38, 313
3:3	157
3:4	42
3:5	39, 49, 212n
3:6	39
3:7	21, 39
3:8	39
3:9	39
3:10–11	39
3:12–13	40
3:13	39
3:14–19	42
3:14–15	40, 212
3:14	41
3:15	41, 42, 126, 141, 154, 216
3:16	40, 41
3:15–19	40, 41
3:17	41, 44
3:18	41
3:21–24	40
3:21	40, 42, 43
3:22	41
3:23–24	40, 42
4:1–16	43
4:1	249n
4:3–5	43
4:4–8	126
4:4	191
4:5	43
4:7	43
4:10	44
4:11–12	44
4:12	44
4:15	44
4:19–24	238
4:20–22	45
4:21	259
4:22	259
4:23–24	44, 57, 126
4:23	44
4:25	44, 249n

(Genesis continued)

4:26	44
5	45, 157
5:5	42
5:22–24	44
5:22,24	46
5:29	44
6–9	13
6	42, 44–47, 126, 313
6:1–4	45, 212
6:1	45
6:3	45, 82
6:5–8	45
6:5–6	195
6:5	46
6:6–7	46
6:6	46, 192, 221
6:7	46, 195
6:8	46
6:9	46, 47
6:11	45 n24, 48, 126, 128
6:13–14	46
6:13	13, 126
6:14–16	259
6:18	47
6:22	47, 259
7:1	47
7:5	47
7:8–9	47
7:11–12	13, 47
7:22	19
8:1–2	47
8:1	13
8:4	47
8:9–17	196
8:15–17	47
8:20–21	48
8:21–22	47
8:21	191, 195
8:22	10, 47
9:1–17	34
9:1–6	49
9:1	49
9:2	47
9:3–4	47
9:3	47
9:5–6	35
9:5	47

9:6	48, 264
9:8–17	47
9:20–24	48
9:24–27	49
10–11	74
11	49, 128, 223
11:3–4	49
11:4	49
11:5	223
11:6	49, 223
11:7–9	223
11:9	50
12:1–3	51
12:1	89, 94, 131
12:2	89
12:3	89, 90, 94, 99, 100, 307
12:4	51, 89
12:7	94, 131
13:14–17	94, 131
14:1–12	128
14:14	128
14:15	128
14:17–20	273
14:18–20	309
14:18	129
14:20–24	129
14:20	129
14:22–24	273
15–16	22
15	51, 90, 196
15:1–5	196
15:1	82, 273
15:2–3	273
15:4	90, 273
15:5	273
15:6	51, 90, 196, 273
15:7–21	90, 94, 131
15:7	196, 273
15:8	273
15:9–21	274
15:9–11	197
15:12–16	197
15:12–13	82
15:13	224
15:14	69, 224
15:16	69, 131
15:17	197
15:18	197

15:18–21	131	24:3–4	254
15:18	34, 71	24:5	254
16:2	90	24:7–8	254
16:4–6	90	24:8	254
16:7–14	90, 91	24:10–11	254
16:10	91	24:12–14	254
17	90	24:15	254
17:7–14	34	24:15–25	254
17:8	94, 131	24:26–27	254
17:15–19	91	24:30–60	255
17:17	91	24:48	2555
17:20	91	25:21	91, 249n
18	51, 221, 274	25:22	91
18:10–14	249n	25:23	91, 230
18:12–15	91	25:26	91
18:14	272	25:28	92
18:16–19	51	25:29–34	92
18:17	274	25:34	92
18:18–19	230	26:3	94, 131
18:18	94	26:4	94
18:19	90	26:5	90
18:20–21	50, 51, 71, 274	27:1–29	92
18:20	50	27:2–4	92
18:21	221	27:22–40	92
18:23–32	195	27:29	93
18:25	51, 274, 313	27:40	231
18:26–32	51	27:46–28:1	238
18:27	51	28–52	92
18:33	274	28:12–15	82
19:1–22	207	28:13	94, 131
19:6–8	52	28:14	94
19:14	52	30:2	249n
19:23–28	50	31:10–13	82
19:24–25	13	32:24–30	82
19:26	52	33:3	93
19:29	52	35:5	82
20:3–9	198	35:12	94, 131
20:3–7	82, 225, 309	36	93
20:7	51 n43	36:6–8	93
21:1–7	91	37	255
21:12	91	37:2	66
21:13	91	37:3–4	66
21:17–21	91	37:5–11	66
21:18	91	37:5–10	225
22:1–18	90	37:5–9	82
22:12	221	37:20	66
22:18	94, 99	37:21–22	66
24	254	37:23–35	66

(Genesis continued)

37:26–27	66, 238
38	238
38:7	56
38:7–10	56
38:6–10	238
38:11–30	238
39–40	66
39:2–6	67
39:21–23	67
39:41	67
40:5	82
40:20–23	68
41–50	240
41	13
41:1–7	82
41:33–36	67
42–50	67
42:43–43:14	68
43:8–10	238
44	238
44:16–34	238
44:18–34	68
45:4–8	68
45:8	318
47:13–23	267
50:19–20	68
50:20	317, 318

EXODUS

1	224
1:7	69
1:8–22	69
1:15–21	69
1:22	69, 243
2:1–10	69
2:6	69
2:11–22	69
2:23	197
2:24–25	70, 197
3–4	70, 192
3:1–2	82
3:7,9,15	70
3:7–9,17	70
3:8	131
3:10	70
3:17	131
3:18	70
3:19–20	70
3:21–22	70
4:1–9	70
4:13–16	70, 192, 195
5–14	70
5:1–6:12	72
6–12	13
6:4–5	70
6:7	72
7:3–5	71
7:8–12	72
7:13–14	71
7:13	71
7:22–23	71
8:8–15	72
8:10	72
8:15	71
8:18–19	72
8:22–23	72
8:25–32	72
9:4–7	72
9:8–11	243
9:11	72
9:13–21	71
9:16	72
9:17	72
9:18–21	72
9:19–21	71
9:26	72
9:30	71
9:34–35	71
10:1–2	72
10:3	71
10:7–11	72
10:7	71
10:20	71
10:23	72
10:24–27	72
10:27–29	71
11–12	71
11:1	243
11:2–3	70
11:3	71, 72
11:4–7	243
11:7	72
11:8	71, 243

11:9–10	71	17:13	129
12:12	243	17:15–16	129
12:13	72	18	309
12:23	72	19:3	34
12:24–27	72	19:5–6	25, 93
12:29–30	243	19:8	25
12:31–33	71, 243	20:1–17	35
12:35–36	10, 70	20:2–7	25
12:38	71	20:2	25, 34
13:17–22	73	20:11	7, 25
14–16	22	20:20	25
14:1–4	73, 129	20:22	34
14:4	72, 73	21:1	35 n32
14:5–8	73	21:2	34
14:5–9	129	22:14	192
14:8	72, 73, 129	23:20–33	94
14:10–12	129	23:23	94, 131
14:13–14	129	23:27–31	94, 131
14:17–21	72	23:27	82
14:17–18	73	23:30–31	25
14:17	71	23:32–33	25
14:18	129	24:1–8	34
14:20	129	24:3,7	25
14:21–28	129	24:3–8	25
14:19–30	73	25–40	22
14:21	14	32	25, 58, 94
14:26–28	14	32:1	22
14:31	72	32:4	58
15:1–10	14	32:7–14	52, 221
15:3	129	32:9–10	58, 94, 230
15:9	129	32:10	274
15:18	73	32:11–13	94
15:22–23	57	32:12	58
15:24–25	24	32:13	58, 94
15:24	57	32:14	221
15:25–26	58	32:26–29	58, 94
15:25	57	32:31–33	59
15:26	244	32:32	94, 295
16:2–3	24	32:33–34	295
16:4–6	24	32:33	59, 94
16:20,27–28	24	32:34	58, 94
17	131	32:35	56, 58, 59, 94, 244
17:1–7	58	33:1–3	131
17:2–7	24	33:19	96
17:7	58	34:11	132
17:8	129	35:30–35	259
17:9	129	35:34	259
17:11	129		

LEVITICUS

1–7	35
1	191
8–10	22
10:1	22
10:1–2	56
11–17	35
19:9–10,23–25	17
25:1–7,11	17
25:19	17
26	34, 59
26:4,19–20	13
26:13	17
26:16	244
26:25	244
26:43	18

NUMBERS

11:1	56
11:4–34	59
11:25–27	83
11:33	59, 244
12:1–16	59
12:6	255
12:10–15	244
13–14	59, 130
13:1–25	130
13:26–33	130
14:3	130
14:4	130
14:9	130
14:10	130
14:11–12	230
14:12	130
14:13–22	130
14:22–35	130
14:25	130
14:28–35	230
14:36–38	130
14:37	56, 59, 244
14:39–45	130
16:5–50	59
16:31–33	56
16:35	56
16:46–50	244
16:46–49	59
20:2–13	59
21–25	130
21	130
21:4–9	59
21:6	56
22–24	309
22:4–7	260
22:8–13	260
22:9–12	82
22:19–20	260
22:20	82
22:21–35	260
22:38	260
23:3–5	82
23:7–11	130
23:12	260
23:16	82
23:19–24	130
23:19	192
24:1–2	260
24:2–4	82
24:3–4	260
24:5–9	130
24:14	260
24:15–16	260
24:18–19	231
25:1–3	130, 260
25:4–11	130
25:8–9	56, 244
25:17–24	260
31:16	130, 260

DEUTERONOMY

4:24	202
7:3–4	132
7:7–8	70
8:2–3	24
9:6	233
17:14–20	26, 264
28	13, 34, 59, 233
28:21–22	244
28:27–28	244
28:35	244
28:59–61	244
29:4	233

29:29	x	13:24	132
30:6	198, 233	13:25	82, 132
31:16–18	233	14:1–3	132
31:19–32:45	59	14:4	82, 133
31:27	233	14:6	82, 133
		14:19–16:3	133
		14:19	82, 133
		15:14	82
		16:4–22	133

JOSHUA

1:1–2	131	16:17–20	133
1:2–4	131	16:17	82
2:1–21	71	16:19	133
2:11	132	16:20	133
5:13–14	132	16:22	133
5:13	131	16:23–24	133
5:14	131	16:30	133
6:1–20	131	20–21	26
6:2	131		
6:18	131		
6:19	131	## RUTH	
6:21	131		
6:22–23	132	4:13	249n
6:24	131		
6:25	132		
7:1	131, 132	## 1 SAMUEL	
7:2–5	132		
7:3–5	255	2:30–31	192
7:11–12	132	6:19	56
7:21	131	8–15	22
7:26	132	8	26
9:14	255	8:4–20	26
9:19–26	255	8:22	26
11:19–20	71	9:1–20	26
		9:15–10:1	26
		9:21	26
		10:2,14–16	26
		10:5–6,9–12	26

JUDGES

		10:5	26
2:18	200	10:6	82, 83
6:11–23	207	10:7	26
7:2	133n	10:8	26
13:1	132	10:10–11	82
13:2–23	132	10:10	83
13:3–21	207	10:19–24	26
13:3	82	11:1–11	26
13:4–5	133	11:14–15	26
13:5	132	12:12	26
13:7	133	13	22
13:14	133		

(1 Samuel continued)

13:3	27
13:3–4	26
13:5	26
13:6–10	26
13:13–14	26
14	27
14:1–14	320
15	22, 27, 297
15:11	27, 192, 221, 297
15:29	27, 192, 193, 297
16	27
16:1–13	134
16:12	82
16:14–23	134
16:14	82, 215
16:15–16	83
16:16	215
16:23	83, 215
17:1–31	134
17:11	134
17:15	134
17:24	134
17:26–30	320
17:26	134
17:32	320
17:33–51	134
17:33–36	320
17:36	320
17:45–47	320
17:47	134
18:3–4	196
18:8–9	215
18:10–11	215
18:10	83
18:12	215
18:15	215
18:17–27	215
18:29	215
19:9–10	215
19:9	83
19:11–17	215
19:23–24	83
19:23	83
23:9	223
23:11	223–224
23:11–12	224
23:13	224
28:11–19	157

2 SAMUEL

5	134
6	22
6:1–7	239
6:6–7	56
6:19	56
7–12	22
7:14	242
7:16	242
12:1–14	267
12:7–9	22
23:1–2	259
24:1–4	229
24:1	214
24:2–3	214
24:10	214
24:11–13	214
24:15	214, 244
24:16	214
24:18–25	214
24:19	214
24:29	214

1 KINGS

3	274
3:5	275
3:5–15	255
3:9	275
3:11	275
3:12	275
3:13	275
3:14	275
5–11	22
10:29–39	226
11:1–9	241
11:11	241
11:12–13	241
11:14	241
11:23–25	241
11:27–28	242
11:29–32	242
11:40	242
12:4	242
12:5	242
12:7	242
12:8–16	242

12:15	242	**2 KINGS**	
12:20	242		
12:22–24	226	1:2–4	244
12:24	242	1:9–12	56
12:26–33	59, 226	1:13–15	56
13:1	226	2:1–12	244
13:2	226	4:18–37	244
13:4	244	4:42–44	20
13:3–6	226	5	310
13:6	244	5:1–14	244
14:1	244	5:27	244
14:12	244	8:7–9	229
14:17	244	8:10	229
15:23	244	8:12	229
16:30	276	8:13–15	229
16:31–18:40	59	10:32–33	229
16:33	277	12:17	229
16:34	244	13:3–7	229
17–18	320	13:14	244
17:1	13, 277	13:17	227
17:2–18:15	277	13:21	244
17:4–6	10	15:5	244
17:17–22	244	17:7–23	59
18	237	18–19	59
18:16–40	277	18:19–36	277
18:38–39	237	19:4	277
18:41–45	13	19:5–7	277–278
18:41	277	19:7–8	278
18:41–44	277	19:9–13	278
19:4	295	19:10–13	278
19:5–8	295	19:15–19	278
19:15–18	295	19:15	278
19:15	230	19:20	278
19:16–17	265	19:20–31	278
19:18	97	19:22	278
21:19	227	19:23–24	278
22	204	19:25	278
22:2–4	204	19:28	278
22:5	204	19:35–36	278
22:6	204	19:37	278
22:7	204	20:1–6	221, 244
22:8	204	20:1	278
22:13	204	20:2–3	279
22:15	204	20:5–6	279
22:16	204	20:7	279
22:19–23	198, 204	20:8–11	279
		20:12–19	279
		20:16–18	280

SCRIPTURE INDEX

(2 Kings continued)

21–25	59
21:1–9	280
21:10–15	280
22:1	226
23:15–16	226–227
23:26–27	280
23:29–30	239

1 CHRONICLES

13:7–11	239
13:9–10	182
15:2	239
15:12–13	239
21:3	214
21:6	214
21:8	214
21:9–12	214
21:14	214, 244
21:15	214
21:17	214
21:18–26	214
21:27	214
21:28–22:1	214
22–29	214
28:11–19	259
29:14	257

2 CHRONICLES

16:12	244
17:10	239
20	134, 320
20:1–2	134
20:3	135
20:6	135
20:12	135
20:15–17	135
20:21	135
20:22–23	135
26:21	244
35:20–24	239
35:22	239
36:13–20	62

Ezra

1:1	266, 293
1:2–3	266

Nehemiah

1:4	291
2:1–2	269
2:1–8	266

ESTHER

1:1	268
1:13–18	268
1:19–2:4	268
1:19	268
2:1–18	268
2:21–23	269
2:23	268
3:1	269
3:4–5	269
3:4	269
3:6–15	269
3:8	269
4:1–4	269
4:8	269
4:14	269, 270
5:1–14	269
6	309
6:1–11	269
6:12–7:10	270
6:13	269
8:8	268

JOB

1–2	23, 217
1:1	27
1:3	27, 309
1:5	27
1:6	27, 45 n21, 203, 213
1:7–22	28
1:7	28
1:8	28, 29
1:9–11	28, 213
1:12	28, 213
1:13–19	28
1:15	213
1:17	213

SCRIPTURE INDEX

1:21	29, 30	8:3–6	15
1:22	28	8:6–8	7
2:3	28, 29	9	63
2:5	28	16	159
2:6	28	16:9–11	158
2:7	28	19	7
2:9	28	22	142
2:10	28, 30	22:18	232
2:11–3:19	28	22:27–28	142–143
2:12–13	156	24:1–2	7
3–31	29	30:9	157
3	309	33:6–9	7
3:1–16	251	37:1–2	35
3:20–21	251	37:9–10	35
4:11	309	41:9	239
9:2	151	50:9–12	190–191
10:3	151	50:14–15	191
19:25–26	158	51:11	82
24	151	51:16–19	191
32–37	29	62:12	165
33:14–15	256	74:13–14	4 n10
38–41	11, 29, 151, 213	78:40	46 n27
42:2–3	29	78:40–41	60 n5
42:2	214	82	203–204
42:3	152, 214	82:1	204
42:4	214	82:5	204
42:5	30	82:6	204
42:6	30	82:7	204
42:7–8	29, 152	90	160
42:8–9	30	90:1–2	157
42:8	213	90:4	157, 158, 162
42:10	29	90:5–6	157
42:11	30	90:5	157
		90:7–9	157
		90:9	157
		90:10	157
PSALMS		90:11	157
2	62, 79, 216, 287	90:12	158
2:1–3	62	90:13–15	158
2:4	62	90:15	157
2:5–6	63	95:9	24
2:7	63	102:26	157
2:8	63, 144, 287	102:27	194
2:9	63	104	9–10
2:10–12	63	104:21	10
2:12	63	105:17–19	68, 318
6:5	157	105:27–35	13
8	88	107:24–30	13

(Psalms continued)

107:33–35	13
110:1	164
115:2–3	78
115:3	xix
115:12	78
127:1	314
135:6	xix n., 73
135:8–12	73
139:1–9	232
139:1	232
193:2	232
139:3	232
139:4	232
139:13–16	232
139:13–15	18
139:13	249n, 250
139:14–16	249
139:14	247
139:16	232
141:2	129

PROVERBS

1:7	314
3:5–6	252
16:3	252
16:33	26, 128
19:21	127, 252
21:1	266, 268
21:13	295
21:30	251
24:12	165

ECCLESIASTES

3:17	157
6:6	157
7:2	157
9:2–6	157
9:10	157
12:1–7	157
12:14	157

ISAIAH

1–6	222
1:2–3	60 n57, 200n
1:18	xi
6:3	207
6:10	233
7:4–9	198
7:10–17	198
8:16–18	97
10:5–19	309
10:5	77
10:7	78
10:12	78
10:13–14	78
10:15–16	78
10:20–22	97
11	222
11:1–5	222
11:2	83
13–23	222
14:3–27	309
14:12	211–212
14:12–14	212n
14:13	212
14:13–14	211
14:14	212
14:15	212
14:24–25	77
14:26–27	78
19:18–25	78
22	222
25:7–8	158
26–31	222
28:5	97
31	309
34	222
35	222
37:21–35	309
38:1–6	244
39–41	222
40:3–5	137
40:5–19	222
41:8–9	98
41:8	197
41:25–26	227
42:1–7	222
42:1	83, 98

42:6	98	59:5	136
42:14	201	59:6–7	136
43:1	98	59:8	136
43:23–24	201	59:9–15	136
44–45	151	59:15–16	136
44	222	59:16–17	136
44:3	83	59:19	136
44:7	223	60–64	222
44:22–23	222–223	61:1	83
44:28–45:1	227	63:9	201
44:28	237	63:10	46 n27, 86, 196
45	222	65:1–2	60 n57, 200n
45:1–14	309	65:17–25	222
45:4	237	65:17	146
45:6–7	150	65:24	284
45:17	150	66:7–11	216
45:21	223, 227		
45:22–23	150–151		
45:23	227	## JEREMIAH	
46–47	309		
46:10	228	1:4–5	262
46:11	228	1:6	262
47	222	1:7	262
48	222, 228	1;14–16	262
48:9	201	1:14–15	74
48:11	14	2:1	196
49:1–7	222	2:2–3:2	60 n57
49:3	98	2:2	200
49:5–6	99	2:5	200
49:6	144n	2:29	200
52:13- 53:12	222	2:31	200, 221
53:8	108	2:32–3:3	196
54	222	3:7	221
54:7–8	200	3:19–20	60 n57, 200n, 221
54:13	110	4:6	74
55:6–7	310	4:7	75
55:10–11	228	4:9	262
57:15–21	170	4:11	75
57:21	170	4:13	75
58	295	4:19	201
58:2	295	7:5	221
58:3	295	8:4–7	60 n57
58:6–7	295	8:18–9:1	201
58:10	295	9:7	60
59	135	9:10	200
59:1–2	136	11:18–20	262
59:3	136	12:1–4	262
59:4	136	12:7	200–201

(Jeremiah continued)

13:1–11	262
14:13	262
15:6	201
18	53, 90, 96, 150, 193
18:1–12	96, 262
18:5–10	96
18:6	53, 96
18:7–10	35, 221
18:7–8	53
18:9–10	53
18:11–12	53
18:13–15	60 n57, 200n
18:18	262
18:19–23	262
20:1–6	262
20:7–18	262
21:3–4	262
22:4–5	221
23:1–2	262
23:5	262
23:9–32	262
25:1–11	262
25:8–11	53
25:12–14	53
25:12	262
26:1–28:17	262
26:3	221
27:1–11	309
27:5–7	75
27:5–6	237–238
27:5	53, 265
27:6	53
27:8–13	75
28:14	75
29:8–11	238
30:1–31:40	262
31	60
31:20	200
31:31–34	198, 233
32:1–44	262
32:17	272
36:1–32	262
46–51	74, 309
48:30–32	201
48:35–36	201
49:7–22	93

EZEKIEL

1:4–24	207
3:16–21	53
11:19–20	198
12:3	221
16:8–14	196
16:15–19	196
18:1–32	53
18:1–32	53
18:23–32	61
18:23	53, 107
18:32	107
20	52
21:18–23	198
21:18–22	238
22:30–31	52
23:3–8	196
23:4–5	196
28:12–17	211
28:12	212
28:13	212
28:16	212
28:17	212
28:19	212
33:11	107
36–48	222
36–37	60
36:25–27	233
36:26–27	112, 198, 235
36:27	83
37:14	83

DANIEL

1–3	22
1–4	55
1:3–5	75
1:8–20	76
1:20	76
2–4	310
2	54
2:1–13	76
2:4	82, 309
2:14–23	76
2:24–28	76
2:31–45	76

2:39-45	222	9:24	206
2:47	76	9:25-27	292
3	49, 267	9:26	206
3:1-7	76	10-12	204
3:8-16	76	10	206, 216
3:17-18	76	10:1	293
3:19-23	76	10:2-3	293
3:29	76	10:4-21	207
4	54, 55, 77, 266	10:5-6	293
4:4-19	77	10:12-14	150
4:5-6	54	10:13	207, 212, 217
4:7-8	55	10:20-21	150, 207
4:19-26	77	10:20	212
4:19-27	55	10:21	217
4:25	55	11:2-45	222
4:17	77, 265	12:1	206, 217, 293
4:25,26,32	77	12:2	159
4:25	55, 265	12:9-12	206
4:27	77		
4:28-37	265		
4:28-34	77	## HOSEA	
4:29-30	55		
4:31-33	55	1:2	196
4:32	228, 265	2:2-5	196
4:34-37	55	2:2	196
4:34-35	77	2:7	196
4:35	55	2:16	196
4:36	55	2:19	196
4:37	77	2:20	196
6	267, 310	11:1-9	60 n57
6:8	268	11:1-4	200n
6:12	268	13:14	159
7-12	293		
7:23-27	206, 222		
8:15-26	207	## JOEL	
8:20-25	222		
8:26	206	1-2	13
9	292	2:28-29	83
9:2	292		
9:3	292		
9:4	292	## AMOS	
9:5-14	292		
9:15-16	292	1:3-2:15	74
9:17-18	292	1:3-2:3	309
9:18-19	292	3:2	113
9:21-27	207	3:6	x
9:22-23	292	3:7	51 n43
9:24-27	206, 222	3:9	309

(Amos continued)

5:1–2	200
7:1–6	221
9:7	74, 141, 309

OBADIAH

10–14	93
11–14	231

JONAH

	35
1–2	239
1	192
1:1–4	54
1:6–16	54
1:16	310
1:17	54
1:18	54
3	310
3:1–3	198, 240
3:1–2	54
3:4	54
3:5–9	54
3:9	54, 193
3:10	54, 192–193, 221, 232
4:2	54, 193, 232
4:3	295
4:8	295
4:9–11	295
4:11	54

MICAH

3:8	83
5:2	229
6:3	60 n57, 200n

HABAKKUK

1:2–4	151
1:3–7	53
1:6	151
1:13	151
1:15–16	53, 151
1:17	151
2:8	151
2:13–14	151

HAGGAI

1	191

ZECHARIAH

3:1	217

MALACHI

1:2–3	93
2:14	196
3:16–18	97

MATTHEW

1:3	238
1:19–24	240
1:20–24	207, 255
1:20	82
1:21	108
2:1–12	309
2:4–6	229
2:12–20	153
2:12	82, 256
2:13–15	240
2:13	82, 207, 255
2:14–23	153
2:16	216
2:19–20	207
2:19–23	240, 255
2:19	82
3–4	23
3:11	83, 99
3:13–14	99
3:16–17	30
3:16	83
4:1–23	30

SCRIPTURE INDEX

4:1–11	215	11:21–24	224
4:1	23, 30, 83	12:17–21	99
4:3–7	20	12:18	83
4:3,6	30	12:22	244
4:8–9	30, 212	12:24–26	215
4:11	207	12:28	20, 83
4:23–24	20	13:38–39	215
5:17–48	35	13:40–43	168
5:25–26	170	13:41–42	171
5:45	9	13:54–58	245
6	284	13:55	153
6:5–6	284	14:15–21	20
6:6	284	14:25–27	20
6:7	284	14:35–36	20
6:8	284	15:22–28	245
6:9–10	284	15:32–38	20
6:11–13	284	16:18	139, 141, 175, 181, 291
6:13	215, 293	16:21	223
6:14–15	284	16:23	31, 215
6:16–18	284	17:14–20	245
6:17–18	284	17:18	244
6:18	284	18:8–9	171
6:25	284	18:34	170
6:26,28–30	9	19:3–12	35
6:26	284	19:8	34
6:28–30	284	19:26	272, 285
6:30–32	284	20:17–19	223
6:33	284	20:28	153
6:34	284	21:18–22	20
7:7–8	310	22:1–14	113
8:5–10	245	22:2	113
8:16	20	22:3	113
8:24–27	20	22:4–6	114
8:26	20	22:7	114
9:1–8	244	22:8	114
9:8	20	22:10	102, 114
9:20–22	245	22:11–13	102
9:29	245	22:11	114
9:34	215	22:14	102, 113
10:1	20, 245	22:15–22	267
10:8	20	22:21	267
10:11–15	168	22:44	164
10:18	20	23:33–36	60
10:28	171	23:35	44
10:29–30	11–12	23:37–38	60
10:32–33	124	24:1–2	223
11:4	20	24:2	61
11:20–24	13, 199, 308	24:12	177

(Matthew continued)

24:15–26	61
24:36	161
24:37–39	163
24:48–51	172
25	168
25:30	172
25:31–32	164, 168
25:32	168
25:34–35	168
25:34	168
25:40	168
25:41–46	146
25:41	168, 172
25:45	168
25:46	164, 168, 171
26:1–2	80
26:5	31
26:21–25	81, 231
26:23–28	153
26:24	80, 81
26:28	80
26:33	225
26:34	225
26:36–44	31
26:38	31
26:39–44	80
26:39	31
26:31	80
26:45	80
26:46	31
26:53–54	80
26:53	31
26:63–65	80
26:64	139
26:69–75	225
26:75	225
27:3–10	81
27:12–18	80
27:15–26	153
27:19	80, 310
27:25	61
27:26	80
28:2–7	207
28:18–20	300
28:18–19	144n
28:18	139
28:19	162

MARK

1:8	83
1:10–11	30
1:10	83
1:12	30, 83
1:25	14
1:35	281
3:29	171
4:37–38	14
9:14–29	215
9:37	168
9:41	168
9:42–49	172
10:45	108, 153
11:13–14	284
11:13	284
11:15	138n
11:20–21	284
11:22–25	284–285
11:22–24	291
12:30	x
13:1–2	223
13:34–35	35
14:18–21	81, 231
14:21–24	80
14:21	81, 220
14:29	225
14:30	225
14:31	225
14:33–39	80
14:61–65	80
14:66–72	225
14:72	225
15:6–15	80
16:15–16	300
16:19	139

LUKE

1:1–3	263
1:11–20	207
1:11	82
1:26–38	207, 216
1:31–33	137
1:35	99
1:37	272

1:51–53	141	13:16	215, 244
1:51–52	136–137	13:28	172
2:1–4	152	13:34–35	199
2:1	229	13:34	199
2:3	229	14:23	198
2:4–5	229	15:3–7	95
2:7	153	15:12–13	198
2:8–15	207	16:22–31	172
2:11	99	17:2	172
2:13–14	207	18:1	294
2:34–35	216	18:5	294
3:4–5	137	18:7	294
3:16	83, 99	18:9	106
3:21–22	30	18:10	106
3:22	83	18:11	106
4:1–13	215	18:13	106
4:1–3	137	18:14	106
4:1	83	18:27	272
4:3–4,9–12	20	19:45	138n
4:5–6	212	21:5–6	223
4:6	135, 215	22–23	23
4:11	30	22:1–23	81
4:13	31	22:1–6	81
4:14	31, 83	22:3	81
4:18–21	31	22:4–44	80
4:18–19	137–138	22:20–22	80, 153
4:18	83	22:22	81
4:33–36	138	22:31	225, 281
4:38–40	138	22:32	225
4:41	138	22:33	225
4:43	138	22:34	225, 281
6:12–13	281	22:39–46	31
6:13	99	22:42	153, 282
6:38	257	22:43–44	282
8:3	153	22:44	31
9:35	99	22:54–62	225
9:50	168	22:61–62	225
9:52–55	57	22:70–71	80
9:58	153	23:5–12	80
10:8–12	168	23:13–25	80
11:13	83, 290	23:25–27	203
12:4–5	168	23:28–31	61, 80
12:10	168	23:31–33	23
12:20	172	23:41	153
12:38–40	199	23:47	153
12:46–48	170–171, 172	24:4–7	207
12:59	172	24:7	31
13:3,5	13	24:43	207

(Luke continued)

24:46–47	138, 300
24:46	31
24:49	83, 139, 300

JOHN

1:2–3	8
1:4–5	308–309
1:14	152, 194
1:18	152, 203
1:29	99, 108
1:33	83, 99
1:34	99
2:16	111
2:24–25	111
3:3	109
3:5–8	109
3:8	84
3:14–18	109
3:14–15	153
3:14	153
3:16	108, 144n, 152
3:19–20	111
3:34	83
3:36	109
4	241
4:23	191
4:42	99
5:10–18	111
5:18	111
5:19	281, 282
5:24	109
5:44	111
5:45–47	111
6:37	109
6:41–42	111
6:44	109, 110
6:45	110
6:48	99
6:52	111
6:64	231
6:65	109
6:70	81, 239
7:4–5	111
7:15	153
7:17	110
7:21–24	111
7:37–39	83, 139, 290
7:40–43	111
7:70	99
8:28	153
8:33–41	111
8:42	110
8:44	215
8:48–59	111
9:1–11	320
9:1–3	244–245
9:3	245
9:22	111
10:8–18	118
10:8	111
10:10	117, 153
10:11–18	80
10:11–15	153
10:11	108
10:15	108
10:17–18	31, 100
10:18	153
10:26	111
10:27–29	117
10:27	111
10:28	290
10:30	152
10:31–39	111
10:36	100
11	282
11:1–44	320
11:4	282
11:6–15	282
11:23	282
11:25	282
11:33–35	282
11:38	282
11:39–41	282
11:41–42	283
11:43	283
11:47–48	111
11:48–50	80
11:50	80
11:51–52	80, 108
12:4–6	81
12:23–33	80, 153
12:24	153
12:27–28	282

12:27	153
12:28	153
12:31–33	282
12:31	153, 215
12:32	108, 109, 110, 144n. 169n, 284
12:33	153
12:37–41	111
12:37	199
12:38–40	199
12:42	111
12:43	111
12:45	152
13:2	81
13:11	231
13:18–27	81
13:18	99
13:19	231
13:21–30	231
13:21–27	231
13:27	81, 231n
13:34–35	35
13:37	225
13:38	225
14:6	108
14:7	152
14:9	152, 203
14:12	289
14:13–14	289
14:16–17	83, 282, 289
14:30	153
15:5	314
15:13–15	197
15:13–14	108
15:16	99
15:19	99
15:26	83
16:7	83
16:11	153
16:15	83
17	283
17:1–2	283
17:4	283
17:5	283
17:6–19	283
17:9	108, 283
17:12	81
17:15	283
17:20–23	179, 283
17:20–21	283
17:21	283
17:22–23	180
17:23	283
18:15–18	225
18:25–27	225
18:28–19:16	310
18:39–40	80
19:1–16	153
19:4	153
19:6	153
19:7	80
19:10–11	81
19:11	265
19:12	80
19:15	80
19:22–24	231
19:28	231
19:34	231
19:36	231
19:37	231
20:21–23	139
20:21	300
20:22	83
21:24	263

ACTS

1:1	139
1:2–3	286
1:4–8	290
1:4–5	83, 286
1:4	286, 300
1:5,8	83
1:6–8	95
1:6	161
1:8	144n, 161–162, 176, 286, 288, 300
1:12–15	176
1:14	83, 286, 302
1:16–19	81
1:26	26
2–5	23
2	286
2:1	84, 302
2:2–3	84

(Acts continued)

2:4	84, 303	4:24	287
2:5–12	300	4:25–27	287
2:5	303	4:27–28	79
2:6–12	84, 303	4:27	62, 287
2:13	303	4:28	287
2:14–41	237	4:30	287
2:14	303	4:31	287
2:17–18	84	4:32–37	32, 304
2:17	255, 303, 304	4:33–35	257–258
2:18	304	4:36	241
2;21	304	5	182
2:23	62, 79, 222, 231	5:1–2	32
2:25–31	159	5:1–11	57, 139, 176
2:33–36	83, 139	5:3–5	86
2:33	83, 139, 290	5:3,9	23, 32
2:36–38	79	5:5–11	244
2:36	61, 303	5:7–42	32
2:37	198, 237, 300, 303	5:12–16	300
2:38–39	84, 304	5:12	300
2:38	61, 83, 290, 303	5:40=42	267
2:40	61, 303	5:9	86
2:41	61, 286, 300, 303	5:29	267
2:42–47	303, 304	5:31	97, 114, 115
2:42	286	6	139
2:44–45	32	6:1–6	32
3:1–4:4	198	6:1–7	139
3:1–11	245	6:1	176, 300
3:1–10	320	6:7	61, 300
3:13–26	61	6:8–8:3	139
3:13–14	79	6:11–8:3	32
3:16	245	7	139, 176
3:17	79, 215	7:38	176
3:18	62, 79	7:55	32
3:19–20	79	7:56	139
3:19	304	7:57–60	288
3:21	161, 163	7:58	288
3:26	300	7:60	288
4–8	303	8:1–3	176
4–5	176	8:3–5	139
4	139	8:4–40	139
4:1–20	32	8:5	139
4:2	159	8:6–13	300
4:4	61, 300	8:6–8	140
4:8,31	32	8:9–13	176
4:10	79, 139	8:12	300
4:22	245	8:14–17	140
4:23–31	287	8:15–17	84
		8:26–39	95, 310

8:26–29	140	11:4–14	300
8:26–35	300	11:5–10	85
8:28–38	85	11:5	288
8:29	85	11:12	85
8:30–37	140	11:13	85
8:39–40	140	11:15–18	300
8:39	304	11:15–17	139
9	32	11:15	84
9:1–6	288	11:17	84
9:3–6	82, 139	11:18	95, 114, 115, 176, 300
9:10–12	82, 139	11:19–21	139
9:15–16	291	11:21	95
9:15	177	11:22–30	304
9:17	84	11:27–30	32, 85, 241
9:23–25	176	11:28	13
9:29–30	176	11:29	258
9:30–38	287	12	139, 253, 289
9:31	139, 300	12:1–2	176
9:33–34	245	12:2	288
9:34	139	12:3	288
9:35	300	12:4	288
9:36–41	245	12:5	288
9:36	288	12:6–11	288
9:39	288	12:6–10	207
9:40–42	288	12:12–16	288
9:40	288	12:19	288
9:42	288, 300	12:22–23	57
10–11	176	12:23	244
10	54n50, 139, 241, 310	13–19	176
10:1–33	300	13:2–4	241
10:2	85, 95, 288, 300	13:2	85, 139
10:3–6	85	13:4	85, 241
10:9–19	82, 85	13:6–11	176
10:9–10	288	13:7	300
10:13–15	176	13:8–12	300
10:19–20	85	13:8–11	244
10:22	85, 300	13:13–52	241
10:28	176	13:27–29	80
10:30–33	85	13:27	61, 62
10:30–31	288	13:28	153
10:35	85, 300	13:31–33	62
10:38	83, 215, 244	13:35–37	159
10:44–47	84	13:42–47	95
10:44	300	13:42–44	177
10:46–47	84	13:43	300
10:46	300	13:44	300
11	139	13:45	95, 176
11:2	176, 300	*(Acts continued)*	

13:47	300	16:26–30	300
13:48	95, 109	17:1–5	95
13:49	300	17:2–4	300
13:50	109, 176	17:2	301
13:52	84, 304	17:4	177, 300
14:1–5	95	17:5–9	176
14:1	177, 245, 300	17:10–13	95
14:3	300	17:11–12	300
14:4–6	176	17:12	177, 300
14:8–20	198	17:13	176
14:8–10	245	17:16–23	176
14:11–13	176	17:16–18	320
14:15	8	17:17	301
14:15–17	10	17:18	159
14:16	74, 307	17:23	260
14:17	307	17:24–25	190
14:19–20	176	17:24	8
14:21	177, 300	17:25	10
14:26–27	241	17:26–28	74, 89, 308
15:1	176	17:26	141, 234
15:8	84	17:27	260
15:9	176	17:28	260, 308
15:12	95	17:29	308
15:14	95, 300	17:30–31	35
15:15	176	17:30	308, 311
15:19–21	35	17:31	165
15:28–29	35	17:32–34	177
15:41	240	18:4–11	95
16:4–5	240	18:4	198, 301
16:5	300	18:6	176
16:6–7	85, 252	18:8–10	177
16:6–8	240	18:8	300
16:6–10	140	18:9–10	256
16:6	209	18:9	82
16:7	139	18:10	95, 300
16:9–10	85, 240, 252	18:12–17	176, 310
16:9	82, 256	18:21	209
16:13–15	140	18:27	103
16:14–15	257	19	209, 240
16:14	300	19:1–10	177
16:16–34	291	19:1–5	209
16:16–24	140, 257	19:1	209
16:16–18	176	19:6	84, 209
16:19–24	176	19:8–10	95
16:19	110	19:8	209, 300
16:25	140	19:9	176, 209, 301
16:25–34	257	19:10	177, 209, 300, 304
16:26–34	140	19:11–12	209, 245, 300

19:13–20	300	**ROMANS**	
19:13–19	176		
19:15–17	210	1–5	105
19:17–20	304	1:5	177
19:17	210	1:8	177
19:18–19	210, 304	1:10	252
19:20	210, 304	1:13	177, 252
19:23–41	176	1:16	107, 116, 177
19:23–31	176	1:18–32	165
19:24–27	211, 304	1:18–28	35
19:26	304	1:18–3:20	165
19:28–34	211	1:18	105
19:30–34	211	1:19–20	307
19:31	211	1:21	22
20:3	176	1:22	307
20:9–10	245	1:24–32	307
20:19–20	177	1:24	105
20:19	176	1:26	105
20:22–23	85	1:28	105
20:26	300	1:32	307–308
20:28	108, 117	2:1–4	165
20:29–30	117	2:5–16	35
20:29	17	2:5	105, 165
20–28	253	2:6–11	105
21–28	177	2:6	165
21:4	85	2:7–8	166
21:10–14	85	2:9–16	309–310
21:20	61, 97, 177	2:11	166, 314
22:24–29	267	2:12–16	35
23:11	82, 291	2:12	166, 308
23:12–35	267	2:13–15	166
24:10–26	310	2:14–15	308
24:11	267	2:14–16	168
25:8–12	267	2:16	166
26:1–32	310	2:28–29	95
26:13–19	82	3:9	105
27:22–26	253	3:22	106
27:22–24	207	3:23	105
27:30–32	253	3:24	105
27:42–43	253	3:25	106, 159
28:14–31	176	3:26	106
28:17–19	267	4:21	272
28:25–27	173	5	159
		5:1–2	112

SCRIPTURE INDEX

(Romans continued)

Reference	Page
5:3–4	296
5:5	112
5:6–10	106
5:8	160
5:12–21	43
5:12	159
5:14	160
5:15–21	99
5:15	106
5:17	106, 169
5:18–19	169n
5:18	160, 169
5:19	160
6:23	106
8	247
8:1–17	85
8:6	112
8:7–8	112
8:9	112
8:13	113
8:16	120
8:17	113
8:19–23	292
8:20–21	41
8:26–27	85, 290
8:28–30	113, 290
8:28–29	291, 317
8:28	xx, 141, 181, 247
8:29–30	128
8:29	22
8:31–39	290
8:34	118, 290
8:35	118
8:36	44
8:38	118
9–11	95
9	94
9:1–5	290
9:3–5	94
9:3	94
9:6–20	290
9:6–9	94
9:6	94
9:7–9	91
9:8	95
9:10–13	92
9:13	93
9:15	96
9:16–18	94, 96
9:19–21	96
9:20	249
9:22	59, 96
9:23–26	96, 177
9:23–25	290
9:29	97
9:30–32	96, 106
9:30	290
10:1–15	290
10:1	290
10:3–4	97
10:4	301
10:9	139
10:12–13	106
10:14–15	177
10:16	290
10:19–21	290
11:1	97, 290
11:2	113, 222
11:5	97, 290
11:7–15	97
11:7–10	290
11:7	290
11:11–32	290
11:11–12	290
11:11	177
11:15	177
11:17–24	97
11:20	97
11:22	97
11:23	97, 141
11:25–26	98, 145, 169
11:25	141, 162, 177
11:26	141, 162
11:28–29	97
11:29	97, 145
11:32	97n, 98, 107, 113, 145, 169, 177
11:33	x
11:35	191
12:1	191
13:1–7	35
13:1–2	264
13:1	263
13:4–6	264
13:7	264

13:8–11	35	14:37	263
15:8–12	177	14:39	85, 86
15:18–21	177	15	163
15:22–29	85	15:3	159
15:23–28	252	15:12–13	164
15:31–32	252–253	15:20–21	159
16:20	154, 177	15:21–23	164
16:25–26	177	15:22–23	164
		15:22	99, 169
		15:23	164

1 CORINTHIANS

		15:24–25	160
		15:25	146
1:11	263	15:26	160, 164
2:7	127	15:28	169
2:8	215	15:29–54	164
3:10–12	170	15:38	19
3:12–15	170	15:45–49	30
3:15	170	15:52	169n
3:21–23	181	15:54–55	160
4:19	85, 252	15:54	164
5:1	263	15:56	160
5:9	263	16:7–8	252
7:1	263		
7:10	263		
7:12	263	## 2 CORINTHIANS	
7:21	249, 315		
7:24	249, 315	1:15–17	85
7:25	263	1:23–2:2	85
8:6	8	3:6–18	35
9:20–22	301	4:3–4	115
10:13	319	4:4	215, 317
11:18	263	5:14–15	107
11:29–32	244	5:14	154
12:4	85	5:17	154
12:9	246	5:18	154
12:11	85, 183	5:19	107, 154, 169, 194
12:18	19	8:1–7	257
12:22	248	8:2	257
12:28	246	8:13–15	258
12:30	246	9:8–11	256, 258
12:31	86	10:3–5	116
14:1–5	85	12–13	85
14:1	86, 183, 256	12	295
14:2	85	12:1–4	82
14:13–19	85	12:7	296, 318
14:14–15	290	12:8	296
14:27–32	85	12:9	296, 318
14:32	85	12:10	296

GALATIANS

2	261
2:2	85
3:8	229
3:16–19	141
3:16	99
3:28	250
4:13–14	248
4:15	248
5:16–18	86
5:17	86
5:22–23	86
5:25	86
6:7–8	35

EPHESIANS

1:3–14	100
1:3–12	177
1:3	100, 101
1:4	100, 101, 167
1:5	101
1:6	101
1:7	101
1:8	101
1:9–11	127
1:9–10	169–170
1:9	101
1:10	102
1:11	101, 127, 177
1:13–14	101
1:13	101
1:15–23	xi
1:18–19	177
1:21	178
1:22–23	176, 178, 181
1:20–26	164
2–3	95
2:1	108
2:1–3	101, 178
2:3–5	104
2:4–9	101
2:4–10	178
2:5	108
2:8–9	104
2:8	114
2:11–13	101
2:11–12	178
2:13–18	178
2:19	178
2:20–22	139
2:20	176, 178, 180, 181
2:21–22	178
3:3–6	178
3:4–6	229
3:6	101, 102
3:8–11	178
3:9–11	229
3:11	101, 127, 143, 206
3:18–19	178
3:20–21	178
3:20	272
4:3–6	179
4:7	179
4:10	179
4:11	179, 183
4:12–13	179
4:14–16	179
4:15	176
4:27	215
4:30–31	86
5:6	172
5:23	176, 196
5:25–37	180
5:25	108, 176
6:10–20	180
6:11–12	294
6:11	206
6:12	115, 131, 206, 215
6:13	206
6:15	116
6:18–20	116
6:18	294

PHILIPPIANS

1:6	117
2:8–11	138–139
2:10–11	169
2:12–13	117
3:4–5	250
3:8	250
4:10	257

4:11–12	316	2:3–7	267–268
4:13	257	2:3–6	107
4:14	257	4:1–4	177
4:15–16	257	4:10	108
4:18–19	257	5:23	245
4:18	257	6:17–19	258

COLOSSIANS

1	8
1:16	206
1:19–20	145, 169
1:23	120
2:10	208
2:15	154, 208, 210
2:27	245
3:25	314

1 THESSALONIANS

2:17–18	85
2:18	216
4:16	164
5:3	164, 172
5:19–22	86

2 THESSALONIANS

1:6–9	146, 172
1:7–10	164
2:1–11	162
2:10–12	173
2:12	111
2:13–14	104
3:10	256
5:2–3	163

1 TIMOTHY

1:13	288
2:1–6	291
2:1–2	263
2:1	116
2:2	267

2 TIMOTHY

1:9–10	106, 159
1:9	127, 234
1:10	234
2:13	118
2:14	39
2:25–26	117
3:1–8	177
3:6	212
3:15–17	261
4:16–17	310
4:20	245

TITUS

1:2	21, 127, 234, 312, 314
1:3	234
2:11	107, 169n
3:1	264

HEBREWS

1:3	8, 139
2:4	301
2:5–8	88
2:9	108, 159
2:10	31
2:14–15	159
2:17	120, 159
2:18	31
3:6	120
3:7–11	121
3:7–4:2	173
3:12–14	121
4:3	121
4:11	121
4:14	121

(Hebrews continued)

4:15	31, 120, 121
4:16	121
5:8–9	31
5:9–10	120
5:11–6:3	121
6:4–6	121
6:9–10	122
6:11–12	122
6:17–20	122
6:18	21, 314
6:20	120
7:23–8:2	120
7:25	108, 118
8:7–13	35
8:13	62
9:11–14	120
9:24–26	120
9:26	159
9:28	159
10:5–10	35
10:10–18	120
10:12–13	160
10:18	35
10:19	122
10:21	120
10:22	122
10:23	122
10:26–27	122
10:29	123
10:35	123
10:36–39	123
11	320
11:4	43
11:6	310
11:7	47, 320
11:8–12	90
11:23	320
11:27	296
11:31	320
12:5–13	296
12:5–11	202
12:5–8	316
12:10–11	316
12:10	174
12:14	174
12:16–17	123
12:29	202
13:7–8	194

JAMES

1:2–5	296
1:2	33
1:4	33
1:5	276
1:6–8	276
1:12	33
1:13–14	33
1:13	21, 314
1:17	192, 314
1:19	33
2:6	110
2:23	197
4:3	275
4:7	215, 319
4:13–16	253
5	277
5:10–11	33
5:14–16	315
5:14–15	246
5:15–16	244
5:15	275
5:16–18	276
5:17–18	13

1 PETER

1:1	235
1:1–2	102, 222
1:2	235
1:3	102
1:4–5	118
1:4	102
1:5	102
1:6–9	103
1:6–7	30
1:9	103
1:10–12	103
1:10–11	262
1:11	222
1:20	103, 127, 234
2:4–8	176
2:4	99, 176

2:5	103
2:6	103
2:8	103
2:9	102
2:13	264–265
2:14	264–265
2:17	264–265
3:7	295
5:8–9	215

2 PETER

1:1	103
1:3	103
1:4	103
1:5	103
1:8	103
1:9	103
1:10–11	103
1:20–21	261
2:1	117
2:4	207, 212
2:7–8	52
3	162
3:4	162
3:7	162
3:8–9	162
3:8	160
3:9	107, 141, 145
3:10	163
3:12	162
3:13	146

1 JOHN

1:5	21, 202, 314
1:7	118
2:1–2	118
2:2	107, 159
2:3–6	119
2:9–11	119
2:10	118
2:15	119
2:18	118
2:19	118, 119
2:21	118
2:22–23	118
2:22	118
2:24	120
2:26	118
2:27	118, 120
2:29	119
3:3	119
3:4–9	119
3:7	119
3:10–18	119
3:23	119
3:24	119, 120
4:2–3	118
4:4	215
4:7–12	119
4:8–10	314
4:10	107, 159
4:13	120
4:15	120
4:16–21	119
4:16	202, 312
5:1	119, 120
5:2–3	119
5:4	119
5:10–13	120
5:10–12	108
5:13	119
5:14–15	276, 289
5:16–17	119, 289
5:18	119, 215
5:19	135, 215, 317

JUDE

6	45 n22, 207, 212
24	118

REVELATION

1:1–2	82
1:1	207
1:5	217, 219
1:10–18	82
1:18	160
1:20	123
2–3	33, 144, 180

(Revelation continued)

2:2–3	33
2:4–5	33, 123
2:4	123
2:5	33
2:7	124
2:9	146, 215
2:10	33, 146, 215
2:11	124
2:13	146, 215
2:14–16	123, 146
2:16	123
2:17	42
2:20–23	123, 146
2:22–23	124
2:24	146, 215
2:26	124
3:1–3	124
3:5	124, 167
3:9	146, 215
3:12	124
3:15–17	124
3:16	124
3:19–20	124
3:20	124
3:21	124
4:4	207
4:6–8	207
4:8–9	207
4:10–11	207
4:11	8, 191
5:6–10	218
5:9–10	144
5:9	217, 218, 219
5:10	219
5:11–12	207
6:1	207
6:3	207
6:3–8	146
6:5	207
6:7	207
6:8	146, 160
6:9	146
6:9–11	146, 160
6:11	160
7:1–3	207
7:9–17	169
7:9	97n, 144, 154, 162, 311
7:11–12	207
7:13–14	207
7:14–17	154–155
7:14	144, 146, 217
8:2–6	207
8:7–12	13
9:11	146
9:13–19	146
10:1–11	207
11:6	13
11:7–10	146
11:13	13, 146
11:15	217
11:16–18	207
11:18	18, 146
11:19	142
12	141, 212, 215, 216
12:1	216
12:2	216
12:3–4	146, 215
12:3	216, 217
12:4–5	218
12:4	216
12:5	216, 218
12:6	216, 218
12:7–9	131, 144, 207, 212, 217
12:7–17	146
12:7	218
12:8–9	217
12:9	28, 137, 212, 216
12:10	217, 219
12:11	144, 212, 217, 218
12:12	217
12:13–13:18	146
12:13–17	215
12:13–16	218
12:14	218
12:16	218
12:17	218
13–14	267
13	212, 318
13:1–4	146, 215
13:3	146
13:5	218
13:7–10	215, 218
13:7	218
13:8–10	218
13:8	124, 127, 167, 218, 234

13:10	167, 218	20:4	145, 146, 160
13:11	146	20:7–9	173
13:15–18	218	20:7–10	146
13:17	167	20:10	146, 173
14:6–12	207	20:11–15	35, 166
14:9–11	146, 172, 267	20:11	166
14:14–20	207	20:12–13	146
14:18–20	146	20:12	124, 166
15:4	144	20:13	160, 166
15:6–16:1	207	20:14	160
16	146	20:15	124, 146, 166–167
16:5–7	146	21–22	154, 163
16:12–14	146	21	155, 164
16:13–16	146	21:1	142, 146
17:1–18	207	21:2	180
17:6	146	21:3–4	144, 155
17:12–16	146	21:4	146
17:15–18	146	21:5	142
17:17	319	21:7–8	167
18	146	21:8	146, 172
18:1–3	207	21:9–22:5	207
18:8–10	146	21:9–11	180
19:1–3	207	21:24,26	74, 144
19:7–8	180	21:27	167, 172
19:8	181	22:2	155
19:9	207	22:5	219
19:17–21	146	22:6	207
19:20	146	22:14–15	167
20	167, 173	22:15	146, 172
20:1–3	146, 173, 207	22:16	207
20:2	28	22:18–19	263
20:3	173		

www.ingramcontent.com/pod-product-compliance
Lightning Source LLC
Chambersburg PA
CBHW071142300426
44113CB00009B/1057